Annotated Teacher's Edition

Shining Star

A

Anna Uhl Chamot

Pamela Hartmann

Jann Huizenga

with

Ann Hilborn

Angela Seale

Longman

longman.com

Contents

Shining Star A

Pearson Education, 10 Bank Street, White Plains, NY 10606

Vice president, director of instructional design: Allen Ascher
Editorial director: Ed Lamprich
Acquisitions editor: Amanda Rappaport Dobbins
Project manager: Susan Saslow
Senior development editors: Virginia Bernard, Howard Gutner, Joan Poole, Bill Preston
Vice president, director of design and production: Rhea Banker
Executive managing editor: Linda Moser
Production manager: Ray Keating
Senior production editor: Sylvia Dare
Production editor: Jane Townsend
Director of manufacturing: Patrice Fraccio
Senior manufacturing buyer: Edith Pullman
Photo research: Kirchoff/Wohlberg, Inc.
Design and production: Kirchoff/Wohlberg, Inc.
Cover design: Rhea Banker, Tara Mayer
Text font: Franklin Gothic 10/11
Illustration and Photo credits: Page T279

ISBN: 0-13-049945-5

Printed in the United States of America
4 5 6 7 8 9 10-BAM-08 07 06

Program Authors

Anna Uhl Chamot is professor of secondary education and faculty adviser for ESL in George Washington University's Department of Teacher Preparation. She has been a researcher and teacher trainer in content-based second-language learning and language-learning strategies. She codesigned and has written extensively about the Cognitive Academic Language Learning Approach (CALLA) and spent seven years implementing the CALLA model in the Arlington Public Schools in Virginia.

Pamela Hartmann is a teacher and writer in the field of Teaching English to Speakers of Other Languages (TESOL). She has taught ESL and EFL in California and overseas since 1973. In addition, she has authored several books in the fields of TESOL and cross-cultural communication.

Jann Huizenga is an educator and consultant in the field of TESOL, with a special interest in teaching reading. She has worked as a teacher trainer at Hunter College in New York City, at the University of New Mexico at Los Alamos, and overseas. She has written numerous books for ESL students.

Program Consultants

Ann Hilborn has been a classroom teacher for thirty years. Her experience includes curriculum writing, grant writing, professional development workshops, and coordination of ESL programs in a large urban high school in Houston, Texas. She writes and consults with publishers, school administrators, and teachers.

Angela Seale is an educational consultant specializing in English as a Second Language. Her expertise is in providing professional staff development to teachers of ESL students.

An Excellent Array of Print and Technology Resources

Longman ESL is dedicated to the needs of English language learners and produces materials that meet the standards and support teachers in every aspect of instruction. **Shining Star** *offers manageable, customizable support to motivate students to succeed in English, in all areas of the academic curriculum, and in their daily lives.*

Print Resources:

- **Student Edition**
- **Annotated Teacher's Edition**
- **Student Workbook**
- **Assessment Guide**
- **Resources for Teachers and Students**
    Daily Lesson Plans
    Newcomer Worksheets
    Letters Home
    Transparencies
    Graphic Organizers
    Daily Language Practice Activities
    Answer Keys
- **Classroom Library**

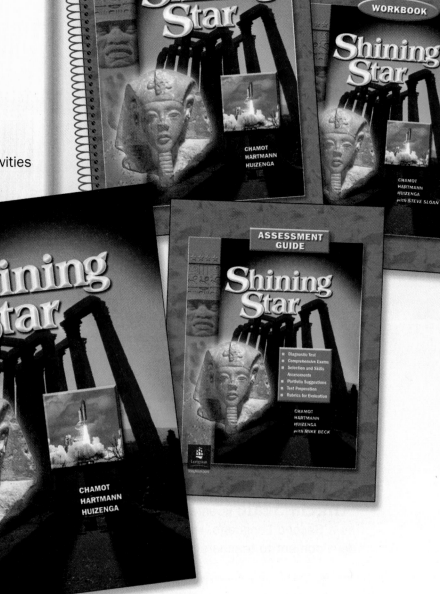

TRANSPARENCIES
Shining Star

- Daily Language Practice
- Graphic Organizers
- Writing Models with Overlays

CHAMOT
HARTMANN
HUIZENGA

RESOURCES FOR TEACHERS
Shining Star

- Lesson Plans
- Student Book Answer Key
- Workbook Answer Key

CHAMOT
HARTMANN
HUIZENGA

RESOURCES FOR YOUR STUDENTS
Shining Star

- Letters Home
- Selection Summaries
- Graphic Organizers
- Newcomer Worksheets

CHAMOT
HARTMANN
HUIZENGA

Daily Language Practice - WEEK 8

DAY 1
An ocean or a lake are very different habits.

DAY 2
amphibians lives in land and in water

Name _____ Date _____

H THE WEATHER

Say the weather.

It's rainy. It's sunny. It's cloudy. It's windy. It's snowy.

Draw a line from the weather to the clothes.

umbrella   shorts   T-shirt   sunglasses
It's snowy.

snow boots   jacket
It's rainy.

raincoat
It's sunny.

Write the weather.

1. _____ 2. _____
It's _____ It's _____

Shining Star Newcomer Worksheet H

DAY 1

Use Daily Language Practice Transparency for Week 7.

Refer to pages 46–47 of the Student Book as you introduce the Unit Theme "The Natural World." Discuss with students the meaning of the word *natural*. Read and discuss the Background information on page 48 of the Prepare to Read spread. Have students respond to the questions in the Make Connections section. Introduce the Key Words on page 49 and model for students how to use the information on the chart to tell the meaning of each word. Have students use the Vocabulary activity on the CD-ROM for additional practice with the Key Words. Make copies of the Letter Home for Unit 2 and send them home with students.

Homework
Have students complete the Vocabulary exercises on pages 00 and 00 of the Workbook.

In addition, ask students to complete the Viewpoint activity on ATE page 46, in which they are asked to look at the art on the Unit Opener pages and name and describe the living and nonliving things they see. Then have students list some of the natural and artificial ... Tell them to divide the items on their list into three ... and nonliving things made ...

Name _____ Date _____

Dear Family,

For the next few weeks, our class will be studying the natural world. We will talk about living things, such as people, animals, and plants. We will also talk about how living things work with nonliving things, such as the sun, the air, and water.

You can help your child learn more about the natural world. Talk to your child about the environment in your region of the United States or your country of origin. You may give information about:

- plants and trees that grow in the region
- animals that live in the region
- what the region was like long ago and how people have changed it

Also talk about how things in the natural world help people to live. For example, plants make oxygen and medicines, and rivers and lakes supply water for drinking and farming. This activity will help your child better understand the connection between people and the natural world, and why people should protect the environment.

As part of this unit, students will talk about a process, or how to make or do something.

You can help by providing examples like these:

- a copy of instructions that show how to assemble something in your home
- a recipe from your region or country of origin

Students will also write an essay about their environment. You can help by providing things like these:

- photographs of places in the region where you live
- a map of the region that shows cities, mountains, lakes, rivers, forests, coastlines, etc.

At the end of this unit, your child may work alone or with other students on a project. Your child may need to search the Internet or find other information at the school library to do this project. I am also encouraging your child to read other books about the natural world. Ask your child to talk with you about the school projects he or she is doing and the additional books he or she is reading for this unit.

Thank you for helping us with our unit about the natural world.

Sincerely,

Teacher _____

Level 2, Unit 2, The Natural World

1

And . . .
Technology Resources:
- Interactive Student CD-ROM
- Reading Selections on Audio CD and Audiocassette
- Focus and Connect Video Program
- On-line Student and Teacher Resources at http://www.longman.com/shiningstar

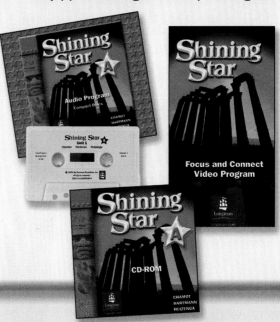

Shining Star A — Audio Program — Compact Discs
CHAMOT HARTMANN HUIZENGA

Shining Star — Unit 1 — Chamot Hartmann Huizenga

Shining Star A — Focus and Connect Video Program — Longman

Shining Star A — CD-ROM
CHAMOT HARTMANN HUIZENGA

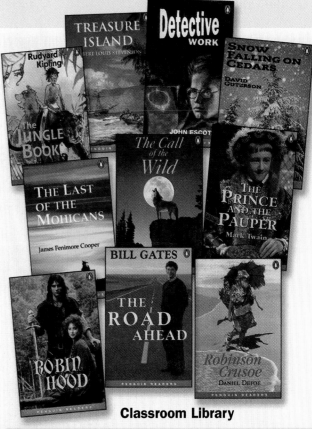

TREASURE ISLAND — ROBERT LOUIS STEVENSON
Detective WORK — JOHN ESCOTT
SNOW FALLING ON CEDARS — DAVID GUTERSON
The JUNGLE BOOK — Rudyard Kipling
The Call of the Wild
THE LAST OF THE MOHICANS — James Fenimore Cooper
THE PRINCE AND THE PAUPER — Mark Twain
BILL GATES — THE ROAD AHEAD
ROBIN HOOD
Robinson Crusoe — DANIEL DEFOE

Classroom Library

An Outstanding Blend of Literature and Content

Only Longman's **Shining Star** *provides your students with a balanced approach to learning English through authentic literature and informational readings.*

Classic literature opens your classroom to lives and cultures across time and space, including ancient myths and legends, poetry, and songs.

Contemporary literature is relevant to students' lives and fosters a love and appreciation of the written word.

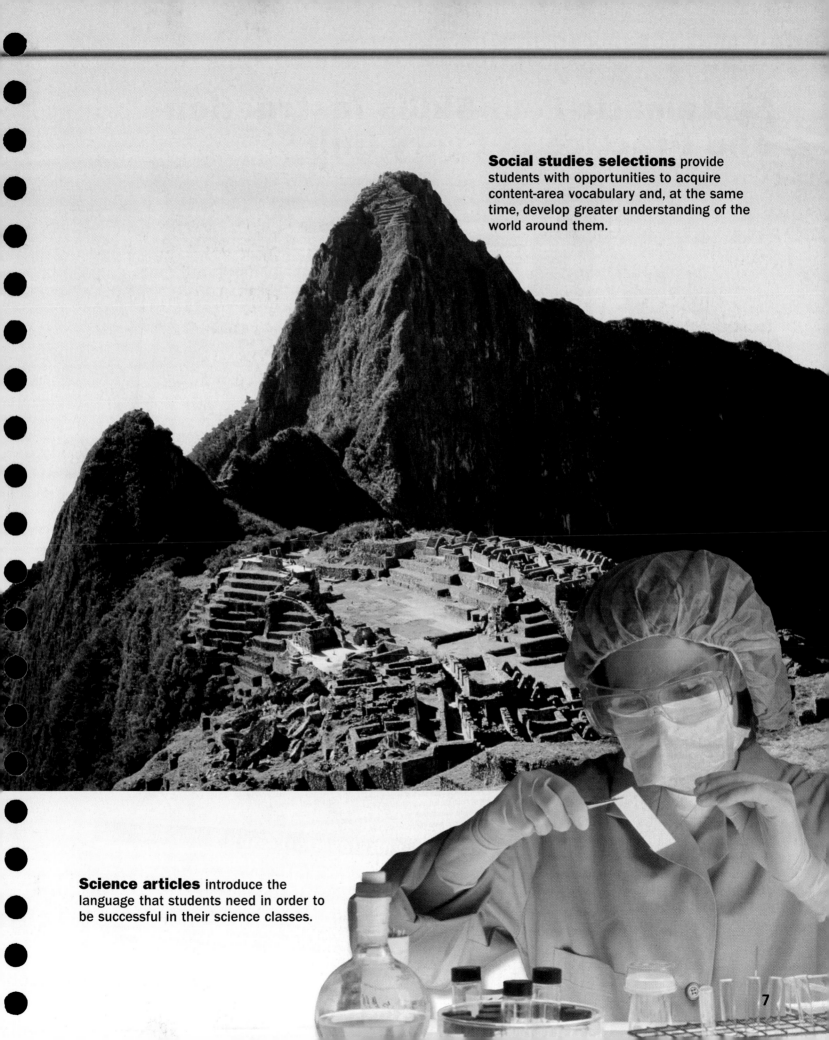

Social studies selections provide students with opportunities to acquire content-area vocabulary and, at the same time, develop greater understanding of the world around them.

Science articles introduce the language that students need in order to be successful in their science classes.

7

Systematic Four-Skills Instruction and Practice in Every Unit

Reading activities provide an achievable, step-by-step approach to reading literature and informational texts.

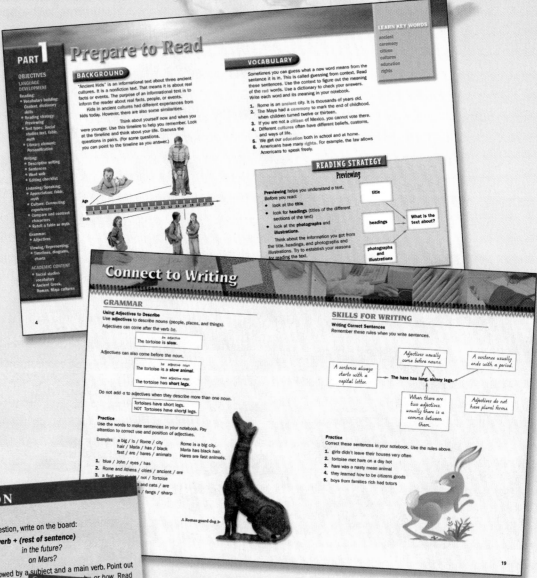

Grammar and writing instruction includes spelling, phonics, and vocabulary development.

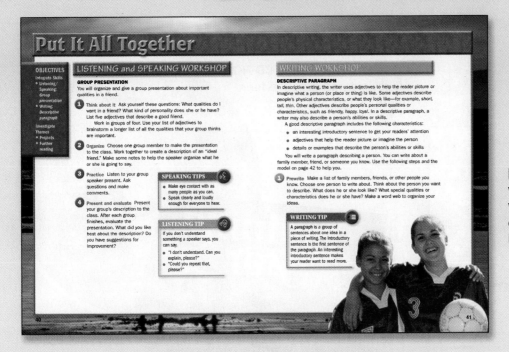

Listening and speaking workshops and **writing workshops** give students opportunities to use language in new contexts.

SPEAKING TIPS

- Make eye contact with as many people as you can.
- Speak clearly and loudly enough for everyone to hear.

Strategies and tips help students with all facets of language acquisition.

LISTENING TIPS

If you don't understand something a speaker says, you can say,

- "I don't understand. Can you explain, please?"
- "Could you repeat that, please?"

WRITING TIP

A **paragraph** is a group of sentences about one idea in a piece of writing. The introductory sentence is the first sentence of the paragraph. An interesting introductory sentence makes your reader want to read more.

Support for All Students

Reproducible newcomer worksheets for basic language acquisition

Interactive student CD-ROM for review and practice for multiple learning styles

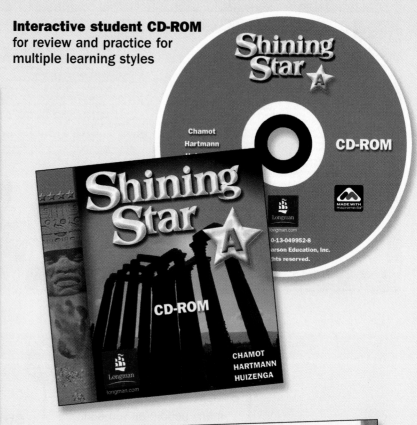

Newcomer teaching suggestions for support in every unit

Point-of-use teaching suggestions to scaffold instruction

READING SUMMARIES
from *My Side of the Mountain*

ENGLISH
This story tells about Sam, a boy who runs away from home and heads for his great-grandparents' land in the mountains. Sam starts walking alone through a forest. He faces many challenges on the first day, such as trying to catch fish and make a place to sleep. He can't light a fire, so he goes to bed hungry, cold, and miserable.

SPANISH
Esta historia habla de Sam, un niño que se escapa de casa y se dirige a la tierra de sus bisabuelos en las montañas. Sam empieza por caminar solo por el bosque. En el primer día se enfrenta a muchos retos tal como agarrar un pez y hacer un lugar para dormir. No consigue encender un fuego por lo que se va a dormir hambriento, con frío y desgraciado.

VIETNAMESE
Câu chuyện kể về Sam, một cậu bé bỏ nhà để tới vùng đất của cụ tổ tiên trong núi. Sam bắt đầu phải đi bộ một mình qua khu rừng. Trong ngày đầu tiên, cậu phải đối mặt với nhiều thử thách như phải cố gắng bắt cá cho đến việc tự tạo chỗ ngủ. Vì không biết nhóm lửa nên cậu bé phải đi ngủ trong đói khát, lạnh lẽo và khốn khổ.

from *My Side of the Mountain*

CHINESE
本故事講述小男孩山姆離家出走，投奔在大山裡的曾祖父。山崎開始在森林中獨行。第一天他面臨許多挑戰，例如抓魚和安排睡覺的地方。他不會點火，因此他只能帶著饑餓、寒冷和濃慘睡去。

HMONG
Zaj dab neeg no qhia txog Sam, ib tug tub hluas uas ncaim nws lub tsev mus nrhiav nws poj koob yawm txwv tej teb chaws nyob pem roob. Sam pib taug kev mus nws ib leeg xwb mus dhau ib lub hav zoov. Thawj thawj hnub ntawd nws raug kev cov nyom ntau, xws li nws yuav tsum sim nuv ntses thiab pua chaw rau nws pw. Nws tsis txawj rauv taws, ces nws yuav tsum yoo mov hmo ntuj, no no nws thiab nws txom nyem.

CAMBODIAN
[Cambodian text]

Copyright © 2004 by Pearson Education, Inc.

Summaries of each reading available in English, Spanish, Cantonese, Vietnamese, and Hmong to increase student understanding and success

All reading selections recorded on the *Shining Star* Audio Program

Shining Star ✦
Unit 1
Chamot Hartman Huizenga

Shining Star ✦
Audio Program
Compact Discs
CHAMOT
HARTMANN
HUIZENGA

Shining Star ✦
Audio Disc 1

Assessment Tools for Success

Shining Star *gives teachers the tools they need for evaluating and assessing their students.*

- Diagnostic Test
- Comprehensive Midterm and Final
- Four-Skills Part and Unit Tests
- Test Prep Worksheets for standardized test practice

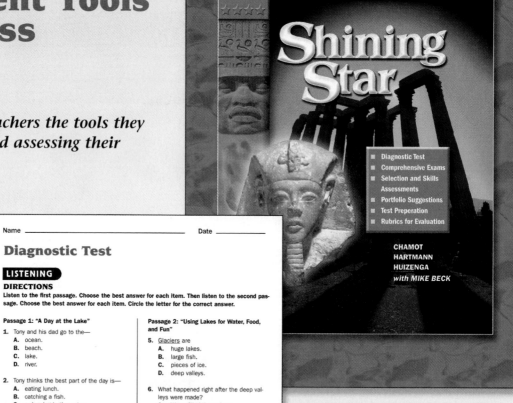

ASSESSMENT GUIDE

Shining Star

- Diagnostic Test
- Comprehensive Exams
- Selection and Skills Assessments
- Portfolio Suggestions
- Test Preperation
- Rubrics for Evaluation

**CHAMOT
HARTMANN
HUIZENGA**
with MIKE BECK

Name _____ Date _____

Diagnostic Test

LISTENING

DIRECTIONS

Listen to the first passage. Choose the best answer for each item. Then listen to the second passage. Choose the best answer for each item. Circle the letter for the correct answer.

Passage 1: "A Day at the Lake"

1. Tony and his dad go to the—
   A. ocean.
   B. beach.
   C. lake.
   D. river.

2. Tony thinks the best part of the day is—
   A. eating lunch.
   B. catching a fish.
   C. swimming in the water.
   D. listening to his dad's stories.

3. You can tell from the passage that Tony's dad—
   A. is funny.
   B. is a good cook.
   C. d

Passage 2: "Using Lakes for Water, Food, and Fun"

5. Glaciers are
   A. huge lakes.
   B. large fish.
   C. pieces of ice.
   D. deep valleys.

6. What happened right after the deep valleys were made?
   A. Water filled the valleys.
   B. People skated on the ice.
   C. Glaciers moved slowly.
   D. Birds came to the lakes

Test Preparation

ANSWERING QUESTIONS ABOUT A PASSAGE

Strategy: Preview the Title, Passage, and Questions

Some tests have passages, or readings, such as short stories, poems, or history or science texts. The tests also have questions or items that ask about the passages. Before you read each passage, preview the title, the passage, and the questions. When you preview, you look at the title, the passage, and the questions to find out what the passage is about and what the questions ask.

Previewing the title, the passage, and the questions helps you:
- decide how to read the passage.
- think about what you need to know to answer the questions.

Practice this strategy by answering the questions on the next page. Follow these steps:

1. Look at the title and the first sentence in each paragraph in the passage. Ask yourself, "Is this passage fiction or nonfiction? What is this passage mostly about?"

2. Then decide how to read the passage. If the passage is nonfiction, or if it tells about something you don't know much about, you should read the passage slowly and carefully. If the passage is fiction, or if it tells about something you already know, you can probably read the passage more quickly.

3. Look at any art that goes with the passage. Ask yourself, "What does the art tell me about the passage?"

4. Look at the questions. Find out what information you need to know to answer the questions. For example, find out if this information as you read the passage.

5. Read the passage. Don't worry if you do not understand all the words. You need to understand enough information to answer the questions.

6. Follow the directions to answer each question. Look back at the passage as often as you like to help you answer the questions. You don't have to reread the whole passage. Look for information that helps you answer the questions. If you are allowed to write in your test, underline key words that help you answer the questions.

7. Don't spend too much time on a question. If you can't decide what the best answer is, circle the number of the question. If you have time at the end of the test, you can go back and finish any questions you circled.

GO ON

Test Preparation/Strategy: Preview the Title, Passage, and Ques

---

Name _____ Date _____

Midterm Test

LISTENING

DIRECTIONS

Listen to the first passage. Choose the best answer for each item. Then listen to the second passage. Choose the best answer for each item. Circle the letter for the correct answer.

Passage 1: "A Trip to the Mountains"

1. What was the trip called?
   A. Mile-High Trip
   B. Lookout Mountain Trip
   C. Rocky Trip
   D. Mother-Daughter Trip

2. What can people see from the top of Lookout Mountain?
   A. Aunt Mary's cabin
   B. The animals at the Denver Zoo
   C. The whole city of Denver below
   D. The tallest mountain in Canada

3. You can tell from this passage that the person telling the story—
   A. did not like to ski.
   B. liked the zoo best of all.
   C. thinks Ohio is more interesting than Denver.
   D. likes visiting a place that is different from Ohio.

4. You can tell that the passage uses first-person point of view because—
   A. it tells about a trip.
   B. it uses the pronoun I.
   C. it tells about Denver.
   D. it compares Colorado to Ohio.

Passage 2: "Rocky Mountains"

5. A mountain chain is—
   A. a very tall mountain.
   B. a group of mountains.
   C. something you use to climb a mountain.
   D. something you use to ski down a mountain.

6. The tops of the Rocky Mountains are covered with—
   A. snow.
   B. forests.
   C. lakes.
   D. rivers.

7. This passage is—
   A. a letter.
   B. a play.
   C. nonfiction.
   D. a poem.

8. You can tell from this passage that the author thinks the Rocky Mountains are—
   A. a scary place to drive through.
   B. too dangerous for most people.
   C. a good place for people to visit.
   D. the best place for people to live.

GO ON

Midterm Test/Listening

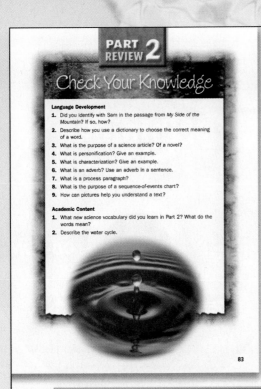

PART REVIEW 2

Check Your Knowledge

Language Development

1. Did you identify with Sam in the passage from *My Side of the Mountain*? If so, how?
2. Describe how you use a dictionary to choose the correct meaning of a word.
3. What is the purpose of a science article? Of a novel?
4. What is personification? Give an example.
5. What is characterization? Give an example.
6. What is an adverb? Use an adverb in a sentence.
7. What is a process paragraph?
8. What is the purpose of a sequence-of-events chart?
9. How can pictures help you understand a text?

Academic Content

1. What new science vocabulary did you learn in Part 2? What do the words mean?
2. Describe the water cycle.

83

ASSESS

You can assess students' knowledge of the unit in several different ways.

Portfolio: Have students place their process paragraphs in their portfolios to compare with later process writing. Have students answer the Check Your Knowledge questions on a separate sheet of paper and add it to their portfolios.

Traditional: Students can complete the Check Your Knowledge questions in class. After students complete Check Your Knowledge, use the Assessment Package. Students can complete the Part Test on pages 41–44. For further practice, have students complete the Test Preparation worksheets.

Performance: Have students who complete the Check Your Knowledge questions in class work in a group to develop their responses. Meet with each group to monitor learning. Be sure to ask students about the thinking behind their answers.

TEST-TAKING TIP

Remind students that when they finish taking a test they should check to make sure they have answered all the questions. See the Test Preparation pages in the Assessment Guide for additional test-taking strategies.

METACOGNITION

Suggest that students use scratch paper to make notes and diagrams that will help them draft their Academic Content answers before they write the final version on the answer sheet.

REACHING ALL STUDENTS

LANGUAGE LEVELS

Beginning: Shorten the Check Your Knowledge questions and clarify the information that is needed to answer each one correctly. For example, for question 2 ask, *Why do you use a dictionary? Suppose you look up a word and it has more than one meaning. How do you decide which one is correct?*

Advanced: Have pairs of students work together to complete Check Your Knowledge. Ask one student to read a question and have the other rephrase it to clarify what is being asked. Then have students compare their answers and determine whether they have answered each question correctly and completely. Students should fix incorrect answers after they reread the relevant pages in their textbook.

T83

Traditional, portfolio, and performance assessment suggestions in the Annotated Teacher's Edition

Listening passages for every assessment recorded on the *Shining Star* Audio Program

Outstanding Technology Resources

Shining Star *technology resources motivate students with a wide array of media, including audio, video, and software.*

Interactive CD-ROM offers practice and reinforcement for all skills and strategies taught in the student text and features activities, games, and grammar resources for every unit.

Shining Star A

Chamot
Hartmann
Huizenga

CD-ROM

VPG
Longman
longman.com
ISBN 0-13-049952-8
© 2004 by Pearson Education, Inc.
All rights reserved.

Internet home page at http://www.longman.com/shiningstar includes additional resources for teachers and students.

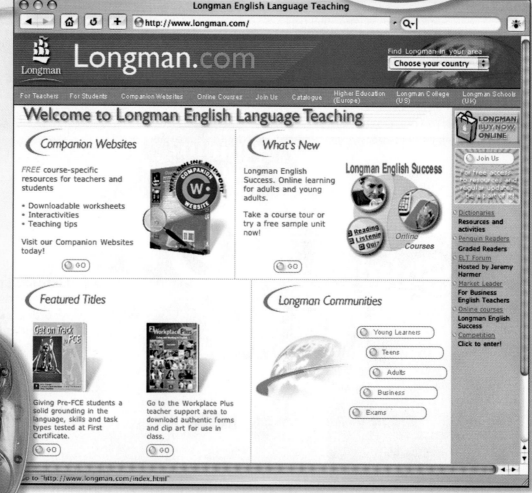

14

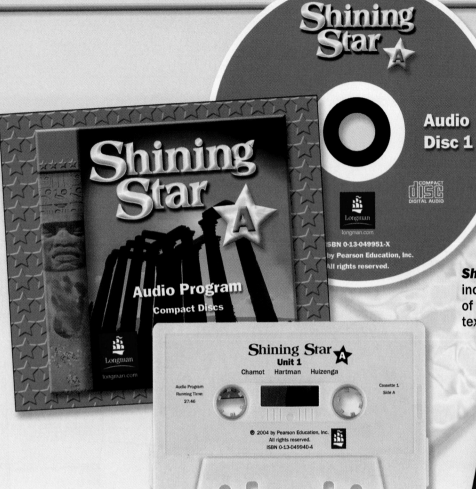

Shining Star Audio Program includes professional recordings of all selections in the student text.

The *Shining Star* **Focus and Connect Video Program** grabs students' attention to explore each unit theme.

Support for Classroom Management

Shining Star gives teachers abundant tools and support for managing time, individualizing instruction, and designing engaging lessons.

Annotated Teacher's Edition:

- Unit Resource Manager for print and technology components

- Part 1/Part 2 Teaching Guide and component correlation

- Newcomer teaching suggestions to give all your students access

- Point-of-use teaching suggestions, including scaffolding and cooperative grouping

- Alternative assessment suggestions that allow students to demonstrate their knowledge

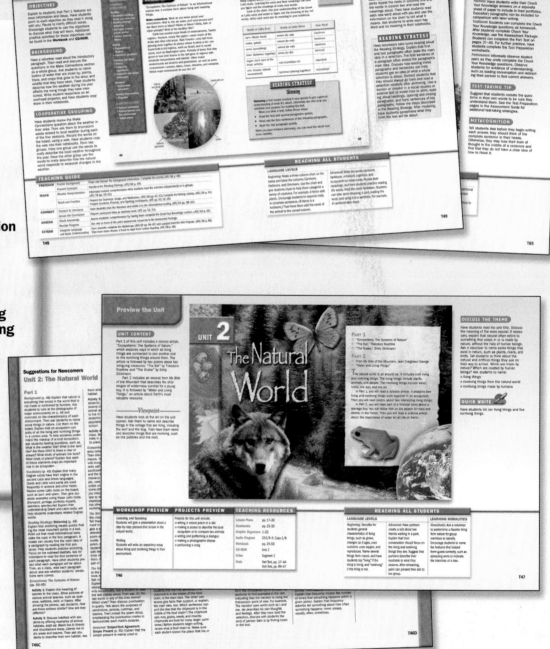

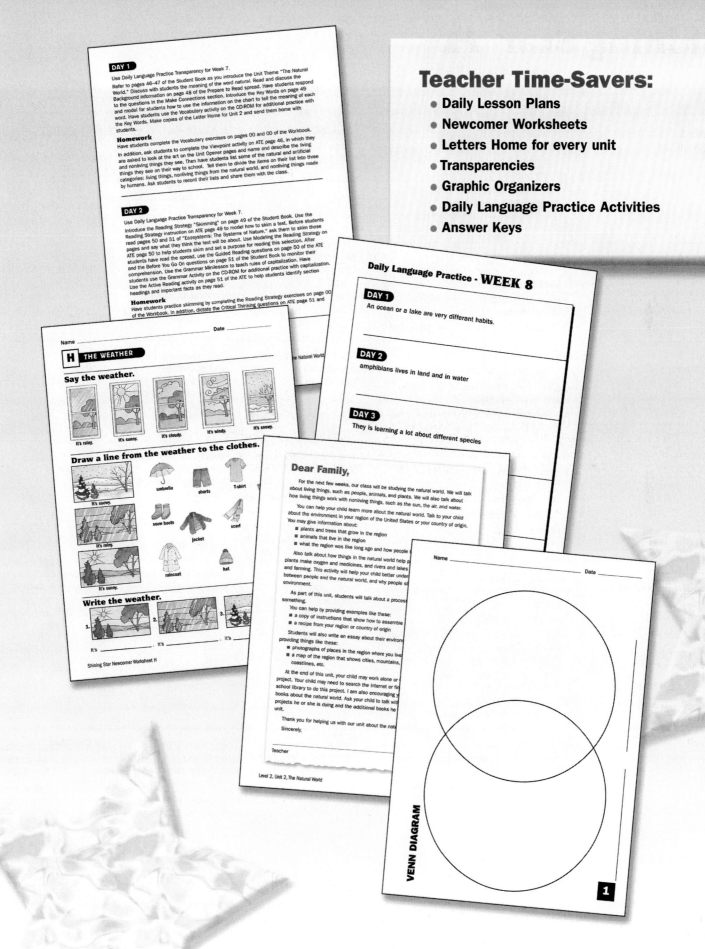

Teacher Time-Savers:

- Daily Lesson Plans
- Newcomer Worksheets
- Letters Home for every unit
- Transparencies
- Graphic Organizers
- Daily Language Practice Activities
- Answer Keys

DAY 1

Use Daily Language Practice Transparency for Week 7.
Refer to pages 46–47 of the Student Book as you introduce the Unit Theme "The Natural World." Discuss with students the meaning of the word natural. Read and discuss the Background information on page 48 of the Prepare to Read spread. Have students respond to the questions in the Make Connections section. Introduce the Key Words on page 49 and model for students how to use the information on the chart to tell the meaning of each word. Have students use the Vocabulary activity on the CD-ROM for additional practice with the Key Words. Make copies of the Letter Home for Unit 2 and send them home with students.

Homework

Have students complete the Vocabulary exercises on pages 00 and 00 of the Workbook.
In addition, ask students to complete the Viewpoint activity on ATE page 46, in which they are asked to look at the art on the Unit Opener pages and name and describe the living and nonliving things they see. Then have students list some of the natural and artificial things they see on their way to school. Tell them to divide the items on their list into three categories: living things, nonliving things from the natural world, and nonliving things made by humans. Ask students to record their lists and share them with the class.

DAY 2

Use Daily Language Practice Transparency for Week 7.
Introduce the Reading Strategy "Skimming" on page 49 of the Student Book. Use the Reading Strategy instruction on ATE page 49 to model how to skim a text. Before students read pages 50 and 51 of "Ecosystems: The Systems of Nature," ask them to skim those pages and say what they think the text will be about. Use Modeling the Reading Strategy on ATE page 50 to help students skim and set a purpose for reading this selection. After students have read the spread, use the Guided Reading questions on page 50 of the ATE and the Before You Go On questions on page 51 of the Student Book to monitor their comprehension. Use the Grammar Minilesson to teach rules of capitalization. Have students use the Grammar Activity on the CD-ROM for additional practice with capitalization. Use the Active Reading activity on page 51 of the ATE to help students identify section headings and important facts as they read.

Homework

Have students practice skimming by completing the Reading Strategy exercises on page 00 of the Workbook. In addition, dictate the Critical Thinking questions on ATE page 51 and

...the Natural World

Name _____ Date _____

H   THE WEATHER

Say the weather.

It's rainy.   It's sunny.   It's cloudy.   It's windy.   It's snowy.

Draw a line from the weather to the clothes.

umbrella   shorts   T-shirt

It's snowy.

snow boots   jacket   scarf

It's rainy.

raincoat   hat

It's sunny.

Write the weather.

1. It's _____ It's _____ It's _____

Shining Star Newcomer Worksheet H

Daily Language Practice - WEEK 8

DAY 1

An ocean or a lake are very differant habits.

DAY 2

amphibians lives in land and in water

DAY 3

They is learning a lot about different species

Dear Family,

For the next few weeks, our class will be studying the natural world. We will talk about living things, such as people, animals, and plants. We will also talk about how living things work with nonliving things, such as the sun, the air, and water.

You can help your child learn more about the natural world. Talk to your child about the environment in your region of the United States or your country of origin. You may give information about:

- plants and trees that grow in the region
- animals that live in the region
- what the region was like long ago and how people...

Also talk about how things in the natural world help p... plants make oxygen and medicines, and rivers and lakes... and farming. This activity will help your child better under... between people and the natural world, and why people sh... environment.

As part of this unit, students will talk about a process... something.

You can help by providing examples like these:

- a copy of instructions that show how to assemble...
- a recipe from your region or country of origin

Students will also write an essay about their environ... providing things like these:

- photographs of places in the region where you live...
- a map of the region that shows cities, mountains,...
  coastlines, etc.

At the end of this unit, your child may work alone or... project. Your child may need to search the Internet or fi... school library to do this project. I am also encouraging y... books about the natural world. Ask your child to talk wit... projects he or she is doing and the additional books he... unit.

Thank you for helping us with our unit about the nat...

Sincerely,

Teacher

Level 2, Unit 2, The Natural World

Name _____ Date _____

VENN DIAGRAM

1

Shining Star A

	Selection	Vocabulary	Reading Strategies	Literary Element
Unit 1 Growing Up	• "Ancient Kids" • "The Hare and the Tortoise," Aesop and "Why Rattlesnake Has Fangs," Cheryl Giff • From *Later, Gator*, Laurence Yep • "Amazing Growth Facts"	Key vocabulary terms; Greek & Latin roots; Cognates	Previewing; Predicting	Personification; Point of view
Unit 2 Challenges and Choices	• "Extraordinary People" • "He Was the Same Age as My Sister," Mieke C. Malandra • From *A Boat to Nowhere*, Maureen Crane Wartski • "Sudan's 'Lost Boys' Start New Lives"	Key vocabulary terms; Prefixes; Suffixes	Skimming a text to determine major ideas; Visualizing	Mood; Flashback
Unit 3 Mysterious Ways	• "Fact or Fiction?" • "Truth or Lies?" George Shannon • "Teenage Detectives," Carol Farley and Elizabeth Dearl • Science experiments: "How to Make a Friend Disappear" and "Water Trick"	Key vocabulary terms; Synonyms; Antonyms	Distinguishing fact and opinion; Using a graphic organizer to compare and contast	Suspense; Plot
Unit 4 Conflict	• "World War I" • "Letter Home," Lance-Corporal Frank Earley • "Can We Forget?" Cora Inez Keyes • "Grass," Carl Sandburg • From *Zlata's Diary*, Zlata Filipović • "The Physical World: The Balkans"	Key vocabulary terms; Phrasal verbs; Collocations	Noting causes and effects; Analyzing historical context	Rhyme; Images
Unit 5 We Can Be Heroes	• "Heroes: Yesterday and Today" • "Wind Beneath My Wings," Bette Midler • *Sebastião Salgado* • From *Leaves of Grass*, Walt Whitman • From *The Diary of Anne Frank, The Play*, Frances Goodrich and Albert Hackett, adapted by Wendy Kesselman • "Heroic Art: Pablo Picasso's *Guernica* and the Kids' Guernica Art Project"	Key vocabulary terms; Homophones; Meaning based on root words	Making inferences; Visualizing	Recognizing and analyzing setting
Unit 6 Look Into the Future	• "Life in the Future" • "Interview with an Astronaut: Dan Bursch" • From *The Time Warp Trio: 2095*, Jon Scieszka • "DNA, Genes, and Traits"	Key vocabulary terms; Using print and online resources to find spelling and meaning; Word origins	Summarizing; Reading for enjoyment	Dialogue

Grammar	Writing	Phonics	Spelling
Using adjectives to describe; Using the conjunction *and*; Present tense: regular and irregular verbs; Negative sentences in the present	Writing correct sentences; Writing compound sentences; Writing descriptive sentences; Writing a descriptive paragraph	Short *a, o, i*; Short *u, e*	Spelling short *a, o, i*; Spelling short *u, e* sounds
Using the simple past; Using the conjunction *but*; Identifying parts of speech; Questions in present and past (affirmative, negative information)	Writing a narrative paragraph; Using a variety of sentence types; Writing a personal narrative	Long *a, i* sound: *a-e, ai, ay, i-e, igh*; Long *o*, long *e*, long *u*	Spelling long *a, i* sounds: *a-e, ay, i-e*; Spelling long *o, e, u*
Present progressive + prepositions of location; Adjective placement in compound sentences; Punctuation: periods and exclamation points	Writing a descriptive paragraph; Writing clues; Writing instructions for a science experiment	Blends; Digraphs *sh, ph, th*	Adding *–ing*; Number words
Using *so* as a conjunction; Using pronoun referents; *Wh–* questions; Possessives with apostrophes	Writing a cause-and-effect paragraph; Writing an eyewitness report; Writing a historical report	Digraphs *wh, ng*; Digraphs *ch, tch*	Adding *–ed*; Adding *–es*
The passive voice; Comparative and superlative adjectives; Capitalization; Comparative adverbs	Using time phrases to write a biography; Writing a review; Writing a letter to the editor	Digraphs *wr, kn*; *r*-controlled vowels	Silent letters *wr, kn*; Changing *y* to *–i* to add *–er* and *-est*
Using *will* for the future; Using *be going to* for the future; Word order in questions; Punctuation: comma	Writing notes for a research report; Making a sentence outline; Writing a research report	Diphthong: *ou, ow, oy, oi* Schwa /ə/	Spelling diphthong sounds; Spelling the schwa sound /ə/

Shining Star B

	Selection	Vocabulary	Reading Strategies	Literary Element
Unit 1 Journeys of Discovery	• "The First Americans" • "This Land Is Your Land," Woody Guthrie • "Roll On, Columbia," Woody Guthrie • From *River to Tomorrow,* Ellen Levine • "Reading a Relief Map"	Key vocabulary terms; Cognates; Prefixes	Previewing and predicting; Visualizing	Alliteration; Flashback
Unit 2 The Natural World	• "Ecosystems: The Systems of Nature" • "The Bat," Theodore Roethke • "The Snake," Emily Dickinson • From *My Side of the Mountain,* Jean Craighead George • "Water and Living Things"	Key vocabulary terms; Greek and Latin roots; Suffixes	Skimming; Identifying with a character	Rhyme; Personification; Characterization
Unit 3 Striving For Success	• "Success Stories" • "An Interview with Naomi Shihab Nye," Rachel Barenblat • From *Seedfolks,* Paul Fleischman • "How Seeds and Plants Grow"	Key vocabulary terms; Suffixes with occupations; Idioms	Making inferences; Monitoring comprehension	First-person point of view; Plot
Unit 4 Change	• "Changing Earth" • "The Intersection," Dina Anastasio • "China's Little Ambassador," Bette Bao Lord • "Migration Patterns"	Key vocabulary terms; Phrasal verbs; Synonyms	Noting causes, effects, and solutions; Using your experience to understand a story	Dialogue; Simile
Unit 5 The Frontier	• "The Road to Texas Independence" • From *A Line in the Sand,* Sherry Garland • From *Pecos Bill: The Greatest Cowboy of All Time,* James Cloyd Bowman • "The Cowboy Era"	Key vocabulary terms; Antonyms; Print and nonprint resources for meaning and spelling	Taking notes; Summarizing	Setting; Hyperbole
Unit 6 Explaining the Universe	• "Earth's Orbit" • "How Glooskap Found the Summer" • "Persephone and the Pomegranate Seeds" • *The Great Bear,* Pamela Gerke • "Telescopes"	Key vocabulary terms; Homonyms; Meaning based on word roots	Studying diagrams; Reading plays aloud	Hero or heroine; Conflict; Narrator; Stage directions

Grammar	Writing	Phonics	Spelling
Using pronouns; Using the conjunctions *and* and *or;* Adjective placement; Identifying parts of speech	Writing a descriptive paragraph; Writing a descriptive essay	Long and short *a* and *e;* Long and short *i*	Spelling long and short *a* and *e* sounds; Spelling long and short *i*
Subject-verb agreement: simple present; Using adverbs; Capitalization; Imperatives	Writing an expository paragraph; Writing a process paragraph; Writing an expository essay	Long and short *o* and *u;* Silent *e*	Spelling long and short *o* and *u* sounds; Adding *-ed*
Yes/No and *wh-* questions: simple past; Using compound sentences; *Be* verbs: simple past; Negative past sentences	Writing a narrative paragraph; Writing a personal narrative; Writing a biographical narrative	*r*-controlled vowels *ar, ir, er, ur;* Digraph *wh*	Spelling occupation words; Initial *w-* and *j-*
Using real conditionals: Sentences with *if* clauses; Complex sentences; Future tense; The comma	Writing a formal persuasive letter; Writing an informal persuasive e-mail message; Writing a travel brochure	Schwa /ə/; Voiced and unvoiced final *s*	Spelling the schwa /ə/ sound; Rules for plurals
Comparative and superlative adjectives; Using possessive adjectives and possessive pronouns; Comparatives and superlatives; Subject and object pronouns	Writing notes for a research report; Writing summaries and responses; Writing a research report	Blends; Digraphs *wh, ng, ch, tch, wr, kn*	Changing *y* to *i* to add *-er* and *-est;* Spelling *kn-* words
Using quotations; Using prepositional phrases; Apostrophes with contractions and possessives; Using adverbs for precision	Writing a short myth; Writing a skit; Writing a short story	Digraphs *sh, ph, th;* Diphthongs *oo, ou, ow, oy, oi*	Spelling /t/, /th/, /d/; Adding *-ing*

Shining Star C

	Selection	Vocabulary	Reading Strategies	Literary Element
Unit 1 Points of View	• "Moving Toward Independence: The Boston Tea Party" • "Yankee Doodle" and "The World Turned Upside Down" • From *Daughter of China*, Meihong Xu and Larry Engelmann • "Understanding Cultural Differences," Sandy Cameron	Key vocabulary terms; Cognates; Prefixes	Previewing; Using knowledge and experience to predict	Comparing and contrasting
Unit 2 The Human Spirit	• "Abraham Lincoln" • "Nancy Hanks," Rosemary Carr and Stephen Vincent Benét • "Lincoln," John Gould Fletcher • *Sor Juana Inés de la Cruz*, Kathleen Thompson • "The Peace Corps"	Key vocabulary terms; Suffixes; Homonyms	Taking notes; Making inferences	Rhyme; Simile; Characterization
Unit 3 Voices of Freedom	• "I Have a Dream," Martin Luther King Jr. • "Lady Freedom Among Us," Rita Dove • From *Roll of Thunder, Hear My Cry*, Mildred D. Taylor • "Words of Freedom"	Key vocabulary terms; *Have* + noun; *Be* and *get* (idiomatic)	Summarizing; Visualizing	Metaphor; Mood
Unit 4 Risks and Challenges	• "The Train to Freedom" • "Follow the Drinking Gourd" • "Five New Words at a Time," Yu-Lan (Mary) Ying • From *The Little Prince: The Play*, Rick Cummins and John Scoullar, adapted from the novel by Antoine de Saint-Exupéry • "Performance Anxiety"	Key vocabulary terms; Meanings based on roots; Synonyms	Skimming for main ideas; Analyzing text structure	Stage directions
Unit 5 Reach for the Stars	• "Earth and the Milky Way" • *The Starry Night* (painting), Vincent van Gogh • "On van Gogh's *Starry Night*," Martha Staid • "Escape at Bedtime," Robert Louis Stevenson • "The Ten Chinese Suns" • "Re" • "Why the Sun Is So High in the Heavens" • "Solar Eclipses"	Key vocabulary terms; Antonyms; Greek and Latin roots	Using a K-W-L-H chart; Identifying causes and effect	Personification; Theme
Unit 6 Shifting Perspectives	• "Light" • "A Reflection in Art: Jan van Eyck's Double Portrait" • "Mirror, Mirror: Mambo No. 5," Gustavo Pérez Firmat • From *The Story of My Life*, Helen Keller • "Sowing the Seeds of Peace," Mandy Terc	Key vocabulary terms; Number words including ordinals; Using print and online resources to find spellings, etc.	Monitoring comprehension; Listening to texts	Point of view

Grammar	Writing	Phonics	Spelling
Using the simple past; Subject-verb agreement in the simple present; Regular and irregular verbs in the present; Question forms: present and past	Writing a narrative paragraph; Writing a journal entry; Writing a personal narrative	Long and short vowels *a, i*; Long and short vowels *e, o, u*	Spelling long and short *a* and *i* sounds; Spelling long and short *e, o,* and *u* sounds
Using real conditionals: Sentences with *if* clauses; Modals of advice; Identifying parts of speech; Adjective clauses	Persuasive paragraph; Giving advice in an informal e-mail; Writing a letter to the editor	Liquid *l* and *r*; Digraph *wh*	Spelling double *l*s and *r*s; Initial *w–, j–*
The present perfect; Using gerunds and infinitives; Past participles; Past progressive	Writing essays; Writing a poem; Writing a descriptive essay	Blends *st, cl, sl*; Digraphs *th-, ph-, sh*	Words with *cl, sl, st, ch, sh, th, wh*
Using prepositions and prepositional phrases; Contractions; Prepositional phrases with time; Possessives	Writing interview questions; Writing dialogue; Writing a biographical narrative	Digraphs *ch, tch, wr, kn*; Voiced and voiceless *s*	Doubling the final consonant and adding *–ing*; Initial *s, sh, z*
Comparative and superlative adjectives; Using the passive voice; Comparative and superlative adverbs; Compound and complex sentences	Writing a research report comparing and contrasting two subjects; Writing a research report using a variety of sources; Writing a research report using note cards	*r*-controlled vowels; Voiced *–ed* endings	Changing *y* to *i* before adding *–er, –est*; Doubling the final consonant and adding *–ed*
Subject and object pronouns; Compound and complex sentences; Nominative and objective cases; Using the simple future	Writing responses; Writing a personal narrative; Writing a short story	Unvoiced *–ed*; Diphthongs *ou, ow, oy, oi*	Adding *–ed*; Schwa sounds

How to Teach Learning Strategies to English Language Learners

Anna Uhl Chamot
The George Washington University

English language learning (ELL) students face many challenges to academic achievement. Not only must they learn academic English, but they must also learn content subject matter and skills. In addition, ELL students are now expected to meet many of the same national and state standards and assessments as native English speakers. **Shining Star** *provides challenging content-based language development and learning strategies that help students achieve these goals.*

Why teach learning strategies?

One way to accelerate the academic language learning of ELL students is to teach them how to learn more effectively and efficiently. Learning strategies are techniques for understanding, remembering, and using information and skills. Learning strategies are particularly important for ELL students as they seek to master both language and academic content simultaneously, as they do in *Shining Star.*

Strategy instruction, incorporated throughout *Shining Star,* can help students by:

- showing them techniques for "how to learn"
- developing their independence and confidence as learners
- increasing their academic motivation as they become more successful in school
- developing their awareness of their own thinking and learning processes

When students develop metacognition, the awareness of the learning processes and strategies that lead to success, they are more likely to plan how to proceed with a learning task, monitor their own performance on an ongoing basis, find solutions to problems encountered, and evaluate themselves upon task completion.

Shining Star incorporates learning strategies into student activities. The chart on page 25 identifies the strategies taught and provides brief definitions. Strategies with an asterisk are presented explicitly in the student textbook in strategy boxes for reading and writing. The strategies without asterisks are presented implicitly in a wide range of language development activities.

Learning Strategies for ELL Students

STRATEGY NAMES	DESCRIPTION AND EXAMPLES
Organizational Planning	Setting a learning goal; planning how to carry out a project, write a story, or solve a problem
*Predicting	Using parts of a text (such as illustrations, titles, headings, organization) or a real life situation and your own background knowledge to anticipate what is likely to occur next
Self-management	Seeking or arranging the conditions that help you learn
*Using Your Knowledge and Experience	Using your knowledge and experience to understand and learn something new, brainstorming relevant words and ideas, making associations and analogies; writing or telling what you know
*Monitoring Comprehension	Being aware of how well a task is going, how well you understand a topic while listening or reading, or how well you are expressing your ideas when writing or speaking
*Skimming for Main Ideas	Focusing on specific aspects of a task, such as identifying key words or ideas or scanning a text for particular information
Using/Making Rules	Applying a rule (phonics, decoding, grammar, linguistic, mathematical, scientific, and so on) to understand a text or complete a task; figuring out rules or patterns from examples
*Taking Notes	Writing down key information in verbal, graphic, or numerical form, often as concept maps, word webs, timelines, or other types of graphic organizers
*Visualizing	Creating mental pictures and using them to understand and appreciate descriptive writing
Cooperation	Working with classmates to complete a task or project, demonstrate a process or product, share knowledge, solve problems, give and receive feedback, and develop social skills
*Making Inferences	Using the context of an oral or written text and your own knowledge to guess meanings of unfamiliar words or ideas
Substitution	Using a synonym, paraphrase, or circumlocution when you want to express an idea and do not know the exact word(s) you need
*Using Resources	Using reference materials (books, dictionaries, encyclopedias, videos, performances, computer programs and databases, the Internet) to find information or complete a task
Classification	Grouping words, concepts, physical objects, numbers, or quantities according to their attributes; constructing graphic organizers to show classifications
*Asking Questions	Negotiating meaning by asking for clarification, explanation, confirmation, rephrasing, or examples
*Summarizing	Making a mental, oral, or written summary of something you listened to or read; retelling a story or other text in your own words
*Self-evaluation	After completing a task, judging how well you did, whether you reached your goal, and how effective your learning strategies or problem-solving procedures were

How can learning strategies be taught?

Since learning strategies are mental processes with few observable manifestations, teachers often cannot tell whether a student is learning how to use them. Strategies such as applying one's prior knowledge or making inferences during reading cannot be observed at all, and students may encounter some difficulty in understanding and using them. *Shining Star* offers these suggestions to help teachers make strategies instruction more tangible:

- Model the strategy by "thinking aloud" as you perform a task similar to the one students will perform.
- Use the strategy names and refer to them consistently by name.
- Tell students why the strategy is important and how it can help them.
- List strategies with brief definitions on a poster or write individual strategies on laminated cards that can be posted on a bulletin board. Refer to the posted strategies when they are taught and practiced.
- Remind students to use strategies as they read, brainstorm, write, focus on grammar, learn vocabulary, and work on projects.
- Provide opportunities for students to discuss strategies— how they use them, additional strategies they use, and which strategies they prefer.

The instructional sequence developed for the Cognitive Academic Language Learning Approach (CALLA) has provided a useful framework for teaching language learning strategies and for the development of *Shining Star*. The sequence provides a five-phase recursive cycle for introducing, teaching, practicing, evaluating, and applying learning strategies. In this approach, highly explicit instruction in applying strategies to learning tasks is gradually faded so that students can begin to assume greater responsibility in selecting and applying appropriate learning strategies. The cycle repeats as new strategies or new applications are added to students' strategic repertoires. The five phases of the CALLA instructional sequence are as follows:

- **Preparation** (**Preteach** in *Shining Star*)
  The purpose of this phase is to help students identify the strategies they are already using and to develop their metacognitive awareness of the relationship between their own mental processes and effective learning. By identifying students' prior knowledge of a topic and evaluating their current use of learning strategies, teachers can diagnose the needs of their students for learning strategies instruction. Activities in the Preparation stage can include class discussions about strategies used for recent learning tasks, group or individual interviews about strategies used for particular tasks, think-aloud sessions in which students describe their thought processes while they work on a task, questionnaires or checklists about strategies used, and diary entries about individual approaches to language learning.

- **Presentation** (**Teach** in *Shining Star*)
  This phase focuses on explaining and modeling the learning strategy or strategies. The teacher conveys information about the characteristics, usefulness, and applications of a particular strategy. Perhaps the most powerful way in which to accomplish this purpose is for the teacher to model his or her own personal use of the strategy. For example, the teacher might think aloud while reading a text displayed on the overhead projector. Strategies the teacher might demonstrate while reading could include making predictions based on the title, using illustrations to recall prior knowledge of the topic, selectively attending to headings and bold-faced text, monitoring comprehension and making decisions about how unfamiliar words, structures, or ideas should be treated, and, finally, evaluating how successful he or she has been in learning from the text. The teacher can ask students to recall the strategies they observed and then further describe the strategies, provide a specific name for each strategy, and explain when the strategy can be used most effectively. This modeling helps students visualize themselves working successfully on a similar task.

- **Practice** (**Connect** in *Shining Star*)
  In this phase, students have the opportunity to practice the learning strategy with an authentic learning task, such as those presented in *Shining Star*. The practice will frequently take place during collaborative work with classmates. For example, a group of students might read a story, then describe the images the story evoked, discuss unfamiliar words encountered and infer meanings through context clues, and take turns summarizing the main points of the story. Strategies can be practiced

with any content or language task and can involve any combination of language modalities. In a content-based ESL program such as *Shining Star*, strategies can be used to understand and remember concepts and skills from curriculum areas such as science, mathematics, social studies, and literature.

- **Self-Evaluation** (**Assess** in *Shining Star*)
  The main purpose of this phase is to provide students with opportunities to evaluate their own success in using learning strategies, thus developing metacognitive awareness of their own learning processes. Activities that develop students' self-evaluation insights include debriefing discussions after strategies practice, learning logs in which students record the results of their learning strategies applications, checklists of strategies used, and open-ended questionnaires in which students can express their opinions about the usefulness of particular strategies.

- **Expansion** (**Extend** in *Shining Star*)
  In this phase students make personal decisions about the strategies that they find most effective, apply these strategies to new contexts in other classes as well as in the ESL class, and devise their own individual combinations and interpretations of learning strategies. By this stage, the goal of learning strategies instruction has been achieved, for students have become independently strategic and are able to reflect on and regulate their own learning. An important feature of the CALLA instructional sequence is that the needs and thoughts of students are central to all instruction. The sequence guides students towards increasing levels of independence, thus fostering attitudes of academic self-efficacy.

Ongoing monitoring of students' use of both instructed and individually developed strategies is essential if teachers are to scaffold their instruction successfully. In scaffolded instruction, teachers begin with explicit instruction and gradually reduce prompts and cues to students. In this way students begin to assume responsibility for and regulation of their own learning. Individual students may need greater or lesser amounts of explicit strategies instruction, depending on the degree to which they have developed strategies independently of instruction. This is why teachers must continually assess their students' ability to use the strategies independently and transfer them to new tasks. When students are able to use instructed strategies without

prompting, they need to explore new strategies, new applications, and new opportunities for self-regulated learning. The quest for self-regulated learning is—as with all aspects of self-knowledge—a life-long endeavor, and even high-achieving adults can continue to develop their repertoire of effective learning strategies.

Suggested Reading

Chamot, A. U., Barnhardt, S., El-Dinary, P. B. & Robbins, J. (1999). *The learning strategies handbook.* White Plains, NY: Addison Wesley Longman.

Chamot, A. U. (1996). *Accelerating achievement with learning strategies.* Glenview, IL: Scott Foresman Addison Wesley.

Chamot, A. U. & O'Malley, J. M. (1994). *The CALLA handbook: Implementing the cognitive academic language learning approach.* White Plains, NY: Addison Wesley Longman.

National Capital Language Resource Center (2002). *The elementary immersion learning strategies resource guide.* Washington, DC: NCLRC.

The Elements of Reading

Pam Hartmann

Left to their own devices, with no direction from a teacher, most ESL students tend to read word by word, painfully looking up every unknown word, usually in a bilingual dictionary. This approach, the grammar-translation method, was actually used for hundreds of years and may have been useful in the learning of a dead language but—as most teachers are well aware—does not allow for true communication or result in a student's becoming a good reader.

Then what *is* a good approach? A good reading program not only teaches students English, but also gives them the strategies to deal with the written language in other classes and, we hope, a sense of the joy of reading.

On the way to becoming independent readers and thinkers, students will often encounter reading passages that seem over their heads. Because of this, they need more than practice with readings at their level. They need *scaffolding*—support questions and activities to help them deal with more difficult material—and explicit direction for what to do with material that appears too hard—in a word, *strategies*.

Strategies

In order to become good readers in English, students need to read—a lot. But they also need to be taught useful strategies and given ample practice in using them. In one's own language, there are good skills that seem to come naturally, such as figuring out the meaning of an occasional new word from its context—even if not perfectly—instead of going to the dictionary for an exact definition. However, these skills seldom translate to the new, target language— in this case, English. It is often the best students who need the most direction from the teacher, because they are often inclined to believe that being a good student requires doing things the hard way and involves discipline and maybe suffering. Therefore, these students need "permission" and encouragement from the teacher to activate good reading strategies.

Students will get more out of a reading passage if they know something about the topic going into it. Pictures, diagrams, and prereading discussion questions help students consider what they already know, spark their curiosity, and suggest questions that they can expect to answer by reading. This skill of "activating schema" includes holding a question or idea in mind while reading. The reading either answers the question or confirms (or corrects) the reader's expectation, and learning takes place.

A related skill is making predictions. Any reader whose mind is engaged by a story or book, such as a great mystery novel, is constantly wondering, "So what happens next?" For a student reading a chapter in a biology textbook, no doubt this is far less likely to occur, but all students will benefit from knowing how to stop occasionally in a reading passage to predict what the next section will tell them.

The skill of identifying the main idea in a reading passage is essential for all students. Without it, meaning is not clear. It requires an ability to distinguish general from specific information, which doesn't always come easily. Often, a book has more than one topic that students might identify as the main idea. Students sometimes choose an obscure, minor point as the "main idea" because, as they explain, "it's interesting." A variety of exercises can help students find the main idea. If students choose the wrong one, the teacher needs to help them find the "umbrella" idea that includes *all* of the important information of the passage.

In individual paragraphs with a clearly stated *topic* sentence, students can practice finding this sentence which is often, but not always, the first. Identifying topic sentences is a reading skill that also helps prepare students to create topic sentences when the assignment is to write their own paragraphs.

For a text of any length—a paragraph, a section of a chapter, an entire chapter, or a story—students can identify the central topic of the passage, or what it's about, using a noun or noun phrase. Then they list everything the passage says about the topic and "add up" these details to formulate a sentence describing the larger idea that the passage conveys. This is far more difficult than answering a multiple-choice question or identifying the topic sentence, but it is a step toward becoming an independent reader.

Filling in a chart or graphic organizer is a useful way to guide more visually-oriented students toward first finding main ideas and important details and then demonstrating this understanding.

Reading in phrases instead of word by word is another skill that can be taught. In doing this, students learn to group words by their meanings so that it is possible to understand more and read faster. By focusing on phrases, students can also better remember new vocabulary. Recent brain research provides evidence that the brain remembers "chunks" (i.e., phrases) better than it does "bits" (i.e., individual words).

These and many other skills—recognizing sequence, making inferences, and distinguishing fact from opinion, to name a few—are all a part of the overall ability to think critically and are, therefore, essential for success in any class.

Extensive Reading

If it is the textbook that offers practice with *intensive* reading and necessary strategies, it is the *extensive* reading component that gives students the chance to read longer texts outside the classroom and to put into practice the strategies that they've been learning. In extensive reading, students read a novel, for example, and then report on it to the teacher or class.

A variation on this is "sustained silent reading" or "free reading." Free reading offers students the joy of reading. It involves showering students with books. The students are given a wide variety of books to choose from—fiction and nonfiction, novels, short story books, history, romance, war stories, even comic books. Each student chooses one and reads for pleasure, knowing that there will be no tests, no written reports. Students might, from time to time, informally share what they like about the book they've chosen with a small group of students. The students carry this book everywhere and read whenever there is a chance. The teacher usually sets aside ten to fifteen minutes of class time, several days a week, in which students can simply read—for fun. The only rule is that the books should not be boring or too hard. They should be at the students' level or perhaps somewhat lower to allow them to relax and turn pages without feeling the need to go to the dictionary. As soon as students decide that a book is boring or hard (or, of course, when they finish it), they bring it back and exchange it for a new book. Teachers are often surprised at the number of books students read and at the improved attitude toward reading when given such a choice.

Without explicitly taught strategies, students fall into bad habits; they have trouble finding meaning and become frustrated. Without access to a stream of books that they truly enjoy, students cannot develop a love of reading. But when both elements are included in the right amounts, students become efficient, energized, critical readers with a lifelong appreciation for the written word. It is finding the balance between these elements that is the art of teaching reading.

Suggested Reading

Bamford, J. & Day, R. R. (1997, May). Extensive reading: What is it? Why bother? *The Language Teacher, 21 (5),* 6–8, 12.

Brinton, D. M., Snow, M. A. & Wesche, M. B. (1989). *Content-based second language instruction.* Rowley, MA: Newbury House.

Carrell, P. L. (1998, March). Can reading strategies be successfully taught? *The Language Teacher, 22 (3),* 7–14.

Ernst-Slavit, G., Moore, M. & Maloney, C. (2002, October). Changing lives: Teaching English and literature to ESL students: To enhance learning for ESL students the authors provide selected background knowledge and strategies. *Journal of Adolescent & Adult Literacy, 46,* 116.

Eskey, D. (1995, March). Colloquium on research in reading in a second language. Paper presented at TESOL '95, Long Beach, CA, USA.

Kern, R. G. (1994). The role of mental translation in second language reading. *Studies in Second Language Acquisition, 16 (4),* 441-461.

Krashen, S. (1993). *The power of reading: Insights from the research.* Englewood, CO: Libraries Unlimited.

Lewis, M. (1997). *Implementing the lexical approach: Putting theory into practice.* London: Language Teaching Publications.

Nation, I. S. P. (1990). *Teaching & learning vocabulary.* Boston: Heinle & Heinle.

Redford, S. & Quinn, K. (1998). Developing a vocabulary-based communicative course. In *JALT '97: Trends and transitions,* 89-94.

Richard-Amato, P. (1988). *Making it happen.* White Plains, NY: Longman.

Scarcella, R. (1990). *Teaching language minority students in the multicultural classroom.* White Plains, NY: Longman.

Teaching the Program

Shining Star is a three-level English language-learning program based on the systematic development of skills and strategies. In *Shining Star*, English learners will read a wide variety of thematically linked selections, including classic contemporary literature as well as informational readings. Each selection will enable students to learn the vocabulary, grammar, viewing, listening, speaking, and writing skills they need to transition into the mainstream curriculum.

Each unit of *Shining Star* develops language use through a systematic structure that unfolds the content of the program gradually and logically. Students and teachers are supported with explicit, direct, and clear instruction, as well as a number of outside resources for classroom enrichment. Systematic scaffolding is provided in the Annotated Teacher's Edition to maximize learning for all students.

Student Textbook

Each of the six units in the *Shining Star* Student Textbook is based on a relevant, high-interest theme. The unit is divided into two parts, with at least four reading selections. Part 1 of each unit contains a content reading with a connected literature selection. Part 2 contains a literature selection with a connected informational reading. Each part includes strategies for reading the selections, as well as vocabulary-building activities and instruction to help students make connections between selections. Grammar, usage, and mechanics instruction, a writing assignment, and a self-assessment opportunity round out each part of the unit.

After students complete the unit, they have opportunities to combine their language skills and apply their understanding of the unit theme in a Listening and Speaking Workshop, a Writing Workshop, Unit Projects, and Suggestions for Further Reading about the theme.

Annotated Teacher's Edition

The spiral-bound Annotated Teacher's Edition of *Shining Star* contains reproduced student pages with point-of-use teaching suggestions. The Annotated Teacher's Edition also provides explicit instructions for:

- direct teaching
- demonstration
- scaffolding
- modeling
- cooperative grouping
- preteaching and reteaching
- suggestions and techniques for addressing various language proficiencies
- suggestions and techniques for addressing various learning modalities

A Resource Manager and Suggestions for Newcomers are included before each unit in the Annotated Teacher's Edition. Because your time is important, the Resource Manager will help you design and implement the lesson plan using the wide array of print and technology resources that are available with the *Shining Star* program. The Suggestions for Newcomers pages are designed to help you address the needs of students who are new to the English language. These suggestions, along with the Newcomer Worksheets in the Resources for Your Students, will help you create a meaningful learning environment for new students.

Each part of every unit in the Annotated Teacher's Edition is designed to enhance student comprehension and retention using the following time- and research-tested approach:

- preteach
- teach
- connect
- assess
- extend

This structure presents content in a logical order to help students make connections within a content area and across the curriculum. While taking into account the skills your students have already mastered, it helps you control the amount of new information that is introduced in each unit, as well as the extension and application of all new material.

Student Workbook

The student Workbook contains skill-building activities for vocabulary and word analysis, for grammar, usage, and mechanics, and for writing. Also included are active reading log pages for two of the readings in each unit.

Audio Program

Available on both cassette and CD, every selection in the *Shining Star* program has been professionally recorded to build listening and reading skills and to help you engage your students. A listening assessment passage for each unit is also included in the Audio Program.

Assessment Guide

In addition to measuring student progress, the *Shining Star* Assessment Guide has been carefully crafted to help you make important instructional decisions throughout the academic year. You can use it at the beginning of the year to determine entry-level language ability. Summative assessment is provided with every part and every unit. These tests consist of multiple-choice items and essay questions. Each item is tagged according to the skill it covers, so you can customize the tests to fit the needs of individual students. A cumulative midterm and final are also provided to determine whether students have achieved the goals defined by a group of standards. Suggestions and sample forms are included for portfolio assessment to monitor progress and measure student performance over time. Worksheets that enable students to practice taking standardized tests are also included in the Assessment Guide.

Resources for Teachers

Along with the Annotated Teacher's Edition, the Resources for Teachers gives you support for your instruction. The step-by-step lesson plan summarizes the standards covered in the unit and references all of the materials used, such as transparencies, workbooks, audio program, CD-ROM, video, and other materials that support you in teaching all your students. Answer keys for every activity in the Student Textbook are included in this resource, along with video scripts, segment timestamps, and viewing suggestions.

Resources For Your Students

The *Shining Star* program makes it easy to communicate with your students' parents and provides resources to meet the individual needs of each learner. Included in these resources are Letters Home that describe the activities and projects in every unit. The letters are available in English and Spanish in the print version and can be found in other languages at www.longman.com/shiningstar. Summaries of each reading selection from the Student Textbook are also available in this resource in English, Spanish, Hmong, Vietnamese, Cambodian, and Cantonese. Reproducible Newcomer Worksheets that focus on basic social and academic language and Graphic Organizer forms that were created to facilitate comprehension are also included.

Transparencies

Included in the *Shining Star* Transparencies booklet are Daily Language Practice transparencies, authentic student Writing Models with overlays for each writing assignment, and Graphic Organizers. The Daily Language Practice transparencies are intended to provide your students with a warm-up language activity. You can use these transparencies at the beginning of each class to recycle and reteach grammar, usage, and mechanics skills, including spelling and punctuation. The Writing Models reproduce the student writing models included in each writing assignment in the Student Textbook. Overlays with teaching annotations are also provided. The Graphic Organizer transparencies will facilitate class instruction.

Video

The *Shining Star* Focus & Connect Video Program offers an engaging way to introduce your students to the theme of each unit. High-interest video segments build background and help students understand the unit themes.

Student CD-ROM

The interactive CD-ROM provides additional practice and support for all sections of the Student Textbook. Activities and games reinforce concepts and language, giving students the opportunity to write, save, print, and/or email their work to the teacher. An adaptive story is included to extend the skills and language the student has acquired. Timed standardized test practice builds student test-taking skills. Student work is tracked for each session.

Bibliography

Anderson, Thomas, and Bonnie Armbruster. "On Selecting 'Considerate' Content Area Textbooks." In *Remedial and Special Education* 9 (January/February 1988): 47.

Anderson, Thomas, and Bonnie Armbruster. *Reading Comprehension, from Research to Practice.* Edited by Judith Orasanu, 151–162. Mahwah, N.J.: Lawrence Erlbaum Associates, 1986.

Auerbach, Elsa. *Making Meaning, Making Change: Participatory Curriculum Development for Adult ESL Literacy.* Washington, D.C.: Center for Applied Linguistics, 1992.

Bartlett, F. C. *Remembering: A Study in Experimental and Social Psychology.* New York: Cambridge University Press, 1995.

Berg, E. C. "Preparing ESL Students for Peer Response." In *TESOL Journal* 8 (2), 1999.

Breen, Michael P., ed. *Learner Contributions to Language Learning: New Directions in Research.* New York: Longman, 2001.

Brinton, Donna M., and Peter Master, eds. *New Ways in Content-Based Instruction.* Alexandria, Va.: Teachers of English to Speakers of Other Languages, 1997.

Chamot, Anna Uhl, et al. *The Learning Strategies Handbook.* White Plains, N.Y.: Longman, 1999.

Clemmons, J., et al. *Portfolios in the Classroom: A Teacher's Sourcebook.* New York: Scholastic, 1993.

Cohen, Andrew D. *Strategies in Learning and Using a Second Language.* New York: Longman, 1998.

Cummins, Jim. *Empowering Minority Students.* Sacramento: Calif.: California Association for Bilingual Education, 1989.

Cummins, Jim. "Language Proficiency, Bilingualism, and Academic Achievement." In *The Multicultural Classroom: Readings for Content-Area Teachers,* edited by P. A. Richard-Amato and M. A. Snow. White Plains, N.Y.: Longman, 1992.

Cummins, Jim. "Linguistic Interdependence and the Educational Development of Bilingual Children." In *Review of Educational Research* 49 (2), 1979.

Cummins, Jim. *Negotiating Identities: Education for Empowerment in a Diverse Society.* California Association for Bilingual Education, 1996.

Cummins, Jim, and Dennis Sayers. *Brave New Schools: Challenging Cultural Illiteracy Through Global Learning Networks.* New York: St. Martin's Press, 1995.

Dole, J. A., K. J. Brown, and K. Trathen. "The Effects of Strategy Instruction on the Comprehension Performance of At-Risk Students." In *Reading Research Quarterly* 31 (1996): 62–88.

Doughty, C., and J. Williams. *Focus on Form in Classroom Second Language Acquisition.* New York: Cambridge University Press, 1998.

Fathman, A. K., M. E. Quinn, and C. Kessler. *Teaching Science to English Learners, Grades 4–8.* National Clearinghouse for Bilingual Education, 1992.

Freeman, David E., and Yvonne S. Freeman. *Between Worlds: Access to Second Language Acquisition.* Portsmouth, N.H.: Heinemann, 1994.

Gardner, Howard. *Frames of Mind: The Theory of Multiple Intelligences.* New York: Basic Books, 1993.

Glazer, S. M., and C. S. Brown. *Portfolios and Beyond: Collaborative Assessment in Reading and Writing.* Norwood, Mass.: Christopher-Gordon, 1993.

Gonzalez, Virginia, et al. *Assessment and Instruction of Culturally and Linguistically Diverse Students with or At-Risk of Learning Problems.* Boston: Allyn & Bacon, 1997.

Grabe, W. "Current Developments in Second Language Reading Research." In *TESOL Quarterly* 25 (1991): 375–406.

Hudelson, Sarah. *Write On: Children Writing in ESL.* Englewood Cliffs, N.J.: Prentice Hall Regents, 1989.

Kessler, Carolyn, ed. *Cooperative Language Learning: A Teacher's Resource Book.* Englewood Cliffs, N.J.: Prentice Hall Regents, 1992.

Larsen-Freeman, Diane, and Michael H. Long. *An Introduction to Second Language Acquisition Research.* New York: Longman, 1991.

Lightbown, Patsy, and Nina Spada. *How Languages Are Learned,* rev. ed. New York: Oxford University Press, 1999.

McCaleb, Sudia P. *Building Communities of Learners: A Collaboration Among Teachers, Students, Families, and Community.* New York: St. Martin's Press, 1994.

Miller, G. "How School Children Learn Words." In *Proceedings of the Third Eastern States Conference on Linguistics,* edited by F. Marshall. Columbus, Ohio: The Ohio State University, 1986.

O'Malley, J. Michael, and Anna Uhl Chamot. *Learning Strategies in Second Language Acquisition.* New York: Cambridge University Press, 1990.

O'Malley, J. M., and L. Valdez Pierce. *Authentic Assessment for English Language Learners: Practical Approaches for Teachers.* Reading, Mass.: Addison-Wesley, 1996.

Oxford, Rebecca, ed. *Language Learning Strategies Around the World: Cross-Cultural Perspectives.* Honolulu, Hawaii: Second Language Teaching and Curriculum Center, 1996.

Pressley, Michael J., and V. Woloshyn, eds. *Cognitive Strategy Instruction That Really Improves Children's Academic Performance,* 2d ed. Cambridge, Mass.: Brookline Books, 1995.

Reid, J. M., ed. *Learning Styles in the ESL/EFL Classroom.* Boston, Mass.: Heinle & Heinle, 1995.

Richard-Amato, Patricia A., and Marguerite Ann Snow, eds. *The Multicultural Classroom: Readings for Content-Area Teachers.* White Plains, N.Y.: Longman, 1992.

Rigg, Pat, and Virginia G. Allen, eds. *When They Don't All Speak English: Integrating the ESL Student into the Regular Classroom.* Urbana, Ill.: National Council of Teachers of English, 1989.

Rong, Xue Lan, and Judith Preissle. *Educating Immigrant Students: What We Need to Know to Meet the Challenges.* Thousand Oaks, Calif.: Corwin Press, 1998.

Rubin, J. "A Review of Second Language Listening Comprehension Research." In *Modern Language Journal* 78 (1994): 199–221.

Rumelhart, D. E. "Schemata: The Building Blocks of Cognition." In *Theoretical Issues in Reading Comprehension: Perspectives from Cognitive Psychology, Linguistics, Artificial Intelligence, and Education,* edited by R. J. Spiro, B. C. Bruce, and W. F. Brewer. Mahwah, N.J.: Lawrence Erlbaum Associates, 1980.

Scarcella, Robin. *Teaching Language Minority Students in the Multicultural Classroom.* Englewood Cliffs, N.J.: Prentice Hall Regents, 1990.

Short, D. J. "Assessing Integrated Language and Content Instruction." In *TESOL Quarterly* 27 (4), 1993.

Short, D. *New Ways of Teaching English at the Secondary Level.* Alexandria, Va.: Teachers of English to Speakers of Other Languages, 1998.

Snow, M. A., and D. Brinton. *The Content-Based Classroom: Perspectives on Integrating Language and Content.* White Plains, N.Y.: Longman, 1997.

Spandel, Vicki. *Creating Writers: Through 6-Trait Writing Assessment and Instruction,* 3d ed. New York: Longman, 2001.

Spangenberg-Urbschat, Karen, and Robert Pritchard, eds. *Kids Come in All Languages: Reading Instruction for ESL Students.* Newark, Del.: International Reading Association, 1994.

Sternberg, Robert J. *The Triarchic Mind: A New Theory of Human Intelligence.* New York: Viking Press, 1988.

Warschauer, Mark. *E-Mail for English Teaching: Bringing the Internet and Computer Learning Network into the Language Classroom.* Alexandria, Va.: Teachers of English to Speakers of Other Languages, 1995.

Wenden, Anita. *Learner Strategies for Learner Autonomy: Planning and Implementing Learner Training for Language Learners.* New York: Prentice Hall, 1991.

Wendt, Dirk, "An Experimental Approach to the Improvement of the Typographic Design of Textbooks." In *Visible Language* 13 (2), 1979.

Shining Star A

Anna Uhl Chamot

Pamela Hartmann

Jann Huizenga

Longman

longman.com

Shining Star

Pearson Education, 10 Bank Street, White Plains, NY 10606

Vice president, director of instructional design: Allen Ascher
Editorial director: Ed Lamprich
Acquisitions editor: Amanda Rappaport Dobbins
Project manager: Susan Saslow
Senior development editors: Virginia Bernard, Bill Preston
Vice president, director of design and production: Rhea Banker
Executive managing editor: Linda Moser
Production manager: Ray Keating
Senior production editor: Sylvia Dare
Production editor: Patricia W. Nelson
Director of manufacturing: Patrice Fraccio
Senior manufacturing buyer: Edith Pullman
Photo research: Kirchoff/Wohlberg, Inc.
Design and production: Kirchoff/Wohlberg, Inc.
Cover design: Rhea Banker, Tara Mayer
Text font: 12.5/16 Minion
Acknowledgments: See page 278.
Illustration and photo credits: See page 279.

Library of Congress Cataloging-in-Publication Data
Chamot, Anna Uhl.
    Shining star / Anna Uhl Chamot, Pamela Hartmann, Jann Huizenga.
        p. cm.
    Includes index.
    Contents: A. Level 1. — B. Level 2. — C. Level 3.
    ISBN 0-13-093931-5 (pt. A) — ISBN 0-13-093933-1 (pt. B) — ISBN
0-13-093934-X (pt. C)
    1. English language—Textbooks for foreign speakers.   [1. English
language—Textbooks for foreign speakers. 2. Readers.]   I. Hartmann,
Pamela.   II Huizenga, Jann. III. Title.

    PE1128.C48 2003
    428.2'4—dc21

                                                        2002043460

ISBN: 0-13-093931-5

Printed in the United States of America
1 2 3 4 5 6 7 8 9 10–RRD–08 07 06 05 04 03

About the Authors

Anna Uhl Chamot is professor of secondary education and faculty adviser for ESL in George Washington University's Department of Teacher Preparation. She has been a researcher and teacher trainer in content-based second-language learning and language-learning strategies. She codesigned and has written extensively about the  Cognitive Academic Language Learning Approach (CALLA) and spent seven years implementing the CALLA model in the Arlington Public Schools in Virginia.

 **Pamela Hartmann** is a teacher and writer in the field of Teaching English to Speakers of Other Languages (TESOL). She has taught ESL and EFL in California and overseas since 1973. In addition, she has authored several books in the fields of TESOL and cross-cultural communication.

Jann Huizenga is an educator and consultant in the field of TESOL, with a special interest in teaching reading. She has worked as a teacher trainer at  Hunter College in New York City, at the University of New Mexico at Los Alamos, and overseas. She has written numerous books for ESL students.

Consultants and Reviewers

To the Student

Welcome to
Shining Star

This program will help you develop the English skills you need for different school subjects. Each unit has selections about a variety of topics, including science, social studies, and math. There are also literary selections. These selections will help you understand the vocabulary and organization of different types of texts such as stories, poems, and nonfiction articles. They will give you the tools you need to approach the content of the different subjects you take in school.

Before starting to read a selection, you will do activities that help you relate your background knowledge to the new information in the text. You will also study some of the new words in the text to give you a head start as you begin to read. Finally, you will learn a reading strategy that will help you read with greater understanding.

While you read, ask yourself, "Am I understanding this? Does it make sense to me?" Remember to use the reading strategy! Your teacher may also play a recording of the selection so that you can listen to it as you read.

After you read, you will check your understanding of the text. Then you will work on activities to help improve your English skills in grammar, phonics, and spelling.

To extend your ability in English, you will participate in several types of activities related to the selections in each unit. Some of these activities involve listening and speaking, while in others you will produce different kinds of writing. Each unit also has a number of projects in which you can practice your artistic, musical, dramatic, scientific, mathematical, language, social, and thinking talents. You'll also see some suggestions for further reading related to the theme of the unit.

We hope that you enjoy *Shining Star* as much as we enjoyed writing it for you!

Anna Uhl Chamot
Pamela Hartmann
Jann Huizenga

Contents

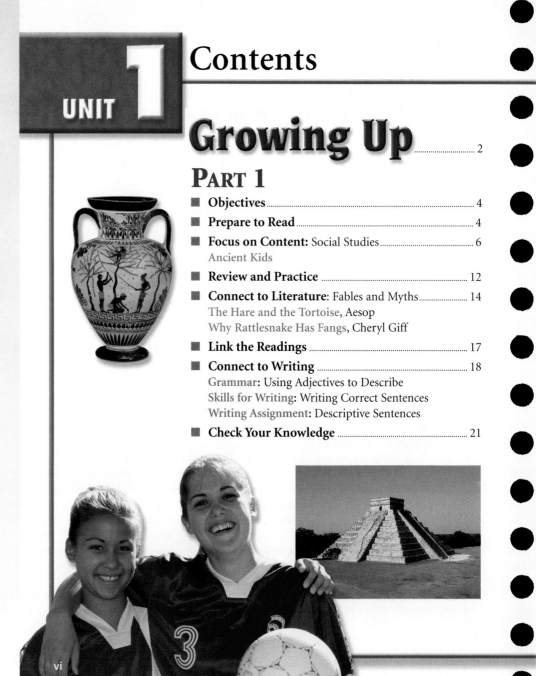

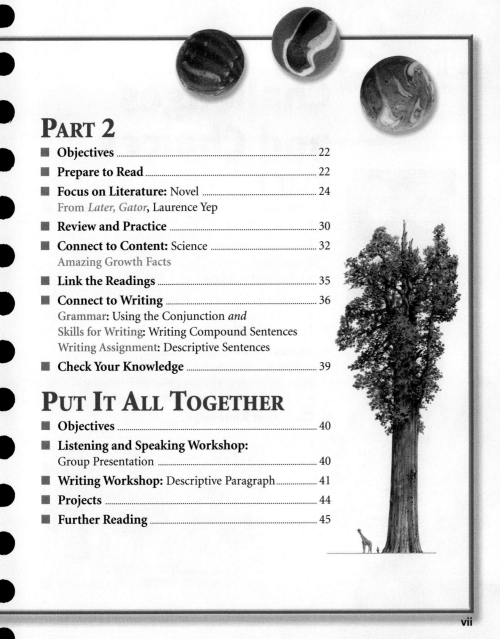

UNIT 2

Challenges and Choices

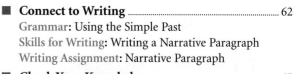

PART 2

PUT IT ALL TOGETHER

x

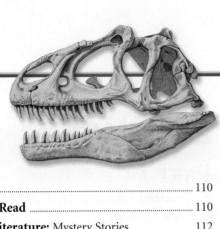

PART 2

PUT IT ALL TOGETHER

xi

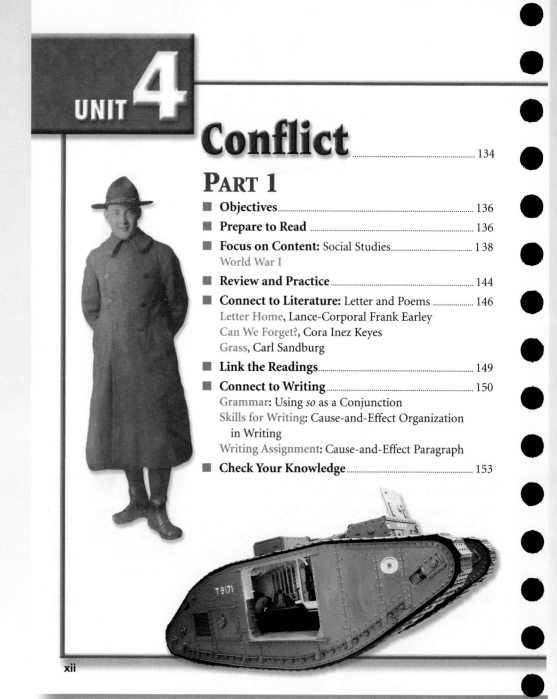

UNIT 4

Conflict

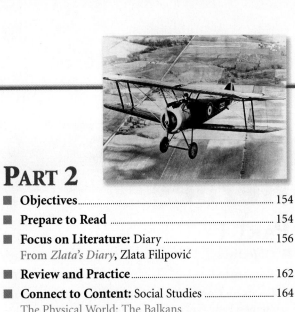

PART 2

PUT IT ALL TOGETHER

UNIT 5

We Can Be Heroes

xiv

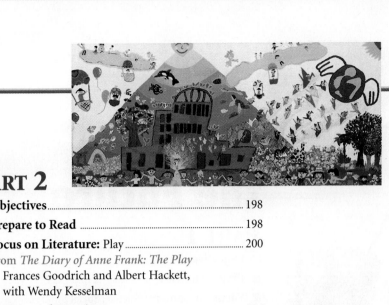

PART 2

PUT IT ALL TOGETHER

xvi

PART 2

PUT IT ALL TOGETHER

Level 1 Unit 1

Growing Up

Make enough duplicate copies of the Letter Home for Unit 1 so that each student has a copy to take home. Show Video Segment 1.

PART 1 TEACHING GUIDE

PRETEACH	**Provide Background**	• Read and discuss the Part Objectives and Background Information. (SB p. 4; ATE p. T4)
	Present Concepts	• Introduce the Key Words and Reading Strategy. (SB p. 5; ATE p. T5; WB pp. 2, 4) • Pronounce the Vocabulary words. (ATE p. T5) • Model how to use context clues to define Key Words. (ATE p. T5)
TEACH	**Monitor Comprehension**	• Informally monitor comprehension through Guided Reading and Critical Thinking questions. (ATE pp. T6–T17) • Monitor students' comprehension through Critical Thinking, Metacognition, Discussion, and Extension activities. (SB p. 13, 17; ATE pp. T3, T7, T9, T11–T13, T15, T17, T21)
	Teach and Practice	• Use individually tailored activities for beginning and advanced students. (ATE pp. T3, T5, T7, T9, T11, T13, T15, T17, T19, T21) • Pair beginning, intermediate, and advanced students through Cooperative Grouping activities. (SB pp. 13, 17; ATE pp. T4, T13, T17) • Develop viewing skills using photos and illustrations and present the Viewpoint activities. (ATE pp. T2, T7, T9, T10, T15) • Complete the Vocabulary, Phonics, Grammar, and Spelling lessons. (SB pp. 5, 18; ATE pp. T5, T8, T10, T18, T20; WB pp. 10-11, 14) • Introduce the Writing Strategy and apply students' ability to write a narrative paragraph using the Writing Model and Writing Assignment. (SB pp. 19-20; ATE pp. T19–T20; WB pp. 12-13; Transparency # 21)
CONNECT	**Connect to Literature**	• Develop students' ability to analyze characteristics of genres through pairing of selections. (SB pp. 14-16; ATE pp. T14–T16) • Provide students with interactive reading support and practice. (WB pp. 5-9)
	Across the Curriculum	• Develop students' ability to extend the content of the reading selections through extended math, social studies, science, health, and art activities. (ATE pp. T9, T11)
ASSESS	**Check Knowledge**	• Use the Before You Go On, Check Your Knowledge, Link the Readings, and Review and Practice features to assess students' comprehension of the selection. (SB pp. 7, 9, 11, 15, 17, 21; ATE pp. T17, T21)
	Monitor Progress	• Use the Assessment Options, Test-Taking Tip, and the test. (ATE p. 21; AG pp. 29–32)

CONTENT TERMS

Present and elicit definitions of these content-specific terms:

• ritual	• decorated	• crops	• dust
• influenced	• hunt	• nature	
• average	• conversion chart	• heart	

PART 2 TEACHING GUIDE

PRETEACH	**Provide Background**	• Read and discuss the Part Objectives and Background Information. (SB p. 22; ATE p. T22)
	Present Concepts	• Introduce the Key Words and Reading Strategy. (SB p. 23; ATE p. 23; WB p. 16, 18) • Pronounce the Vocabulary words. (ATE p. 23) • Model how to use context clues to define Key Words. (ATE p. 23)
TEACH	**Monitor Comprehension**	• Informally monitor comprehension through Guided Reading and Critical Thinking questions. (ATE pp. T24–T35) • Monitor students' comprehension through Critical Thinking, Metacognition, Discussion, and Extension activities. (SB pp. 31, 35; ATE pp. T25, T27, T29–T31, T33, T35, T39, T44)
	Teach and Practice	• Use individually tailored activities for beginning and advanced students. (ATE pp. T23, T25, T27, T29, T31, T33, T35, T37, T39, T41, T43, T45) • Pair beginning, intermediate, and advanced students through Cooperative Grouping activities. (SB pp. 31, 44; ATE pp. T22, T31, T35) • Develop viewing skills using photos and illustrations and present the Viewpoint activities. (ATE pp. T24, T26, T28, T33) • Complete the Vocabulary, Phonics, Grammar, and Spelling lessons. (SB pp. 23, 36; ATE pp. T23, T24, T26, T28, T36; WB pp. 24–25, 28) • Introduce the Writing Strategy and apply students' ability to write a descriptive essay using the Writing Model and Writing Assignment. (SB pp. 37-38; ATE pp. T37-T38; WB p. 26; Transparency # 22)
CONNECT	**Connect to Content**	• Develop students' ability to analyze characteristics of genres through pairing of selections. (SB pp. 32–34; ATE pp. T32–T34) • Provide students with interactive reading support and practice. (WB pp. 19–23)
	Across the Curriculum	• Develop students' ability to extend the content of the reading selections through extended math, social studies, science, health, and art activities. (ATE pp. T26, T28, T34)
ASSESS	**Check Knowledge**	• Use the Before You Go On, Check Your Knowledge, Link the Readings, and Review and Practice features to assess students' comprehension of the selection. (SB pp. 33, 35, 39; ATE pp. T33, T35, T39)
	Monitor Progress	• Use the Assessment Options, Test-Taking Tip, and the test. (ATE p. T39, AG pp. 33–36)

PUT IT ALL TOGETHER TEACHING GUIDE

EXTEND	**Integrate Skills and Apply Understanding**	• Apply students' ability to give a group presentation using the Listening and Speaking Workshop. (SB p. 40; ATE p. T40) • Apply students' ability to write a descriptive paragraph using the Writing Workshop. (SB p. 41–43; ATE pp. T41–T43) • Have students complete one or more of the Unit Projects. (SB p. 44; ATE p. T44) • Have students choose a theme-related reading selection from the Further Reading suggestions. (SB p. 45; ATE p. T45)

Suggestions for Newcomers

Unit 1: Growing Up

Part 1

Background (p. 4) Answer the questions on p. 4 about yourself, and then ask students to discuss the questions about themselves. Draw a timeline on the board and explain how a timeline works. Read each question aloud, and then refer to yourself and the timeline as you answer it. For example, read question 1: *What year were you born?* Write the year you were born on the timeline. Point to yourself and the timeline, and say, I was born in . . . Model answers to the other questions until you fill up the timeline. Then ask students, *When was I born? How old was I when I started school?*

Vocabulary (p. 5) Give students blank word cards. Write each Key Word on the board, say it, and use it in a sentence. Then have students say the word and write it on a card. Use props and/or simple explanations and gestures to demonstrate the Key Words. Play a game by creating and saying other sentences using the Vocabulary. Have students hold up the card for each Key Word they hear.

Reading Strategy: Previewing (p. 5) Explain that *previewing* a text is getting a general idea of what it is about. Before you ask students to apply the strategy to the reading, model it for them. For example, show the class an article from a magazine that has a clear title, headings, and photos/illustrations. Make sure the article is simple and about a subject students will likely know something about. Preview the article with the students. After reviewing the title, headings, and photos/illustrations individually, ask students what they think the article is about. Then have students look at pp. 6–11. Ask them what they think the reading is about.

Ancient Kids (pp. 6–11)

Activity 1: Have students find the different places on a world map. Explain that the Roman Empire included most of Europe and parts of North Africa and the Middle East.

Activity 2: Discuss what the word *ancient* means. Review the timelines in the text closely, or draw a larger one on the board in order to show how long ago these cultures existed.

Activity 3: Give examples of *chores* you used to do at home. Ask students what chores they do at home and how they help their families.

Activity 4: Make a word web of different kinds of *toys*. Ask students which toys they have played with and have them give examples of other toys.

Activity 5: Explain that *pets* are animals that people keep at their homes. Ask students what kinds of pets they have or have had in the past. Ask what other kinds of animals can be kept as pets. Make a list.

Activity 6: If there are *tutors* at your school, explain what they do. Point out that many people use tutors, including musicians, singers, and athletes.

Comprehension (p. 12) Explain that a *Venn diagram* compares two things—it shows how the things are similar and different. Demonstrate a model comparing two simple things, such as cats and dogs. Ask students to look at the headings on the diagram on p. 12. Ask, *What two things does the diagram compare?* (Greek boys, Greek girls) Explain that the left and right parts of the circles show how Greek boys and Greek girls were different. The middle parts of the circles show how they were similar.

The Hare and the Tortoise (pp. 14–15) Explain that *fables* are stories that teach a lesson or give advice to live by. The lesson, or moral, usually comes at the end of the fable. Point out that fables often have animals that act like people. Ask students for examples of TV shows or movies with animals that act like people. After the students read "The Hare and the Tortoise," ask if anyone knows another fable that teaches a lesson. If so, ask students to share the fable with the class.

Why Rattlesnake Has Fangs (p. 16) Explain that *myths* are ancient stories that explain something. The title often tells what a myth explains. Ask students to read the title and predict what the myth will be about. Afterward, write the names of these animals on the board: *hare* (or *rabbit*), *tortoise, skunk, rattlesnake*. Show pictures of the animals if necessary. Explain that each animal has a way to protect itself—to fight or get away from danger. Ask, *If you try to catch a rabbit, what can it do?* (Run away.) Ask students how other animals protect themselves. *(A tortoise goes into its shell; a skunk has a bad smell.)* After they read, ask if students know other myths that explain things. If so, ask them to share with the class.

Grammar: Using Adjectives to Describe (p. 18) Explain that *nouns* are people, places, or things. Explain that *adjectives* can describe nouns. Use simple objects in the classroom to demonstrate nouns and adjectives. For example, point to a chair and say, *This is a chair.* Then say, *This is a green chair.* Stress the adjectives that describe the object. Ask

students to describe other simple objects in the classroom. Then ask students to look at the picture and caption on p. 18. Ask, *What kind of dog is it? (Possible answers: It's a Roman dog. It's a guard dog. It's a Roman guard dog.)* Point out that in this case, *Roman* and *guard* are two adjectives that describe the noun *dog.* They tell what kind of dog it is.

Skills for Writing and Writing Assignment (pp. 19–20) Explain that some adjectives and nouns describe physical appearance, or the way someone looks. Explain that other adjectives describe personality, or the way someone acts. Describe yourself, using both kinds of adjectives. Write, *What do I look like? = Physical appearance* on the board. Point to yourself and ask the question. Then answer, listing some physical characteristics: *I'm tall/short, thin/heavy. I have dark/light hair, brown/blue eyes,* etc. Then write, *What am I like? = Personality* on the board. Ask the question and list some personality traits: *I'm happy, confident, friendly,* etc. Pantomime if necessary. Then ask students to describe Juan. Make a T-chart on the board. Write, *What does Juan look like?* in the first column and *What is Juan like?* in the second column. Ask for volunteers to complete the chart with adjectives and nouns in the appropriate columns.

Part 2

Background (p. 22) Discuss birthdays with students. Use a calendar to show students when your birthday is and say, *My birthday is on (month, day). I was born on (month, day).* Ask several students, *When is your birthday?* Then discuss what you usually do on your birthday. Talk about some of the presents you have received over the years. Describe some of the most unusual presents you have received. Then ask students about their own birthdays: *What do you like to do? Do you receive presents? Have you ever given gifts to other people?*

Vocabulary (p. 23) Use pictures to help students understand the meanings of the Key Words used in the text. For example, show a picture of a party with *birthday presents,* or show pictures of *reptiles* such as snakes and lizards. To illustrate *imagination,* you might draw a picture of someone thinking of a scene (in a thought bubble) while writing or painting. Use the words *special* and *normal* in contrast to each other in order to explain them. Demonstrate that a birthday is a *special* day, while other days might be *normal* days. Demonstrate the meaning of *get along with* by using contrast as well. Point out that someone might *get* along with or be better friends with one person over another. Continue using vocabulary words in context until students understand their meanings.

Reading Strategy: Predicting (p. 23) Before you review the chart on p. 23, explain that *clues* are hints that lead to a solution. These clues can give the reader an idea of what is going to happen next and can help the reader predict. Use examples. Say, *If you see someone walking to a lake carrying a fishing pole and tackle box, you can predict that they are . . . ? (going fishing)* The lake, the fishing pole, and the tackle box are all clues. List the clues on the board. Explain to students that you can make predictions by using *what you already know* and *personal experience.* From the first example, students would probably already know that you need a fishing pole, a tackle box, and a lake to catch fish. Or, they might have gone fishing themselves and can predict through personal experience.

After the students finish reading the excerpt from *Later, Gator,* begin a class discussion to predict what will happen in the rest of the story. Have students use clues in the text to predict: *What will Teddy do? Will he buy an alligator for his brother? What will Bobby's reaction be?* Then have students use their own experiences to predict what their mother's reaction will be if Teddy buys his brother an alligator. Review how and why the students made these predictions.

From *Later, Gator* (pp. 24–29) Explain that *Later, Gator* is a work of fiction. Fiction is a story that is not real. The author made up the characters and the events in the story.

Activity 1: Have students discuss *pets.* With the students, write on the board animals that are commonly kept as pets. Then discuss responsibility for these pets. Ask students what kind of responsibilities a pet owner has and why an alligator might cause problems as a pet.

Activity 2: Have students identify the main characters in *Later, Gator.* Make a T-chart to describe Teddy and Bobby. Have students list things they know about each character. For example: *Teddy: Older; Doesn't want to buy his brother a present. Bobby: Younger; It's his birthday.*

Activity 3: Explain that the narrator is the person telling the story. In *Later, Gator* the narrator (Teddy) uses a first-person point of view because he takes part in the story. Point out instances in the text where the narrator uses a first-person point of view. *(The narrator uses words like I and me: "She told me to buy something special." "Last Christmas I gave him a pair of socks.")* Read these sentences out loud and point to yourself, demonstrating that because you

are telling the story, you're using first-person. Ask students to find other examples of the first-person point of view in the story.

Comprehension (p. 30) Explain that chronological order tells the order in which events occurred. Guide students through your own day to help explain chronological order. On the board, write the events of your morning. For example: *I got out of bed; I showered; I ate breakfast; I got dressed; I drove to school,* etc. Pantomime if necessary. Number these events to show the order in which they occurred. Introduce words like *first, after, next, then,* and *last.* Then ask students about the chronological order of your day. For example: *What did I do after I took a shower? What did I do after I ate breakfast? What did I do last?* etc. Then ask students to give a chronological order of some of the events of their school day.

Amazing Growth Facts (pp. 32–34) Explain that informational texts give us facts. Facts are things that are known and can be proved. Review facts about a subject they most likely know something about. For example: *the United States: It is made up of fifty states; It is located in North America;* etc. In the reading, students learn about the different growth rates of plants and animals. After you read the text, ask students what facts they learned. Have students compare growth rates of the plants and animals mentioned in the text. Introduce comparative adjectives such as *larger, smaller, longer, shorter, same, different, faster, slower,* etc. Then have students use the illustrations and text to answer questions such as, *Is the adult Nile crocodile larger or smaller than the adult golden eagle? Do humans grow at a faster or slower rate than a kangaroo? Is Pacific giant kelp taller or shorter than bamboo?*

Grammar: Using the Conjunction *and* (p. 36) Explain that the word *and* joins words or phrases in a sentence. Describe two things that you are wearing. *(I am wearing socks and shoes.)* Point to yourself to demonstrate that the subject is *I.* Then point to each item as you mention it. Describe things you like to do. *(I like to run and play tennis.)* Pantomime if necessary. Continue giving examples until students understand the conjunction *and.* Ask students to identify two things they are wearing by using the conjunction *and.*

Skills for Writing and Writing Assignment (pp. 37–38) Explain that a comma is used to separate clauses or words in a list. It is one of the most commonly used punctuation marks in English. On the board, write several sentences that use commas in a list. For example: *The American flag is red, white, and blue. At the store I bought milk, eggs, doughnuts, and orange juice.* Explain that a comma can also be used to separate

clauses or parts of a sentence that contain a subject and verb. Explain that a subject is who or what the sentence is about. The verb is the action the subject is doing. Write out a simple sentence on the board, circling the subject and underlining the verb. For example: *She hit the ball. Then she ran to first base.* Explain that a compound sentence uses two independent clauses. These independent clauses can stand on their own as sentences, because they have a subject and a verb. They can be joined together by using a comma and the conjunction *and.* Write out the first simple sentences as one compound sentence, circling the subjects and verbs. *(She hit the ball, and then she ran to first base.)* Then write out several simple sentences about yourself. Have students identify the subject and verb in each sentence. Then ask them how they can turn the two simple sentences into one compound sentence.

Put It All Together

Listening and Speaking Workshop: Group Presentation (p. 40) Before the class breaks into groups, describe what qualities you look for in a friend and why. Review main idea and *supporting details.* Explain that students should come up with a main idea about their "ideal friend." Then they should back up this main idea with supporting details. As the students practice their presentations, other members of the group should ask questions. From these questions, encourage students to review their presentations and make the necessary changes. Have students answer questions about their presentation, such as, *What is the main idea? What are the supporting details? Are these clear in the presentation?*

Writing Workshop: Descriptive Paragraph (pp. 41–43) Review the purpose of adjectives and descriptive phrases with the class. Use yourself as an example. On the board, write several adjectives and descriptive phrases that describe your physical appearance, personality, and skills. Then write a short paragraph about yourself. Before students begin writing their descriptive paragraphs, demonstrate with an example. Pick a person that the entire class is most likely familiar with, such as a celebrity or the principal of your school. Use this person as an example and walk through the exercise with the class. Begin by describing the person physically. Have students brainstorm adjectives or descriptive phrases that describe this person. Write these on the board. Then have students use these descriptions to write one or two sentences about the individual.

UNIT CONTENT

The first part of this unit includes a selection entitled "Ancient Kids." This nonfiction article explores what it was like to be a child growing up in ancient Greece and Rome, and in the Maya culture. It is followed by an ancient Greek fable, "The Hare and the Tortoise," and by a myth entitled "Why Rattlesnake Has Fangs." Aesop's fable about the plodding tortoise who teaches the overconfident hare a well-deserved lesson has delighted children for thousands of years. "Why Rattlesnake Has Fangs" is a myth of the Native American Pima tribe in Arizona.

The second part of the unit offers two additional selections. An excerpt from the novel *Later, Gator* is followed by "Amazing Growth Facts," a nonfiction article. Point out that these selections explore other ways that people, plants, and animals change and grow.

—Viewpoint—

Have students carefully examine the collage on the unit opener. Ask them to identify and describe the different pictures that make up the collage. Ask them what the pictures illustrate about the stages people go through as they grow up.

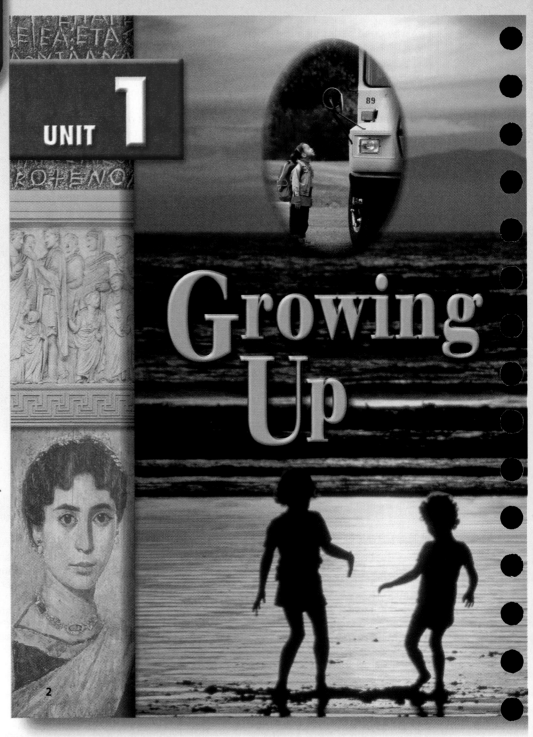

UNIT 1

Growing Up

2

WORKSHOP PREVIEW	PROJECTS PREVIEW	TEACHING RESOURCES	
Listening and Speaking Students will give a presentation about the personality traits they value in a friend. **Writing** Students will write a description of someone they know.	Projects for this unit include: ● making a timeline ● writing a story about how an animal got a special body part ● acting out a fable ● collecting amazing facts about how plants and animals grow ● making a poster illustrating daily life in an ancient culture	**Lesson Plans** **Summaries** **Graphic Organizers** **Audio Program** **Workbook** **CD-ROM** **Video** **Tests**	pp. 3–16 pp. 17–26 pp. 1–20 CD1/1–6; Cass.1/A pp. 1–28 Unit 1 Segment 1 Part Test, pp. 29–36 Unit Test, pp. 79–87

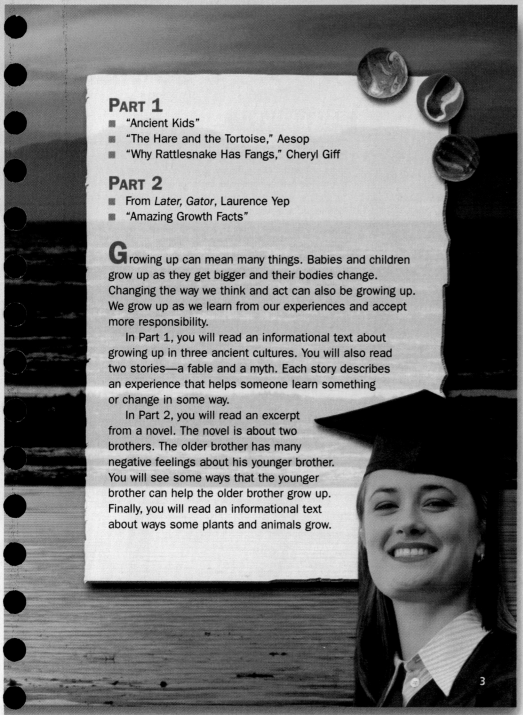

PART 1
- "Ancient Kids"
- "The Hare and the Tortoise," Aesop
- "Why Rattlesnake Has Fangs," Cheryl Giff

PART 2
- From *Later, Gator*, Laurence Yep
- "Amazing Growth Facts"

Growing up can mean many things. Babies and children grow up as they get bigger and their bodies change. Changing the way we think and act can also be growing up. We grow up as we learn from our experiences and accept more responsibility.

In Part 1, you will read an informational text about growing up in three ancient cultures. You will also read two stories—a fable and a myth. Each story describes an experience that helps someone learn something or change in some way.

In Part 2, you will read an excerpt from a novel. The novel is about two brothers. The older brother has many negative feelings about his younger brother. You will see some ways that the younger brother can help the older brother grow up. Finally, you will read an informational text about ways some plants and animals grow.

DISCUSS THE THEME

Have a volunteer read aloud the unit title, "Growing Up." Then have students discuss what they think of when they hear these words. Point out that when people grow up, they grow more than just physically. They also learn more about their feelings and the world around them. Ask students:
- to describe ways in which they are growing up
- what changes they have seen in their brothers, sisters, or friends
- how it feels to grow up
- what they think helps a person to grow up

QUICK WRITE

Ask students to write a few sentences or a short paragraph about an experience they have had growing up. It might include a discovery they made or a game or activity that they suddenly outgrew or lost interest in.

EXTEND THE LESSON

Have students bring in family photos or magazine pictures that depict people of various ages. Invite them to try and guess the approximate ages of the people in the photos. Ask what clues they used to figure out each person's age. Students with family photos should identify each family member and verify his or her age.

REACHING ALL STUDENTS

LANGUAGE LEVELS

Beginning: Label several stacks of index cards with abilities and changes that are associated with childhood and growing up, such as *talk, walk, read, go to school, learn to ride a bicycle, lose a first baby tooth, go on a first date.* Hand out the cards to groups of students. Have them talk about the ages at which each of these events might take place. Then have them put the cards in order from first to last event.

Advanced: Invite students to discuss how people can change. Encourage students to share personal examples of times when they have changed after learning something. Model an example from your own life, such as a time when you learned something from someone else and it made you change how you felt or acted. For example, you might describe how you overcame a fear of technology when you first learned to use a computer.

Preteach

OBJECTIVES

Explain to students that in part 1, they will be reading about how people lived and grew up long ago. Read the list of objectives, encouraging students to follow along. Emphasize the words that are italicized, such as *previewing* and *personification,* and define them for students. Additional practice activities for these objectives can be found in the **Workbook** and **CD-ROM.**

BACKGROUND

Ask students to read the Background text with you aloud. Then have students look at the series of pictures on the page. Ask volunteers to describe what they see in each picture. As a class, discuss the experiences that people have at different ages. Then read aloud and discuss each question. *(Accept all reasonable answers.)*

COOPERATIVE GROUPING

Pair intermediate and advanced students with beginning students. Ask partners to read the Background page together and discuss their answers to the questions. Invite students to share their answers.

OBJECTIVES

LANGUAGE DEVELOPMENT

Reading:
- Vocabulary building: *Context, dictionary skills*
- Reading strategy: *Previewing*
- Text types: *Social studies text, fable, myth*
- Literary element: *Personification*

Writing:
- Descriptive writing
- Sentences
- Word web
- Editing checklist

Listening/Speaking:
- Appreciation: *fable, myth*
- Culture: *Connecting experiences*
- Compare and contrast characters
- Retell a fable or myth

Grammar:
- Adjectives

Viewing/Representing:
- Timelines, diagrams, charts

ACADEMIC CONTENT
- Social studies vocabulary
- Ancient Greek, Roman, Maya cultures

BACKGROUND

"Ancient Kids" is an informational text about three ancient cultures. It is a nonfiction text. That means it is about real facts or events. The purpose of an informational text is to inform the reader about real facts, people, or events.

Kids in ancient cultures had different experiences from kids today. However, there are also some similarities.

Make connections Think about yourself now and when you were younger. Use this timeline to help you remember. Look at the timeline and think about your life. Discuss the questions in pairs. (For some questions, you can point to the timeline as you answer.)

Age

0 1 2 3 4 5 6 7 8 9 10 11 12 13 14 15 16 17 18

Birth

1. What year were you born?
2. How old were you when you started school?
3. What toys did you play with when you were younger? What games or sports did you play?
4. How old are you now?

4

TEACHING GUIDE

PRETEACH	Provide Background	Read and discuss the Background information. Complete the activity. (ATE/SB p. 4)
	Present Concepts	Introduce the Reading Strategy. (ATE/SB p. 5)
TEACH	Monitor Comprehension	Informally monitor comprehension while students read the selection independently or in groups. (ATE/SB pp. 6–11)
	Teach and Practice	Present the Grammar, Usage, and Mechanics. (ATE/SB pp. 18, 19) Complete the Writing activity. (ATE/SB p. 20) Present Grammar, Phonics, and Spelling minilessons. (ATE pp. 8, 10, 20)
CONNECT	Connect to Literature	Have students read the literature and relate it to the informational reading. (ATE/SB pp. 14–16)
	Across the Curriculum	Present curriculum links as students read. (ATE pp. 9, 11)
ASSESS	Check Knowledge	Assess students' comprehension by having them complete the Check Your Knowledge section. (ATE/SB p. 21)
	Monitor Progress	Use one or more of the print assessment resources in the Assessment Package.
EXTEND	Integrate Language and Apply Understanding	Have students complete the Workshops (ATE/SB pp. 40–43) and choose a project from the Unit Projects. (ATE/SB p. 44) Then have them choose a book to read from Further Reading. (ATE/SB p. 45)

VOCABULARY

Sometimes you can guess what a new word means from the sentence it is in. This is called guessing from context. Read these sentences. Use the context to figure out the meaning of the red words. Use a dictionary to check your answers. Write each word and its meaning in your notebook.

1. Rome is an **ancient** city. It is thousands of years old.
2. The Maya had a **ceremony** to mark the end of childhood, when children turned twelve or thirteen.
3. If you are not a **citizen** of Mexico, you cannot vote there.
4. Different **cultures** often have different beliefs, customs, and ways of life.
5. We get our **education** both in school and at home.
6. Americans have many **rights**. For example, the law allows Americans to speak freely.

LEARN KEY WORDS

ancient
ceremony
citizen
cultures
education
rights

READING STRATEGY
Previewing

Previewing helps you understand a text. Before you read:

- look at the **title**
- look for **headings** (titles of the different sections of the text)
- look at the **photographs** and **illustrations**

Think about the information you got from the title, headings, and photographs and illustrations. Try to establish your reasons for reading the text.

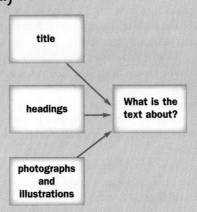

title → What is the text about?

headings → What is the text about?

photographs and illustrations → What is the text about?

5

VOCABULARY

Pronounce each of the Key Words in the box at the top of the page and have students repeat each word after you. Then call students' attention to the red Key Words in the sentences. Tell students to listen as you read each sentence, emphasizing the Key Word. Provide a model to help students identify the context clues that will help them understand the meaning of a key word: Ancient *is a word that describes a city, the city of Rome. The next sentence tells me that the city is thousands of years old. So the word* ancient *must mean "very old."*

As a follow-up activity, write the Key Words on the board and have students work in pairs, writing each word on an index card. Then have students close their books. Have one student in each pair hold up an index card, while his or her partner uses the word on the card in a sentence. Have students take turns creating sentences for the Key Words until all of them have been used.

READING STRATEGY

Write *previewing* on the board. Explain to students that previewing means to study the parts of a text before you read. Have a volunteer read the text box. Discuss the organizer in the text box with students.

Then have students preview pages 6 and 7. Call on volunteers to identify the following features in the text: the selection title and subtitle, the main idea of the timeline, and the illustration captions. Explain that these text features will help them to predict what they are about to read. Then ask students whether this selection is fiction or nonfiction. Discuss with them how identifying a text as fiction or nonfiction can help them to establish a purpose for reading.

REACHING ALL STUDENTS

LANGUAGE LEVELS

Beginning: Form two teams. Have students preview two pages in the selection and then close their books. Alternating teams, ask individual students questions such as *How many pictures are on page __? How many headings are on page __?* Award a point for each correct answer.

Advanced: Display the first page of a chapter in a text-book that contains visuals and boldfaced words or subheads. Point to and read aloud the title and headings. Ask students whether the text is fiction or nonfiction based on these features. Then have them open their texts to pages 8 and 9 and preview the title, headings, and illustrations.

LEARNING MODALITIES

Visual: As students preview the selection, ask them to study all of the illustrations to note whether they depict the present or a time long ago. Then have students explain what clues in the illustrations helped them to reach this conclusion.

READING SUMMARY

The nonfiction article describes what it was like to grow up in ancient Greece and Rome, and in the Maya culture. It describes the lives of children in these ancient societies, focusing on the different experiences of boys and girls.

SCAFFOLDING

Have students listen to the CD/tape as they read silently, following along. Then ask them to read aloud with partners, taking turns to read each paragraph.

MODELING THE READING STRATEGY

Previewing: Model how to preview the timeline on page 6. Say, *I notice that the timeline begins just over 4,000 years ago, at 2000 B.C.E. According to the timeline, the period known as ancient Greece begins at this point and goes through 323 B.C.E., the highlighted part of the timeline. Now I know that when I read about ancient Greece, I am reading about this period in history.*

GUIDED READING

1. What special thing did a father do when a baby was born in ancient Greece? *(a ritual dance while holding the baby)*
2. Who usually decided whom a girl would marry, the girl or her father? *(her father)*
3. Why did boys have to memorize everything they learned? *(There were no schoolbooks.)*

FOCUS ON CONTENT • **Social Studies**

Preview the text. Look at the title and headings. What is the topic? What three ancient cultures will you read about? What do the pictures tell you about the topic? What can you learn from the timelines on pages 6, 8, and 10? What is your purpose for reading this text?

ANCIENT KIDS
GROWING UP IN ANCIENT GREECE

ANCIENT GREECE

| 2000 B.C.E | 323 B.C.E | 0 | 2000 C.E. |

When a baby was born in ancient Greece, the father did a **ritual** dance, holding the newborn baby. For boy babies, the family decorated the house with **wreaths** of olives. For girl babies, the family decorated the house with wreaths made of wool.

There were many differences in the lives of boys and girls as they grew up. One main difference was that girls did not go to school and boys did. Some girls learned to play musical instruments.

Mostly, girls helped their mothers with **chores** in the house or in the fields. They didn't leave their houses very often. Sometimes they went to festivals or funerals. They also visited neighbors.

Girls stayed home with their parents until they got married. Girls' fathers usually decided who they would marry.

Boys stayed home until they were six or seven years old. They helped grow **crops** in the fields, and they learned to sail boats and to fish.

▲ Some girls learned to read and write at home.

---

ritual, based on religious rules
wreaths, decorative circles made of flowers, plants, or other items
chores, small jobs
crops, wheat, corn, fruit, etc., that a farmer grows

6

MULTICULTURAL NOTE

Have students reread the first paragraph on page 7. Then explain that the lyre is a stringed musical instrument that was found throughout the ancient Near East. Some people played lyres with their fingers while others plucked the strings with a stick called a plectrum, which is like a guitar pick. During the Middle Ages, the lyre's popularity spread across Europe, taking a slightly different form: In some European countries the lyre was played with a bow. Ask students to name musical instruments they have played or heard that are similar to the lyre. List their ideas on the board. Have volunteers come to the board and circle the stringed instruments.

When boys were about seven years old, they started their formal education. They went to school and learned reading, writing, and mathematics. They had to **memorize** everything because there were no school books! They memorized the poetry of Homer, a famous poet. They also learned to play a musical instrument, such as a **lyre**.

At school, boys learned about the arts and war. They also learned how to be good citizens. At the age of eighteen, boys went to **military school** for two years.

Children played with many toys, such as rattles, clay animals, pull-toys on four wheels, yo-yos, and **terra-cotta** ② dolls. Children also had pets, such as birds, dogs, goats, tortoises, and mice.

▲ A student and his teacher working together

memorize, remember the exact words
lyre, ancient instrument, similar to a guitar
military school, school where students learn to fight in wars
terra-cotta, baked red clay

◄ People placed these clay figures in the graves of children to keep them company in the afterlife.

BEFORE YOU GO ON . . .

1 How were boys' and girls' lives different in ancient Greece?
2 What toys did children play with?

HOW ABOUT YOU?
● Did your family have any special ceremonies when you were born?

7

CRITICAL THINKING

Have students respond orally or in writing to these questions:
● How were the lives of children who grew up in ancient Greece different from yours? How were they similar? *(Differences: Girls did not go to school; a girl's father decided whom she would marry; they had no schoolbooks. Similarities: toys, pets, and the subjects that boys studied in school)*
● In your opinion, were children treated fairly in ancient Greece? Why or why not? *(Possible answer: Girls were treated unfairly, because they were not allowed to go to school.)*

Viewpoint

Ask students to study the art on page 6 and read the caption. Ask, *In what ways is this girl similar to a girl today? In what ways is she different?* On the board, draw a two-column chart with the headings *Similar to* and *Different.* Have volunteers come to the board and record and read aloud their ideas.

ACTIVE READING

Have students create a three-column chart in their notebooks. Ask them to write *Ancient Greeks, Ancient Romans,* and *Ancient Maya* as headings. Tell students to list important ideas in the appropriate columns of the chart as they read. Model how to complete the first column. Reread the first paragraph on page 6. Ask students to identify the main idea in this paragraph. *(Boy babies were welcomed differently from girl babies in ancient Greece.)* Have students write this idea in the first column and then complete it.

REACHING ALL STUDENTS

LANGUAGE LEVELS

Beginning: Display pictures of as many of the following items as possible to help students better understand the vocabulary in the selection: a rattle, clay animal, pull-toy on four wheels, yo-yo, and terra-cotta pot (to show what the dolls were made of). Encourage students to describe the items and match them to the vocabulary words on the page.

Advanced: Invite student groups or pairs of students to choose a toy described on page 7. Have students do research to find out about the history of the toy and its evolution through today. Ask pairs or groups to share at least three interesting facts they learned about the toys, especially facts that deal with ancient Greece.

GROWING UP IN ANCIENT ROME

ANCIENT ROME

| | 753 B.C.E | 0 | 476 C.E. | 2000 C.E. |

ANCIENT GREECE

| 2000 B.C.E | | 323 B.C.E | 0 | 2000 C.E. |

When a Roman baby was born, a relative put the baby at the feet of the father. The father picked up the baby to accept it into the family. The baby was named nine days after birth.

The oldest man in a family—the father, the grandfather, or an uncle—was the "head of the family." However, women were also important to family life. They managed the house and household finances. In the early years of ancient Rome, women did not have many rights. In later years, they had more rights. They were allowed to own land and to have some types of jobs. They could manage some businesses. But they were still not allowed to hold jobs in the government or to become lawyers or teachers.

Girls and boys wore a special locket, called a *bulla*, around their necks. The bulla protected them from evil. A girl wore the bulla until her wedding day. A boy wore the bulla until he became a citizen. A boy became a citizen at age sixteen or seventeen. The family had a big celebration on this day.

In the third century, the Greeks **influenced** Roman education. Some Greeks lived in southern Italy. Greek teachers introduced the Romans to literature and philosophy.

---

influenced, had an effect on; changed

▲ Roman children dressed like their parents. They wore long shirts called *tunics*.

◀ Marble heads of a Roman girl and boy ▼

8

▲ Glass and clay marbles

School was not free. Most children in ancient Rome were not from rich families. They were poor. In poor families, parents taught their children at home. Many poor children did not learn to read or write.

Rich families sent their children to school at age seven to learn basic subjects. Girls did not continue in school after they learned the basic subjects. They stayed at home, where their mothers taught them how to be good wives and mothers. **①**

Boys from rich families continued their education in formal schools or with **tutors**. They became lawyers or worked in government. **②**

What did children do after school? They played with friends, pets, or toys. Toys included balls, hobbyhorses, kites, **models** of people and animals, hoops, stilts, marbles, and knucklebones. War games were popular with boys. Girls played with dolls. They also played board games, tic-tac-toe, and ball games.

What kind of pets did children play with in ancient Rome? Dogs were the **favorite** pets. Other pets were birds, such as pigeons, ducks, quail, and geese. Some children even had monkeys.

◄ Dolls were popular toys.

---

tutors, teachers of one student or a small group of students
models, small copies
favorite, preferred over all others; best loved

BEFORE YOU GO ON . . .

① What did girls do when they grew up?
② What kind of work did boys from rich families do?

HOW ABOUT YOU?
- What do you do after school?

9

CRITICAL THINKING

Have students respond orally or in writing to these questions:
- How were the lives of Roman children like your own? *(They went to school. They learned to read and write. They played with friends, pets, and toys.)*
- Do you think you would have enjoyed living as a child in ancient Rome? Why or why not? Give information from the text to support your answer. *(Possible answer: No. Based on the fact that girls stayed home to learn to be good wives and mothers, I don't feel they were given enough choices.)*

Viewpoint

Ask students to look at the marbles and the doll illustrated on page 9. Discuss with students whether children today might play with these toys. Then have students compare the ancient toys with today's toys.

across the curriculum

SOCIAL STUDIES Focus students' attention on the timeline on page 8. Have students find 753 B.C.E. and 476 C.E. Explain that B.C.E. stands for Before the Common Era, or before year 0, and C.E. stands for Common Era, or after the year 0. Point out that the Roman Empire began in 753 B.C.E. and ended in 476 C.E. Have students find zero on the timeline. Guide students to discover that the numbers to the left of the zero go from larger to smaller. Ask students how the numbers change as they move from zero to the right of the timeline. Then help students use the timeline to determine how many years the civilization of ancient Rome lasted.
(753 + 476 = 1,229 years)

REACHING ALL STUDENTS

LANGUAGE LEVELS

Beginning: Make a three-column chart on the board with the following headings: *School, Toys and Games, Pets.* Invite students to think about their own lives, come to the board, and list the following: what they learn at school, a toy or game they like, and a pet that they or a friend own. Then explain that these pages tell about the schools, toys, and pets of children who lived long ago in ancient Rome.

Advanced: Invite students to create and present a three-minute skit entitled "A Day in the Life of a Roman Child." Brainstorm with students about what school might be like and what after-school activities a Roman child might participate in, based on the facts in the text. Encourage students to use ideas in the text to write the skit. Allow them time to practice before presenting the skit to the class.

MODELING THE READING STRATEGY

Previewing: Ask students to recall the steps for previewing. Remind them that they will look at the headings and pictures to help them figure out what the selection will be about, and whether it is fiction or nonfiction. Have them preview pages 10 and 11 and tell a partner what they think this section of the reading will be about. Then have students read the section.

GUIDED READING

1. What separate responsibilities did Maya men and women have? *(Men worked hard to support their families, and they paid taxes. Women cooked, made cloth and clothing, and took care of the children.)*
2. What did Maya girls and boys learn from their parents? *(Girls learned how to weave and cook. Boys learned to hunt and fish. Both boys and girls learned to grow food.)*
3. What objects could be found on children's toys but were not used by the Maya in their work or transportation? *(wheels)*

─── *Viewpoint* ───

Explain to students that the Maya built large cities throughout the present-day countries of Mexico and Guatemala. Then call on a volunteer to read the caption under the picture of the pyramid on page 10. Ask students to describe how this building looks different from buildings they would find in a city today.

GROWING UP IN THE ANCIENT MAYA CULTURE

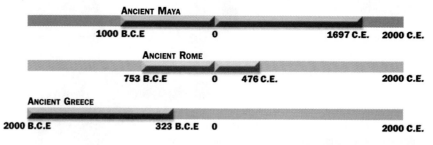

ANCIENT MAYA

| 1000 B.C.E | 0 | 1697 C.E. | 2000 C.E. |

ANCIENT ROME

| 753 B.C.E | 0 | 476 C.E. | 2000 C.E. |

ANCIENT GREECE

| 2000 B.C.E | 323 B.C.E | 0 | 2000 C.E. |

1   The Maya people lived in a large area of southern Mexico and Guatemala. They lived in enormous cities and created extraordinary art and **architecture**. You can visit the **ruins** of some ancient Maya cities, such as Chichén Itzá in Mexico.

The father was the head of the family. Maya men worked hard to support their families, and they paid **taxes** to the **government**. Women in Maya society cooked, made cloth and clothing, and took care of children.

When a boy was about five years old, the Maya tied a small white bead to the top of his head. When a girl was about five, the Maya tied a red shell around her waist. When boys and girls were twelve or thirteen years old, the **2** village had a big ceremony that marked the end of childhood. During the ceremony, a priest cut the beads from the boys' heads. Mothers removed the red shells from the girls' waists. After the ceremony, boys and girls could get married. Young men painted themselves black until they were married.

▲ The Maya city of Chichén Itzá became a center for buying and selling goods.

All women did some weaving and spinning. They made things for their families and to sell. ▼

---

architecture, building design
ruins, the parts of buildings that are left after the rest have been destroyed
taxes, money paid to the government
government, people who rule a city or a country

10

SPELLING MINILESSON

Spelling Short *a, o, i*

Dictate the following CVC words from the selection, inviting students to write each one: *not, fish, can, dogs, had, did.* As you dictate, emphasize the short vowel sounds. Then demonstrate how to use a dictionary to check to see if a word is spelled correctly. Say the first sound in the word *not.* Identify for students which beginning letter this sound represents and have them turn to that page in the dictionary. Then say the vowel sound. Use the guidewords to determine the dictionary page, and run your finger along the page until you find the word. Spell the word aloud. Have students work in pairs to look up the rest of the words. Ask each pair to record the correct spelling of each word in their notebooks.

◄ This Maya vase shows a jaguar.

▲ Dog on wheels

In Maya culture, school was free. Boys and girls learned from their parents, too. Girls learned how to weave and cook. Boys learned to hunt and fish. Children also learned how to grow food. At age seventeen, boys joined the army to learn about war and fighting.

Children played games and they played with toys. Some of their toys had wheels. Surprisingly, the Maya did not use wheels in their work or transportation. However, toys, such as animal pull-toys, had wheels.

Animals were important in everyday life and religion. The Maya used animals in their art. They decorated various items with pictures of foxes, owls, jaguars, hummingbirds, eagles, and other animals. The Maya ate some dogs. But they used most dogs for hunting. The Maya thought that dogs could **guide** people on the journey to the afterlife. They buried dogs with their owners.

---

guide, show the way

CRITICAL THINKING

Have students respond orally or in writing to these questions:
● Why do you think the Maya had a special ceremony to mark the end of childhood? *(Possible answer: This is a very special time in a person's life. A child gains new rights but also more responsibilities.)*
● How would the use of wheels have affected the Maya's work and transportation? *(Possible answer: Wheels would have made their work easier and their transportation faster.)*

WEBSITES

For more information, log on to http://www.longman.com/shiningstar for links to other interesting websites about ancient Greece, ancient Rome, and the ancient Maya culture.

BEFORE YOU GO ON . . .

1 In which modern-day countries did the ancient Maya live?

2 Why did boys and girls have a special ceremony when they turned twelve or thirteen?

HOW ABOUT YOU?
● Can you cook? If so, what can you cook?

11

across the curriculum

GEOGRAPHY Display a world map. Have students locate the United States on the map. Then read aloud the first sentence on page 10 of the Student Book. Have students find Mexico and Guatemala on the map. If there are students from Guatemala or Mexico in your class, ask them to talk about the climate and history of their country. Emphasize how close Mexico and Guatemala are to the southern border of the United States.

REACHING ALL STUDENTS

LANGUAGE LEVELS

Beginning: Have students create new word dictionaries in which they can record new vocabulary and definitions. Tell them to label a separate page in their notebook for each letter of the alphabet. Explain that on each page they will write new words beginning with that letter. Have them draw a picture of the word or write the definition.

For each selection that they read, have students record at least five words in their new word dictionaries. These words should not be Key Words or those already defined at the bottom of the text. Have students work in pairs to find the meanings of the words—either from context clues or in a dictionary—before they record them in their notebooks.

Review

COMPREHENSION

Have students reread the section on ancient Greece on pages 6 and 7 to recall how the lives of Greek boys and girls were similar and different. Ask them to copy the Venn diagram in their notebooks and add additional information from the selection. Point out that information about Greek boys goes on the left side, information about Greek girls goes on the right side, and information about both boys and girls goes in the center. Then have students respond to these questions:

1. Where did boys in ancient Greece learn to read and write? Where did girls learn to read and write? *(at school; at home)*

2. What toys did ancient Greek boys and girls play with? *(rattles, clay animals, pull-toys on wheels, yo-yos, terra-cotta dolls)*

3. What pets did Greek boys and girls have? *(birds, dogs, goats, tortoises, mice)*

CRITICAL THINKING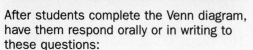

After students complete the Venn diagram, have them respond orally or in writing to these questions:

● Why do you think all girls didn't learn to read and write at home? *(Possible answers: Families could not read. There was too much work to do. Perhaps some people did not think girls should read.)*

● How is a Venn diagram useful? When might you use a Venn diagram? *(Possible answers: A Venn diagram helps me see how some things are similar and different. I would use one whenever I needed to compare and contrast something.)*

COMPREHENSION

Reread pages 6–7 of "Ancient Kids." Copy the Venn diagram into your notebook. Fill in more information for Greek boys (on the left side), Greek girls (on the right side), and both Greek boys and girls (in the center). Then compare diagrams in pairs.

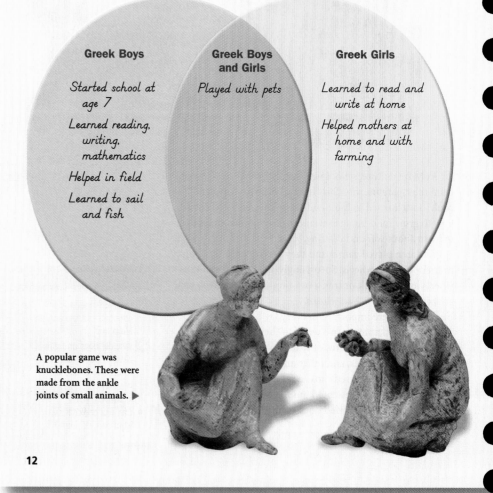

Greek Boys

Started school at age 7

Learned reading, writing, mathematics

Helped in field

Learned to sail and fish

Greek Boys and Girls

Played with pets

Greek Girls

Learned to read and write at home

Helped mothers at home and with farming

A popular game was knucklebones. These were made from the ankle joints of small animals. ▶

12

EXTENSION

Copy the chart into your notebook. In the left column, write kids' activities in ancient Greece, ancient Rome, or the ancient Maya culture. In the right column, write *same* if you do the activity and *different* if you don't. Explain.

Ancient Kids	Me
Maya boys learned to hunt.	Different. I don't hunt.
Roman kids played with pets.	Same. I have a cat.

DISCUSSION

Discuss in pairs or small groups.

1. What are some examples of ceremonies in "Ancient Kids"? What ceremonies are important today?

2. How was a girl's life different from a boy's life in each of these cultures? How are the lives of boys and girls different today?

3. What did you do to preview the text? Did previewing help you understand the text? Explain.

4. Would you prefer to live in ancient Greece, ancient Rome, or the ancient Maya culture? Why?

13

EXTENSION

Have students look at the chart. Point out that the first column includes some details from the selection. Explain that the second column shows how young people today are different from or similar to children who lived in ancient times. Have students work independently to copy and complete the chart, comparing the ancient children with themselves.

DISCUSSION

Have students read the questions and discuss them in pairs. Ask volunteers to share some of the important points they made during the discussion.

METACOGNITION

Ask students:

1. How did previewing help you to read this selection?

2. Which graphic organizer was easier for you to use, the Venn diagram or the two-column chart? Why do you think so?

3. How does making a chart to organize information help you remember what you have read?

REACHING ALL STUDENTS

LANGUAGE LEVELS

Beginning: Invite students to fold a piece of drawing paper in half and draw a picture of an "ancient kid" playing a game on the left and a picture of themselves playing a game on the right. Before completing the Extension chart, guide students to describe their pictures and tell how the activities depicted are alike and different.

Advanced: Invite students to discuss their completed Extension charts with partners. Model how to write a combined sentence using information from one row (both left and right columns) of the chart. For example, *Maya boys learned to hunt, but I don't hunt,* or *Roman kids played with pets, and I have a pet.* Challenge students to interpret their chart and write a combined sentence for each row.

Connect

READING SUMMARY

In this classic Greek fable, Tortoise challenges the overconfident Hare to a race. When Hare stops for a nap, the steady Tortoise wins.

MODELING THE READING STRATEGY

Previewing: Ask students to work in pairs or small groups to preview the selection. Remind them to read the title and look at the pictures. Have them tell what they think the selection is about.

SCAFFOLDING

Ask students to tell what they know about tortoises and hares, including where they live, what they eat, and how quickly they move. Guide students to list adjectives that describe each animal. Then have students draw pictures of both animals and label the pictures with the adjectives. Tell students to listen to the CD/tape as they read the story silently. Ask them to volunteer to read aloud.

GUIDED READING

1. How does the tortoise move? (*slowly, steadily*)

2. How does the hare move? (*fast*)

3. Who wins the race? (*Tortoise*)

CONNECT TO LITERATURE **Fables and Myths**

Fables and myths are fiction. That means they are stories about imaginary people (or animals) and events. Most fables and myths are part of the "oral tradition"—they are told by parents to children. Their purpose is to entertain and instruct. Often fables have a "moral," or lesson, at the end.

Aesop's
The Hare and the Tortoise

1   On a hot, sunny day, Hare saw Tortoise **plodding** along on the road. Hare **teased** Tortoise because she was walking so slowly.

    Tortoise laughed. "You can tease me if you like, but I bet I can get to the end of the field before you can. Do you want to race?"

    Hare agreed, thinking that he could easily win. He ran off. Tortoise plodded **steadily** after him.

2   Before long, Hare began to feel hot and tired. "I'll take a short **nap**," he thought. "If Tortoise passes me, I can **catch up to** her." Hare lay down and fell asleep.

    Tortoise plodded on steadily, one foot after another.

    The day was hot. Hare slept and slept in the heat. He slept for a longer time than he wanted. And Tortoise plodded on, slowly and steadily.

---

plodding, walking slowly
teased, made fun of; laughed at
steadily, at the same speed
nap, a short sleep
catch up to, go faster and pass

14

Finally, Hare woke up. He had slept longer than he wanted, but he still felt **confident** that he could reach the **finish line** before Tortoise.

He looked around. Tortoise was nowhere in sight. "Ha! Tortoise isn't even here yet!" he thought.

Hare started to run again. He leaped easily over roots and rocks. As he ran around the last corner and stopped to rest, he was amazed to see Tortoise, still plodding steadily on, one foot after another, nearer and nearer the finish line.

Now Hare ran as fast as he could. He almost flew! But it was too late. He threw himself over the finish line, but Tortoise was there first.

"So what do you say?" asked Tortoise. But Hare was too tired to answer.

MORAL: Slow and steady wins the race.

LITERARY ELEMENT

Personification is giving human traits to animals or things. Can you find personification in "The Hare and the Tortoise"?

confident, sure; certain
finish line, end of the race

About the Author

Aesop

Aesop was a slave in ancient Greece. He was a great storyteller. He told stories about animals to teach people lessons. Some historians believe that Aesop gained his freedom because of his stories. His fables are still popular today.

BEFORE YOU GO ON . . .

1. Who are the two characters in this story?
2. Why does Hare decide to take a nap?

HOW ABOUT YOU?
- Who did you want to win the race? Why?

15

CRITICAL THINKING

Have students respond orally or in writing to these questions:
- What did you learn from this story? *(Possible answers: Never give up. You can do anything if you really try.)*
- Which character do you like better, Tortoise or Hare? Why? *(Possible answer: Tortoise, because she does not tease Hare and she never gives up.)*

—————Viewpoint—————

Have students look at the picture and describe the tortoise and the hare. Ask students if they have ever heard a story that included either one of these characters before. Call on volunteers to describe the stories.

LITERARY ELEMENT

Call on a volunteer to read the definition of *personification* aloud. Point out that one characteristic of fables is that they are stories in which animals behave and speak like people. Invite students to share their knowledge of stories, TV shows, and movies in which animals act like people, such as the *Star Wars* features or the book *The Phantom Tollbooth.*

ABOUT THE AUTHOR

Scholars continue to debate the facts surrounding Aesop's life, including his very existence. Some scholars contend that the word *Aesop* referred to the story genre, rather than to the original author. They believe several people wrote these tales.

REACHING ALL STUDENTS

LANGUAGE LEVELS

Beginning: Write *Hare* inside a circle on the board. Ask students to describe the character. Write their descriptive words on "spokes"—lines that radiate from the circle. Ask students to copy this word web into their notebooks and to add one more descriptive word.

Advanced: Ask students to determine what kind of friend Tortoise or Hare would be based on their words and actions in the text. Invite students to complete the following sentence and to elaborate on their ideas: *I think Tortoise/Hare would be a good/bad friend because __.*

LEARNING MODALITIES

Auditory: Read aloud the fable. Ask students to listen for words that describe the two characters. Then form pairs. Have one partner describe either Tortoise or Hare. Ask the other partner to determine which character is being described and to explain his or her answer.

Connect

In this retelling of a Native American myth, Rattlesnake starts out as a helpless animal who is treated badly by the other animals. With the help of the powerful Sun God, Rattlesnake finds two thorns and places them in his mouth as fangs. His rattle warns others that he is nearby, but his fangs protect him.

MODELING THE READING STRATEGY

Previewing: Ask students to work in pairs or small groups to preview the selection. Remind them to read the title and look at the pictures. Have them tell what they think the selection is about, and whether it is fiction or nonfiction.

GUIDED READING

1. What did the Sun God forget to give Rattlesnake? *(a way to protect himself)*

2. How do the other animals treat Rattlesnake when he has no weapon? *(They tease him, throw him around, and kick him.)*

3. How does Rattlesnake solve his problem? *(He puts thorns in his mouth and rattles a warning.)*

This is a myth of the Native American Pima tribe in Arizona. Like a fable, a myth is a short fictional story. Myths explain something about nature or the world.

Why Rattlesnake Has Fangs

Cheryl Giff

Rattlesnake used to be the gentlest little animal. The Sun God forgot to give Rattlesnake a **weapon** to protect himself, and he was called the Soft Child.

The animals liked to hear him rattle, so they teased him all the time. One day at a ceremonial dance, a mean little rabbit said, "Let's have some fun with Soft Child."

He started to throw helpless little Rattlesnake around.

"Catch," yelled Skunk as he threw Soft Child back to Rabbit.

They had a good time, but Rattlesnake was unhappy and there was nothing he could do about it.

The Sun God felt sorry for the sad little snake, and he told him what to do.

"Get two sharp **thorns** from the devil's claw plant and put them in your mouth."

---

fangs, big, sharp teeth
weapon, something you use to fight with
thorns, sharp spikes on a plant

Rattlesnake picked the devil's claw and put the thorns in his upper jaw.

"Now you will have to rattle to give a **warning**," the Sun God told him. "**Strike** only if you have to."

The next day, Rabbit started to kick the snake and throw him around the way he always did.

Rattlesnake began to rattle his warning, but Rabbit just laughed and kicked him again. Soft Child remembered the thorns he held in his mouth. He used them on Rabbit.

After that, every animal backed away from Rattlesnake, and he was not called Soft Child any longer.

To this day, Rattlesnake strikes only if he has to, but everyone fears him.

---

warning, sign that something bad will happen
strike, hit

BEFORE YOU GO ON . . .

1. How does the Sun God help Rattlesnake?

2. What does this myth explain?

HOW ABOUT YOU?
- Are you afraid of snakes? Explain.

16

Link the Readings

Think about "Ancient Kids," and reread the fable and the myth. Then copy the chart into your notebook and complete it.

Title of Selection	Type of Text (Genre)	Fiction or Nonfiction	Purpose of Selection	Culture
"Ancient Kids"	informational text	nonfiction	to inform	Greek, Roman, Maya
"The Hare and the Tortoise"	fable	fiction	to instruct and entertain	
"Why Rattlesnake Has Fangs"	myth		to instruct and entertain	

DISCUSSION

Discuss in pairs or small groups.

1. List the animals from the readings in your notebook. Which is your favorite? Which don't you like? Why?

2. Take turns telling a fable or myth. Use your own words. You can use "The Hare and the Tortoise," "Why Rattlesnake Has Fangs," or another fable or myth.

3. With your partner, discuss how you previewed "The Hare and the Tortoise" and "Why Rattlesnake Has Fangs." Did previewing help you understand the stories? How?

17

REFLECTION

Point out the chart at the top of page 17 and read the headings aloud with students. Demonstrate how to read the chart, starting with the left-hand column and reading from top to bottom. Then ask:

1. Which story is a fable? ("The Hare and the Tortoise")
2. Which selection informs the reader? ("Ancient Kids")

COOPERATIVE GROUPING

Pair intermediate and advanced students with beginning students. Ask each pair to copy the chart in their own notebooks and work together to find the missing information. Ask volunteers to explain why they chose each answer.

DISCUSSION

Have students discuss each point in pairs or small groups. Model how to answer question 2 by telling a fable or myth like "King Midas." Then encourage students to practice telling a fable or myth to their group members. After they have completed their discussion, ask volunteers to share their fables or myths with the class.

CRITICAL THINKING

Remind students that the phrase "growing up" can refer to more than growing taller. Have students discuss the different meanings of "growing up" in the nonfiction selection, and also how the hare and the rattlesnake "grew up" in the literature selections. Point out that learning a lesson about life is a way of growing up.

REACHING ALL STUDENTS

LANGUAGE LEVELS

Beginning: To help students answer Discussion question 1, have them brainstorm adjectives that describe the animals in the fable and the myth (tortoise, hare, rattlesnake, skunk, rabbit). Write their ideas on the board under the name of each animal. Then have pairs or groups answer the discussion question.

Advanced: Invite students to make a two-column chart to show what the animals in the fable and myth learned. Have students list all the animal characters in the first column and what they learned in the second column.

Connect to Writing

GRAMMAR

Ask students to read the top of page 18 with you. Explain that adjectives are words used to describe a person, place, or thing. They provide details that make writing more interesting and informative. Then have students find examples of adjectives in "Ancient Kids," "The Hare and the Tortoise," and "Why Rattlesnake Has Fangs." Ask students to record the examples they find in their notebooks. Invite students to share their examples with the class.

Then ask students to read the bottom half of the page and use the words in the list to write sentences with adjectives.

SCAFFOLDING

Provide a context for understanding adjectives. Show students an item, such as a shoe, that will allow them to think up a number of adjectives that could describe it. List the adjectives they mention on the board. Then invite students to work in pairs to write two sentences about the item using some of the adjectives from the board.

GRAMMAR

Using Adjectives to Describe

Use **adjectives** to describe nouns (people, places, and things).

Adjectives can come after the verb *be*.

> *be* adjective
> The tortoise is **slow**.

Adjectives can also come before the noun.

> *be* adjective noun
> The tortoise is a **slow animal**.
>
> *have* adjective noun
> The tortoise has **short legs**.

Do not add *-s* to adjectives when they describe more than one noun.

> Tortoises have short legs.
> NOT Tortoises have short$ legs.

Practice

Use the words to make sentences in your notebook. Pay attention to correct use and position of adjectives.

Examples: a big / is / Rome / city   Rome is a big city.
           hair / Maria / has / black   Maria has black hair.
           fast / are / hares / animals   Hares are fast animals.

1. blue / John / eyes / has
2. Rome and Athens / cities / ancient / are
3. a fast animal / is / not / Tortoise
4. pets / good / Dogs and cats / are
5. have / Rattlesnakes / fangs / sharp

A Roman guard dog ▶

18

SKILLS FOR WRITING

Writing Correct Sentences
Remember these rules when you write sentences.

A sentence always starts with a capital letter.	*Adjectives usually come before nouns.*
	A sentence usually ends with a period.

The hare has long, skinny legs.

When there are two adjectives, usually there is a comma between them.

Adjectives do not have plural forms.

Practice
Correct these sentences in your notebook. Use the rules above.

1. girls didn't leave their houses very often
2. tortoise met hare on a day hot
3. hare was a nasty mean animal
4. they learned how to be citizens goods
5. boys from families rich had tutors

19

Write the following sample sentence on the chalkboard and read it aloud: *Hare and Tortoise raced across the field on a cold, rainy day.* Then call on volunteers to come to the board. Have one student circle the nouns in the sentence while another identifies and underlines the adjectives. When they have finished, read the rules for writing correct sentences aloud with students. Then write this incorrect sentence on the board:

boys in Greece learned to play instruments musicals

Have students correct the sentence using the rules for writing correct sentences.

(Boys in Greece learned to play musical instruments.)

Form student pairs to correct the five sentences at the bottom of the page. Then have students apply these rules to sentences or paragraphs they have written in their notebooks.

SCAFFOLDING

Model how to use the rules for writing to correct the following sentence:

mothers removed the shells reds from the girls' waists

Explain each step as you use the rules to correct the sentence.

REACHING ALL STUDENTS

LANGUAGE LEVELS

Beginning: Have students work with partners to identify the adjectives in corrected sentences 1 to 5. Ask them to read the adjectives aloud and then write them in their notebooks. Invite volunteers to list the adjectives on the board.

Advanced: Before inviting students to write two sentences that describe a character from the fable or myth, remind them of the rules for writing correct sentences. Then have students work in pairs to make sure they have applied all the rules for writing correct sentences.

Teach

WRITING ASSIGNMENT

Descriptive Sentences

Have students reread pages 14-16 and make a list of ten adjectives that the authors use to describe the characters in these stories.

WRITING STRATEGY

Explain that making a word web can help students prepare to write a description of a person or place. Have students identify the person who is described on the web and then answer the questions beneath it. Then, before students begin writing, model how they can check the sentences in their first draft. Write the following sentences on the board and read them aloud with students:

My Aunt Joan is a small, quiet woman, but don't let her size fool you. She's as strong as anybody I know.

Then say, *When writing a description, I make sure that the first word in each new sentence starts with a capital letter. If I use two adjectives, I separate them with a comma. I also make sure that adjectives come before the nouns they describe.*

Next, ask students to write a short character description using adjectives from their word web.

USING THE EDITING CHECKLIST

Read the Editing Checklist aloud with students. Ask students to use the checklist to revise their writing.

WRITING ASSIGNMENT

Descriptive Sentences
You will write six sentences to describe a family member, a friend, or yourself.

1. **Read** Look for adjectives in the stories on pages 14–16. In your notebook, list adjectives that describe each character.

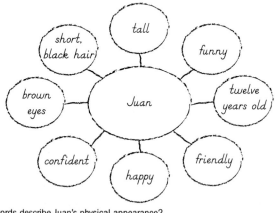

> *Writing Strategy: Word Web*
> A word web helps you prepare to write a description. It helps you plan before you write. Look at the word web about Juan.
>
> (word web: Juan — short, black hair; tall; funny; twelve years old; friendly; happy; confident; brown eyes)
>
> 1. What words describe Juan's physical appearance?
> 2. What words describe Juan's personality?

2. **Make a word web** Draw a word web in your notebook. Write the name of the person you are describing in the center circle. Write adjectives that describe the person in circles around it.

3. **Write** Use your word web to write six sentences about the person. Remember the rules for writing correct sentences.

EDITING CHECKLIST

Did you . . .

▶ start each sentence with a capital letter?

▶ end each sentence with a period?

▶ put adjectives in the correct place?

20

GRAMMAR MINILESSON

Present Tense: Regular and Irregular Verbs

Review regular and irregular verbs with students. Then write these sentences on the board:

I eat an apple.	*She eats an apple.*
You like the water.	*It likes the water.*
We watch a movie.	*She watches a movie.*

Point out the regular verbs in each sentence pair, and have students identify sentences with verbs that have an *s* at the end. Tell students to use the base form of the regular verb with *I, you, we,* and *they.* Add *-s* or *-es* only with the third person singular. Have students find five examples of regular verbs in their textbook and write the sentences in their notebooks.

Then write the following sentences that contain irregular verbs on the board: *I am happy; You are happy; He is happy; It is happy; We are happy; They are happy.* Point out that these are the correct forms of the verb *be.* Ask students to describe items from the classroom using irregular verbs.

Check Your Knowledge

Language Development

1. What is one way to find the meaning of a new word?
2. Describe previewing a text. How does previewing help you understand the text?
3. What is the purpose of informational texts? Of fables? Of myths?
4. What is personification? Give an example.
5. How can a word web help you write?
6. What are adjectives? Give three examples. Where do they usually come in a sentence?
7. What do the timelines in "Ancient Kids" tell you?

Academic Content

1. What new social studies vocabulary did you learn in Part 1? What do the words mean?
2. What three cultures did you read about in "Ancient Kids"?
3. How is your life different from the life of a girl or boy in the ancient Maya culture?
4. Who was Aesop?

21

OBJECTIVES

Read the list of objectives, encouraging students to join in. If necessary, define any difficult words for students. Have pairs of students work together to restate the list of things they will learn. Additional practice can be found in the **Workbook** and **CD-ROM.**

BACKGROUND

Ask students to read the first paragraph as a choral reading. Explain that *Later, Gator* is set in San Francisco's Chinatown. Tell students that the characterizations of the family and the portrayal of the culture are realistic and likable in this fast-paced story. Then ask students to look at the chart as you read aloud the headings. Ask them what kind of information they will be recording in the chart. *(information about gifts they have received)* Have students complete the chart and share it with a partner. Partners can compare the gifts they have received and discuss the events and occasions that their families celebrate with gifts.

COOPERATIVE GROUPING

Group beginning students with intermediate or advanced students. Ask groups to read the Background page and complete the chart. Ask each group to discuss presents they have received.

PART 2 — Prepare to Read

OBJECTIVES

LANGUAGE DEVELOPMENT

Reading:
- Vocabulary building: *Context, dictionary skills*
- Reading strategy: *Predicting*
- Text types: *Novel, science article*
- Literary element: *Point of view*

Writing:
- Descriptive writing
- Graphic organizers: *Word web, charts*
- Editing checklist

Listening/Speaking:
- Appreciation: *Story, article*
- Discussing ideas
- Compare and contrast

Grammar:
- Conjunction *and*
- Compound sentences

Viewing/Representing:
- Illustrations, charts, diagrams, photographs

ACADEMIC CONTENT
- Science vocabulary
- Growth in plants and animals
- Measurements

BACKGROUND

Later, Gator is a novel. A novel is fiction. Novels are usually longer than fables or myths. *Later, Gator* is about a boy who gives his little brother a very unusual present. You will read an excerpt—or small part—of this novel.

Make connections Think of presents people have given you. Then copy the chart into your notebook and complete it. Share your chart with a partner.

Present	When did you get it?	Who gave it to you?	Did you like it?

22

TEACHING GUIDE

PRETEACH	Provide Background	Read and discuss the Background information. Complete the activity. (ATE/SB p. 22)
	Present Concepts	Introduce the Reading Strategy. (ATE/SB p. 23)
TEACH	Monitor Comprehension	Informally monitor comprehension while students read the selection independently or in groups. (ATE/SB pp. 24–29)
	Teach and Practice	Present the Grammar, Usage, and Mechanics. (ATE/SB pp. 36, 37) Complete the Writing activity. (ATE/SB p. 38) Present Grammar, Phonics, and Spelling minilessons. (ATE pp. 24, 26, 28)
CONNECT	Connect to Content	Have students read the informational reading and relate it to the literature. (ATE/SB pp. 32–34)
	Across the Curriculum	Present curriculum links as students read. (ATE pp. 26, 28, 34)
ASSESS	Check Knowledge	Assess students' comprehension by having them complete the Check Your Knowledge section. (ATE/SB p. 39)
	Monitor Progress	Use one or more of the print assessment resources in the Assessment Package.
EXTEND	Integrate Language and Apply Understanding	Have students complete the Workshops (ATE/SB pp. 40–43) and choose a project from the Unit Projects. (ATE/SB p. 44) Then have them choose a book to read from Further Reading. (ATE/SB p. 45)

VOCABULARY

Read these sentences. Use the context to figure out the meaning of the red words. Use a dictionary to check your answers. Write each word and its meaning in your notebook.

1. When he turned twelve years old, he got lots of **birthday presents**—toys, books, and clothes.
2. They **get along with** each other very well. They never fight.
3. When you write fiction, you have to use your **imagination**.
4. It is **normal** to feel tired after running a long way.
5. I hate **reptiles**, especially snakes and lizards.
6. His birthday is a **special** day. He eats cake and gets presents.

LEARN KEY WORDS

birthday presents
get along with
imagination
normal
reptiles
special

READING STRATEGY

Predicting

You will understand a text better if you **predict**, or guess what will happen next, as you read. Follow these steps:

- stop sometimes and ask yourself, "What will happen next?"
- look for clues in the story and illustrations
- think about what you already know
- think about your own experiences

Then continue reading to see if your prediction is correct.

```
        what you
         know
         so far

clues from          predictions
  text

        your own
       experiences
```

23

VOCABULARY

Read the Key Words aloud, and have students repeat them after you. Then read the sentences and have students raise their hands when they hear the Key Word in each sentence. Model for students how to find the context clues in the sentences in number 2: *In the first sentence, I cannot find any context clues that would help me figure out the phrase "get along with." However, if I look at the second sentence, I read, "They never fight." This means that people who get along with each other never or hardly ever fight, so they must be friends.* Then have students find the context clues in sentence 1, and explain how to find words in the dictionary. Have students work with partners to complete the activity in their notebooks.

READING STRATEGY

Tell students that when you predict as you read you make a guess about what will happen next based on clues from the story and your own experience with a similar situation. Read aloud the information about predicting. Then review the flowchart, modeling each step in the process. Read aloud the title and the introduction to *Later, Gator.* Have a volunteer describe the pictures on the first page. Ask students to use these clues to predict what will happen in the story. Have them record their ideas in a three-column chart labeled *Story Clues, My Predictions,* and *Story Outcome.*

REACHING ALL STUDENTS

LANGUAGE LEVELS

Beginning: Wrap a bell or other easy-to-identify item as if it were a gift. Display the wrapped gift and tell students that it is a present. Discuss other words for *present,* such as *gift.* Then shake the gift, and ask students to predict what might be inside the wrapping. Ask, *What do you predict is inside the wrapping? Why do you think so?* Open the gift so students can check their predictions. Then model how to fill out an entry about the present in the chart on page 22. Encourage students to talk about presents they have received. Have students complete their own charts.

READING SUMMARY

In this excerpt from the novel *Later, Gator*, Teddy's younger brother Bobby is about to have his eighth birthday. When his mother pressures him into buying a special gift, Teddy plans to buy an alligator to scare Bobby.

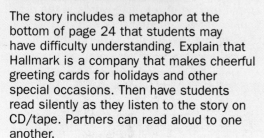

SCAFFOLDING

The story includes a metaphor at the bottom of page 24 that students may have difficulty understanding. Explain that Hallmark is a company that makes cheerful greeting cards for holidays and other special occasions. Then have students read silently as they listen to the story on CD/tape. Partners can read aloud to one another.

GUIDED READING

1. How does Bobby feel when he receives socks as a present? *(He likes them.)*
2. How do most people feel about Bobby? *(Everyone likes him except Teddy.)*
3. Why is Mother upset with Teddy? *(She doesn't like the way he treats his little brother.)*

—Viewpoint—

Invite students to describe what they see in the picture. Ask what the picture shows them about the relationship between Teddy and his brother.

FOCUS ON LITERATURE Novel

Preview the text. As you read, try to find clues in the text and illustrations that help you predict what will happen next.

from Later, Gator

Laurence Yep

2 *In this story, Teddy, the narrator, is jealous of his younger brother, Bobby, because everyone likes him. When their mother asks Teddy to buy Bobby a birthday present, Teddy plans to buy him something that he hopes will scare Bobby.*

The alligator was Mother's fault. She told me to buy something special. Mother, as usual, **blames** me. She says that I've got more imagination than brains.

That's not my little brother's problem. Last Christmas I gave him a pair of socks. Bobby was too dumb to understand the insult. Instead of getting mad, he said to me, "They're **neat-o** and just what I wanted."

Yeah, sure, I thought to myself.

Bobby had to put on his new socks right away and wriggle his toes at me. "They're very warm and comfortable. Thank you," he said.

Do you see what I mean? Bobby is a walking Hallmark card.

---

blames, says someone did something bad
neat-o, great (slang)

24

GRAMMAR MINILESSON

Negative Sentences

Write the following on the board:

Simple Sentence	*Negative Sentence*	*Negative Contraction*
Bobby was normal.	*Bobby was not normal.*	*Bobby wasn't normal.*
He could read.	*He could not read.*	*He couldn't read.*
I can afford it.	*I cannot afford it.*	*I can't afford it.*

Tell students that the word *not* can be used to make a sentence negative, or the opposite of what it would mean without the word *not*. Ask volunteers to read these sentences aloud. Help students see that *not* changes the meaning of each sentence in the second column by comparing it with the previous sentence. Then point out the contractions for *was not, could not,* and *cannot*. Help students see that the contractions shorten the words so that they sound more like the way we usually speak.

A *narrator* tells a story from his or her *point of view.*
● In first-person point of view, the narrator tells his or her own story using *I* and *my.*
● In third-person point of view, the narrator tells someone else's story using *he* or *she.*

Mother had understood, though. So this year, on Friday, the week before Bobby's eighth birthday, she took me aside. "Why can't you get along with your little brother? What has he ever done to you?"

"Nothing," I confessed. That was the trouble. What kind of little brother doesn't **bug** his big brother? Bobby was not normal.

Mother clicked her tongue. "Everybody else likes your brother. He's so sweet."

"Bobby's a regular mint chocolate bar, all right," I said, and thought to myself, And I am a raisin cookie.

"Then why haven't you ever bought him something special?" Mother demanded. She would make a good **prosecutor**.

"You always said it's the **spirit** that counts," I grumbled.

Mother frowned. "Only a mean person buys a cheap pair of white cotton socks."

"He liked the baseball."

Mother folded her hands in front of her. "Which you then used and lost."

"The Christmas before I got him comic books," I pointed out.

---

bug, annoy; bother
prosecutor, lawyer who asks questions in court
spirit, thought or attitude

"Which he couldn't read."

"I read them to him," I said. Mother just looked at me until I admitted, "Sometimes."

"You treat him like he's an enemy. Don't you love your brother?" Mother asked.

"Of course I do," I lied. (But really, how can I love a little angel who makes me feel mean and selfish and bad?)

"Then show your love," Mother said. **1** "Get something Bobby wants."

I tried to **weasel out of** it. "I can't afford the official **Willie Mays** baseball glove."

"No, I mean something he wants even more. I've talked it over with your father, and he's agreed that Bobby is now old enough to have a pet," Mother said.

She went to a cabinet and took out a big paper bag. From the bag, she slid out a kidney-shaped plastic tray. A wall of transparent plastic some three inches high ran around the edge of the tray. Part of the bottom rose up into an **island** in the center. A plastic palm tree grew from the island's middle.

---

weasel out of, avoid
Willie Mays, famous baseball player
island, land surrounded by water

BEFORE YOU GO ON . . .

1 What does Mother want Teddy to do?

2 Who is the narrator of the story?

HOW ABOUT YOU?
● Do you have a younger brother or sister? If so, describe him or her.

25

Have students respond orally or in writing to these questions:
● Why does Teddy think his brother Bobby lacks imagination? *(Possible answer: Bobby didn't understand his gift was supposed to be an insult.)*
● Do you think Teddy would be happy if Bobby bugged him? *(Possible answer: No, he would probably complain about that, too.)*

MODELING THE READING STRATEGY

Predicting: Discuss with students what takes place in the story at the end of page 25. Then ask, *What kind of pet do you think Teddy's mother has in mind? Why do you think so? What do you think will happen next in the story?* Have students write down the clues they find on their charts. Then have them make predictions about what will happen next in the story.

LITERARY ELEMENT

Explain to students that if an author is telling his or her own story, using pronouns like *I* and *my,* the story is written in the first-person point of view. If the author tells someone else's story, and uses pronouns like *he* and *she,* the story is written in the third person. Ask students to identify the point of view in *Later, Gator* as well as the person telling the story. *(The story is written in the first-person point of view. The narrator, Teddy, is telling the story.)* Then relate an event in two ways—first person and third person. When you have finished, have students identify the point of view in which you are speaking.

REACHING ALL STUDENTS

LANGUAGE LEVELS

Beginning: Lead students to find story clues by previewing the title and pictures. Read the introductory paragraph. Have students predict what will happen and record the clues and predictions in their charts. Ask students to check their predictions after reading the next section and record what happens in the *Story Outcomes* column. Then have students write new predictions based on what they have read so far.

Advanced: Have students make a two-column chart to illustrate how both Teddy and his mother describe Bobby. Ask students why they have different feelings for Bobby. Discuss how Teddy's point of view affects the story and how it might be different if Teddy's mother had written it. Then have students rewrite the first two paragraphs on page 25 from Teddy's mother's point of view. Have volunteers read their paragraphs aloud.

Teach

GUIDED READING

1. What does Teddy's mother buy for Bobby's birthday present? *(a turtle home)*

2. What does Teddy's mother tell him to do after he washes the dishes? *(buy Bobby's pet)*

————*Viewpoint*————

Ask students to look closely at the picture on page 26. Then have students reread the description at the bottom of page 25 and top of page 27, which tells about the gift that Teddy's mother bought for Bobby. Ask, *What other kinds of animals might be able to live in the turtle home?*

across the curriculum

SCIENCE Brainstorm with students a list of reptiles and words that could be used to describe them. Record their ideas on a large sheet of paper, and invite volunteers to use magazine cutouts and drawings to illustrate the list as a resource for reading. Be sure the word *alligator* appears on the list. Make available level-appropriate books about reptiles for students to use as a resource.

26

PHONICS MINILESSON

Short *u, e*

Say /ŭ/ and have students repeat it. Explain that this sound is called short *u*. Then write the following words on the chalkboard and read them aloud: *fun, just, huge, hung, cute, cut.* Have students repeat each word and raise their hands when they hear a word that contains the short *u* vowel sound. Ask partners to work together to find these words in the story on page 27. Have volunteers read aloud the sentences that contain these words.

Say /ĕ/ and have students repeat it. Explain that this sound is called short *e*. Then write the following words on the chalkboard and read them aloud: *pet, eat, rest, egg, tree, edge.* Have students repeat each word and raise their hands when they hear a word that contains the short *e* vowel sound. Ask partners to work together to find these words in the story on page 27. Then call on volunteers to read aloud the sentences that contain these words.

"I got the idea when he was watching a nature show on TV. He likes animals," Mother said. "He always wants to go to the zoo or the Academy of Sciences." **1** The academy was in Golden Gate Park and had an aquarium, a hall with stuffed animals, and a reptile section.

It wasn't fair, I told myself. I figured he watched educational shows to please our parents and to make me look bad. I'll take the Three Stooges over a nature show anytime.

"Then I saw an ad in the newspaper," Mother said, "and I bought this. It's a turtle home. You go down to the department store. They've got turtles on sale. You can buy him a pet."

Feeling miserable but caught, I promised.

For the rest of the week, I put it off. There was no fun in giving Bobby something he wanted. Instead, I just hung **2** around the apartment and moped.

On the morning of his birthday, he was up bright and early and jumping around, pretending to catch fly balls over the shoulder like Willie Mays. He had made so much noise that I had got up early, too, even though it was Saturday.

Mother served his favorite breakfast. We each had a scrambled egg with rice and slices of Chinese sausage. The problem was that Mother served it every morning. It was typical of Bobby to play up to Mother that way. I would have asked for scrambled eggs, bacon, and toast.

Three Stooges, popular TV comedians
miserable, very unhappy
moped, felt sad

When Father asked Bobby what he wanted to do on his birthday, Bobby volunteered to help him in the fish shop. Any normal kid would have asked for money for a movie—for him and for his older brother. Boy, he really drove me crazy.

After Father and Bobby left for work, Mother stood over me. "Well, did you buy Bobby's pet?" she asked.

I squirmed on my chair. "I didn't want to get it too soon. If Bobby found it, it would ruin the surprise."

"I thought so." Mother handed me a folded-up piece of paper. "I cut out the ad from the newspaper so you would know where to go. After you wash the dishes, go down and buy Bobby's pet."

"That's Bobby's chore today," I whined.

"It's his birthday," Mother said. "I have to buy tonight's dinner. When I come home, I want to find that turtle waiting for me. You can leave it in our bedroom until we give out the presents." She wasn't going to leave me any way to escape. "If you need money, go down to the garbage cans. I saw lots of empty soda bottles."

---

volunteered, offered to do something
drove me crazy, made me angry
squirmed, turned and twisted
escape, get away from something

BEFORE YOU GO ON . . .

1 Why does Mother think Bobby likes animals?

2 Why doesn't Teddy want to buy Bobby a turtle?

HOW ABOUT YOU?
- What do you like to do on your birthday? **Answers will vary.**

27

CRITICAL THINKING

Have students respond orally or in writing to these questions:
- Do you think Bobby watches nature shows just to make Teddy miserable? Why or why not? *(Possible answer: No. He probably really likes them. Teddy feels embarrassed because he'd rather watch* The Three Stooges.*)*
- How do you think Bobby feels about Teddy? *(Possible answers: He looks up to him; he tries to be cheerful so that Teddy will like him.)*

MODELING THE READING STRATEGY

Predicting: Show students the graphic organizer about Predicting on page 23. Focus attention on the box that reads "what you know so far." Point out that this means students can change their predictions as they get more information from the story. Ask students to think about what they learned when they read page 27. Were their predictions correct? What new predictions can they make about what will happen next in the story?

ACTIVE READING

Point out that although Bobby has little dialogue in the story, the author includes many details that describe his character. Have students create a character web for Bobby in their notebooks. Ask them to write *Bobby* in the middle of a circle and to include details about his character on lines that radiate from the circle.

REACHING ALL STUDENTS

LANGUAGE LEVELS

Beginning: To reinforce the highlighted vocabulary on page 27, write the words *moped, miserable,* and *squirmed* on the chalkboard. Call on volunteers to pantomime the meaning of each of these words in front of the group while students guess the meaning.

Advanced: Form student groups of three. Have each student choose a different character—Teddy, Mother, or Father. Invite them to complete the following sentence as if they were the character they chose: *Today is Bobby's birthday. I feel _____ because _____.*

LEARNING MODALITIES

Auditory: Discuss the meaning of the following idioms with the group. Then have volunteers use them in oral sentences.
- put it off *(waited to do it)*
- play up to Mother *(try to please Mother)*
- drove me crazy *(made me angry)*

Teach

GUIDED READING

1. What two animals are featured in the newspaper ad Teddy's mother gave to him? *(turtle, alligator)*

2. What question does Teddy ask the department store operator? *(If I buy a pet, can I return it?)*

──────── *Viewpoint* ────────

Invite students to look closely at the illustration on this page. Ask them what they think Teddy is thinking based on his expression in the illustration.

across the curriculum

MUSIC The title of this story comes from a song sung in the 1950s by Bill Haley's Comets, titled "See Ya Later, Alligator." Students might enjoy listening to and learning this song. For more information, visit http://www.longman.com/shiningstar

---

After Mother left, I heaved a big sigh. Going into the kitchen, I turned on the radio for music and began washing the dishes.

As I was finishing up, I saw the newspaper ad on the table. It was for a department store in the Stonestown mall, where Mother worked. It would take me most of the morning to get out there.

Above the address was a big drawing of a boy and girl **gazing** happily at a turtle. It was grinning back from a plastic bowl like the one Mother had bought. In big type, the ad announced the turtles were on sale

for fifty cents. Then I saw the small print: BABY ALLIGATORS ON SALE. And like an **omen**, the radio began playing a funny song from the past. "See you later, alligator," the radio sang. "After a while, crocodile."

If there had been a light bulb over my head, it would have suddenly shone as bright as the sun. Carefully I reviewed Mother's words. As far as I could remember, she had said to buy Bobby a pet. I chuckled. Poor Mother. She thought she had trapped me, but she had given me a **loophole**.

---

gazing, staring

omen, sign that something will happen
loophole, something that lets you escape

28

<spiral binding>

SPELLING MINILESSON

Spelling Short *u, e* Sounds

Explain that many words containing the short *u* and short *e* sounds follow certain spelling patterns. Write the following patterns on the board, and have students read and spell out the examples that follow the patterns.

CVC: *wet, fun*
CCVC: *shed, club*
CVCC: *sent, rung*

Have students find the words *left, bulb, sun,* and *when* on pages 28 and 29. Point out the short *u* and short *e* spelling patterns in each of these words. Then ask students to look for words with the short *u* and short *e* spelling patterns throughout the story and record them in their notebooks. Pairs of students can share and compare their lists. Examples include *dumb, get, bug, them, then, rest, just, much, help, well, cut, fun, pet, run.*

A plan began to build in my mind. First, though, I called up the department store having the sale. When I got the **operator**, I asked her, "I'd like to buy my brother something special from your pet department. If he doesn't like it, can I return it?"

"You can return anything within seventy-two hours after the sale." She added, "But the pet has to be alive."

"It won't be here long enough to die," I laughed, and hung up. I imagined what would happen tonight when Bobby opened his present. He would probably run **shrieking** from the room.

In my mind, I played out many **marvelous** scenes, ranging from a **horrified** Bobby to an **outraged** one. In any case, I would have to return it and get my money back. At the same time Mother would learn her lesson too.

It was the perfect gift. I could keep my promise to Mother because it would be nature stuff as well as something special. I could keep my promise to myself because it would be weird enough.

---

operator, someone who answers phone calls
shrieking, screaming
marvelous, good; wonderful
horrified, very upset
outraged, extremely angry

About the Author

Laurence Yep

Laurence Yep is a Chinese-American writer. He writes stories for children and adults. He was born in 1948, in California. When he was young, Yep really did buy his little brother an alligator as a pet!

❶

BEFORE YOU GO ON . . .

❶ What does Teddy think Bobby will do when he opens the present?

❷ Does Teddy have a good imagination? Explain. **Answers will vary.**

HOW ABOUT YOU?

● Would you like to get an alligator as a birthday present? Why or why not?

29

CRITICAL THINKING

Have students respond orally or in writing to these questions:

● What animal do you think Teddy will buy for Bobby? *(Possible answer: alligator)*

● What is your opinion of Teddy? *(Possible answer: He is jealous and selfish.)*

● Knowing how Bobby acted when Teddy gave him other gifts, how do you think Bobby will act when he gets Teddy's gift? *(Possible answer: He will probably like it.)*

MODELING THE READING STRATEGY

Predicting: After students read pages 28–29, ask them whether their predictions were correct. If not, discuss with students what clues on the previous pages could have helped them to make other predictions.

ABOUT THE AUTHOR

Laurence Yep grew up in an African-American neighborhood in San Francisco and commuted to a bilingual school in Chinatown. At times, Yep felt lost in the clash of cultures that he was experiencing. Through his writing, Yep is able to invoke his family connections, explore his Asian American roots, and define his place in his cultural community.

WEBSITES

For more information, log on to http://www.longman.com/shiningstar for links to other interesting websites about reptiles.

REACHING ALL STUDENTS

LANGUAGE LEVELS

Beginning: Ask students to study the pictures throughout this story. Have them choose two pictures that help tell the story. Ask them to write captions for these pictures.

Advanced: Invite students to predict what might happen next, based on clues the author has provided throughout the story. Then invite them to work in pairs to write the next part of the story. When they have finished, call on volunteers to read their stories aloud.

LEARNING MODALITIES

Kinesthetic: Invite students to act out the story. Have students work in groups of three to play the parts of Teddy, his mother, and Bobby. Students can write their dialogue on index cards to help them remember their lines. Encourage a narrator to reread nondialogue sections of the story aloud to keep the story flowing.

Review and Practice

COMPREHENSION

Invite volunteers to take turns reading aloud the Comprehension directions. Then read aloud the list of events from the story. Ask students to number the events in chronological order (the order that they occurred in the story). Tell students to refer back to the story if they need help.

Have students respond to these questions:

1. Which two events happened near the beginning of the story? *(Teddy gives Bobby a pair of socks; Mother asks Teddy to buy a pet for Bobby.)*

2. Which events happened in the middle of the story? *(Bobby eats breakfast; Bobby helps in the fish shop; Mother gives Teddy a newspaper ad; Teddy does the dishes.)*

3. Which two events happened at the end of the story? *(Teddy has an idea; Teddy calls the department store.)*

CRITICAL THINKING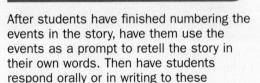

After students have finished numbering the events in the story, have them use the events as a prompt to retell the story in their own words. Then have students respond orally or in writing to these questions:

● How do you think Bobby will feel when he gets the alligator? *(Possible answers: He might like it; he might be scared of it; he might feel bad if he can't keep it.)*

● Why does Teddy buy gifts for Bobby that most kids would not like? *(Possible answer: Teddy resents Bobby.)*

COMPREHENSION

Reread the excerpt from *Later, Gator.* Number the events in chronological (time) order. Remember, the story includes events that took place before Mother asks Teddy to buy a special present for his brother. Write the sentences in your notebook.

_____ Bobby eats his birthday breakfast.

_____ Teddy's mother asks him to buy Bobby a pet.

___1___ Teddy gives Bobby a pair of white socks for Christmas.

_____ Teddy does the dishes because it's Bobby's birthday.

_____ Teddy calls the department store.

_____ Mother gives Teddy a newspaper ad with directions on it.

_____ Teddy has an idea that makes him happy.

_____ Bobby volunteers to help in the fish shop.

30

EXTENSION

1. Look at the words in the box. Do you know what they mean? If not, look them up in your dictionary.

| friendly | jealous | funny | selfish |
| helpful | thankful | kind | mean |

Copy these word webs into your notebook. Write adjectives that describe the boys in the empty circles. Use words from the box. Then compare word webs in small groups.

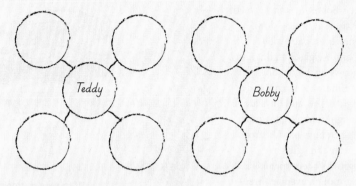

2. Compare yourself to Bobby and Teddy.

DISCUSSION

Discuss in pairs or small groups.

1. Is an alligator a good pet? Why or why not?
2. What predictions did you make as you read the story? Were your predictions correct? What were some clues you used to make predictions? How do you predict *Later, Gator* will end?

31

EXTENSION

Have students look at the incomplete character webs. Explain that the words in the box are adjectives that describe Teddy and Bobby. Ask students to work in pairs to choose words from the box and create webs about the two brothers. Then have students work independently to create webs that describe themselves. Later they can share their finished webs with their partners.

DISCUSSION

Have students read the questions and discuss them in pairs or small groups. After they have completed their discussion, ask volunteers to present their answers to the rest of the class.

METACOGNITION

Ask students:

1. How did context clues help you figure out the meaning of words you didn't know?
2. How did the first-person point of view help you better understand the character of Teddy? How would the story have been different if it were told from Mother's or Bobby's point of view?
3. Did making a character web about Bobby help you as you read the story? Why or why not?

REACHING ALL STUDENTS

LANGUAGE LEVELS

Beginning: Read aloud the list of words in the box in the Extension activity. Ask students to repeat each word, correcting pronunciation as necessary. Demonstrate how to find the first word, *friendly,* in a dictionary using the guide words at the upper corners of the pages. Then have students locate the remaining words in the dictionary and write down the guide words that appear on the page where each word is found.

CONNECT TO CONTENT Science

This is an informational text. It gives some facts about growth. Look at the title, headings, and pictures. What do you think the text is about?

AMAZING GROWTH FACTS

It is one of the wonders of nature that all living things **increase** in size. Think about how a tiny acorn can grow into an enormous oak tree. Sometimes this growth is very fast, other times it is very slow.

The **average** newborn baby is 50 centimeters long and weighs 3.4 kilograms. When the baby grows up, he or she increases to three times that **length** and 18 times that **weight**. Girls and boys are about the same **height** and weight until early adulthood. Then boys usually grow taller and weigh more than girls.

Bamboo can grow 90 centimeters in one day—the height of an average three-year-old child.

Pacific giant kelp (a kind of seaweed) can grow as much as 45 centimeters in one day.

An ant can lift more than 100 times its weight. One hundred times the weight of a 64-kilogram person would be the same weight as three cars!

increase, become bigger
average, usual or normal
length, how long something is
weight, how heavy something is
height, how tall something is

▲ If we were as strong as ants, we could lift three cars!

Bamboo: 30 m

Pacific giant kelp: 60 m

Average man: 1.75 m

32

A baby kangaroo is the size and weight of a paper clip (1 gram). An adult kangaroo is 30,000 times heavier (30 kilograms). If a human grew at this rate, a 3.4-kilogram baby would weigh 102,000 kilograms as an adult—that's as much as a large whale! An average man weighs about 80 kilograms.

The egg of a golden eagle and the egg of a Nile crocodile are both 8 centimeters long. But look how much bigger the crocodile grows!

A 26-centimeter baby crocodile can grow into a 5-meter adult crocodile. If humans grew at the same **rate** as Nile crocodiles, a 50-centimeter baby would grow into a 9.5-meter adult—more than 5 times as tall as the average person!

---

rate, speed

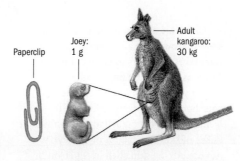

Paperclip   Joey: 1 g   Adult kangaroo: 30 kg

BEFORE YOU GO ON . . .

1. Using the Conversion Chart, convert the metric measurements in the text to imperial measurements.
2. Which grows fastest in one day—humans, bamboo, or Pacific giant kelp? Which grows biggest—eagles, crocodiles, or humans?

HOW ABOUT YOU?
- What growth fact do you find most interesting?

Conversion Chart

metric		imperial
1 millimeter	=	0.039 inches
1 centimeter	=	0.39 inches
1 meter	=	3.28 feet
1 gram	=	0.035 ounces
1 kilogram	=	2.2 pounds

Egg: 8 cm   Chick: 13 cm   Adult golden eagle: 88 cm

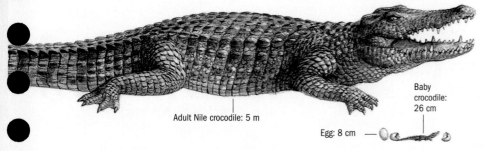

Adult Nile crocodile: 5 m

Egg: 8 cm   Baby crocodile: 26 cm

33

GUIDED READING

1. How much does an average baby weigh? *(3.4 kilograms/7.5 pounds)*
2. How many centimeters can bamboo grow in a day? *(90 centimeters/3 feet)*
3. How much does an adult kangaroo weigh? *(30 kilograms/66 pounds)*

CRITICAL THINKING

Have students respond orally or in writing to these questions:
- How tall would you be tomorrow if you grew like bamboo? *(current height plus 90 centimeters/3 feet)*
- Do you think this article is based on the writer's opinion or on facts that you can check? How do you know? *(It is based on facts, because they can be checked in a reference book.)*

Viewpoint

Ask students to study the art on these two pages. Ask them to identify and describe what they see in each illustration on the page. Then have them tell what the pictures reveal about how certain plants and animals grow.

REACHING ALL STUDENTS

LANGUAGE LEVELS

Beginning: Help students become familiar with common units of measure and gain an understanding of the concepts described in this article. Invite them to use meter sticks and show the length of an average baby, the number of centimeters bamboo can grow in one day, and the length of a fully grown Nile crocodile. Provide weights and/or scales to help students understand how much an average human baby and an average baby kangaroo weigh.

Advanced: Form student pairs. Have one student in each pair reread page 32 while the other student rereads page 33. Ask students to write down three facts from their assigned page that they think are the most interesting. Have partners share their ideas.

Clams are among the longest living and slowest growing of all **creatures**. A deep-sea clam takes 100 years to grow 8 millimeters. That's as big as your fingernail!

Do you ever wonder where the dust in your home comes from? Much of it **is made up of** the 50,000 or so microscopic **flakes** of skin that fall off of you every minute. All the skin **shed** by a person in a 70-year lifetime weighs almost as much as the average 6-year-old child (20 kilograms).

In the average human life of 70 years, a heart pumps enough blood around the body to fill the fuel tanks of 700 **jumbo jets**. The food that we eat in our lifetime is equal in weight to the weight of 6 elephants! A horse's **intestines** are about 27 meters long. A human's intestines are about 7.5 meters long. Luckily, the intestines are curled up inside the body. Otherwise, people and horses would look very strange!

---

creatures, animals or insects
is made up of, consists of; contains
flakes, small, thin pieces
shed, lost by
jumbo jets, very big airplanes
intestines, tubes that take food from your stomach out of your body

▲ Slow-growing clam

▲ A lifetime of shed skin

Intestines

▲ Average human ▲ Average horse

34

Link the Readings

Reread "Amazing Growth Facts." Think about the two texts you read as you look at the chart. Then copy the chart into your notebook and complete it. Discuss your information with a partner.

Title of Selection	Type of Text (Genre)	Fiction or Nonfiction	Purpose of Selection	What I Liked About It
From *Later, Gator*	novel		to entertain	
"Amazing Growth Facts"	informational text	nonfiction	to inform	

DISCUSSION

Discuss in pairs or small groups.

1. Alligators grow to about 5 meters (13 ft.) long and live for about eighty years. Do you think that Teddy's idea to give Bobby an alligator as a pet was a good one? Why or why not?

2. Which reading did you find more interesting—the excerpt from *Later, Gator* or "Amazing Growth Facts"? Why?

Giant sequoia: 84 m ▶

Giraffe: 5.8 m ▶

Human: 1.6 m ▲

35

REFLECTION

Point out the characteristics of novels and informational texts to students. Explain that a novel is a long work of fiction. It usually contains characters and events that are made up but that could occur in real life. An informational text is a work of nonfiction, such as a textbook or a biography. It contains facts about real people and events.

Read aloud the directions with students. Review how to read and fill in the chart, and have students complete the activity. Then ask:

1. What is the purpose of a novel? *(to entertain)*

2. What is the purpose of an informational text? *(to inform)*

DISCUSSION

Have students read the questions and discuss them in pairs or small groups. After they have completed their discussion, ask volunteers to share their ideas.

REACHING ALL STUDENTS

LANGUAGE LEVELS

Beginning: Provide students with examples of novels and informational texts. Then discuss with them the characteristics of these two literary genres. Work with students to create two webs on the chalkboard that illustrate these characteristics. Add any of the following characteristics of novels that students do not mention, such as *not all facts; fiction; longer than short stories; entertains; interesting characters; plot (events that tell a story); imaginary (not real)*. Add any of the following characteristics of informational texts that students do not mention, such as *facts, nonfiction, instructs*. Display the webs in the class for reference. Encourage students to use the webs when they complete the Reflection chart.

GRAMMAR

Call on a volunteer to read the definition of a conjunction aloud. Explain that a conjunction is a word that connects other words, groups of words, and sentences together. Read aloud the uses of *and* that are explained above each box. Then have students read the sentences in each box aloud. Next, have students find examples of the conjunction *and* in *Later, Gator* and "Amazing Growth Facts." Ask students to copy the sentences that contain the conjunction in their notebooks and underline the words, groups of words, or sentences that each conjunction connects. Then have students complete the activity at the bottom of page 36.

SCAFFOLDING

Model how to circle a conjunction and underline the words that the conjunction connects with the following activity. Pass out pages from a newspaper, and ask students to circle each use of the conjunction *and* that they find. Then have students underline the words, groups of words, or sentences that the conjunction connects.

Connect to Writing

GRAMMAR

Using the Conjunction *and*

A **conjunction** connects words, groups of words, and sentences. Use *and* to connect words in a sentence.

> The socks were warm **and** comfortable.
> Bobby makes Teddy feel mean **and** selfish.
> Teddy bought socks **and** books.

Use *and* to connect groups of words in a sentence.

> Bobby likes to play ball **and** to watch nature shows.
> Teddy read the ad **and** called the store.

Use *and* to connect sentences. When *and* is used to connect two sentences, you usually put a comma before it.

> Bobby got up early, **and** he ate breakfast.
> Teddy went to the store, **and** he bought a present.

Practice

Copy the sentences into your notebook. Circle the conjunction *and*. Then underline the words, groups of words, or sentences that the conjunction connects.

Example: Teddy used (and) lost Bobby's baseball.

1. Bobby likes eggs and rice.
2. Mother got an ad and gave it to Teddy.
3. Teddy listened to his mother, and he bought a pet for Bobby.
4. Teddy had a plan, and it was a big surprise.
5. Teddy washed the dishes and bought a present.
6. Teddy was older and smarter.
7. Teddy turned on the radio, and he heard a funny song.

36

SKILLS FOR WRITING

Writing Compound Sentences

When you combine two simple sentences by using *and*, change the period of the first sentence to a comma and change the first letter of the second sentence into a lowercase letter. The new sentence is called a **compound sentence**. It is made up of two simple sentences.

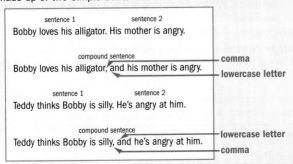

sentence 1   sentence 2
Bobby loves his alligator. His mother is angry.

compound sentence
Bobby loves his alligator, and his mother is angry.   — comma
          — lowercase letter

sentence 1   sentence 2
Teddy thinks Bobby is silly. He's angry at him.

compound sentence
Teddy thinks Bobby is silly, and he's angry at him.   — lowercase letter
          — comma

Practice

Read the sentences. Combine them to make compound sentences. Write them in your notebook.

Example: Teddy likes eggs and bacon. Bobby does too.
          Teddy likes eggs and bacon, and Bobby does too.

1. Bamboo grows quickly. Clams grow slowly.
2. Some growth facts are strange. Some are funny.
3. Bobby likes alligators. His mother likes turtles.
4. Teddy gets angry at Bobby. Bobby smiles at Teddy.
5. Bobby liked the socks. He likes the books too.

WRITING TIPS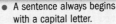

- A sentence always begins with a capital letter.
- A sentence usually ends with a period.

SKILLS FOR WRITING

Have groups of three read the information about combining simple sentences using the word *and.* Then restate the rule for creating compound sentences. Review the example sentences in the box by having students in each group take turns reading sentence 1, sentence 2, and the compound sentence. After each compound sentence is read, ask students to identify the conjunction and the punctuation that has been added to the new sentence. Then ask a volunteer to read the information in the Writing Tips box for correctly punctuating a sentence. Have students work independently or in their groups to complete the Practice exercises. Students should record the compound sentences in their notebooks.

SCAFFOLDING

Ask students to work in pairs to create a web for organizing the ideas presented on this page. Have them write *Compound Sentences* in the central circle. Then have them fill in the surrounding circles with features and rules, such as *Change the period to a comma.*

37

REACHING ALL STUDENTS

LANGUAGE LEVELS

Beginning: Have students work with partners to read the Practice sentences they copied into their notebooks. Then have them put a box around each simple sentence, underline the conjunction *and,* and circle the comma in each compound sentence.

Advanced: Have student pairs look through magazines for examples of compound sentences with the conjunction *and.* Ask students to underline *and* and circle the comma that precedes it.

Teach

Descriptive Sentences

Tell students to read the directions at the top of page 38. If necessary, have students reread the compound sentences on page 37.

WRITING STRATEGY

Call on a volunteer to read the information in the Writing Strategy aloud. Show students how to use the chart to form compound sentences. After students make a sentence-combining chart, have them combine the six simple sentences into three compound sentences.

USING THE EDITING CHECKLIST

Form student pairs. Have pairs read the Editing Checklist together and use it to check each other's compound sentences. Remind partners to check for the correct use of capital letters, commas, and the conjunction *and*.

EXTEND THE LESSON

Ask students to work in small groups to collect facts about alligators. Ask each student in the group to write one simple sentence. Have the group combine sentences to make compound sentences.

WRITING ASSIGNMENT

Descriptive Sentences

You will write three compound sentences to describe a family member, a friend, or another person you know.

1. **Read** Reread the compound sentences on page 37. What word is used to combine the sentences? What punctuation mark is used between the two parts of the sentences?

Writing Strategy: Sentence-Combining Chart

A sentence-combining chart will help you join two simple sentences. Read the sentences. Then look at the chart.

Bobby is happy. Everyone loves him.
Teddy is mean. His mother is angry at him.

Simple Sentence	,	and	Simple Sentence
Bobby is happy	,	and	everyone loves him.
Teddy is mean	,	and	his mother is angry at him.

1. What conjunction joins the two sentences?
2. What punctuation mark separates the two parts of the sentence?

2. **Make a sentence-combining chart** Draw a sentence-combining chart in your notebook.

3. **Write** Write six simple sentences describing a family member, a friend, or another person you know. Then use your six simple sentences and your sentence-combining chart to make three compound sentences. Check your sentences in pairs.

EDITING CHECKLIST
Did you . . .
- begin each sentence with a capital letter?
- end each sentence with a period?
- use a comma to separate the two parts of the compound sentence?

38

PART REVIEW 2

Check Your Knowledge

Language Development

1. How can you check word definitions when you use context to figure out their meanings?

2. How can you use predicting as a reading strategy? Give an example.

3. In *Later, Gator,* what do you predict will happen when Bobby opens his present from Teddy?

4. What is a novel? How is it similar to a fable or myth? How is it different from a fable or myth?

5. What is point of view? From whose point of view is *Later, Gator* told?

6. What is a conjunction? Give an example of a compound sentence that you make using a conjunction.

7. Do the illustrations in "Amazing Growth Facts" help you understand the comparisons? Why or why not?

Academic Content

1. What new science vocabulary did you learn in Part 2? What do the words mean?

2. Do humans, animals, and plants grow at the same rate? Give some examples.

Statue of Liberty ▶

▲ Sequoia

39

Put It All Together

EXTEND THE LESSON

Have students scan the Put It All Together section on pages 40–43. Tell them that these end-of-unit pages review how to write descriptively and punctuate sentences. Special emphasis is given to listening, speaking, and writing skills.

LISTENING AND SPEAKING WORKSHOP

Form small groups, pairing students of mixed proficiencies. Have students read the workshop directions together. Then have them go through each step. Let students use index cards or quarter sheets of paper to make notes for their speakers. Encourage students to practice presenting in front of their own groups.

COOPERATIVE GROUPING

Form groups of three students. Have group members choose one of the following roles: leader, presenter, recorder. Ask each group to read through the workshop together before starting to work on their presentations.

TEACHING THE TIPS

Speaking Tips: Invite a volunteer to read the Speaking Tips on page 40. Invite students to make a poster to display in class reminding a speaker to look directly at the audience and to speak clearly.

Listening Tips: Read the Listening Tips on page 40 with students. Invite students to role-play both good and bad listening habits based on the tips.

RESEARCH SKILLS

Nonprint: Suggest that students watch the evening news and take notes about how the speaker acts while presenting. For example, you might suggest that students notice how few extra gestures or hand movements the speaker makes and how he or she looks at the audience. Encourage all group members to return with suggestions to offer their speaker.

Put It All Together

OBJECTIVES

Integrate Skills
* Listening/ Speaking: *Group presentation*
* Writing: *Descriptive paragraph*

Investigate Themes
* Projects
* Further reading

LISTENING and SPEAKING WORKSHOP

GROUP PRESENTATION
You will organize and give a group presentation about important qualities in a friend.

1 **Think about it** Ask yourself these questions: What qualities do I want in a friend? What kind of personality does she or he have? List five adjectives that describe a good friend.

Work in groups of four. Use your list of adjectives to brainstorm a longer list of all the qualities that your group thinks are important.

2 **Organize** Choose one group member to make the presentation to the class. Work together to create a description of an "ideal friend." Make some notes to help the speaker organize what he or she is going to say.

3 **Practice** Listen to your group speaker present. Ask questions and make comments.

4 **Present and evaluate** Present your group's description to the class. After each group finishes, evaluate the presentation. What did you like best about the description? Do you have suggestions for improvement?

SPEAKING TIPS

* Make eye contact with as many people as you can.
* Speak clearly and loudly enough for everyone to hear.

LISTENING TIP

If you don't understand something a speaker says, you can say,

* "I don't understand. Can you explain, please?"
* "Could you repeat that, please?"

40

WRITING WORKSHOP

DESCRIPTIVE PARAGRAPH

In descriptive writing, the writer uses adjectives to help the reader picture or imagine what a person (or place or thing) is like. Some adjectives describe people's physical characteristics, or what they look like—for example, *short, tall, thin*. Other adjectives describe people's personal qualities or characteristics, such as *friendly, happy, loyal*. In a descriptive paragraph, a writer may also describe a person's abilities or skills.

A good descriptive paragraph includes the following characteristics:

- an interesting introductory sentence to get your readers' attention
- adjectives that help the reader picture or imagine the person
- details or examples that describe the person's abilities or skills

You will write a paragraph describing a person. You can write about a family member, friend, or someone you know. Use the following steps and the model on page 42 to help you.

1 **Prewrite** Make a list of family members, friends, or other people you know. Choose one person to write about. Think about the person you want to describe. What does he or she look like? What special qualities or characteristics does he or she have? Make a word web to organize your ideas.

WRITING TIP

A **paragraph** is a group of sentences about one idea in a piece of writing. The introductory sentence is the first sentence of the paragraph. An interesting introductory sentence makes your reader want to read more.

41

WRITING WORKSHOP

Descriptive Paragraph
Explain to students that they will be writing a description of a person they know. Point out that the sample paragraph will give them ideas for how to organize their thoughts before they write. See pages 18–20 and pages 36–38 for additional support for descriptive writing. Additional practice activities can be found in the **Workbook** and **CD-ROM.**

PROCESS WRITING

Form student pairs. Have partners take turns reading the information about descriptive writing and the sample paragraph. Then ask volunteers to restate the writing task in their own words. Have student pairs read the five steps in the writing process on these pages. Help students use the conjunction *and* to connect sentences. Encourage students to use a descriptive web to organize their thoughts before they write.

TEACHING THE TIP

Writing Tip: Before trading papers, have partners read the Writing Tip and look at the introductory sentences in their descriptive paragraphs. Encourage students to discuss whether the introductory sentence makes them want to read further. Ask them to work together to brainstorm ideas for making the first sentence in their paragraphs more interesting.

REACHING ALL STUDENTS

LANGUAGE LEVELS

Beginning: Encourage beginning students to participate as active listeners during the presentations. Encourage them to write down any words or phrases they heard during the presentations that need more clarification. Suggest that they review their notes on the presentation with a partner after class.

Advanced: Encourage advanced students to check all the notes that are written by members of their group and to make sure that ideas are stated clearly and correctly.

Put It All Together

Sentence Fluency: Read the model paragraph aloud with students. Then call on a volunteer to read aloud the call-outs in the right-hand margin. Discuss the adjectives the writer uses to describe his friend Greg. Have students think of other adjectives the writer could have used and list them on the board.

Before students revise their descriptive paragraphs, explain that *sentence fluency* is the rhythm and flow of language—how it sounds to the ear. For example, if a writer uses only short, uninteresting sentences, readers will soon fall asleep: *Joe went to school. Joe rode the bus there. Joe's first class was English.*

Write the following organizing tips on the board. Tell students to use the tips as they revise their writing.

- Use a variety of simple and complex sentences in your descriptive paragraphs.
- Vary the beginnings of your sentences by occasionally using pronouns in place of proper names.
- Check that your writing can be read aloud without difficulty. It should sound natural and have an easy flow.

Before you write a first draft of your descriptive paragraph, read the model. Notice the characteristics of a descriptive paragraph.

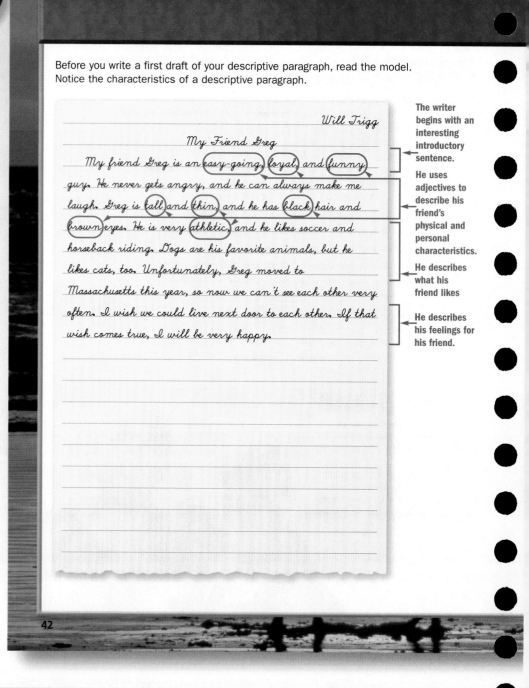

Will Trigg

My Friend Greg

My friend Greg is an easy-going, loyal, and funny guy. He never gets angry, and he can always make me laugh. Greg is tall and thin, and he has black hair and brown eyes. He is very athletic, and he likes soccer and horseback riding. Dogs are his favorite animals, but he likes cats, too. Unfortunately, Greg moved to Massachusetts this year, so now we can't see each other very often. I wish we could live next door to each other. If that wish comes true, I will be very happy.

The writer begins with an interesting introductory sentence.

He uses adjectives to describe his friend's physical and personal characteristics.

He describes what his friend likes

He describes his feelings for his friend.

42

T42

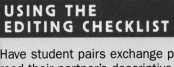
2 **Draft** Use the model and your word web to write your descriptive paragraph.

- Start your paragraph with an interesting introductory sentence, so your reader will want to read your description. Notice how the student starts his paragraph. How does he get you interested in reading about his friend?

- Use adjectives to describe the person's physical and personal characteristics, so your reader can imagine what he or she is like.

- Include details or examples of his or her abilities and interests.

Have student pairs exchange papers and read their partner's descriptive paragraph silently. Then ask partners to review the checklist and follow the steps.

ASSESS

Portfolio: Include the descriptive paragraphs in students' assessment portfolios for comparison with later assignments.

3 **Edit** Work in pairs. Trade papers and read each other's paragraphs. Use the questions in the editing checklist to evaluate each other's work.

EDITING CHECKLIST

Did you . . .

▶ write an interesting introductory sentence?

▶ use adjectives to describe the person?

▶ use *and* correctly?

▶ capitalize the first letter of words in the title?

▶ begin each sentence with a capital letter?

▶ end each sentence with a period?

4 **Revise** Revise your paragraph. Add information and correct mistakes if necessary.

5 **Publish** Share your paragraph with your teacher and classmates.

REACHING ALL STUDENTS

LANGUAGE LEVELS

Beginning: Encourage students to write two or three descriptive sentences. Allow students to use inventive spelling in their writing. Praise their efforts and try not to be too critical of their work. Let them read their completed sentences to you.

Advanced: During the revision stage, encourage pairs or small groups of advanced students to compare their paragraphs with the student sample on page 42. Ask them to look for the strengths in each paragraph and to suggest ways that both paragraphs might be improved. Tell students to ask themselves, *Have I included details and examples that describe my subject's abilities? Does my paragraph include adjectives to help the reader picture the person I'm writing about?*

Unit Projects

EXTEND THE LESSON

Home-School Connection: Students can interview older family members at home, either in person or by telephone. Remind students to ask permission before making long-distance telephone calls. Tell students to prepare their interview questions before the interview.

WEBSITES

For more information, log on to http://www.longman.com/shiningstar for links to other interesting websites.

PROJECTS

Work in pairs or small groups. Choose one of these projects.

1. Talk to older family members or friends about their childhood. What do they remember about growing up? What did they wear? What games did they like to play? What did they do after school? Make a timeline about their life.

2. Reread "Why Rattlesnake Has Fangs." Think of another animal with a special body part, like a monkey (tail) or a butterfly (wings). Write a story about how that animal got its special body part. Draw pictures to go with your story.

3. Go to the library and find a book of fables. Choose one fable with two or three animal characters. With one or two friends, act out the fable for your classmates. Find a piece of music that goes along with your story. Play it in the background as you act out the story.

4. Collect more "amazing facts" about how plants and animals grow. Look in books, in magazines, and on the Internet. Include pictures.

5. Use the Internet to find out more about ancient cultures. Type in key words like *ancient Greece, ancient Rome*, or *ancient Maya*. Find out more about the daily lives of the people who lived in ancient times. Make a poster illustrating your research. Share your poster with your class.

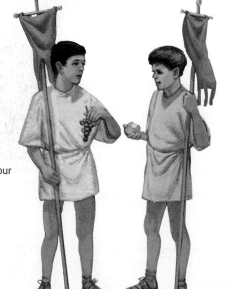

44

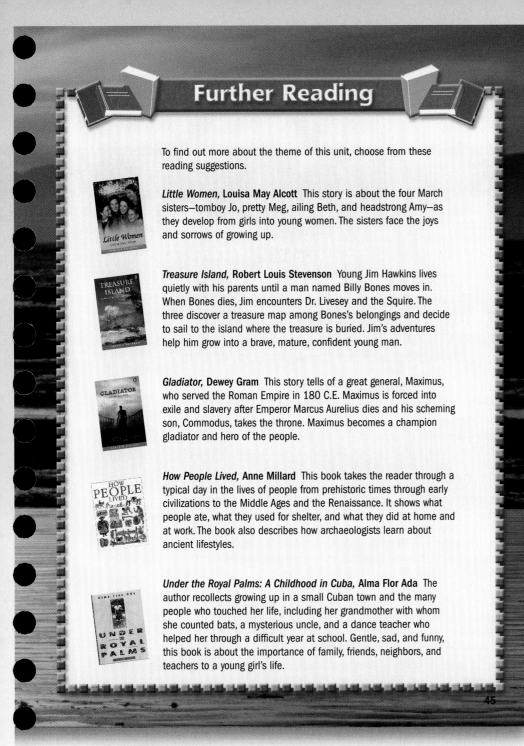

Further Reading

To find out more about the theme of this unit, choose from these reading suggestions.

Little Women, **Louisa May Alcott** This story is about the four March sisters—tomboy Jo, pretty Meg, ailing Beth, and headstrong Amy—as they develop from girls into young women. The sisters face the joys and sorrows of growing up.

Treasure Island, **Robert Louis Stevenson** Young Jim Hawkins lives quietly with his parents until a man named Billy Bones moves in. When Bones dies, Jim encounters Dr. Livesey and the Squire. The three discover a treasure map among Bones's belongings and decide to sail to the island where the treasure is buried. Jim's adventures help him grow into a brave, mature, confident young man.

Gladiator, **Dewey Gram** This story tells of a great general, Maximus, who served the Roman Empire in 180 C.E. Maximus is forced into exile and slavery after Emperor Marcus Aurelius dies and his scheming son, Commodus, takes the throne. Maximus becomes a champion gladiator and hero of the people.

How People Lived, **Anne Millard** This book takes the reader through a typical day in the lives of people from prehistoric times through early civilizations to the Middle Ages and the Renaissance. It shows what people ate, what they used for shelter, and what they did at home and at work. The book also describes how archaeologists learn about ancient lifestyles.

Under the Royal Palms: A Childhood in Cuba, **Alma Flor Ada** The author recollects growing up in a small Cuban town and the many people who touched her life, including her grandmother with whom she counted bats, a mysterious uncle, and a dance teacher who helped her through a difficult year at school. Gentle, sad, and funny, this book is about the importance of family, friends, neighbors, and teachers to a young girl's life.

45

FURTHER READING

- *Little Women* is appropriate for beginning students.
- *Treasure Island* and *Gladiator* are appropriate for intermediate students.
- *How People Lived* and *Under the Royal Palms: A Childhood in Cuba* are appropriate for advanced students.

REACHING ALL STUDENTS

LANGUAGE LEVELS

Beginning: Ask students to make a web as they read each chapter in their Further Reading selection. Encourage students to use the graphic organizer to record the main ideas from the chapter.

Advanced: Encourage students to keep a reading journal in which they write their personal interpretations of each chapter in their Further Reading selection. Ask students to make connections between what they read and their own experiences.

Level 1 Unit 2
Challenges and Choices

Make enough duplicate copies of the Letter Home for Unit 2 so that each student has a copy to take home. Show Video Segment 2.

PART 1 TEACHING GUIDE

PRETEACH	**Provide Background**	• Read and discuss the Part Objectives and Background Information. (SB p. 48; ATE p. T48)
	Present Concepts	• Introduce the Key Words and Reading Strategy. (SB p. 49; ATE p. T49; WB pp. 30, 32) • Pronounce the Vocabulary words. (ATE p. T49) • Model how to use context clues to define Key Words. (ATE p. T49)
TEACH	**Monitor Comprehension**	• Informally monitor comprehension through Guided Reading and Critical Thinking questions. (ATE pp. T50–T61) • Monitor students' comprehension through Critical Thinking, Metacognition, Discussion, and Extension activities. (SB pp. 57, 61; ATE pp. T48, T51, T53, T55–T57, T59, T61)
	Teach and Practice	• Use individually tailored activities for beginning and advanced students. (ATE pp. T47, T49, T51, T53, T55, T57, T59, T61, T63, T65) • Pair beginning, intermediate, and advanced students through Cooperative Grouping activities. (SB pp. 57, 61; ATE pp. T48, T57, T61) • Develop viewing skills using photos and illustrations and present the Viewpoint activities. (ATE pp. T46, T51, T53, T55, T59) • Complete the Vocabulary, Phonics, Grammar, and Spelling lessons. (SB pp. 49, 62; ATE pp. T49, T54, T58, T60, T62; WB pp. 38–39, 42) • Introduce the Writing Strategy and apply students' ability to write a narrative paragraph using the Writing Model and Writing Assignment. (SB pp. 63–64; ATE pp. T63–T64; WB pp. 40–41; Transparency # 24)
CONNECT	**Connect to Literature**	• Develop students' ability to analyze characteristics of genres through pairing of selections. (SB pp. 58–60; ATE pp. T58–T60) • Provide students with interactive reading support and practice. (WB pp. 33–37)
	Across the Curriculum	• Develop students' ability to extend the content of the reading selections through extended math, social studies, science, health, and art activities. (ATE pp. T52, T54, T60)
ASSESS	**Check Knowledge**	• Use the Before You Go On, Check Your Knowledge, Link the Readings, and Review and Practice features to assess students' comprehension of the selection. (SB pp. 59, 61, 65; ATE pp. T61, T65)
	Monitor Progress	• Use the Assessment Options, Test-Taking Tip, and the test. (ATE p. 65; AG pp. 37–40)

CONTENT TERMS

Present and elicit definitions of these content-specific terms:

- brain
- composer
- refugee
- rescue
- continent
- unfamiliar
- goal
- regional
- congratulate
- lectures
- mission

PART 2 TEACHING GUIDE

PRETEACH	**Provide Background**	• Read and discuss the Part Objectives and Background Information. (SB p. 66; ATE p. T66)
	Present Concepts	• Introduce the Key Words and Reading Strategy. (SB p. 67; ATE p. T67; WB pp. 44–46) • Pronounce the Vocabulary words. (ATE p. T67) • Model how to use context clues to define Key Words. (ATE p. T67)
TEACH	**Monitor Comprehension**	• Informally monitor comprehension through Guided Reading and Critical Thinking questions. (ATE pp. T68–T79) • Monitor students' comprehension through Critical Thinking, Metacognition, Discussion, and Extension activities. (SB pp. 75, 79; ATE pp. T69, T71, T74–T75, T77, T79, T83–T84)
	Teach and Practice	• Use individually tailored activities for beginning and advanced students. (ATE pp. T67, T69, T71, T73, T75, T77, T79, T81, T83, T85, T87, T89) • Pair beginning, intermediate, and advanced students through Cooperative Grouping activities. (SB pp. 75, 79; ATE pp. T66, T75, T79) • Develop viewing skills using photos and illustrations and present the Viewpoint activities. (ATE pp. T68, T71–T72, T77) • Complete the Vocabulary, Phonics, Grammar, and Spelling lessons. (SB pp. 67, 80; ATE pp. T67, T72, T80; WB pp. 52–53, 56) • Introduce the Writing Strategy and apply students' ability to write a descriptive essay using the Writing Model and Writing Assignment. (SB pp. 81–82; ATE pp. T81–T82; WB p. 54; Transparency # 25)
CONNECT	**Connect to Content**	• Develop students' ability to analyze characteristics of genres through pairing of selections. (SB pp. 76–78; ATE pp. T76–T78) • Provide students with interactive reading support and practice. (WB pp. 47–51)
	Across the Curriculum	• Develop students' ability to extend the content of the reading selections through extended math, social studies, science, health, and art activities. (ATE pp. T70, T76)
ASSESS	**Check Knowledge**	• Use the Before You Go On, Check Your Knowledge, Link the Readings, and Review and Practice features to assess students' comprehension of the selection. (SB pp. 78–79, 83; ATE pp. T79, T83)
	Monitor Progress	• Use the Assessment Options, Test-Taking Tip, and the test. (ATE p. T83; AG pp. 41-44)

PUT IT ALL TOGETHER TEACHING GUIDE

EXTEND	**Integrate Skills and Apply Understanding**	• Apply students' ability to present a group presentation using the Listening and Speaking Workshop. (SB p. 84; ATE p. T84) • Apply students' ability to write a descriptive paragraph using the Writing Workshop. (SB pp. 85–87; ATE pp. T85–T87) • Have students complete one or more of the Unit Projects. (SB p. 88; ATE p. T88) • Have students choose a theme-related reading selection from the Further Reading suggestions. (SB p. 89; ATE p. T89)

Suggestions for Newcomers
Unit 2: Challenges and Choices

Part 1

Background (p. 48) Write the word *challenge* on the board. Point to the pictures on p. 48. Ask students to tell what is happening in each picture. Help students notice details that describe what the people are doing. Have students use their personal experiences to draw conclusions about what each person might be feeling. For example, as you pantomime the actions, say, *This man is playing basketball. He is throwing the ball into the basket. It is difficult or hard. It is a* challenge. Continue with the other pictures. Suggest an appropriate challenge-related word or words for each picture. Encourage students to describe, act out, or draw pictures of situations when they've faced difficulties or challenges. They might use the sentence pattern: *I (am learning English). It is difficult. It is a challenge.*

Vocabulary (p. 49) Make sets of ten word cards. Each set contains a prefix: *un-, extra-, dis-, in-, under-;* and a high-frequency word, such as *like, ordinary, correct, age, happy.* Demonstrate adding a prefix to a familiar word to create a new word. Begin with high-frequency words. Display the root word card. Tell its meaning in simple terms and pantomime it or have volunteers use it in a sentence. Model and use TPR commands to add prefixes to the root. For example, say, *Put dis- in front of like.* Help students understand the new word.

Have students refer to the chart on p. 49. Point out the prefixes in column 1. Remind students that the word parts in column 1 are called prefixes. Since the roots for the Key Words in column 3 may not be familiar to newcomers, use simple terms and pantomime to convey meaning. Ask volunteers to imitate your actions as you repeat the meaning. For example, say, *Juan can walk across the room. Juan is able to walk across the room. Juan has the ability to walk across the room.* Give several other sample sentences. Add the prefix to the root as you write the new word on the board. Ask volunteers to underline the root word and circle the prefix. Use simple terms and pantomime to convey the meaning of the new word.

Reading Strategy: Skimming a Text (p. 49) Skim the selection on p. 50. Trace with your finger and point to the bold-faced name, the picture, the caption, and the date. Ask questions using *wh-* words—*who, what, where, when.* For example, as you skim, ask, *Who is this about? When did these events occur?* Remind students that some questions will be answered when they read the selection. Use stopping points such as important familiar words and proper nouns. Summarize the page, repeating your question and giving short answers. Write the questions and possible answers on chart paper.

Extraordinary People (pp. 50–55) Skim each section as modeled in the Reading Strategy. Begin a separate chart for each person featured. Read the selection aloud, section by section. Use pantomime, pictures, or explanations to introduce new words. Add the words to the appropriate chart. Have students reread the selection as they listen to the CD/tape. Choose stopping points such as the end of a paragraph to interrupt the reading. Refer to each chart. Discuss and answer the questions written on the chart. Have volunteers dictate answers or draw pictures.

Comprehension (p. 56) Newcomers may benefit by concentrating on only two or three of the people featured. Use the chart on p. 56 as a scaffold to help students understand the main idea. Copy the headings on the board. Above *Person* write *Who?* Above *Challenge* write *What?* Above *Choice* write *What? How?* Refer to the reading on pp. 50–55. Use TPR commands to complete the first column of the chart. For example, say, *Show me Rosa Parks. Write her name in column 1.* Point to column 2 and ask students, *What did Rosa Parks do?* Use a word web to elicit one- or two-word responses and challenge-related words. Have students dictate or draw pictures to complete column 2. Introduce the concept of choices using everyday language and situations. Display pairs of objects such as a T-shirt/sweatshirt, apple/potato chips, water/soft drink. Model possible exchanges with a volunteer.

> **A:** What is this?
> **B:** T-shirt/sweatshirt.
> **A:** I'm cold. What should I wear?
> **B:** A sweatshirt.

Explain that the people in the reading made choices, just as we make choices everyday. Tell students this is *how* they met a challenge. Complete column 3 with students. Ask questions and explain the choices in simple terms. Allow students to respond using single words, phrases, pointing to the text, and/or pantomiming.

He Was the Same Age as My Sister (pp. 58–60) Review vocabulary students have learned to describe feelings. Discuss which words are associated with good feelings and which are associated with bad feelings. Say these words at random. Have students flash a "thumbs-up" or "thumbs-down" to classify each feeling either as good or bad.

Show photographs of your family and friends. Talk about them as you tell a story. For example, you might say, *I have two children. Jason is older than Jessica. He is twelve years old. Jessica is nine. This is Jessica's birthday party. These are her friends. Jessica was happy.* Work with a volunteer to tell a story about his or her family and friends. Encourage the volunteer to use words that express emotions and feelings.

Introduce the concept of personal narrative. Tell students that the author is telling a true story. It took place in Holland. Locate Holland on a map. Read the title and author of the selection aloud. Point out that in a personal narrative the author uses *me, my,* and *I.* Point out these words in the text.

Have students look carefully at the picture on p. 59 and describe what is happening and how the people must feel. Help students notice details in the soldier's expression and then have them use their own experiences to draw conclusions. For example, say, *This soldier is crying. He is sad. He feels sad. I feel sad when people are fighting.*

Grammar: Simple Past (p. 62) Point out the verbs that end in *-ed* on pp. 58–60 and read aloud the sentences in which they appear. Explain that verbs that end in *-ed* tell about things that happened in the past. Demonstrate actions and then make statements about them using simple past verbs, such as, *I opened the window. I walked across the room. I raised my hand.* Have students repeat your actions and words.

Skills for Writing and Writing Assignment (pp. 63–64) Explain to students that a personal narrative describes events, usually in the order that they occurred—that is, in chronological order. Introduce sequence words that reveal chronological order—*first, next, after, then, finally.* Demonstrate sequence words by describing the life events of someone you admire. List his or her achievements chronologically. Use the simple past to describe what the person did. Link the events using the sequence words. Before students start writing, have them create a list of people they admire. It could include family members, sports stars, or people they have read about or seen on TV. Encourage students to choose one person and write notes about some events in the person's life. Explain that they will then use these notes as the basis of their narrative paragraph.

Part 2

Background (p. 66) Preview the reading and look at the illustrations on pp. 66–72. Explain that this story takes place in Vietnam about forty years ago. Point out the map on p. 66 and help students locate Vietnam on a classroom map. Point out and write the characters' names on the board. Have students describe each character, including gender, possible age, size, and what the person is doing.

Vocabulary (p. 67) Introduce the Key Words *beggars, rags,* and *rifles* using the illustrations and pictures. Help students relate the words to the appropriate pictures by pointing to a picture and saying the corresponding word aloud. Have volunteers demonstrate *to run* and *to run away (from).* Practice using other two-part verbs, such as *walk/walk away.*

Draw a rough outline of a person's body on the board. Ask students to name parts of the body. Label the body parts as students suggest them. If they have difficulty, point to a body part and suggest options. For example, say, *Is this an arm or a leg?* Read each label aloud and have students repeat it. When internal organs are named, point out that the stomach is the same as the *belly,* and the brain is where *memory* is located.

Reading Strategy: Visualizing (p. 67) Display objects with sensory attributes. Include objects associated with the story, such as a rag, a bowl of rice. Write these words on the board: *see, touch, hear, taste,* and *smell.* Point to the part of the body that does each thing. Model, and then use TPR to link the sensory words to the objects. For example, say, *Touch the rag. Smell the rag.* Make a word web using the sensory words. Invite students to react to what they see, touch, hear, taste, and smell. Add their word associations in additional circles. Suggest sentence patterns using the word web. For example, *I taste the (rice). It tastes (good).*

Model visualization for students: *When I read, I try to see, or picture in my mind, what is happening.* Point out the illustration on pp. 68–69 and read the last paragraph on p. 69: *This part of the story tells about what Hong said to Kien. I try to picture all the things that are happening—the sound of Hong speaking, the smell of Kien's rags.* As you read the selection, discuss words and phrases that describe how things feel, taste, see, touch, and smell.

From *A Boat to Nowhere* (pp. 68–73) As you read the story, refer to the character chart on p. 66, add new information, and revise it as necessary. Make a family tree to show the relationship of Mai and Loc's family. You may need to explain that their parents were killed in the war. Have students draw from personal experiences of extended households to help them understand the relationship of Tam, Duc, Hong, and Kien.

Comprehension (p. 74) Introduce or review chronology. Make photocopies of the three illustrations in the story and make sets of chronological word cards, such as *first, next, then, last.* Place them in random order on the chalk tray. Discuss the illustrations, ask questions, and have students match the chronological words to the illustrations. For example, say, *Tell me about this picture. When did it take place?* Reshuffle the words and pictures and have volunteers arrange them in chronological order.

If newcomers show mastery of the strategy, adapt the student activity on p. 74. Write the sentences on sentence strips. Help students sort the sentence strips into chronological order, using the illustrations and chronological word cards as prompts.

Sudan's "Lost Boys" Start New Lives (pp. 76–78) Point to the map of Africa on p. 76. Ask students what they know about Africa. Review skimming the article as you point out familiar words, look at pictures, and paraphrase the captions. Ask, *What do you think happens to the boy in the picture on page 77?*

Grammar: Conjunction *but* (p. 80) Help students locate the word *but* on p. 69 in *A Boat to Nowhere.* Explain that *but* usually connects two ideas that are different or contrasting. Model a dialogue such as, *Math is hard. Math is fun. Math is hard but fun. Mario is big. Mario can run fast. Mario is big, but he can run fast.* Have pairs take turns asking and answering similar exchanges.

Skills for Writing and Writing Assignment (pp. 81–82) Explain to students that a simple sentence has one idea, and a compound sentence has two or more ideas that are connected by a conjunction. Review challenges and challenge-related words. Have students use pictures to draw, write, or dictate a challenge they've faced. Help students rework fragmentary responses into full-sentence statements. Encourage students to retell their personal experience using sequence words. Students should try to use both simple and compound sentences to describe their challenge.

Put It All Together

Listening and Speaking Workshop: Panel Discussion (p. 84) Newcomers can form their own panel. Have them refer to the Writing Assignment above. Use the graphic organizers and Word Bank lesson to help students define a challenge. Have students dictate and then list their challenges. Provide them with a sentence starter, such as, *We have many challenges. A challenge is _____. These are our challenges.* Students can take turns as the panel spokesperson and participants.

Writing Workshop: Personal Narrative (p. 85) Show examples of fiction (storybooks, comic books) and personal narratives (magazine and newspaper interviews, letters, postcards, e-mails). Then model dialogue students can use to help them distinguish between a story and a personal narrative.

A: What do you like to (read)?

B: I like to read (magazines).

A: Is this comic book true?

B: No.

Use a T-chart to compare different types of writing and build language. For example, compare a storybook to a newspaper article, fact to fiction, and so on.

Brainstorm problems that students have faced or solved. Guide students through drafting a group personal narrative. Use chronological words to sequence the steps for solving the problem. As a group, edit, revise, and rewrite the narrative. Place it on poster board and have students illustrate it.

UNIT CONTENT

The first part of this unit includes "Extraordinary People," a selection of short biographies about people who have overcome many different challenges. Explain to students that these individuals achieved their dreams in spite of the obstacles they faced. Students will also read Mieke Malandra's "He Was the Same Age as My Sister," a short story that describes an experience the author had in Holland during World War II.

The second part of the unit includes *A Boat to Nowhere,* a work of historical fiction by Maureen Crane Wartski, and the magazine article "Sudan's 'Lost Boys' Start New Lives." Tell students that both selections are about children who have been orphaned as a result of war, and who must find a way to survive on their own.

Viewpoint

Ask students to look at the art on the unit opener and describe what they see. Then have students discuss why they think these photographs were chosen to represent the theme "Challenges and Choices."

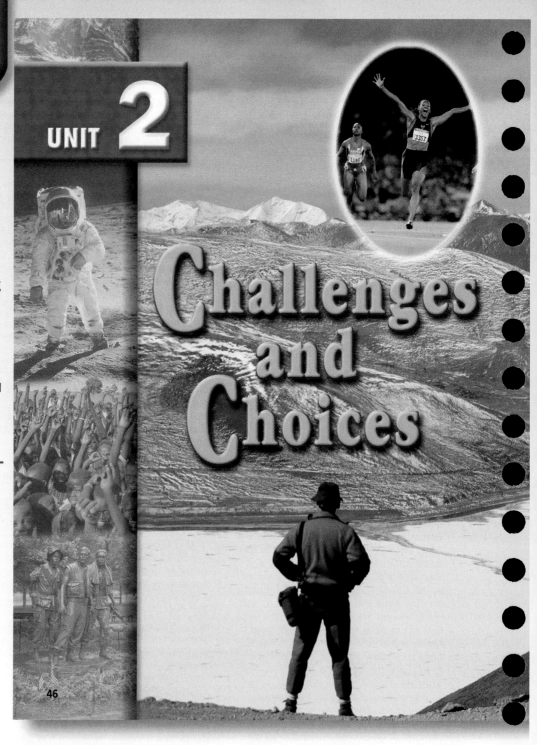

UNIT 2

Challenges and Choices

46

WORKSHOP PREVIEW

Listening and Speaking
Students will engage in a panel discussion to explore the meaning of *challenge.*

Writing
Students will compose personal narratives about challenges they have faced.

PROJECTS PREVIEW

Projects for this unit include:
- researching and presenting information about World War II, the Vietnam War, or the Sudanese civil war.
- role-playing an interview
- creating a piece of artwork that depicts a setting, character, or event
- taking notes about daily challenges
- making a personal collage

TEACHING RESOURCES

Lesson Plans	pp. 17–28
Summaries	pp. 27–32
Graphic Organizers	1–20
Audio Program	CD1/7–10; Cass.1/B
Workbook	pp. 29–56
CD-ROM	Unit 2
Video	Segment 2
Tests	Part Test, pp. 37–44
	Unit Test, pp. 89–97

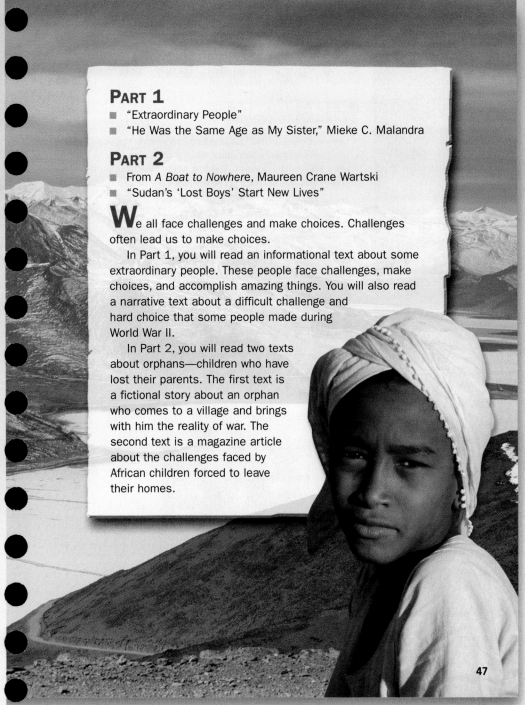

PART 1
■ "Extraordinary People"
■ "He Was the Same Age as My Sister," Mieke C. Malandra

PART 2
■ From *A Boat to Nowhere*, Maureen Crane Wartski
■ "Sudan's 'Lost Boys' Start New Lives"

We all face challenges and make choices. Challenges often lead us to make choices.

In Part 1, you will read an informational text about some extraordinary people. These people face challenges, make choices, and accomplish amazing things. You will also read a narrative text about a difficult challenge and hard choice that some people made during World War II.

In Part 2, you will read two texts about orphans—children who have lost their parents. The first text is a fictional story about an orphan who comes to a village and brings with him the reality of war. The second text is a magazine article about the challenges faced by African children forced to leave their homes.

47

DISCUSS THE THEME

Read aloud the unit title, "Challenges and Choices." Explain to students that a challenge is a difficult task or experience that tests a person's abilities. Then call on volunteers to relate a time when they have felt challenged, either in school or while engaging in some other activity. Have students brainstorm to come up with a list of challenges people often face as they grow up, and write them on the board. Then explain to students that a challenge can have more than one solution, and that people can make choices about the best way to meet and overcome a challenge. Ask students:

● to tell a partner about a challenge they have recently faced
● to describe the choice they made trying to meet the challenge
● to determine if they would make the same choice today
● to brainstorm with their partner some possible choices they could have made to overcome this challenge

QUICK WRITE

Ask students to list two different challenges they have faced. Have students list the choices they made trying to overcome these challenges.

REACHING ALL STUDENTS

LANGUAGE LEVELS

Beginning: Have students brainstorm to come up with challenges and positive choices they make each day. Examples might include choosing to ignore teasing, or working rather than playing after school. Have students draw a picture to illustrate their idea. Tell them to write a sentence under the picture to describe it. Then have partners discuss the pictures and other good choices they have made when facing challenges.

Advanced: Pair intermediate and advanced students with beginning students. Ask pairs to write the name of a person they respect in their notebooks and then list the qualities they admire about that person, as well as the challenges he or she has overcome. Allow students time to complete their lists and then ask them to discuss with partners their reasons for admiring the people they chose.

OBJECTIVES

Explain to students that in Part 1, they will be reading about people that they might study in history, civics, or science class. Read the list of objectives, encouraging students to join in. If necessary, pause to explain any words that students find difficult. When you have finished, ask students to restate what they will learn. Additional practice activities can be found in the **Workbook** and **CD-ROM.**

BACKGROUND

Have students read the Background paragraph and carefully examine the photos. Call on volunteers to describe the activity in each photo *(a speed-skater falling, several people racing in wheelchairs, a person playing basketball).* Ask students how the photos might relate to the theme of the unit. *(The people in each photo are facing some kind of challenge.)* Read each question and encourage class discussion.

COOPERATIVE GROUPING

Pair beginning students with those who are reading at an intermediate or advanced level. Have each pair read the Background page and discuss the questions. Once students have agreed on their individual answers to questions 2–4, choose a volunteer from each pair to share their responses with the class.

PART 1 · Prepare to Read

OBJECTIVES

LANGUAGE DEVELOPMENT

Reading:
- Vocabulary building: *Prefixes*
- Reading strategy: *Skimming for major ideas*
- Literary element: *Mood*
- Text types: *Social studies article, personal narrative*

Writing:
- Making notes
- Chronological order
- Narrative paragraphs

Listening/Speaking:
- Compare and contrast
- Discuss personal experiences

Grammar:
- Simple past of regular and irregular verbs
- Punctuation and capitalization

Viewing/Representing:
- Maps, charts, illustrations

ACADEMIC CONTENT
- Social studies vocabulary
- Important people in history
- World War II

BACKGROUND

"Extraordinary People" is an informational text. It gives biographical information about several important people from the past and the present. The text will tell you about the challenges and choices these extraordinary people made.

Make connections We all face challenges and make choices every day, in different ways. Look at these pictures and answer the questions.

1. What challenges are these people facing?
2. Have you ever faced any of these challenges?
3. How do you think these people feel about their challenges?
4. What challenges do you face in your life?

48

TEACHING GUIDE

PRETEACH	Provide Background	Read and discuss the Background information. Complete the activity. (ATE/SB p. 48)
	Present Concepts	Introduce the Reading Strategy. (ATE/SB p. 49)
TEACH	Monitor Comprehension	Informally monitor comprehension while students read the selection independently or in groups. (ATE/SB pp. 50–55)
	Teach and Practice	Present the Grammar, Usage, and Mechanics. (ATE/SB pp. 62, 63) Complete the Writing activity. (ATE/SB p. 64) Present Grammar, Phonics, and Spelling minilessons. (ATE pp. 54, 58, 60)
CONNECT	Connect to Literature	Have students read the literature and relate it to the informational reading. (ATE/SB pp. 58–60)
	Across the Curriculum	Present curriculum links as students read. (ATE pp. 52, 54, 60)
ASSESS	Check Knowledge	Assess students' comprehension by having them complete the Check Your Knowledge section. (ATE/SB p. 65)
	Monitor Progress	Use one or more of the print assessment resources in the Assessment Package.
EXTEND	Integrate Language and Apply Understanding	Have students complete the Workshops (ATE/SB pp. 84–87) and a project from the Unit Projects. (ATE/SB p. 88) Have students choose a book to read from Further Reading. (ATE/SB p. 89)

LEARN KEY WORDS

disability
extraordinary
incapable
uncommon
underachiever
unusual

VOCABULARY

Some words in English have prefixes. A prefix is a group of letters at the beginning of a word that changes its meaning and makes a new word. If you know the meaning of the prefix, it can help you understand the new word.

Prefix	Meaning	Word	New Word
dis-	opposite or negative	ability	disability
extra-	more than usual	ordinary	extraordinary
in-	opposite	capable	incapable
under-	less than usual	achiever	underachiever
un-	not	usual common	unusual uncommon

READING STRATEGY

Skimming a Text to Determine Major Ideas

Skimming a text is a strategy that good readers use when they read a new or difficult text. Skimming, like previewing, helps you to become more familiar with the text. It also helps you set your purpose for reading the text.

To skim a text:

- read it very quickly to get the main ideas only
- don't stop at words you don't know—skip over them

You'll be surprised at how much of a text you can understand when you skim. When you've finished skimming, you can go back for a more careful reading.

VOCABULARY

Read the Key Words, enunciating clearly, and have students repeat them after you. Ask a volunteer to read aloud the paragraph about prefixes and the table of examples that follow. Then have students brainstorm another list of words that begin with the same prefixes. Record student responses on a large sheet of paper with colored markers. Post the chart on the wall. As students read and discuss the selections, have them add any new words they find with these prefixes to the chart.

READING STRATEGY

Have three students take turns reading the Reading Strategy aloud. Then remind students that after they skim a text, they should ask themselves questions such as, *What is this about? Where in the text do I need to slow down my reading rate? What do I want to find out when I go back and read?* For easy reference, tell students to write each question on a different index card. Have them label the cards *Skimming Questions* and bind them with a rubber band. Students can refer to the cards as they read. (Before they begin the selection, you may wish to invite volunteers to describe the reading strategy in their own words.)

49

REACHING ALL STUDENTS

LANGUAGE LEVELS

Beginning: Write the following word pairs on the board: *tie/untie, connect/disconnect, flexible/inflexible.* Model the meaning of each word pair as you say the words aloud—tie and then untie your shoe, connect and disconnect a plug into an outlet, bend a paper clip and then try to bend a pencil. Ask student pairs to choose one word pair and draw pictures to illustrate the meanings of the words they chose. Have pairs display their pictures and use the words they chose in a sentence.

Advanced: Make sets of ten word cards with two words in each set that begin with one of these prefixes: *un-, extra-, dis-, in-, under-.* Have pairs of students shuffle the cards and sort them by prefix. Then challenge students to choose one of the prefixes, examine the words, and make an educated guess about the meaning of the prefix based on the meanings of the two words. Provide students with dictionaries and have them check their work.

READING SUMMARY

This selection looks at the lives of ten remarkable people. It examines the obstacles and challenges each person overcame in order to reach his or her goals.

SCAFFOLDING

Have students read the text silently as they listen to the CD/tape. Repeat this procedure as necessary. Then have students take turns reading aloud each paragraph.

MODELING THE READING STRATEGY

Skimming: Model how to skim page 50 before students begin reading. Say, *I'm going to look over this page quickly to see what it's about.* As you skim silently, stop once or twice and say, *I'll skip over the word* boycott *right now. When I go back and read the article, I'll check the glossary or the other words around it.* After skimming the text, *say, After skimming this page I can tell that it's about Rosa Parks, a woman who was arrested when she wouldn't give up her seat on a bus.* Have students follow your model and skim page 51.

GUIDED READING

1. Where was Rosa Parks sitting on the bus? *(in the middle of the bus)*
2. What did Rosa Parks say about her arrest? *("I did not get on the bus to get arrested. I got on the bus to go home.")*
3. What kind of scientist was Albert Einstein? *(a physicist)*

FOCUS ON CONTENT   **Social Studies**

First, preview the text. Then skim it. Try to keep reading until you've finished the section on each person. Don't stop when you see a word you don't understand. The second time you read through the text, you can use the glosses and context clues to figure out the meanings of new words.

Extraordinary People

▲ Rosa Parks is often called the "Mother of the Civil Rights movement."

Rosa Parks (1913–) left work and **boarded** a bus in Montgomery, Alabama, on a December evening in 1955. In those days in Alabama, African Americans and white people were separated on buses. White people sat in the front of the bus, and African-American people sat in the back. On this particular evening, Parks sat in the front row of the "colored" section.

1 The bus became crowded, and the bus driver told Parks to give her seat to a white passenger. But she **refused**.

Parks was **arrested** by the police. But she was a well-known woman in the community and **civil rights** leader Dr. Martin Luther King Jr. heard what happened. He led a bus **boycott**. Parks's actions helped to end **segregation** in America's South. It was the beginning of a new era of the **Civil Rights movement**. Rosa Parks did not plan her historic act. "I did not get on the bus to get arrested," she has said. "I got on the bus to go home."

◆ ◆ ◆ ◆ ◆

---

boarded, got onto
refused, said no
arrested, took someone away because he or she did something wrong
civil rights, equal rights for all people
boycott, organized refusal to do something
segregation, the separation of whites and blacks
Civil Rights movement, political struggle from the 1950s to the 1970s

50

Explain that Rosa Parks's refusal to give up her seat on the bus encouraged African Americans to boycott the bus system in Montgomery, Alabama, until they received equal treatment. Many white people in Montgomery also joined the boycott, which lasted 381 days. Protesters chose to walk or carpool in order to support the cause of equal rights for all races. This nonviolent boycott ended with a federal law that states that people cannot be discriminated against when using public transportation.

Tell students that people in other nations have also chosen peaceful ways to bring about change. For example, another nonviolent revolution took place in India under the leadership of Mohandas Ghandi. Explain that through his campaign of passive resistance (a peaceful protest) India received its independence from Great Britain in 1947. Have students consider both situations and discuss the possible challenges that peaceful protesters might face as they work to bring about change.

Have students respond orally or in writing to these questions:
- Why do you think people believed that Rosa Parks's arrest was unfair? *(Possible answer: She should have been able to sit wherever she wanted on the bus.)*
- What kind of challenges did Albert Einstein face? *(Possible answers: People didn't think he was very bright. He struggled in school. He had trouble finding work.)*

Viewpoint

Albert Einstein (1879–1955) was a famous **physicist**. Einstein tried to find the answers to many questions about the **universe**.

When Einstein was a child, he did not seem especially smart. In fact, his parents worried because he learned to talk so late. He was also an underachiever at school. He hated going to classes and taking tests. He graduated from college but then couldn't find a teaching job. But he kept working on his mathematical **theories** even though people thought he wasn't smart. Later people realized he was a **genius**.

After Einstein died, scientists removed his brain. They found that Einstein's brain was unusual. Some parts were different and some were larger than average. These differences may have helped Einstein become such an extraordinary thinker.

❖ ❖ ❖ ❖ ❖

▲ Albert Einstein is one of the most famous scientists in history.

---

physicist, scientist who studies forces like heat, light, and movement
universe, everything that exists
theories, ideas that try to explain something
genius, someone who has extraordinary talents

BEFORE YOU GO ON . . .

1. Why was Rosa Parks arrested?
2. In what way was Albert Einstein's brain unusual?

HOW ABOUT YOU?
- Would you like to talk to Einstein or Parks? What questions would you ask them?

51

REACHING ALL STUDENTS

LANGUAGE LEVELS

Beginning: Demonstrate how to use a web to recall information from the text. Draw a web on the board, writing *Albert Einstein* in the middle of a circle with lines that extend out from it. Ask students to discuss what they have learned about Albert Einstein. Write each piece of information on a separate branch of the web. Encourage students to use the web to retell the information to a partner. Have students copy the web into their notebooks.

MODELING THE READING STRATEGY

Skimming: Have students skim pages 52 and 53 by looking at the photos, captions, and boldfaced headings. Ask volunteers to report what they learned from skimming the text.

GUIDED READING

1. How does Stephen Hawking communicate? *(He uses a voice synthesizer.)*
2. What dangerous situation did Robert Peary and Matthew Henson face? *(falling into icy water)*
3. Why was it hard for Helen Keller to learn to communicate? *(She became unable to see and hear at a very young age.)*
4. How did Mozart spend most of his childhood? *(He traveled around Europe performing music.)*

across the curriculum

GEOGRAPHY Have students locate the North Pole in an atlas. Then have them discuss why Peary and Henson would want to find the North Pole. After opinions are shared, point out the location of the Atlantic and Pacific Oceans in relation to the North Pole. Tell students that one purpose for the North Pole quest was to find a faster route between these two oceans.

Stephen Hawking (1942–) is a famous physicist. He has a disease that affects his **nerves** and muscles. Hawking cannot walk. He is incapable of talking without a voice synthesizer—a special kind of computer that produces sound. However, his disability doesn't stop him from living an active life. Hawking travels, teaches, and writes books. He says that his disability gives him the freedom to think more about physics and the universe.

Hawking has written many science books, including *A Brief History of Time* and *The Universe in a Nutshell*. Many people think he is a genius.

◆ ◆ ◆ ◆ ◆

▲ Stephen Hawking uses a special wheelchair to get around.

Early in the twentieth century, the North Pole was still undiscovered. Many
1 explorers wanted to be the first ones there. No one is certain, but **Robert Peary** (1856–1920) and **Matthew Henson** (1866–1955) were probably the first people to reach the North Pole. Both men **endured** dangerous conditions on their expedition. Traveling to the North Pole is very difficult because you have to walk across large areas of ice. Ice can break apart and move **without warning**. Both men fell into dangerous icy water and were rescued. But on April 6, 1909, they reached their **goal**—the North Pole— the very top of the world!

◆ ◆ ◆ ◆ ◆

▲ Peary (above) and Henson (below) traveled 644 kilometers (400 mi.) in 37 days.

52

---

nerves, parts of your body that control movement and feeling
endured, faced with courage
without warning, unexpectedly; unpredictably
goal, something that you want to achieve

When **Helen Keller** (1880–1968) was nineteen months old, she became sick with a **fever**. The sickness left her without sight or hearing. She couldn't see or hear. Because she was so young when she lost her sight and hearing, it was hard for her to learn to communicate. Also, because she could not see, she couldn't use sign language—the language of hearing-impaired people. She also couldn't "read lips," as many hearing-impaired people do. She was very **frustrated**. But she was extremely intelligent and learned different ways to communicate. For instance, she learned to understand speech by touching the speaker's lips and throat. She learned that everything had a name and that these names were words.

Keller gave lectures (with her teacher's help) and wrote many books.

▲ Helen Keller was the first sight- and hearing-impaired person to graduate from college.

◆ ◆ ◆ ◆ ◆

Wolfgang Amadeus Mozart (1756–1791) was born in Salzburg, Austria. When he was three years old, he began to play the harpsichord. When he was five, he wrote his first song.

Because of his unusual talent, Mozart had a very uncommon childhood. By the time he was six years old, he was traveling around Europe performing concerts for royal families. He became a brilliant musician and **composer**.

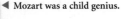

◀ Mozart was a child genius.

During Mozart's life, people didn't recognize his genius. He was extremely poor and not well known. Today, he is recognized as one of history's great composers. People everywhere still enjoy his music.

◆ ◆ ◆ ◆ ◆

---

fever, high temperature
frustrated, upset because you can't do something
composer, person who writes music

BEFORE YOU GO ON . . .

1 What did Robert Peary and Matthew Henson want to achieve?

2 In what ways was Mozart's childhood uncommon?

HOW ABOUT YOU?
- Would you prefer to be a scientist or a musician? Why?

53

CRITICAL THINKING

Have students respond orally or in writing to these questions:
- Stephen Hawking believes that he benefited from his illness. Do you think that he did? Why or why not? *(Possible answer: Yes, because he could spend more time thinking.)*
- How do you think Peary and Henson probably felt when they reached the North Pole? Why? *(Possible answer: They felt proud and excited, because they endured many hardships to get there.)*

──────── *Viewpoint* ────────

Have students look at Helen Keller on page 53. Ask them to compare Helen Keller's method of learning with theirs. How is it the same? In what ways is it different?

EXTEND THE LESSON

Two of the people featured on pages 52 and 53 have physical challenges. Ask pairs of students to discuss how a physical disability might make a person a better problem solver. Then call on volunteers to share their ideas with the class.

REACHING ALL STUDENTS

LANGUAGE LEVELS

Beginning: Tell students that Helen Keller could not see or hear so she had to touch a speaker's lips in order to know what the person was saying. Then have students gently touch their own throat and lips as they read the first sentence about Helen Keller. Discuss how challenging it would be to use this method to communicate.

Advanced: Have students imagine what it would be like to be Mozart and have your genius go unrecognized. Ask students to tell what they might do as Mozart to become recognized and appreciated.

LEARNING MODALITIES

Visual: Ask students to pick one person from the text and draw a comic strip that illustrates some of the highlights from that person's life.

Teach

MODELING THE READING STRATEGY

Predicting: Remind students that when they make a prediction, they are making an educated guess about what they are reading or are going to read. Have students skim the photographs on pages 54–55 and write predictions as to what this passage will be about. After students have finished reading, review whether their predictions were correct.

GUIDED READING

1. What does Ellen Ochoa do for a living? *(She's an astronaut.)*
2. When was Adriana Fernandez born? *(1971)*
3. What mountain did Erik Weihenmayer climb? *(Mount Everest)*
4. What goal did Erik Weihenmayer reach in 2002? *(He climbed the highest mountain on every continent in the world.)*

across the curriculum

HISTORY   Call students' attention to the fact that Adriana Fernandez had to miss the Olympic Games in 1996. Form student groups to research the history of the Olympic Games by using an encyclopedia, a sports reference book, or the Internet. Ask groups to find out the following information and record it in their notebooks: types of contests that were held in the first Olympic Games, places they were held, and three interesting facts about the early Games. Then call on volunteers to share their information with the class.

Ellen Ochoa (1958–) has an extraordinary job. She is an astronaut—someone who travels in space. She studied physics and **engineering** in college. In 1987, she was in the top 100 out of 2,000 applicants to the National Aeronautics and Space Administration (NASA) space program. In 1990, NASA chose Ochoa and twenty-two others to begin training at the Johnson Space Center in Houston, Texas.

1 Ochoa has gone on three missions and has flown in space more than 700 hours. (This is the same as flying fourteen times to the moon and back.) In just one year (1999), she flew more than 11 million kilometers (7 million mi.) in space! Ochoa was the first Hispanic woman ever to become an astronaut. She tells students: "If you stay in school, you have the **potential** to achieve what you want in the future."

◆ ◆ ◆ ◆ ◆

▲ Astronaut Ellen Ochoa is also a musician!

▲ Adriana Fernandez won the New York City Marathon in 1999.

Adriana Fernandez (1971–) is a Mexican runner who is famous all over the world. In 1995, Fernandez won a gold medal at the Pan American Games. In 1996, she set a Mexican national record and won the Houston Tenneco event. Fernandez was injured, however, and lost her chance to compete at the Olympic Games in Atlanta in 1996.

But Fernandez didn't **give up**. In 1998, she finished in second place at the New York City Marathon. Finally, in November 1999, Fernandez won the New York City Marathon. She is the first Mexican woman to win this internationally known marathon.

◆ ◆ ◆ ◆ ◆

---

engineering, the science that plans the way machines, roads, etc., are built
potential, possibility; opportunity
give up, stop trying

54

PHONICS MINILESSON

Long *a* and *i* Sounds: *a-e, ai, ay, i-e, igh*

Read aloud the following sentences, which contain examples of the long *a* sound:

    Shane played games on the train.

    Please stay in that space.

    Are you waiting for the same bus?

Read the sentences a second time, and ask students to raise their hands when they hear the sound /ā/. Then ask students to repeat each sentence after you. Repeat the process with the long *i* sound:

    He likes to dive off the board.

    Turn right on High street.

    She devotes her life to helping others.

Ask students to look for other long *a* and long *i* words in "Extraordinary People."

Erik Weihenmayer (1968–) lost his sight when he was thirteen years old. Later he discovered that he was a **skilled** athlete. Weihenmayer can sky dive, wrestle, and ski. In 2001, Weihenmayer achieved his dream of climbing to the top of the highest mountain in the world—Mount Everest.

Since his climb, Weihenmayer has received hundreds of e-mails. "It's amazing, this response," he said. "It seems it woke up so many people. If you have the right talent and the right ability, you should be given the opportunity to do what you want to do in life. . . . I've never seen myself as a blind guy who climbs. I see myself as a mountaineer and I happen to be blind."

In September 2002, Weihenmayer achieved his ultimate goal of climbing all "seven summits"—the tallest mountains on each of the seven continents.

◆ ◆ ◆ ◆ ◆

skilled, capable; excellent

> **BEFORE YOU GO ON . . .**
>
> ❶ Why is Ellen Ochoa an extraordinary person?
> ❷ In what way is Erik Weihenmayer unusual as a mountain climber?
>
> **HOW ABOUT YOU?**
> • Of the people you read about, which did you find most interesting? Why?

▼ Erik Weihenmayer climbing Mount Everest

55

CRITICAL THINKING

Have students respond orally or in writing to these questions:

● How did Ellen Ochoa's education help her achieve her goals? *(Possible answer: Being an astronaut requires a strong science background.)*

● Why might Adriana Fernandez have been tempted to quit running after her second injury? *(Possible answer: She might have been discouraged because she missed an important race.)*

● Which of these ten people do you think was the most extraordinary? Why? *(Answers will vary.)*

—Viewpoint—

Have students look at the picture of Ellen Ochoa in the space shuttle. Ask students to tell what they see and discuss whether or not they would like to work as an astronaut.

WEBSITES

For more information, log on to http://www.longman.com/shiningstar for links to other interesting websites about extraordinary people.

REACHING ALL STUDENTS

LANGUAGE LEVELS

Beginning: Write the following challenges on the board: *cannot see or hear; faced tough NASA testing program; was injured and had to miss Olympic Games.* Ask volunteers to read each phrase. Have students revisit the text and decide which person faced each challenge. Invite students to share the answers.

Advanced: Have students reread the text and make a list in their notebooks of adjectives that could be used to describe Ellen Ochoa, Adriana Fernandez, and Erik Weihenmayer. Then have them use these adjectives in sentences that explain the obstacles these people faced, and how they overcame them.

LEARNING MODALITIES

Auditory: Have students work in small groups to retell what they learned after reading pages 54 and 55. Then encourage students to take turns telling the rest of their group about the person they found most inspiring, and the reasons behind their choice.

Review

COMPREHENSION

Choose a volunteer to read the directions and the first example about Rosa Parks aloud. Have students work in small groups to complete the chart in their notebooks. Remind them to refer to the selection if they need to find information they cannot recall. When each group has completed the chart, have them designate a spokesperson to share their ideas with the class. Write the ideas on the board and discuss them with students. Then ask the class to agree on the best set of responses to complete the chart. Have students respond to these questions:

1. Which people overcame physical challenges? *(Stephen Hawking, Helen Keller, Erik Weihenmayer, Adriana Fernandez)*

2. Who was looking for a path from the Atlantic to the Pacific Ocean? *(Peary and Henson)*

CRITICAL THINKING

Have students respond orally or in writing to these questions:

● Why do you think Helen Keller decided to become a speaker and give lectures? *(Possible answer: It was a way for her to teach others.)*

● How are Helen Keller's and Erik Weihenmayer's challenges different? *(Possible answer: Erik can make use of technology that wasn't available to Helen.)*

● Albert Einstein expressed admiration for anyone who thought creatively. Why do you think creative thinking is important in science? *(Possible answer: The ability to think of new solutions is critical.)*

Review and Practice

COMPREHENSION

Each of the people you read about in "Extraordinary People" faced a challenge and made a choice. Copy this chart into your notebook. Then reread "Extraordinary People" and complete the chart.

Person	Challenge	Choice
Rosa Parks	She was an African American living in a segregated society.	She chose not to give her seat to a white person even though the driver said she would be arrested.
Albert Einstein		
Stephen Hawking		
Robert Peary and Matthew Henson		
Helen Keller		
Wolfgang Amadeus Mozart		
Ellen Ochoa		
Adriana Fernandez		
Erik Weihenmayer		

56

Choose an extraordinary person you have read about. Draw a timeline of his or her life using the information you have. Think about:

- chronological events
- important dates
- challenges the person faced
- choices the person made

DISCUSSION

Discuss in pairs or small groups.

1. Which two people are physicists? What made them extraordinary?
2. Why is Rosa Parks's action so important in American history?
3. How is life challenging for a person with a physical disability, like Helen Keller, Stephen Hawking, or Erik Weihenmayer?
4. Intelligence, physical strength, determination, and creativity are all important qualities. Choose three people from "Extraordinary People." Which qualities does each have? Which quality do you think is the most important?
5. Do you know any extraordinary people? What makes them extraordinary? Compare the people you chose with those of your partner or group.

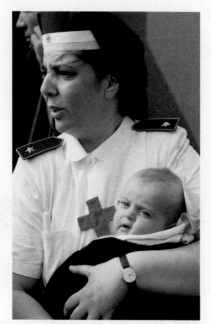

57

EXTENSION

Have students choose a favorite person they have read about in this selection. Give students drawing paper and have them create a timeline of the person's life. Encourage students to research additional information as time permits. Ask them to focus on the key points listed on page 57. If students need help making a timeline, explain that a timeline is a horizontal line that represents a person's lifespan, or another historical period. Important events that took place in that period of time are marked with lines or dots on the timeline in chronological order. Below each line or dot is a short description of the event.

DISCUSSION

Have students work in pairs or small groups to answer and discuss the questions. Explain to them that a correct answer is one that you can prove by using evidence in the text to support it. After students have had ample time to discuss the questions, invite volunteers from each group to share their group's ideas with the class.

METACOGNITION

Ask students:

1. What new vocabulary did you learn from the passages?
2. Did the photographs in the selection help you to visualize the challenges these people faced? Why or why not?
3. How did skimming help you preread the text?

REACHING ALL STUDENTS

LANGUAGE LEVELS

Beginning: To create a simple variation of the timeline, ask students to draw small sketches that show the main events in the person's life. Remind students to leave enough space for each picture when they redraw their timeline. Then have students glue the drawings on their timeline in the order that the events occurred.

Advanced: Provide an opportunity for students to visit the library or Internet to research a person for whom they will create a timeline. Invite students to add information from their research, as well as information from their text, to the timeline.

Connect

READING SUMMARY

This selection describes a series of events that took place on an autumn afternoon near the end of World War II. The story is set in Holland and takes place when the author was a child.

SCAFFOLDING

Have students listen as you model reading aloud the selection with natural intonation. Be sure to alter your voice to express mood. Then ask students to take turns reading aloud paragraphs to a partner.

MODELING THE READING STRATEGY

Skimming: Have students examine the illustration and the map on pages 58–59. Then have them skim the text to determine the major ideas in this selection. When students have finished skimming the text, discuss with them what they think the story will be about.

GUIDED READING

1. What kinds of food do the people of Holland eat in the last years of the war? *(potato peels, cabbage leaves, soup)*
2. Who are the German soldiers searching for? *(men)*
3. Who is standing in the street? *(women and children from the neighborhood)*

CONNECT TO LITERATURE **Personal Narrative**

In this section, you will read a personal narrative. In a personal narrative, the narrator, or person telling the story, tells about something that he or she experienced. Because this narrative is about a real event, it is nonfiction. This experience took place near the end of World War II—in October 1945. Nazi Germany was occupying Holland.

He Was the Same Age as My Sister

Mieke C. Malandra

I'm nearly sixty-seven years old, but every October when the weather **turns**, I am eleven again.

In the last year of the war, fall in Holland was cold and wet. No lighted stoves, no coal. No lamps to make the room seem warm, no electricity. No supper worth the name. The soup from the central

---

turns, changes

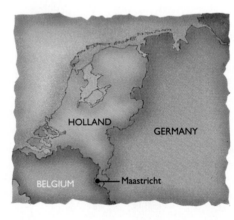

kitchen, a mixture of potato peels and cabbage leaves in water without salt, was cold by the time we got it home.

That day in October, just when it began to get dark, army trucks closed off our street, as they had done many times before, and a **platoon** of German soldiers started a house-to-house search for men.

"**Raus**! Raus!" The **loudspeaker** drove us outside to stand on the sidewalk while soldiers ran through our houses, poking in **attics** and closets. "Raus! Raus!" My little brothers forgot to grab their coats. Jacob's little body warmed me.

Our street filled up with women and children. We could talk freely, since the soldiers didn't understand Dutch, but we kept our voices low. Jokes flew around. I didn't understand what they were talking

---

platoon, part of an army
Raus, German for "get out"
loudspeaker, piece of equipment that makes a person's voice louder
attics, rooms at the top of a house under the roof

58

GRAMMAR MINILESSON

Identifying Parts of Speech

Tell students that in the English language, there are eight main kinds of words. These words are called parts of speech. They include nouns, verbs, pronouns, adjectives, adverbs, conjunctions, prepositions, and interjections. Define and give students an example of each term. Then make an eight-column chart on the board with the parts of speech as headings. Have students find examples of each kind of word from the reading selection or from another source and list them under the appropriate headings. Have students copy the chart into their notebooks.

about, but I liked the laughter. Then news was exchanged. They're in Maastricht! Why won't they come north?

It got colder. The soldiers had nearly come to the end of the street, and no men had been found. We became quiet. And then we heard someone crying. All the mothers turned. It was the sound of a crying child. On the **stoop** of Mr. van Campen's house sat a soldier, his rifle propped up next to him, his face hidden in his coat. He tried to swallow his **sobs**, but then he gave up.

---

stoop, stairway or porch at the entrance of a house
sobs, the sounds someone makes when crying

LITERARY ELEMENT

The *mood* of a story is its atmosphere or feeling. The mood can be sad, funny, scary, tense, happy, hopeless, etc. Writers create mood with descriptive language, by telling what people are doing or saying, and what's happening.

BEFORE YOU GO ON . . .

1. How old is the narrator? How old is she during the story?
2. Try to predict what the mothers will do.
   Answers will vary.

HOW ABOUT YOU?

- Where do you think all the men in the village have gone?

59

Have students respond orally or in writing to these questions:

- What does the author mean by "I am eleven again"? (Possible answer: She is reminded of the events that occurred the October that she was eleven.)
- Why aren't the stoves and lamps lit? (Possible answer: All the fuel went to the war.)
- Why are the German soldiers searching for men? (Possible answer: They are looking for Dutch men to serve as soldiers in the German army in the last days of the war.)

Viewpoint

Have students look at the pictures on pages 58 and 59. Ask them to tell what they think life was like in Holland during World War II. Invite students to discuss which group of children was in greater danger—those in the German army or those in the occupied city. Ask students to explain their answers.

LITERARY ELEMENT

Invite volunteers to read the text inside the Literary Element box. Have students find words or phrases in the story that reveal the mood of the selection. Students might focus on phrases that describe the setting in the second and fourth paragraphs, such as *cold and wet; no lighted stoves, no coal,* or on the description of the German soldier on page 59: *. . . his face hidden in his coat. He tried to swallow his sobs.*

REACHING ALL STUDENTS

LANGUAGE LEVELS

Beginning: Briefly describe the events that led up to World War II. Then point out Holland and Germany on a map. Encourage students to discuss what it might have been like to be a mother or child driven out onto the sidewalk while soldiers who don't even speak your language are searching your house.

Advanced: Have students look up information about other hardships people in Europe faced during World War II, and what it might have been like to live as a private citizen in a country that was occupied by the German army. Invite students to share and discuss their findings.

Connect

GUIDED READING

1. How old is the soldier? *(sixteen years old)*
2. What do the Dutch mothers bring the boy? *(a potato, bread, an apple)*
3. Why is he crying? *(He is very hungry.)*

ABOUT THE AUTHOR

Mieke C. Malandra lives in Lebanon, Pennsylvania. She was born in Holland and lived there during World War II.

across the curriculum

MATH Explain to students that prefixes are important in math and can help them understand math vocabulary. For example, the prefix *dis-* means opposite or negative. *Disjoint sets* are sets that have no common numbers between them, as in this example:

Set A = (2, 4, 6)   Set B = (3, 5)

ACTIVITY: Suggest that students compile glossaries of math terms with prefixes that they want to remember, such as *in*clined plane, *un*known value, *con*nected set, and *penta*gram. Tell them to use a dictionary and a math textbook and to follow these steps: 1) List the term, using italics for prefixes; 2) Include the meaning of the prefix; 3) Supply the definition; 4) Offer an example. When they have finished, have students trade papers with a partner so they can review each other's work.

A mother walked over and talked to him softly in German. "What's wrong?" she asked. She bent over him as he spoke, and when he was finished, she stood straight up and **announced** to us, "This war must nearly be over. He's sixteen years old and hasn't had anything to eat today." Two or three mothers slipped away from the group and went into their houses. A German officer came walking down the street half a **block** away. I was scared—and very cold. The mothers managed to get back in time. A cold cooked potato, a piece of bread, and a wrinkled apple were passed through the group to the boy.

The officer came closer. The boy turned into a soldier again. "**Danke**," he said, and then climbed to his feet and grabbed his rifle.

The truck engines started up. We could go inside. For the rest of the war, for the rest of my life, I have remembered that soldier who cried. He was the same age as my sister.

---

announced, told
block, the distance between two streets
Danke, German for "thank you"

60

About the Author

Mieke C. Malandra

Mieke C. Malandra was born in Utrecht in Holland, the third of six children. She was six years old when World War II started. She now lives in the United States where she works part-time at a school. She wrote this story for her grandson.

BEFORE YOU GO ON . . .

1. Why is the young German soldier crying?
2. What do the women in the town do? Why did they do it?

HOW ABOUT YOU?
- Did you feel sorry for the soldier? Why or why not?
Answers will vary.

SPELLING MINILESSON

Long *a* and *i* Sounds: *a-e, ay, i-e*

Tell students that they are going to explore different ways to spell the sounds /ā/ and /ī/. Tell students that the sound /ā/ can be spelled with the pattern *a-e,* or *ay.* The sound /ī/ can be spelled with the pattern *i-e.* Have students find the words *today* and *same* in the selection. Point out that both have the long *a* sound, but they use different combinations of letters to represent the sound. Ask students to identify which letters represent the sound /ā/ in *today* and *same.* Then have students find the words *life* and *time* in the story. Point out that both have the sound /ī/ and use the pattern *i-e.*

Encourage students to locate additional words from the story that contain the sounds /ā/ and /ī/ and to write them in their notebooks.

Link the Readings

REFLECTION

Reread "He Was the Same Age as My Sister." Then copy the chart into your notebook. Look back at the texts and complete the chart.

Title of Selection	Type of Text (Genre)	Fiction or Nonfiction	Purpose of Selection	Something I Liked/Didn't Like About It
"Extraordinary People"			to inform	
"He Was the Same Age as My Sister"				

DISCUSSION

Discuss in pairs or small groups.

1. What is extraordinary about Rosa Parks? Discuss what she did.
2. What is special about the mothers in "He Was the Same Age as My Sister"? Discuss what they did.
3. Of the people you read about in Part 1, who would you most like to invite to your house for dinner? Why? What would you talk about?
4. Challenges can be big, like climbing a mountain, or small, like learning to ride a bike. What are some big or small challenges you have faced and the decisions you made?

61

REFLECTION

Have students copy the chart into their notebooks. Ask them to review the selections, complete the chart, and respond to the following questions:

1. Name one way the two readings are alike. *(Possible answer: They both tell about real people facing challenges.)*
2. Which text helped you to better understand the experience of overcoming a challenge? *(Answers will vary.)*

COOPERATIVE GROUPING

Group intermediate and advanced students with beginning students. Have students work in small groups to discuss the stories and complete the chart. Remind students to skim to locate information quickly and accurately. Then choose a volunteer from each group to read their answers aloud.

DISCUSSION

Pair beginning and intermediate students with advanced students. Have students take turns reading the questions and then discuss possible answers. Encourage students to refer to the reading to support their answers. Then have student pairs share their results with the class.

CRITICAL THINKING

Define *fear* for students. Ask them whether facing one's fears can be a challenge. Guide students to discuss the fears that Mieke Malandra and the ten "Extraordinary People" might have faced, as well as the choices they had to make while trying to overcome their fears.

REACHING ALL STUDENTS

LANGUAGE LEVELS

Beginning: Copy the Reflection chart on the board or an overhead projector. Have the class discuss each column together and agree on a common answer for each box. Invite volunteers to record the class answers on the chart.

Advanced: Have students complete the Reflection chart individually and then join a partner to compare answers. Encourage partners to tell each other why they felt the way they did about the item in the last column. Invite partners to share the information with the class.

Teach

GRAMMAR

Have students take turns reading the Grammar section. Then have students scan "Extraordinary People" and "He Was the Same Age as My Sister" to find sentences written in the simple past tense. Have students write three of these sentences in their notebooks.

Read aloud the examples of negative simple past sentences. As a class, brainstorm a list of additional examples showing the use of *did not* or *didn't* in sentences. Call on volunteers to write the sentences on the board.

SCAFFOLDING

Draw two columns on the chalkboard. Write the words *joked, hoped,* and *raked* in the first column, and the words *jumped, needed,* and *walked* in the second column. Have students discuss how the words in the two columns are similar. *(They are all in the simple past tense.)* Then underline the root word in each word. Have students identify how the words in the two columns are different. *(The root words in the first column end in* -e.*)*

Connect to Writing

GRAMMAR

Using the Simple Past

Use the **simple past** to talk about an action that happened in the past and is completed.

> In 2001, Erik Weihenmayer **climbed** Mount Everest.
> Helen Keller **graduated** from college.
> Adriana Fernandez **won** a gold medal in 1995.

Most verbs are regular. To form the simple past of most regular verbs, add **-ed** to the base form.

walk + -ed	**walked**	climb + -ed	**climbed**
play + -ed	**played**	fill + -ed	**filled**

For regular verbs that end with **-e**, add **-d** to the base to form the simple past.

close + -d	**closed**	graduate + -d	**graduated**
use + -d	**used**	recognize + -d	**recognized**

Some verbs are irregular. These verbs have special past forms.

eat	**ate**	keep	**kept**
have	**had**	is	**was**
go	**went**	fall	**fell**
come	**came**	think	**thought**
fly	**flew**	make	**made**
win	**won**	understand	**understood**

For negative simple past sentences, use **did not (didn't) + verb.**

> Albert Einstein **did not like** school very much.
> Rosa Parks **did not give** her seat to a white person.
> The German soldiers **didn't understand** Dutch.

Practice

Look through "Extraordinary People" and "He Was the Same Age as My Sister." Find ten sentences in the simple past. Write them in your notebook. Circle the verbs. Then compare sentences in pairs.

62

T62

SKILLS FOR WRITING

Writing a Narrative Paragraph

Narrative writing tells a story. The story can be either fiction or nonfiction. If it is a story about something from the narrator's own experience, it is called personal narrative. The events are usually told in chronological order—that is, in the order that they happened. These sequence words show chronological order: *First, . . . Next, . . . After, . . . Then, . . . Finally, . . .*

Read about Milica's grandparents. Then discuss the questions.

> Milica Bogetic
>
> My Amazing Grandparents
>
> My grandparents are amazing people. My grandfather was in the army for four years during World War II. After the war, he studied at the Sorbonne in Paris, and then went to Harvard and got a Ph.D. He met my grandmother there. They got married in December 1952. My grandfather taught at the University of Connecticut. He and my grandmother had three children, but the second child died. Then they adopted two more children. After that, my grandmother got a master's degree and worked as a part-time teacher and an editor. Both of my grandparents speak several languages. My grandmother taught English to immigrants. After my grandfather retired in 1992, he taught English to inmates at a prison.

← sequence words

1. What makes this text a personal narrative?
2. What verbs does the writer use?
3. What words and phrases show chronological order?

63

SKILLS FOR WRITING

Read aloud the definition of narrative writing to students. Then ask them to read the essay "My Amazing Grandparents." Tell students to watch for clues that indicate key events in the lives of Milica's grandparents, and the order in which they took place. Then have students work in small groups to answer the questions at the bottom of the page.

SCAFFOLDING

Have small groups of students invent an imaginary character and give it a special name, such as Sammy the Soccer Star or Mara the Mountain Climber. Have groups work together to create an oral presentation that describes that character's day. Write the time order words from page 63 on the board so students can use them to transition from one idea to the next. Have groups share their presentations.

REACHING ALL STUDENTS

LANGUAGE LEVELS

Beginning: Find a recent literature selection that has clear examples of the words and phrases that signal chronological order. Copy the sentences in which the words and phrases appear onto sentence strips and tape them to the board. Have students discuss the clue words in each sentence, and whether the sentences have been placed in the correct chronological order on the board. Then call on a volunteer to put the strips in the correct order. Have the class compare the strips to the original selection to check their work.

Teach

WRITING ASSIGNMENT

Narrative Paragraph

Tell students they are going to choose one person they admire to write about. Encourage students to choose someone they know well.

WRITING STRATEGY

Call on a volunteer to read the directions for the Writing Strategy aloud. Encourage students to notice that the writer did not use complete sentences when making notes about her grandparents. Then, after students make notes about a person they admire, tell them that they will use the notes to write a narrative paragraph about the person. Explain that the paragraph must be written in the simple past and have a clear beginning, middle, and end. Encourage students to use time order words, such as those in the essay on page 63, to provide a transition from one idea to the next. Remind students that they can add ideas or events to their essay that are not in their notes.

USING THE EDITING CHECKLIST

Read the Editing Checklist aloud with students. Have students work with a partner to use the checklist as they revise their writing.

WRITING ASSIGNMENT

Narrative Paragraph

You will write a narrative paragraph about an extraordinary person.

1. **Read** Choose a person you think is extraordinary. You can choose a famous person, a friend, or a family member.

Writing Strategy: Notes

Making notes is a good way to organize information before you write. Notes don't have to be in complete sentences. They can be words or phrases. Look at the notes the writer made before writing the paragraph about her grandparents.

Grandfather—

    was in the army

    studied at the Sorbonne

Grandfather and Grandmother—

    met at Harvard

    had 3 children, adopted 2 more

    were teachers

    speak several languages

---

1. What information from the notes did the writer include in her paragraph?
2. How is the format different from the paragraph on page 63?

2. **Make notes** In your notebook, make notes about your extraordinary person.

3. **Write** Use your notes to write a paragraph. Write your paragraph in the simple past.

EDITING CHECKLIST

Did you . . .

▶ indent the first sentence in your paragraph?

▶ place the events in chronological order?

▶ include the most important events?

▶ use the simple past?

▶ write in complete sentences?

▶ begin each sentence with a capital letter?

▶ end each sentence with a period?

64

PART REVIEW 1

Check Your Knowledge

Language Development

1. How can prefixes help you figure out word meaning?
2. What do you do when you skim a text?
3. What is one reason to make notes before you begin writing?
4. What is the mood of "He Was the Same Age as My Sister"? How does the author create mood in this story?
5. What are three sequence words we use in narrative writing?
6. What letters do you add to the base form of a regular verb to form the simple past? Write a sentence that tells something you did yesterday.

Academic Content

1. What new social studies vocabulary did you learn in Part 1? What do the words mean?
2. Choose one person described in "Extraordinary People." Describe the challenges he/she faced and choices he/she made.
3. What was happening in history at the time of the story "He Was the Same Age as My Sister"?

▲ A fork in the road

65

ASSESS

You can assess students' knowledge of the unit in several different ways.

Portfolio: Students can complete the Check Your Knowledge section and include it in their portfolios.

Traditional: Students can complete the Check Your Knowledge questions as a quiz. After students complete Check Your Knowledge, use the Assessment Package. Students can complete the Part Test on pages 37–40. For further practice, have students complete the Test Preparation worksheets.

Performance: Students can demonstrate understanding through a one-on-one oral interview with the teacher about Check Your Knowledge questions.

TEST-TAKING TIP

Remind students to listen carefully to directions before a test begins. Have students underline key words in the directions. See the Test Preparation pages in the Assessment Guide for additional test-taking strategies.

METACOGNITION

Remind students to think about the Check Your Knowledge questions before they answer them, and to ask themselves whether the best answers might come from the text, from their personal lives, or from their general knowledge of the subject.

REACHING ALL STUDENTS

LANGUAGE LEVELS

Beginning: Have students read the questions before beginning the test. Encourage them to ask any questions they have about unfamiliar vocabulary, especially in the directions.

Advanced: Have students answer the questions. Then have pairs of students work together to discuss their answers. Tell students that they must agree on the correct answer. Encourage students to find information in their textbook that supports their answers.

T65

Preteach

OBJECTIVES

Read the list of objectives aloud, encouraging students to join in. Then tell students that they will be reading two selections that they might study in history class. Ask volunteers to restate the list of things they will learn. Additional practice activities for these objectives can be found in the **Workbook** and **CD-ROM.**

BACKGROUND

Have students read the text aloud and find Vietnam on the map. Ask students to discuss what the dashed line through Vietnam indicates. *(It divides North and South Vietnam.)* Invite any students from Vietnam to share information about their country.

COOPERATIVE GROUPING

Pair intermediate and advanced students with beginning students. Have pairs read the background page and discuss the characters.

PART 2 Prepare to Read

OBJECTIVES
LANGUAGE DEVELOPMENT

Reading:
- Vocabulary building: *Context, dictionary skills*
- Reading strategy: *Visualizing*
- Character chart
- Literary element: *Flashbacks*

Writing:
- Timeline
- Sentence variety
- Personal narrative
- Correct punctuation and capitalization

Listening/Speaking:
- Listening for major idea and supporting evidence
- Compare your understanding with others

Grammar:
- Combine ideas using *but*

Viewing/Representing:
- Maps, charts, illustrations
- Venn diagram, charts

ACADEMIC CONTENT
- Social studies vocabulary
- Vietnam War
- Civil war in Sudan

BACKGROUND

The novel *A Boat to Nowhere* is historical fiction. In most historical fiction, the setting and events are nonfictional but the characters are fictional. The historical background in this story is the Vietnam War during the 1960s and 1970s.

The excerpt from *A Boat to Nowhere* has many characters. This character chart will help you understand the story.

Characters	
Mai	an eleven-year-old orphan girl
Loc	Mai's younger brother
Thay Van Chi	Mai and Loc's grandfather and the village teacher
Tam and Duc	a couple who rescued Mai, Loc, and Thay Van Chi from the forest
Hong	the family's maid and cook
Kien	a fourteen-year-old orphan who has just arrived at Tam and Duc's home

Make connections Look at the map. Where is North Vietnam? Where is South Vietnam?

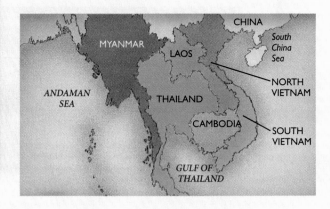

66

TEACHING GUIDE

PRETEACH	Provide Background	Read and discuss the Background information. Complete the activity. (ATE/SB p. 66)
	Present Concepts	Introduce the Reading Strategy. (ATE/SB p. 67)
TEACH	Monitor Comprehension	Informally monitor comprehension while students read the selection independently or in groups. (ATE/SB pp. 68–73)
	Teach and Practice	Present the Grammar, Usage, and Mechanics. (ATE/SB pp. 80, 81) Complete the Writing activity. (ATE/SB p. 82) Present Grammar, Phonics, and Spelling minilessons. (ATE pp. 68, 72, 80)
CONNECT	Connect to Content	Have students read the informational reading and relate it to the literature. (ATE/SB pp. 76–78)
	Across the Curriculum	Present curriculum links as students read. (ATE pp. 70, 76)
ASSESS	Check Knowledge	Assess students' comprehension by having them complete the Check Your Knowledge section. (ATE/SB p. 83)
	Monitor Progress	Use one or more of the print assessment resources in the Assessment Package.
EXTEND	Integrate Language and Apply Understanding	Have students complete the Workshops (ATE/SB p. 84–87) and a project from the Unit Projects. (ATE/SB p. 88) Then have them choose a book to read from Further Reading. (ATE/SB p. 89)

LEARN KEY WORDS

beggars
belly
memory
rags
rifles
run away

VOCABULARY

Read these sentences. Use the context to figure out the meaning of the red words. Use a dictionary to check your answers. Write each word and its meaning in your notebook.

1. **Beggars** ask others for food or money so they can survive.
2. Kien ate bowls of rice until his **belly** was full.
3. Mai's **memory** of losing her mother and father made her sad.
4. Hong burned the dirty old **rags** that Kien wore.
5. The soldiers used **rifles** to fight the enemy.
6. People in the village tried to **run away** from the soldiers.

READING STRATEGY

Visualizing

Visualizing means imagining, or picturing, the characters, events, and places in a text. Writers use descriptive words to help readers visualize. Usually the descriptive words are adjectives, but they can also be verbs or nouns:

- Kien's **narrow black** eyes were **unfriendly**. (adjectives)
- Your belly will **explode** if you eat more. (verb)
- We had a big **home** with **flowers** in the **garden**. (nouns)

Visualizing can help you understand and enjoy a text.

Vietnamese "boat people" arrive in Hong Kong. ▶

67

VOCABULARY

Clearly enunciate each Key Word. After you say it, have students point to the word and repeat it. Then read each sentence aloud, and have students raise their hands when they hear the Key Word. Model how students can use context clues to help them determine the meaning of the Key Word. Say, *In the second sentence, Kien's belly was full after he ate rice. I know that my stomach feels full after I eat,* so belly *must be another word for stomach.* After students complete the activity, have them share the definitions of each key word.

READING STRATEGY

Have students read the Reading Strategy information. Point out that visualizing is a strategy that students can use as they are reading. Explain that visualizing requires careful reading for details that reveal what something looked like or how someone acted. Tell students that they will use what they already know about a topic to help them visualize the selection.

REACHING ALL STUDENTS

LANGUAGE LEVELS

Beginning: Choose a descriptive poem from a book such as *Where the Sidewalk Ends* by Shel Silverstein. Tell students to close their eyes and listen for adjectives and adverbs that help them to picture the poem as you read it aloud. Then have students draw what they visualized. Have volunteers share their drawings with the class, and discuss which words from the poem helped them to visualize the text.

Advanced: Have students describe the steps in a process required to build something or to complete a task. Examples could include such activities as painting a gate, making a bed, or getting a haircut. Encourage students to include clear details so that the group can visualize the process and guess what it is.

Teach

READING SUMMARY

This story is told from the point of view of a young orphan girl during the Vietnam War. When a fourteen-year-old boy arrives at her rural home, she tries to understand why so many of the adults want him to leave.

SCAFFOLDING

As students read *A Boat to Nowhere*, have them create a three-column chart labeled *Mai, Hong,* and *Kien* in their notebooks. In each column, students should record words that describe the personality traits of the main characters. Then have students read silently as they listen to the selection on the CD/tape.

GUIDED READING

1. What is Kien eating? *(rice)*
2. Why does Mai come looking for Kien? *(Grandfather sends her to find him.)*
3. What does Kien need to do before meeting the teacher? *(wash and change clothes)*

——Viewpoint——

Have students look at the picture of Kien eating on page 68. Ask them to describe how he is eating and tell why they think Kien is eating this way. *(Possible answers: He has recently arrived at the village and hasn't eaten in a long time; his clothes look as though he's been walking for days.)*

FOCUS ON LITERATURE — Historical Fiction

First, preview the excerpt from A Boat to Nowhere. *Refer to the chart on page 66 to help you keep track of the characters. Then, as you read the text more carefully, visualize images that the adjectives, verbs, and nouns create. Which images are easy to visualize?*

from A Boat to Nowhere

Maureen Crane Wartski

68

PHONICS MINILESSON

Long *o*, Long *e*, Long *u*

Say /ō/. Have students repeat the sound after you, and explain that this sound is called long *o*. Model the following examples of the long *o* sound by elongating the vowel sound. Have students repeat after you:

> She <u>spoke</u> loudly to the <u>growing</u> boy.

Repeat this activity for long *e* /ē/ and long *u* /ū/ using these sentences:

> <u>Peter</u> <u>needs</u> to <u>clean</u> his room.

> He drank the <u>fruit</u> <u>juice</u> slowly.

Then have students work with a partner to create a chart with a column for each of the three sounds. Have them skim the text for words with the long *o*, *e*, and *u* sounds to complete the chart. Examples include: *feed, flea, no, boat, rude.*

In their small, isolated village in South Vietnam, Mai and her family thought they were safe from the war. Then Kien, a fourteen-year-old **orphan***, came into their lives, bringing tales of terrible conquerors from the North taking over the forest villages.*

Kien could certainly eat!

Mai watched amazed as the boy **wolfed down** four big bowls of rice and held out his bowl for more. Hong grumbled, but filled it up again. She said loudly that she was glad to cook and take care of Thay Van Chi and his family, but feeding a beggar brat she did not enjoy.

"If you're going to work for your rice as you boasted, you'll end up working for years!" she snapped in her loud voice.

Kien paid no attention. He slurped his rice, scooping it up into his mouth as if his

---

to nowhere, not to any place; with no destination
orphan, child whose parents have died
wolfed down, ate hungrily and quickly, like a wolf

---

chopsticks couldn't work fast enough. Mai couldn't help staring. Hadn't he ever learned any **manners**?

"What are you looking at?" Kien's narrow black eyes were unfriendly. "Haven't you ever seen a person eat?"

Mai **blushed**. "Grandfather wants to see you when you've eaten," she said. "He sent me to tell you."

"You'll have to wash first. No one is going to get near the teacher in your condition!" Hong insisted.

Kien gave a snort of laughter. "Too bad. I've grown fond of all my **lice and fleas**," he said.

He held out his rice bowl again, but Hong shook her head. "Your belly will explode if you eat more. Now, here is soap and a towel. Over there is the bathing area. There is a large jug of fresh water. Do you hear me? Now, wash!" Kien shrugged. "Here are some clean clothes. The clothes may not fit, but beggars can't choose. I am going to burn those rags you're wearing. Now, move!"

---

manners, correct way to act
blushed, turned red with embarrassment
lice and fleas, small insects that live on people's or animals' skin or in their hair

---

BEFORE YOU GO ON . . .

1 Why does Kien eat so quickly?
   Answers will vary.
2 Why does Hong say that Kien's belly will explode?

HOW ABOUT YOU?
● Do you like Hong? Why or why not?

69

CRITICAL THINKING

Have students respond orally or in writing to these questions:

● Has Mai known Kien long? How do you know? *(Possible answer: No, she stares at the boy and wonders if he has any manners. She doesn't seem to know him well.)*
● What clues help you know that Kien is poor? *(He is hungry; he is called a "beggar brat"; he has lice and fleas; he is wearing rags.)*

MODELING THE READING STRATEGY

Visualizing: Remind students that when they visualize they look for descriptive words that will help them form a mental picture of the characters, events, and places in the text. Model how to visualize using the following example: *On page 69 the author describes how Kien eats: He wolfed down four big bowls of rice. I know the phrase* wolfed down *means to eat hungrily, like a wolf. This phrase can help me to picture in my mind how Kien looked as he ate the rice.*

ACTIVE READING

Have students make a character web by drawing a circle and writing *Mai* in the center. As students read, have them draw lines that radiate from the circle and record significant events from Mai's life on each line.

REACHING ALL STUDENTS

LANGUAGE LEVELS

Beginning: Have students draw a comic strip that illustrates this portion of the story. Encourage them to include dialogue balloons with dialogue taken from the story. Invite students to share their cartoons and explain what their scenes are about. As students read, have them sketch and discuss other scenes from the story. Explain that students will be drawing pictures of Mai's recollections of her childhood. Later, they can arrange their cartoons in chronological order.

Advanced: Invite a volunteer to read pages 68 and 69 aloud. Ask students to listen for words and phrases that give clues about the length of time Kien has been with the household. Have students write these words and phrases in their notebooks and then share them with the class. Point out that although the story doesn't say exactly how long Kien has been there, clues such as the fact that he hasn't had a chance to shower or change clothes indicate that it has not been long.

T69

GUIDED READING

1. Where is the cooking area? *(behind the house)*
2. In what way is Grandfather important to the village? *(He is the headman and teacher.)*
3. What kind of work does Mai's father do? *(He is a doctor.)*
4. Where was Loc born? *(at the hospital in the city)*

across the curriculum

HEALTH Draw a four-column chart on the board, and title the columns *Fruits, Vegetables, Grains,* and *Meat,* respectively. Tell students that common foods in the Vietnamese diet include melon, pomegranate, pork, and fish. Add these items to the chart in the corresponding columns. Then ask students what grain Kien eats in the story, and add *rice* to the chart. Have students think of examples of each kind of food from different cultures, and add these suggestions to the chart. Then show students a diagram of the food pyramid. Have them copy it and add the foods from their chart to the pyramid. Ask students which foods could be combined to form a healthy diet that conforms to the guidelines on the pyramid.

Kien grinned **impudently**. "Sure, . . ." he said, and **sauntered off**. Hong's face turned a brick red.

"Imagine having to cook for such a one at this time of night!" she grumbled. "Here, Mai. Help me clean up!"

While Mai helped Hong in the cooking area behind the house, she could hear Duc and Big Tam talking with Grandfather. Mai caught the words "Kien" and "bad" and "he should go away."

"They don't want Kien to stay in the Village," Mai said to Hong. "Why?"

"He's a bad boy. Besides, he doesn't **belong** here."

"Loc and I weren't born in the Village," Mai pointed out. "Grandfather brought us here when Loc was just a baby. But *we* belong here!"

"That's different." Hong's face softened, and she turned to smooth back Mai's black hair. "From the time Tam and Duc found you in the forest, you and Loc have been like my own."

Mai nodded, remembering how kind this big, rough woman had been . . . how kind everyone else had been. The Village had **taken them to their hearts**, and soon Thay Van Chi had become the Village's **revered** teacher and its headman. Then why . . .

"Why doesn't anyone like Kien?" Mai wanted to know. "Is it because he's so rude?"

"That and other reasons."

---

impudently, rudely; disrespectfully
sauntered off, walked away
belong, be connected to or part of a place
taken them to their hearts, welcomed them
revered, greatly respected

70

What other reasons could there be? Mai wondered.

Hong began to busy herself **stacking** newly washed pots. Then she stopped to ask, "Mai, do you remember very much about your first home? In the city, I mean, when your parents still lived?"

Mai said, "I remember Mama and Father—a little. Mama was very pretty. She was always singing to me and playing with me. Father was a doctor. We had a big home with flowers in the garden. I was named for the flowers. . . ."

"Do you remember why you left the city?" Hong asked.

"Father had to go away to be a doctor to the soldiers. He . . . he never came back." Even now the memory hurt Mai so much she hurried over this part. "Mama and I went to live with Grandfather in another city. Then Mama went to the hospital and Loc was born." Mai's voice **dropped to a whisper**. "Mama never came back from the hospital. . . ."

"Ah," Hong said, her eyes full of tears.

"Grandfather said that the war had killed both Father and Mama. He took Loc and me away from the city. Loc was just a little baby and he cried a lot." Mai remembered that she had often cried herself as they walked hour after hour, from one town to another.

LITERARY ELEMENT

A *flashback* interrupts the action in narrative fiction. It tells about something in the past. It gives the reader a more complete picture of a character or the current situation.

---

stacking, placing in a pile
dropped to a whisper, became very quiet

BEFORE YOU GO ON . . .

1. How does Hong feel about Mai and her brother, Loc?
2. Who did Mai and Loc live with before they came to the village?

HOW ABOUT YOU?

- Does this part of the story help you visualize? What images come to your mind?

71

CRITICAL THINKING

Have students respond orally or in writing to these questions:

- Why do you think Kien is so rude to others? (*Possible answer: He knows they want him to leave.*)
- How do you think Mai's father died? (*Possible answer: He was probably killed in the war.*)

MODELING THE READING STRATEGY

Visualizing: Read aloud the first two words on page 70. Ask students to describe what they visualize. Then read aloud the rest of the paragraph. Ask students to explain how the additional details changed the picture of the scene that they had in their mind.

—Viewpoint—

Refer students to the picture on page 71. Ask students to describe how the picture illustrates that Mai has become a member of this household. Invite students to discuss other ways the illustrator might have shown the same idea.

LITERARY ELEMENT

Have students read the Flashback text box. Explain that a flashback is used to provide details about important events from the past. It often provides background information to show how a past event influenced a character's current actions or feelings. Ask students how Mai's flashback on page 70 might help her understand Kien's behavior.

REACHING ALL STUDENTS

LANGUAGE LEVELS

Beginning: Tell students to listen for words that describe Mai and Hong. Read aloud the text on page 70 and have volunteers tell what words they hear that describe Mai and Hong. Have students list these words in two different character webs.

Advanced: Have students listen for descriptions of Mai, Hong, and Kien as you read aloud page 70. Then ask volunteers to name each character and tell what they know about him or her. Have students pretend to be a character and write a brief self-introduction. For example, *I am Mai. I lived with my parents when I was very young until . . .* Ask volunteers to share their writing.

Teach

GUIDED READING

1. Who found Mai and her family in the forest? *(Tam and Duc)*
2. Who is at risk in Kien's song? *(the mother, sister, and baby)*
3. How does Mai know that Hong is afraid? *(Hong is shaking and tells Kien to stop.)*

—Viewpoint—

Have students look at the picture on page 72. Tell them to focus on the characters' expressions. Ask them to describe how each character feels in this illustration, and to identify details in the text that support their answers.

WEBSITES

For more information, log on to http://www.longman.com/shiningstar for links to other websites about the Vietnam War.

72

GRAMMAR MINILESSON

Questions in Present and Past

Write the following questions in the simple present on the board. Have students practice saying and answering the following questions with a partner:

Do you have a pencil?   Can you read the title of the story?

Encourage students to answer both in the affirmative (yes) and negative (no). Point out how questions in the simple present can be formed with *do, does,* or *can* plus a subject and the base form of a verb. Then have students form their own questions that begin with *do you* or *can you.*

Repeat the process with the following questions in the simple past:

Did you have a pencil?   Could you read the title of the story?

Point out that questions in the simple past can be formed with *did* or *could* plus a subject and the base form of a verb. Then have students form their own simple past questions that begin with *did you* or *could you.*

Each time they arrived at a new village or town she had asked her grandfather whether they could stay there, but Thay Van Chi had kept on going.

"It took us a long, long time to reach the Village," Mai told Hong. "I don't know how many towns and villages we stayed in . . . and we were often lost. One day we were so lost in the forest that I was sure we'd never find our way. Then Tam and Duc found us. . . ."

There was a silence. Mai could hear Kien **scrubbing** himself some distance away in the bathing area. He sang as he **sluiced** water over himself:

"Oh, rifles are closer, my sister—
*Ah, the **cannon** is **booming**, Mother!*
Why don't you take your baby and run
    away?"

"Stop that noise!" Hong shouted. Mai saw that the big woman was shaking, and suddenly she, too, was afraid. Why was Kien singing of rifles and cannon and running away? Why had Hong asked her to remember the old days?

"What has my remembering about the city to do with Kien not being welcome in the Village?" she asked.

Hong **grunted**. "You ask too many questions," she said in her normal voice. "Go away now. I'm too busy to talk to you."

---

scrubbing, rubbing with a cloth or brush
sluiced, washed with water
cannon, large gun, usually on wheels
booming, making loud noises
grunted, made a short, low sound

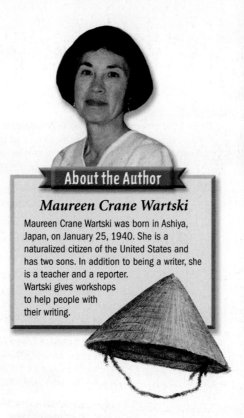

About the Author

Maureen Crane Wartski

Maureen Crane Wartski was born in Ashiya, Japan, on January 25, 1940. She is a naturalized citizen of the United States and has two sons. In addition to being a writer, she is a teacher and a reporter. Wartski gives workshops to help people with their writing.

BEFORE YOU GO ON . . .

1. In Kien's song, why should the mother "run away"? **Answers will vary.**
2. How does Kien's song make Hong and Mai feel?

HOW ABOUT YOU?
- Do you like Kien? Would you like to know him? Why or why not?

CRITICAL THINKING

Have students respond orally or in writing to these questions:
- Why do you think Thay Van Chi continued to travel from village to village for so long? *(Possible answer: He was trying to get as far from the war as possible.)*
- Why do you think Hong asked Mai to recall the old days? *(Possible answer: Hong wants Mai to remember what it is like to be in Kien's position.)*
- Why do you think Hong asked Mai to leave? *(Possible answer: She sees that Mai will not understand why Kien's arrival is so disruptive to the villagers.)*

MODELING THE READING STRATEGY

Visualizing: Have students reread the text and write in their notebooks words and phrases that helped them to visualize the events on page 73. Then call on volunteers to share their work with the class and model how each word or phrase helped them to visualize the events in the story

ABOUT THE AUTHOR

Maureen Crane Wartski, also known as M. A. Crane, has a B.A. degree in English literature. In addition to writing books, Ms. Wartski contributes to children's magazines and lectures on creative writing. She currently resides in North Carolina.

REACHING ALL STUDENTS

LANGUAGE LEVELS

Beginning: Ask students to list challenges that Mai has overcome. Then ask what Mai might be like today if her parents were still alive. Have students record their responses in their notebooks. Have them share their written responses with a partner.

Advanced: Draw a four-column chart on the board. Write *Mai, Kien, Hong,* and *Grandfather* at the top of each column respectively. Have students discuss how each character has been affected by the war so far. Ask volunteers to record class responses on the chart. When they have finished, have students write summaries of the information on the chart.

Review and Practice

COMPREHENSION

Define the term *chronological order* for students. Then call on volunteers to take turns reading the Comprehension directions. Have students read aloud each of the sentences that describe events in the story, and have a volunteer read the sentence that has the number 1 next to it. Point out that this event happened first. Then tell students to copy that sentence in their notebooks. Have students decide together which event happened next and write this sentence in their notebooks. Repeat this procedure until all the sentences have been placed in the correct order. Have students respond to these questions:

1. What is the first event in Mai's life that we know about? *(Mai lives in a big house in the city.)*

2. Does Kien frighten Hong with a song before or after the people of the village welcome Mai and her family? *(after)*

3. Which sentence tells what happens last in the story? *(Kien sings a song that frightens Hong.)*

CRITICAL THINKING

Have students respond orally or in writing to these questions:

- How could you find out what happened next if you weren't sure? *(Possible answer: You could refer back to the story.)*

- What is another way to show the chronological order of this story? *(Possible answer: Create a timeline.)*

COMPREHENSION

Reread the excerpt from *A Boat to Nowhere*. Number the events in chronological order. Remember that some of these events took place before Mai and Loc arrived at the village. Write the sentences in your notebook.

___5___ Hong gives Kien food and Mai watches him eat it.

___6___ Hong makes Kien take a bath.

___7___ The villagers say they don't want Kien to stay.

___3___ Grandfather brings Mai and Loc to the new village.

___8___ Kien sings a song that frightens Hong.

___1___ Mai's father goes to be a doctor for the soldiers.

___4___ The villagers welcome Mai, her brother, and their grandfather.

___2___ Mai, Loc, and their grandfather walk for a very long time and get lost in the forest.

Use the list to retell the story to a partner.

74

EXTENSION

Copy the Venn diagram into your notebook. Reread the story and look at the list of characters on page 66. Fill in the missing characters in Mai's past and present (before and after she came to the village). Which characters are in both Mai's past and present?

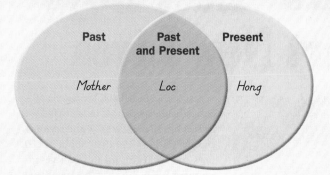

Past

Past and Present

Present

Mother

Loc

Hong

DISCUSSION

Discuss in pairs or small groups.

1. Why do you think Mai has many memories of living in the city?
2. Do you like this story? Do you want to read the rest?
3. Why don't the villagers want Kien to stay?
4. What do you think will happen next in the story?

75

EXTENSION

Look at the Venn diagram and read the directions aloud with students. Have them read the heading in each circle. Ask students to explain how the information in the Venn diagram is similar to the information in the chart on page 66. Invite students to work alone or in pairs to complete the diagram in their notebooks.

DISCUSSION

Have students work in pairs or small groups and take turns reading the Discussion questions. Encourage students to return to the selection to answer any challenging questions. Have students share their answers orally as a class.

METACOGNITION

Ask students:

1. How does the Venn diagram help you organize and remember information?
2. What did you learn about the Vietnam War from this story?
3. What strategy did you use to sequence the events in chronological order? Did the strategy work well? Why or why not?

REACHING ALL STUDENTS

LANGUAGE LEVELS

Beginning: To reinforce chronological order, have students write each class they take on a separate index card. Have them use their cards to describe their daily schedule to a partner: *First I go to math. Next I go to science class. . . .*

Advanced: Discuss with students some possible endings for *A Boat to Nowhere.* To stimulate discussion, ask, *Where do you think Kien came from? Why is he singing about rifles and cannons coming closer?* Then ask students to write down additional events that might lead to a conclusion based on their discussion.

LEARNING MODALITIES

Kinesthetic: Have students determine the correct order of events from the story listed on page 74. Then have volunteers work alone or in small groups to act out the events from the story in the correct chronological order.

Connect

READING SUMMARY

A civil war has raged in the African country of Sudan since the mid-1980s. This article describes events in the lives of a group of children known as the "Lost Boys," who were orphaned when troops destroyed their villages in southern Sudan. After escaping to Ethiopia, many of them came to the United States.

SCAFFOLDING

Have students read silently as they listen to the selection on the CD/tape. Then read the article together as a class.

GUIDED READING

1. On which continent is Sudan located? *(Africa)*
2. What kind of war is taking place in Sudan? *(a civil war)*
3. Where did the boys go after their villages were destroyed? *(They walked to Ethiopia.)*
4. What organization helped about fifty young Sudanese men settle in the United States? *(World Vision)*

across the curriculum

GEOGRAPHY Have students locate Sudan in an atlas and draw a map showing a route the "Lost Boys" might have taken to get from Sudan to Ethiopia and Kenya. Have them find Africa and North America on a globe and trace with their finger the route the boys would then take to America.

This is a magazine article about real people and events. Preview and skim the text. With your classmates, make some predictions about what the article is about. Write them on the chalkboard. Then, in your notebook, write two questions that you think the article will answer. Think of the questions as you read the article.

Sudan's "Lost Boys" Start New Lives

▲ Sudan is the largest country in Africa.

Since the mid-1980s, the people of Sudan have experienced terrible **civil war** caused by religious, **ethnic**, and regional **conflict**. In 1987 and 1988, about 20,000 boys and 2,000 girls left their villages in southern Sudan. They left because their villages were destroyed by **troops** from the northern Khartoum government. Most adults and girls were killed or sold as **slaves**. The boys, mostly between five and ten years old, had nowhere to go and no one to take care of them. They walked hundreds of kilometers through the East African desert. Some boys carried their baby brothers as they walked. Many died of hunger, thirst, disease, or attack by wild animals. To stay alive, they often ate leaves and mud.

---

civil war, war between two or more groups of people who live in the same country
ethnic, racial or cultural
conflict, fight or argument
troops, soldiers; members of the army
slaves, people who are sold for money

76

▲ David Akuei, wearing new clothes, leaves a mud hut in Kenya to travel to the United States.

About 12,000 children reached Ethiopia. In Ethiopia, and later in Kenya, they lived in **refugee camps** for over ten years. They didn't have any parents, so the children formed their own "family" groups. The older children took care of the younger ones. **Relief workers** in the camps named the children the "Lost Boys." This name comes from the book *Peter Pan*. In *Peter Pan*, a group of boys stays together without adults.

---

refugee camps, temporary living areas for people who have to leave their homes because of war
relief workers, people who help victims of a disaster

Now most of these "lost boys" are young men between seventeen and twenty-five years old. About 4,000 of them have moved to the United States. First, the young men fly from Kenya to the United States. Then they go to cities across the United States. Relief **organizations** are helping the men start a new life in freedom and safety.

One organization, World Vision, is helping about fifty young Sudanese men **settle** in the Seattle area of Washington. World Vision first places each young man with an American family for two to four weeks. Then the young men move into apartments. They study English and learn about American culture. They must learn all **aspects** of American life (from using a can opener to finding a job) very quickly. That way, they can learn to live **independently**. This is a very difficult task, especially when they have never seen mattresses, lightbulbs, ice, or a television.

---

organizations, groups such as clubs or businesses
settle, begin to live in a new place
aspects, parts of a situation, idea, problem, etc.
independently, alone, without help

BEFORE YOU GO ON . . .

1. Why did the "Lost Boys" of Sudan have to leave their homes?
2. How did these boys get to Ethiopia?

HOW ABOUT YOU?
- Do you know the story of Peter Pan? If not, do you know any stories about children like the "lost boys"?

77

CRITICAL THINKING

Have students respond orally or in writing to these questions:
- Why do you think it might be important for the "Lost Boys" to stick together even after they come to America? *(Possible answer: They can share experiences and act as each other's family.)*
- Why do you think these children formed family groups in Ethiopia? *(Possible answer: to help each other)*
- Which do you think was harder for the "Lost Boys": to leave their homeland and travel to the refugee camps, or to leave the refugee camps to come to America? Explain your answer. *(Answers will vary.)*

MODELING THE READING STRATEGY

Visualizing: Ask students to close their eyes as you read page 76 aloud. Have them listen for words in the text that will help them to picture what it might have been like for Sudanese children during the war. After reading, ask students to describe what they pictured.

--- *Viewpoint* ---

Have students look at the picture of David Akuei as he leaves Kenya to travel to the United States. Create a flowchart for students to copy into their notebooks to record the journey of the "Lost Boys."

REACHING ALL STUDENTS

LANGUAGE LEVELS

Beginning: Point out that the "Lost Boys" repeatedly show a willingness to help each other. Have students find and discuss two ways that the boys helped each other to survive.

Advanced: Discuss with students what expectations the young Sudanese men might have had when they came to America and how realistic or unrealistic those expectations might have been. Then have students discuss their own expectations when they came to the United States. Have them reflect on how realistic their expectations were.

Connect

GUIDED READING

1. What is the strange white box the young Sudanese men find in the kitchen? *(a refrigerator)*

2. How will the men spend their time in the United States? *(working and going to school)*

3. What do some of the men hope to do? *(They hope to return to Sudan and rebuild their villages.)*

Since they arrived, the young men have been amazed by new discoveries: keys, stoves, stairs, and telephones. Then there is macaroni, canned juice, and the "huge white box" in the kitchen. They tried lifting the strange machine from the bottom. They tried pulling it apart. Then they discovered the handle and opened the refrigerator. It was full of cold, unfamiliar foods.

Some of the young men will use their time in the United States to get a good education and earn money. Then they hope to return to Sudan and rebuild their villages.

▲ Philip Maliah Dar (right) is congratulated by his teacher in an English class at Harvard University.

BEFORE YOU GO ON . . .

1 What were some things that surprised the young men?

2 What did they do with the refrigerator?

HOW ABOUT YOU?

- What did you find interesting about the "lost boys'" experience?

▲ Mou Deng reaches up to catch a snowflake in front of his new home in the United States.

78

MULTICULTURAL NOTE

Explain that farming is an important part of the Sudanese lifestyle, with almost 80 percent of the population employed in agriculture. Most people in Sudan still live by farming or herding. They grow cotton to export and sorghum and millet to eat. The small farms of Sudan are cultivated without machinery, and few have access to modern irrigation and fertilization practices. Discuss what the young Sudanese men can learn in the United States that will be helpful when they return to their homeland to rebuild their villages. Students can look at university catalogues on the Internet to create a course of study for the "Lost Boys."

Link the Readings

Reread "Sudan's 'Lost Boys' Start New Lives." Then think about it and the excerpt from *A Boat to Nowhere* as you look at the chart. Copy the chart into your notebook and complete it.

Title of Selection	Type of Text (Genre)	Fiction or Nonfiction	Purpose of Selection	Country/ Countries
From *A Boat to Nowhere*		*fiction*		*Vietnam*
"Sudan's 'Lost Boys' Start New Lives"	*magazine article*		*to inform*	

DISCUSSION

Discuss in pairs or small groups.

1. Which text did you prefer, the excerpt from *A Boat to Nowhere* or "Sudan's 'Lost Boys' Start New Lives"? Did you prefer it because of the style, the people, or for some other reason? Explain.

2. Compare the lives of the orphans in the excerpt from *A Boat to Nowhere* and "Sudan's 'Lost Boys' Start New Lives." In what ways are their lives similar and different? What kind of challenges do they face? What kind of choices can they make?

3. What objects that we see every day in the United States might be different for people from Vietnam or Sudan?

4. Imagine you have to describe an everyday object, such as a table or an umbrella, to someone who doesn't know what that object is. Describe what the object does and how it works.

▲ Two students take a break from English lessons to work on their soccer skills.

79

REFLECTION

Read the headings of the chart together with students, and discuss their meanings. Then have students copy and complete the chart in their notebooks. Encourage students to reread the selections as needed. Students can use their completed charts to discuss the similarities between the two selections.

1. Which reading selection is nonfiction? *("Sudan's 'Lost Boys' Start New Lives")*

2. What type of text is *A Boat to Nowhere*? *(a novel)*

DISCUSSION

Have students read the questions and discuss their answers. Point out that each of these questions asks readers to use some of their own experiences as they think about the reading, and can have more than one correct answer.

CRITICAL THINKING

Discuss the challenges that the characters faced in the fiction and nonfiction reading selections. Ask students to identify the qualities that helped the characters overcome the challenges they faced.

REACHING ALL STUDENTS

LANGUAGE LEVELS

Beginning: To help students answer Discussion item 4, bring in several common objects, such as a can opener or a toothbrush. Invite students to hold the object and demonstrate how to use it as they explain what it does and how it works.

Advanced: To help students complete Discussion item 2, draw a two-column chart on the board with the headings *Challenges* and *Choices*. Guide students to skim both texts and brainstorm challenges and choices the orphans faced. Record their ideas on the chart and invite students to discuss the questions.

LEARNING MODALITIES

Auditory: Have students form small groups. Encourage students to take turns pretending they are one of the Sudanese "Lost Boys." Have them tell the rest of the group about the customs of American life they find most difficult to adjust to, and those they most enjoy.

Connect to Writing

GRAMMAR

Call on a volunteer to read the definition under "Using the Conjunction *but*" aloud. Make sure students understand that the conjunction *but* is used to connect two contrasting ideas in two contrasting simple sentences. The combined sentence is called a compound sentence. Then write the following simple sentences on the board: *No one in the village liked Kien. They fed him and gave him clean clothes.* Tell students to use the conjunction *but* to combine these two simple sentences into a compound sentence in their notebooks.

Have students scan the text of *A Boat to Nowhere* and write examples of sentences containing the conjunction *but*. After they write the sentences in their notebooks, have students circle the word *but* and underline the contrasting ideas.

Have students work independently or in pairs to complete the Practice exercises. Students should record the sentences in their notebooks.

SCAFFOLDING

Write each of the following words on separate index cards: *sleepy, John, but, was, was, alert, John.* Have each student hold a card. Ask students to arrange themselves to make two simple sentences using the cards. *(John was sleepy. John was alert.)* Tell students that one of the words on the index cards was not needed to make these two simple sentences. *(but)* Then have students make one compound sentence out of the cards. *(John was sleepy, but John was alert.)*

GRAMMAR

Using the Conjunction *but*
The **conjunction *but*** connects two contrasting ideas. Use *but* to connect two contrasting adjectives.

> Kien's new clothes were clean. Kien's new clothes were ragged.
> Kien's new clothes were clean **but** ragged.

Use *but* to combine two contrasting simple sentences. The combined sentence is called a compound sentence. A compound sentence usually has a comma before the conjunction.

> Kien ate several bowls of rice. He was still hungry.
> Kien ate several bowls of rice, **but** he was still hungry.

Practice
Copy these simple sentence pairs into your notebook. Then combine each pair using the conjunction *but.*

Examples:

> The day was hot. The day was windy.
> The day was hot **but** windy.

> The "lost boys" didn't know English. They are learning quickly.
> The "lost boys" didn't know English, **but** they are learning quickly.

1. The village was small. The village was crowded.
2. The "lost boys" didn't have much food. They were grateful for what they had.
3. Many children died in Sudan. Twelve thousand survived.
4. Kien slept for twelve hours. He was still tired.
5. The boat was old. The boat was seaworthy.
6. Kien liked Loc and Mai. He didn't like Hong.

80

SPELLING MINILESSON

Words with Long *o*, Long *e*, Long *u*
Explain that there are many ways to spell the sounds /ō/, /ē/, and /ū/, but most words follow a pattern. Write these patterns on the board and have students identify the words that follow the patterns.

CVVC: *goat, lean, dues*
CVCe: *poke, Pete, June*

Have students look for words with these spelling patterns in the reading selections and list them in their notebooks. Examples include *soap, rude, home, mean, seen, huge, hope.*

SKILLS FOR WRITING

Using a Variety of Sentence Types

Writers use different types of sentences to make their writing more interesting. For example, they use both simple sentences and compound sentences.

> **Simple sentence**
> Hong took care of Mai.
> **Compound sentence**
> Hong was glad to cook for Mai, but she did not want to cook for Kien.

Read the personal narrative. Then answer the questions about the paragraph.

> *Jennifer Rosario*
>
> *My Big Challenge*
>
> Recently, I decided to try out for the Color Guard team at school. I had never done it before, but I decided to practice. ← simple sentence
> First, we did difficult stretches, but I am not very flexible. ← compound sentence
> Then, we worked with the flags, but I'm short and the tosses and the rotations were hard. I was so frustrated, I felt like giving up. I thought I would never succeed, but I kept practicing. I was determined to get better. Finally, the day of the tryouts arrived. I was so scared, I almost didn't go. I did my best. I didn't make the team, but I learned not to give up. Maybe I'll succeed next year.

1. How many simple sentences are there? How many compound sentences?
2. Is the first sentence interesting? Why or why not?
3. What does the writer do in this paragraph to make the writing interesting?

81

SKILLS FOR WRITING

Ask a volunteer to read the directions aloud. Then read the sample paragraph to students. Have them identify sentences that are very short. Call on volunteers to write these sentences on the board. Then have students identify examples of longer sentences. Explain that if all the sentences in a paragraph are the same length, the writing becomes choppy and dull. Have students refer to the paragraph as they answer the questions below it.

SCAFFOLDING

Remind students that a compound sentence is made up of two simple sentences and a conjunction. Have pairs of students choose one of the selections in Part 2 and skim it to find compound sentences that use the conjunction *but*. Students can record their sentences and share them with the group.

REACHING ALL STUDENTS

LANGUAGE LEVELS

Beginning: Write the compound sentence *He wants to go swimming, but he can't find his towel* on the board. Have students identify the two simple sentences in the sentence, and ask a volunteer to underline them. Circle the word *but* and tell students that *but* is a conjunction. It connects two contrasting ideas. Repeat the activity with these sentences:

> *She drank the juice, but she forgot to wash her cup.*
>
> *John speaks three languages, but he doesn't speak French.*
>
> *Carrie had fun at the beach, but she is ready to come home.*
>
> *He often rides his bike to school, but he is walking today.*

Teach

WRITING ASSIGNMENT

Personal Narrative

Invite different students to read each section of the Writing Assignment. Then have students reread the personal narrative on page 81 for words and phrases that express feelings, such as *frustrated* and *scared*. Have them make a list of these "feeling words" in their notebooks. Point out how the words express the author's feelings about being challenged. Have students identify a difficult time or challenge in their own lives that they can write about.

WRITING STRATEGY

Have students take turns reading the Writing Strategy. Explain that using a timeline can help them place events in the correct chronological order. Encourage students to look back at this timeline when they create their own "challenge" timeline in their notebooks. Then ask students to write a narrative piece about a challenge they have faced. Remind them to refer back to their timeline so they can write about their experiences in chronological order. Tell them to add details that will help a reader or listener visualize the people involved, the setting, and the events as they unfolded.

USING THE EDITING CHECKLIST

Ask students to read the Editing Checklist with a partner and use it to revise their writing.

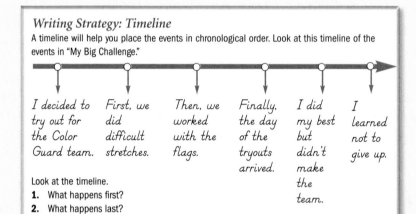

WRITING ASSIGNMENT

Personal Narrative

You will write a paragraph about a challenge you faced and what you learned from the experience.

1. **Read** Reread the model on page 81. How do you know that the writer felt challenged? What clues does the writer include to help you know how she felt?

> *Writing Strategy: Timeline*
> A timeline will help you place the events in chronological order. Look at this timeline of the events in "My Big Challenge."
>
> | I decided to try out for the Color Guard team. | First, we did difficult stretches. | Then, we worked with the flags. | Finally, the day of the tryouts arrived. | I did my best but didn't make the team. | I learned not to give up. |
>
> Look at the timeline.
> 1. What happens first?
> 2. What happens last?

2. **Make a timeline** Think about a challenge you faced. Make a timeline in your notebook. Use the timeline to organize the material into chronological order.

3. **Write** Use your timeline and the model on page 81 to help you write about your experience.

> **EDITING CHECKLIST**
>
> **Did you . . .**
> ▶ tell the events in your story in chronological order?
> ▶ give enough details so that readers get a clear picture in their minds?
> ▶ use a variety of sentence types?
> ▶ use correct punctuation?
> ▶ indent the first sentence?

82

PART REVIEW 2

Check Your Knowledge

Language Development

1. What words does the author use to help you visualize Kien eating in the excerpt from *A Boat to Nowhere*?
2. Which part of the excerpt from *A Boat to Nowhere* is a flashback?
3. How can a timeline help you write about something that happened to you?
4. Give an example of a sentence that uses *but* to join two contrasting ideas.
5. Why is it important to use a variety of sentences in your writing?

Academic Content

1. What new social studies vocabulary did you learn in Part 2? What do the words mean?
2. What do you know about the Vietnam War?
3. What are some ways that the civil war in Sudan has changed the lives of the Sudanese people?

Sudanese women try to feed their families during a drought. ▶

83

Put It All Together

Put It All Together

EXTEND THE LESSON

The Put It All Together section on pages 84–87 consolidates concepts, skills, and strategies from both parts of the unit. Emphasis is on the skills of listening, speaking, and writing as students organize a panel discussion.

LISTENING AND SPEAKING WORKSHOP

Have students make a two-column chart in their notebooks and list challenges they have read about and ones they have faced. Encourage group members to share their lists and agree on a group definition of the word *challenge*. Allow time for students to practice relating their personal challenges. Then have each group present a panel discussion for the whole class.

COOPERATIVE GROUPING

Form small groups of beginning and advanced students. Ask each student to create a list of challenges and then read his or her list to other group members.

TEACHING THE TIPS

Speaking Tips: Help students practice speaking loudly and clearly by having them sit up straight and breathe deeply to calm their nerves.

Listening Tip: Have students practice their listening strategy by writing two key words that will remind them of the question they want to ask or the point they need clarified.

RESEARCH SKILLS

Nonprint: Have students interview a parent or other adult who knew about the problem or difficult choice the student faced. Students can ask the adult to verify information and describe his or her observations about the decisions the student had to make. Have students record interview responses to use as notes when they write their narratives.

OBJECTIVES

Integrate Skills
- Listening/ Speaking: *Panel discussion*
- Writing: *Personal narrative*

Investigate Themes
- Projects
- Further reading

LISTENING and SPEAKING WORKSHOP

PANEL DISCUSSION

You will organize and present a panel discussion about the meaning of the word *challenge*.

1 **Think about it** Make a list of the challenges you read about in this unit. Make another list of challenges you have faced in your life. Read the examples in your two lists. Think about how to define the word *challenge*, and then write a definition.

Work in groups of four. Compare your lists and definitions. Discuss your ideas.

2 **Organize** Organize a panel discussion. Work together to define the word *challenge*. Use ideas from your group members' definitions. Include examples of challenges you read about or challenges you faced to support your definition. Write down your group's definition and supporting examples.

Each group member should plan to tell about a personal challenge from his or her life that illustrates your group's definition.

3 **Practice** Practice your panel discussion. One group member should present your group's definition of *challenge*. Then other group members should take turns telling about a personal challenge. After each person speaks, the other members of the panel can ask the speaker questions or make comments.

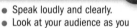

SPEAKING TIPS
- Speak loudly and clearly.
- Look at your audience as you speak.

4 **Present and evaluate** Present your panel discussion to your class. After each panel finishes, evaluate the presentation. What did you like best about the presentation? Do you have suggestions for improvement?

LISTENING TIP

If you don't understand something a speaker says, make a note. Wait until the speaker has finished and then ask your question.

84

T84

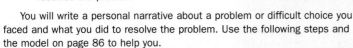

WRITING WORKSHOP

PERSONAL NARRATIVE

In a personal narrative, the writer tells a story about events or people in his or her life. The story is about the writer's personal experience. Usually, the story includes a problem or difficult choice that the writer had to face or make.

A good personal narrative includes the following characteristics:

- a first-person narrator—or "I"—that tells the story
- a clear sequence of events in chronological order
- a problem or difficult choice the narrator faces
- a conclusion that tells how the narrator resolves the problem

You will write a personal narrative about a problem or difficult choice you faced and what you did to resolve the problem. Use the following steps and the model on page 86 to help you.

1 Prewrite Think about a problem or difficult choice you have faced. It can be a choice about a friend or something that happened at school or home. Make notes about it. Where were you? Who was there? What was the problem? What happened as a result of your choice? Read through your notes and then number them in chronological order.

WRITING TIP

Use sequence words to make the time periods and sequence of events clear to the reader. Sequence words usually appear at the beginning or end of a sentence. They show:

- a sequence, or order, of events: first, next, then, last, finally
- movement from one time period to another: before, after, later, while, during
- expressions of time: yesterday, last night, in 1998, on May 24, tomorrow, next week

85

Explain to students that a personal narrative is written in the first-person point of view and describes a personal experience in the writer's life. Have students reread "He Was the Same Age as My Sister" in Part 1 for an example of a strong personal narrative. Additional practice activities can be found in the **Workbook** and **CD-ROM.**

PROCESS WRITING

Explain that the student sample on page 86 is an example of a personal narrative. Have students read the sample narrative as a choral reading. Point out the use of the word *I* as an indicator of first-person point of view. Challenge students to find and name time order words used in the sample. *(first, then, after, finally)* Then have students refer back to the sample to answer these questions:

- *What difficult choice did Kate write about?*
- *What difficult choice will you write about?*
- *How do you know that Kate described her experience in chronological order?*
- *What ideas for your own narrative do you have after reading the sample?*

Have students follow the steps to create a personal narrative.

TEACHING THE TIP

Writing Tip: Read aloud the Writing Tip with students. After they finish their drafts, have students read their story. Ask, *Does any part of your story lack details? Who do you know that might be able to provide those details?* Provide time for students to interview those friends or family members before revising their writing.

REACHING ALL STUDENTS

LANGUAGE LEVELS

Beginning: Have students discuss the readings for Unit 2. Have them identify the person or character they found most inspiring as well as the challenge that person or character overcame. Repeat or rephrase any responses students offer that help them generate additional ideas. You might say, *Raul says the "Lost Boys" were brave and didn't give up even though they lost their families and their homes. What other challenges do you think the "Lost Boys" faced, and how did they overcome them?*

Advanced: Have student pairs take turns videotaping a practice presentation of their panel discussion. Ask each pair to watch their own oral presentation and choose two elements to improve upon when they give their presentation to the class. Students can choose from the list of speaking tips on page 84, or they can choose another area to work on, such as avoiding expressions like *um.*

Put It All Together

Voice: If students need extra help with their narratives, read the model paragraph aloud again. Then call on a volunteer to read aloud the call-outs in the right-hand margin. Discuss the clue words the writer uses to make the sequence of events in the narrative clear. Have students think of other clue words the writer could have used and list them on the board.

Before students revise their own personal narratives, point out that good writers always try to put their "personal stamp" on whatever they write. This is often referred to as the author's *voice*. Remind students that their own writing should reflect their personality and individuality.

Write the following tips on the board. Tell students to use the tips as they revise their writing to make sure their personal voice comes through in their narratives.

- Write about subjects you know well and really care about.
- Express your enthusiasm for the topic you have chosen.
- Make sure you write directly to your readers.
- Use adjectives and verbs that will help your readers feel exactly the same way you feel about your topic.
- Remind students to write legibly using either cursive or manuscript.

Before you write a first draft of your personal narrative, read the following model. Notice the characteristics of a personal narrative.

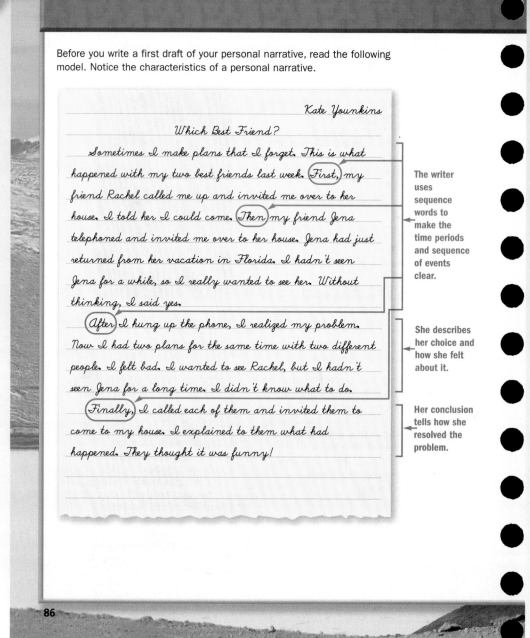

Kate Younkins

Which Best Friend?

Sometimes I make plans that I forget. This is what happened with my two best friends last week. First, my friend Rachel called me up and invited me over to her house. I told her I could come. Then my friend Jena telephoned and invited me over to her house. Jena had just returned from her vacation in Florida. I hadn't seen Jena for a while, so I really wanted to see her. Without thinking, I said yes.

After I hung up the phone, I realized my problem. Now I had two plans for the same time with two different people. I felt bad. I wanted to see Rachel, but I hadn't seen Jena for a long time. I didn't know what to do.

Finally, I called each of them and invited them to come to my house. I explained to them what had happened. They thought it was funny!

The writer uses sequence words to make the time periods and sequence of events clear.

She describes her choice and how she felt about it.

Her conclusion tells how she resolved the problem.

86

T86

2 Draft Use the model and your notes to write your personal narrative.

- Start your narrative in an interesting way, so your reader will want to read your story. Describe the characters and introduce your problem or difficult choice. Notice how the student starts her model narrative. How does she get you interested in her story?

- Describe your problem or choice in the next paragraph. Tell how you felt about the situation.

- Conclude your narrative by describing what you did to resolve the problem. If possible, explain what you learned from this experience.

3 Edit Work in pairs. Trade papers and read each other's personal narratives. Use the questions in the editing checklist to evaluate each other's work.

> ### EDITING CHECKLIST
>
> **Did you . . .**
> - write about events in the order that they happened?
> - use sequence words to help the reader follow the chronology of what happened?
> - capitalize the first letter of every sentence?
> - use correct punctuation?
> - use adjectives to express your feelings?

4 Revise Revise your personal narrative. Add ideas and correct mistakes, if necessary.

5 Publish Share your writing with your teacher and classmates.

87

Form student pairs. Ask partners to read each other's narratives silently before reading the checklist and following the steps. Tell students to look for items on the Editing Checklist one at a time. Circulate and help students go through the checklist.

ASSESS

Portfolio: Include the personal narrative in students' assessment portfolios for comparison with later assignments.

REACHING ALL STUDENTS

LANGUAGE LEVELS

Beginning: Have students go through their personal narrative to look for a variety of sentence types. Encourage students to revise their work to include both simple and compound sentences. Students should be sure to have at least two compound sentences per paragraph.

Advanced: To help students organize their thoughts, have them create a timeline showing the order in which the events in their story took place. Have pairs read each other's timelines. Ask the readers to look for unanswered questions they may still have about their partner's experience and relate them to the writer. Encourage the writer to add the details to the story.

Unit Projects

EXTEND THE LESSON

Home-School Connection: For Project 4, have students share their daily challenges and concerns with family members. As they take notes on these challenges, they can discuss problem-solving strategies and have parents or older siblings help them evaluate the steps they followed to meet the challenge.

WEBSITES

For more information, log on to http://www.longman.com/shiningstar for links to other interesting websites.

PROJECTS

Work in pairs or small groups. Choose one of these projects.

1. Find out more about World War II, the Vietnam War, or the Sudanese civil war on the Internet. Share your findings with the class.

2. Work with a partner. One partner role-plays one of the people in "Extraordinary People." The other partner interviews the person. Ask and answer these questions: *Who are you? What challenges have you faced? What makes you extraordinary?* Take turns playing each role. Present the interview to the class.

3. Choose an art material that you like to work with, such as paint, clay, colored pencils, or paper and glue. Look through the stories you read in this unit. Choose a setting, a character, or an event. Make some artwork showing what you chose. When you're finished, write a sentence or two about your artwork. Present your artwork and writing to the class.

4. Over the course of a few days, take note of daily challenges you face. Record the steps you go through as you meet each challenge. Compare your steps with those of a partner, and evaluate the steps. Were they effective? Sometimes effective? How can you improve them?

5. A collage is a kind of artwork that is made by cutting and pasting together different materials—for example, photos, drawings, written or typed words, or pictures. Some famous artists who made collages are Pablo Picasso, Georges Braque, and Henri Matisse. Find examples of their collages in library books or on the Internet.

   Make a collage about yourself—a combination of words and pictures that shows who you are, what your interests are, and what challenges you have faced.

   - Use words and pictures from newspapers, magazines, personal photos, your own writing or drawings.
   - Cut and paste the pieces onto a piece of paper or cardboard.
   - You can have your name in your collage or not, as you choose.

   Share your collage with your class.

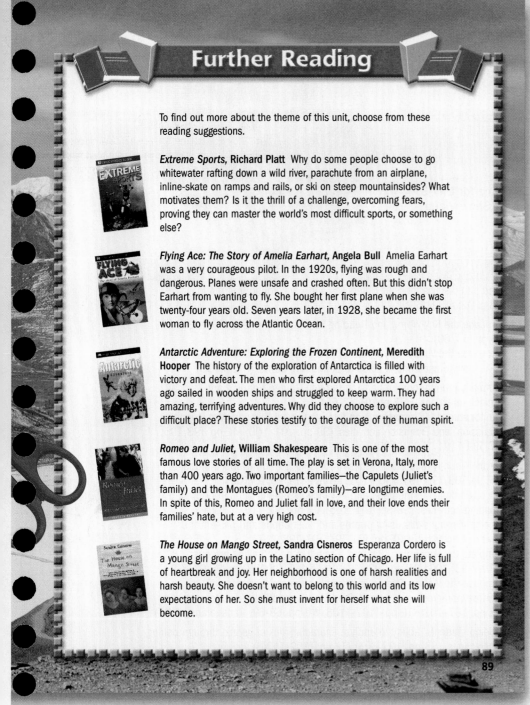

Further Reading

To find out more about the theme of this unit, choose from these reading suggestions.

Extreme Sports, Richard Platt Why do some people choose to go whitewater rafting down a wild river, parachute from an airplane, inline-skate on ramps and rails, or ski on steep mountainsides? What motivates them? Is it the thrill of a challenge, overcoming fears, proving they can master the world's most difficult sports, or something else?

Flying Ace: The Story of Amelia Earhart, Angela Bull Amelia Earhart was a very courageous pilot. In the 1920s, flying was rough and dangerous. Planes were unsafe and crashed often. But this didn't stop Earhart from wanting to fly. She bought her first plane when she was twenty-four years old. Seven years later, in 1928, she became the first woman to fly across the Atlantic Ocean.

Antarctic Adventure: Exploring the Frozen Continent, Meredith Hooper The history of the exploration of Antarctica is filled with victory and defeat. The men who first explored Antarctica 100 years ago sailed in wooden ships and struggled to keep warm. They had amazing, terrifying adventures. Why did they choose to explore such a difficult place? These stories testify to the courage of the human spirit.

Romeo and Juliet, William Shakespeare This is one of the most famous love stories of all time. The play is set in Verona, Italy, more than 400 years ago. Two important families—the Capulets (Juliet's family) and the Montagues (Romeo's family)—are longtime enemies. In spite of this, Romeo and Juliet fall in love, and their love ends their families' hate, but at a very high cost.

The House on Mango Street, Sandra Cisneros Esperanza Cordero is a young girl growing up in the Latino section of Chicago. Her life is full of heartbreak and joy. Her neighborhood is one of harsh realities and harsh beauty. She doesn't want to belong to this world and its low expectations of her. So she must invent for herself what she will become.

89

FURTHER READING

- *Extreme Sports* and *Flying Ace: The Story of Amelia Earhart* are appropriate for beginning students.
- *Antarctic Adventure: Exploring the Frozen Continent* and *Romeo and Juliet* are appropriate for intermediate students.
- *The House on Mango Street* is appropriate for advanced students.

REACHING ALL STUDENTS

LANGUAGE LEVELS

Beginning: For the extraordinary person interview project, have pairs research the person they will be role-playing before writing the questions. Encourage students to ask questions that will generate more than a yes-or-no answer, such as "Why did you decide to move to Virginia at that point?"

Advanced: As students write about their artwork as part of the third project, have them include a paragraph on how they made the art. Encourage students to use sensory words to describe their pieces and the process they used to make them.

Level 1 Unit 3
Mysterious Ways

Make enough duplicate copies of the Letter Home for Unit 3 so that each student has a copy to take home. Show Video Segment 3.

PART 1 TEACHING GUIDE

PRETEACH	**Provide Background**	• Read and discuss the Part Objectives and Background Information. (SB p. 92; ATE p. T92)
	Present Concepts	• Introduce the Key Words and Reading Strategy. (SB p. 93; ATE p. T93; WB pp. 58, 60) • Pronounce the Vocabulary words. (ATE p. T93) • Model how to use context clues to define Key Words. (ATE p. T93)
TEACH	**Monitor Comprehension**	• Informally monitor comprehension through Guided Reading and Critical Thinking questions. (ATE pp. T94–T105) • Monitor students' comprehension through Critical Thinking, Metacognition, Discussion, and Extension activities. (SB pp. 101, 105; ATE pp. T93, T95, T97, T99–T101, T103, T105)
	Teach and Practice	• Use individually tailored activities for beginning and advanced students. (ATE pp. T93, T95, T97, T99, T101, T103, T105, T107, T109) • Pair beginning, intermediate, and advanced students through Cooperative Grouping activities. (SB pp. 101, 105; ATE pp. T92, T101, T105) • Develop viewing skills using photos and illustrations and present the Viewpoint activities. (ATE pp. T91, T94, T97–T98, T103) • Complete the Vocabulary, Phonics, Grammar, and Spelling lessons. (SB pp. 93, 106; ATE pp. T93–T94, T96, T98, T106; WB pp. 66–67, 70) • Introduce the Writing Strategy and apply students' ability to write a narrative paragraph using the Writing Model and Writing Assignment. (SB pp. 107–108; ATE pp. T107–T108; WB pp. 68–69; Transparency # 27)
CONNECT	**Connect to Literature**	• Develop students' ability to analyze characteristics of genres through pairing of selections. (SB pp. 102–104; ATE pp. T102–T104) • Provide students with interactive reading support and practice. (WB pp. 61–65)
	Across the Curriculum	• Develop students' ability to extend the content of the reading selections through extended math, social studies, science, health, and art activities. (ATE pp. T96, T98)
ASSESS	**Check Knowledge**	• Use the Before You Go On, Check Your Knowledge, Link the Readings, and Review and Practice features to assess students' comprehension of the selection. (SB pp. 95, 97, 99–100, 103, 104–105; ATE pp. T100, T105, T109)
	Monitor Progress	• Use the Assessment Options, Test-Taking Tip, and the test. (ATE p. T109; AG pp. 45–48)

CONTENT TERMS

Present and elicit definitions of these content-specific terms:

• pyramid	• pharaoh	• blocks	• monument
• dinosaurs	• experiment	• method	• materials
• molecules	• liquid		

PART 2 TEACHING GUIDE

PRETEACH	**Provide Background**	• Read and discuss the Part Objectives and Background Information. (SB p. 110; ATE p. T110)
	Present Concepts	• Introduce the Key Words and Reading Strategy. (SB p. 111; ATE p. T111; WB pp. 72–74) • Pronounce the Vocabulary words. (ATE p. T111) • Model how to use context clues to define Key Words. (ATE p. T111)
TEACH	**Monitor Comprehension**	• Informally monitor comprehension through Guided Reading and Critical Thinking questions. (ATE pp. T112–T123) • Monitor students' comprehension through Critical Thinking, Metacognition, Discussion, and Extension activities. (SB pp. 119, 123; ATE pp. T113, T115, T117–T119, T121, T123)
	Teach and Practice	• Use individually tailored activities for beginning and advanced students. (ATE pp. T111, T113, T115, T117, T119, T121, T123, T125, T127, T129, T131, T133) • Pair beginning, intermediate, and advanced students through Cooperative Grouping activities. (SB pp. 119, 123; ATE pp. T110, T119, T123) • Develop viewing skills using photos and illustrations and present the Viewpoint activities. (ATE pp. T112, T114, T116, T121) • Complete the Vocabulary, Phonics, Grammar, and Spelling lessons. (SB pp. 111, 124; ATE pp. T111–T112, T114, T116, T124; WB pp. 80–81, 84) • Introduce the Writing Strategy and apply students' ability to write instructions using the Writing Model and Writing Assignment. (SB pp. 129–131; ATE pp. T129–T131; WB pp. 82–83; Transparency # 29)
CONNECT	**Connect to Content**	• Develop students' ability to analyze characteristics of genres through pairing of selections. (SB pp. 120–122; ATE pp. T120–T122) • Provide students interactive reading support and practice. (WB pp. 75–79)
	Across the Curriculum	• Develop students' ability to extend the content of the reading selections through extended math, social studies, science, health, and art activities. (ATE pp. T114, T120)
ASSESS	**Check Knowledge**	• Use the Before You Go On, Check Your Knowledge, Link the Readings, and Review and Practice features to assess students' comprehension of the selection. (SB pp. 113, 115, 117, 118, 121, 122, 123; ATE pp. T119, T123, T127)
	Monitor Progress	• Use the Assessment Options, Test-Taking Tip, and the test. (ATE p. T127, AG pp. 49–52)

PUT IT ALL TOGETHER TEACHING GUIDE

EXTEND	**Integrate Skills and Apply Understanding**	• Apply students' ability to present a group presentation using the Listening and Speaking Workshop. (SB p. 128; ATE p. T128) • Apply students' ability to write instructions using the Writing Workshop. (SB pp. 129–131; ATE pp. T129–T131) • Have students complete one or more of the Unit Projects. (SB p. 132; ATE p. T132) • Have students choose a theme-related reading selection from the Further Reading suggestions. (SB p. 133; ATE p. T133)

Unit 3: Mysterious Ways

Part 1

Background (p. 92) Review with students the difference between *fiction* and *nonfiction*. Point out that fiction is a story that is made up. The characters, events, and plot are all created by the author. Nonfiction is writing that tells about real people, places, and events. Discuss with students some examples of fiction and nonfiction. On the board, make a list of titles and have students identify features of fiction and nonfiction that are common to each one.

Vocabulary (p. 93) Pictures can help students understand the meanings of some Key Words, such as *archaeologist*. To explain words like *clues* and *creature*, use several pictures to illustrate a pattern. For more difficult terms like *disappeared* and *fantasy*, draw a picture on the board or pantomime for the class. Have students develop dictionary skills by having them look up these words in a dictionary. Explain that many words have several entries. Have students pick the best entry for each word used in context.

Reading Strategy: Distinguishing Fact and Opinion (p. 93) Explain the difference between *fact* and *opinion* by having students fill out a T-chart. Start with a subject the students are familiar with, such as *Michael Jordan*. Ask for volunteers to fill in facts about Michael Jordan, such as *He played basketball. He played for the Chicago Bulls*, etc. Ask students, *Can these things be proved? How?* Then ask for volunteers to add their opinions about Michael Jordan. (For example, *He was the world's greatest basketball player. He made basketball look easy*, etc.) Ask students, *Can these things be proved? Why not?* If necessary, have the students fill in more T-charts covering facts and opinions. Use other examples, such as school, the town you live in, the United States, etc.

Fact or Fiction? (pp. 94–99) Explain *mysteries* and *theories* to the class. Explain that *mysteries* are things that are not fully understood. Explain that *theories* are educated guesses to explain these mysteries. Scientists and experts collect what they know and use them to create theories that explain mysteries. Use a mystery and theory that you know of, such as dinosaur extinction. Explain to students that no one knows for sure why the dinosaurs died out; it is a mystery. However, scientists have several theories (giant asteroid, climate change).

Activity 1: With the class, walk through the first section, "Path to the Stars?" Have students identify what the mystery is in this section. Explain that the mystery is, *Why is there a shaft in the pyramid that leads to Orion?* Then ask students what scientists theorize. *(The Egyptians built the shaft so that Cheops could fly from the pyramid to Orion.)*

Activity 2: After students read "Fact or Fiction?" make a two-column chart on the board. For each subhead *(Egyptian Pyramids, Machu Picchu, Bigfoot,* etc.) have students fill in facts they learned from the text.

Activity 3: Have students choose their favorite subject from the selection and write down their own theory. Stress that there are no wrong answers. Then have students support their theory. They can use facts from the text, or information that they already know. Ask for volunteers to share their theories with the class.

Comprehension (p. 100) On the board, make a T-chart of the five *wh-* question words *(When, Where, Who, What, Why)*. Explain what each question will ask. *(Questions that begin with* When *will ask about a time period. Questions that begin with* Who *will ask about a person*, etc.) Use each of the *wh-* questions to ask the students questions. Use the "Path to the Stars?" section as an example. *(When did the pharaoh Cheops build the pyramids? Who noticed the shape of the pyramids was similar to Orion's Belt?* etc.)

Truth or Lies? (pp. 102–104) Discuss *truth* and *lies* with the class. Truth is a statement of fact. Lies are false statements. On the board, give the students a short true/false test. Write both true and false statements about something the students will know about, such as your school or the area in which you live. Then have students identify which statements are true and which are false. Discuss half-truths with the class. Explain that half-truths are found in each of these stories. They are not lies, yet they are not the entire truth. On the board, make a T-chart for each story. In column 1 ask students to identify the half-truth. In column 2 ask students what information was left out. Discuss quotes with the students. Explain that authors use quotes to indicate dialogue or a character's speech. Use the text example to explain the use of quotation marks. Then explain the different punctuation marks that can be used in quotes. Explain that authors identify the speaker by writing *he said, she said*, etc. Mention that authors may also tell how a character is speaking or what he or she is doing while they are speaking.

Grammar: The Present Progressive (p. 106) Give students a brief explanation of the past, present, and future. On the board, write several simple sentences that demonstrate tenses. *(I walked to school yesterday; I am walking to school; I will walk to school tomorrow.)* Pantomime if necessary. Explain that the present progressive is something that is happening right now. Point to yourself and say things like *I am talking; I am speaking; I am standing in front of the class*, etc. Write these sentences on the board. Use hand gestures to signify the subject and action. Circle the present progressive verb being used. Then go around the room and use the students as examples for the present progressive: *She is sitting in the front of the class. He is listening to me speak*, etc. Then ask volunteers to give more examples using the present progressive.

Skills for Writing and Writing Assignment (pp. 107–108) Using objects in the classroom, demonstrate the purpose of prepositions. Begin by pointing to things and using prepositions, such as *The books are* on *the desk; Maria is sitting* behind *Michael; I am standing* in front of *the class*, etc. Then have students write several sentences using prepositions and the present progressive about objects in the classroom. Ask volunteers to share their sentences with the class. Before you begin the writing assignment, have students choose one image in the picture on p. 108. Then have them write two or three sentences on that image using prepositions and the present progressive. *(The airplanes are flying in the air. They are flapping their wings*, etc.) Before they begin writing, have them make a three-column chart based on the questions in the text box on p. 108. Have students write down the questions and fill in the answers in their chart. Make sure the students refer to their chart as they are writing.

Part 2

Background (p. 110) Discuss mysteries and clues with the class. Explain that a mystery is something that is not fully understood. Sometimes mysteries can be solved, sometimes mysteries cannot be solved. Point out that mysteries are often solved by using clues. Clues are hints or things gathered as evidence that help a person solve a mystery. Explain that detectives are people who help solve crimes. Then ask students what tools they use in their everyday lives. How do these tools help them? What are they used for?

Vocabulary (p. 111) Explain that context clues are hints within a sentence that can often tell you what a word means.

They can help solve the mystery of the word's meaning. Use the examples on p. 111 to demonstrate context clues. Review each sentence on the board and ask students what context clues help define the vocabulary word. *(evidence = "such as fingerprints", etc.)* If necessary, write sentences on the board using these words and similar context. Point out the context clues to the class. For more difficult words such as *solution* review the dictionary entries with the students. Explain that many words have several different meanings. Have students try to pick out the correct definition from these entries.

Reading Strategy: Using a Graphic Organizer to Compare and Contrast (p. 111) Explain the difference between comparing and contrasting. Use examples found around the classroom to demonstrate, such as your desk and a student's desk. Use hand gestures to demonstrate the similarities between the two desks. Then do the same to show the differences. Remind students that a Venn diagram can be used to illustrate the differences and similarities between two things. On the board, create a Venn diagram that demonstrates the relationship between two simple things, such as oranges and bananas. Have students volunteer answers on how these two things are the same. *(Both are fruit; you can eat them.)* Then have them offer ideas on how they are different. *(different shape, different color)*

Teenage Detectives (pp. 112–117) Before students begin reading, explain what *plot* is. Point out that *plot* is what happens in a story, including the story problem, the events that lead to solving the problem, and the solution to the problem.

Activity 1: Have students identify the plot in the first story, "The Case of the Surprise Visitor." Guide them to give a general plot outline, not a chronological list of events. Then have students identify the problem in this story.

Activity 2: Before reading the second story, "The Case of the Defaced Sidewalk," have students stop before the solution is given. Ask students to identify the mystery in the story. Then, on the board create a chart labeled *Clues (What the text tells us).* Have students describe the facts of the story. Ask them leading questions, such as, *What do we know about Jenny? What do we know about Mitzi?*

Activity 3: For the third story, have students stop reading before they read the solution. Make a chart on the board listing each of the suspects in the story. *(Mrs. Stearns, Man with truck, Freddie)* Have students list what they know about each suspect. Then ask students if they can guess who the culprit is.

Comprehension (p. 118) Review the meanings of the comprehension chart heading with the class. Explain that the main characters are those that take the most active roles in the story. For example, in "The Case of the Disappearing Signs," make sure students can distinguish between main characters (Max, Nina, Mrs. Decker) and other characters (Mrs. Stearns, Freddie). Ask, *Why is Mrs. Decker a main character? (Because her sign was stolen. She is directly involved with the story's conflict.)* Finally, review *setting* with the class. Explain that setting is where the story takes place. Then review what a criminal is. A criminal is someone who has committed a crime.

How to Make a Friend Disappear (pp. 120–121) Explain that *materials* are things that can be used for something. Give examples of materials that you use while teaching. *(chalk, chalkboard, paper, books, etc.)* Then ask students what materials they use in class. Have them explain what they use these materials for. Explain that *method* is a way to do something, or a way of accomplishing a task. Use classroom materials to demonstrate method for accomplishing something simple. For example, for materials use a sheet of paper and scissors. Then demonstrate how to make paper snowflakes.

Discuss illusions with the class. Explain that illusions are tricks, or mistaken perceptions. Ask students to offer examples of illusions that they know of, such as magician tricks, rainbows, mirages, etc.

Water Trick (p. 122) As you review "Water Trick" with students, demonstrate the experiment in front of the class. Display a wide selection of materials on your desk. Present each one and ask students if it is needed for this experiment. After they have selected the proper materials, ask for volunteers to clearly read the steps to you. Follow the directions that they tell you. Did it work? After the experiment, have volunteers explain the "Why Is It So?" section in their own words.

Grammar: Imperatives (p. 124) Explain that *instruction* teaches you the way to do something, just as you are instructing the students to read and write better English. Explain that *direction* gives you guidance on how to do something, such as how to take certain courses so that you will improve your English. Explain that an *order* tells you to do something, such as complete a worksheet.

Explain that the *subject* is who or what the sentence is about. Go around the room using subjects in simple sentences. *(Alex is sitting in front of the class; I am speaking to the class, etc.)* Point out the subject in each sentence. *(Alex, I)* Use the board if necessary to demonstrate. Explain that when you speak to someone

with an *imperative sentence*, it is understood that the subject is the person you are talking to. When you read something, such a sign that says *Do Not Run*, it is understood that the subject is the person who is reading the sign. Explain that many imperatives are used as cautions: *Don't walk. Slow down*, etc.

Skills for Writing and Writing Assignment (pp. 125–126) Explain that a *flowchart* helps you put things in order. Demonstrate writing a flowchart by performing a simple task around the classroom. Ask students to give step-by-step instructions how to perform this task. Make sure students use imperative statements. As students offer these steps, have them write the steps down on a separate piece of paper. Once the task is completed, ask students to repeat the steps in order. Write them on the board in a chart similar to the one found on p. 126.

Put It All Together

Listening and Speaking Workshop: Instructions to Solve a Problem (p. 128) Begin this exercise by demonstrating with an example. Choose a problem that the students can relate to, such as being late to school. Have students offer ideas on how to solve this problem and write them on the board. Then break the problem down into steps by using a flowchart to show the process that leads to a solution. Review imperative sentences with the class. Use examples around the room to demonstrate the imperative, such as *Open your books, Turn to page 10*, etc. Then ask students to offer other examples of imperative sentences using examples found around the classroom.

Writing Workshop: Instructions for a Science Experiment (pp. 129–131) With the class, review the different parts of the imperative sentences used in the example on p. 130. Identify verbs, nouns, and prepositional phrases and how they are used in these imperative sentences. *(They tell you what to use, how to do it, etc.)* Before students begin writing, review the instructional pictures on p. 131. Identify the verbs, nouns, and prepositional phrases necessary to describe each step of the experiment.

Preview the Unit

UNIT CONTENT

Tell students that the first part of this unit includes a selection that will cover topics they might study in social studies. The article "Fact or Fiction?" explores a number of mysteries from the ancient past, including how the pyramids of Egypt were built and who might have created the mysterious monument of huge stones in England called Stonehenge. In the collection of short stories entitled "Truth or Lies?" students will encounter characters who only tell part of the truth. Each story ends with a question that will prompt students to reread the story and ask, *What is the whole truth?*

The second part of the unit includes a series of mystery stories under the title "Teenage Detectives," as well as two science experiments, "How to Make a Friend Disappear" and "Water Trick." Point out that students will learn how science and mysteries are interrelated.

UNIT **3**

Mysterious Ways

90

WORKSHOP PREVIEW

Listening and Speaking
Students will give a presentation that provides instructions for solving a problem at school.

Writing
Students will write instructions for a science experiment.

PROJECTS PREVIEW

Projects for this unit include:
- writing a mystery story
- drawing and writing about a mysterious place or creature
- conducting an experiment
- listening to a police detective describe his or her job
- performing a Readers' Theater

TEACHING RESOURCES

Lesson Plans	pp. 31–44
Summaries	pp. 33–40
Graphic Organizers	1–20
Audio Program	CD2/1–5; Cass.2/A
Workbook	pp. 57–84
CD-ROM	Unit 3
Video	Segment 3
Tests	Part Test, pp. 45–52
	Unit Test, pp. 99–107

PART 1
- "Fact or Fiction?"
- "Truth or Lies?" George Shannon

PART 2
- "Teenage Detectives," Carol Farley and Elizabeth Dearl
- "How to Make a Friend Disappear" and "Water Trick"

A mystery is something that is hard to explain or understand. In a mystery story, there is a problem to solve, or figure out. The characters in the story—and you, the reader—get clues, or hints, to solve the problem.

In Part 1, you will read an article about some historical mysteries. Is there a monster in a lake in Scotland? What are "lost cities"? Is there really a curse on King Tutankhamen's tomb? You will also read three short mystery stories. In each story, you will get clues to solve the mystery.

In Part 2, you will read three short stories about two cousins who solve mysteries in their neighborhood. In the final reading, you will learn about two science experiments that make mysterious things happen.

91

DISCUSS THE THEME

Read the unit title, "Mysterious Ways," aloud. Call on volunteers to define the word *mysterious* with an example. Then explain that the word *way* has several meanings, such as "a road or path," "a method of doing something," or "what one desires." Point out that a mysterious way can be anything from the unexpected results of a science experiment to an unexplained event or occurrence. Ask students:
- to tell about a time when something happened to them that they could not explain
- to discuss mysterious things they have seen or read about
- to determine why so many people find mysteries interesting and intriguing

Viewpoint

Have students read the first sentence on page 91 that defines the word *mystery*. Then ask them to look at the unit opener collage. Ask how the pictures relate to the concept of mystery.

QUICK WRITE

Ask students to write a sentence describing something that they find mysterious.

REACHING ALL STUDENTS

LANGUAGE LEVELS

Beginning: Hide an object in a bag. Model how to provide clues for students so they can guess what is in the bag. Then have student pairs find a mystery item to put in a bag. Ask partners to work together to develop clues for their item. Partners can present their clues while the class tries to guess what is in the bag.

Advanced: Write the following words on a word wall and discuss their meanings: *problem, clue, solution, solve, detective.* Have students write the words and their meanings in their notebooks. Then encourage students to use the words as they talk about mysteries they have seen or read.

OBJECTIVES

Explain to students that in Part 1 they will be reading about historic and scientific mysteries that they might study in science and social studies class. Read the list of objectives, encouraging students to join in for a choral reading. Explain the meaning of any difficult words or concepts. Ask students to restate the list of concepts and skills they will learn. Additional practice activities for these objectives can be found in the **Workbook** and **CD-ROM.**

BACKGROUND

Call on volunteers to read each section of the Background text. Have students look at the drawing as volunteers read aloud the statistics about the Great Pyramid and how it was built. Then read the questions and have students discuss them.

COOPERATIVE GROUPING

Pair intermediate and advanced students with beginning students. Ask students to take turns reading the paragraphs that describe the Egyptian Pyramids as well as the statistics that surround the illustration of the Great Pyramid at Giza. Have them discuss how they think the pyramids were made. Then have students discuss and answer the questions at the bottom of the page.

PART 1 — Prepare to Read

OBJECTIVES

LANGUAGE DEVELOPMENT

Reading:
- Vocabulary building: *Context, dictionary skills*
- Reading strategy: *Distinguishing fact and opinion*
- Text types: *Informational text, mystery*

Writing:
- Writing strategy: *Asking questions*
- Prepositions and prepositional phrases
- Descriptive paragraph

Listening/Speaking:
- Listen and respond to text
- Discuss a text
- Oral responses to text

Grammar:
- Present progressive
- Prepositional phrases

Viewing/Representing:
- Photos and art

ACADEMIC CONTENT
- Social studies vocabulary
- Historical places and creatures

BACKGROUND

"Fact or Fiction?" is a collection of mysteries that have puzzled people for centuries. They are nonfiction.

One such mystery concerns the Egyptian pyramids. These were monuments to the kings and queens who were buried inside them. About fifty pyramids have survived. How did the Egyptians lift the huge blocks to the top of the structures?

Make connections Look at the picture and some facts about the Great Pyramid at Giza in Egypt. Then discuss the questions.

The pyramid is as tall as a forty-story building.

It is made up of more than 2 million blocks of stone.

Each block weighs about 2,200 kilograms (5,000 lb.)— about the weight of a car.

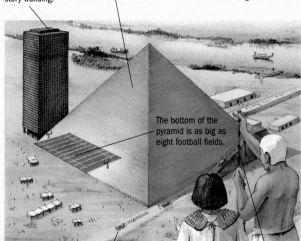

The bottom of the pyramid is as big as eight football fields.

20,000 workers took twenty years to build it.

Workers used logs and ramps.

Workers used a knotted string as a measurement tool.

1. What tools did the builders use to build the pyramids?
2. How do you think workers used logs and ramps to build the pyramids?
3. If a football field is 4,200 square meters (5,000 sq. yd.), how big is the bottom of the pyramid?

92

TEACHING GUIDE

PRETEACH	Provide Background	Read and discuss the Background information. Complete the activity. (ATE/SB p. 92)
	Present Concepts	Introduce the Reading Strategy. (ATE/SB p. 93)
TEACH	Monitor Comprehension	Informally monitor comprehension while students read the selection independently or in groups. (ATE/SB pp. 94–105)
	Teach and Practice	Present the Grammar, Usage, and Mechanics. (ATE/SB pp. 106, 107) Complete the Writing activity. (ATE/SB p. 108) Present Grammar, Phonics, and Spelling minilessons. (ATE pp. 94, 96, 98)
CONNECT	Connect to Literature	Have students read the literature and relate it to the informational reading. (ATE/SB pp. 102–104)
	Across the Curriculum	Present curriculum links as students read. (ATE pp. 96, 98)
ASSESS	Check Knowledge	Assess students' comprehension by having them complete the Check Your Knowledge section. (ATE/SB p. 109)
	Monitor Progress	Use one or more of the print assessment resources in the Assessment Package.
EXTEND	Integrate Language and Apply Understanding	Have students complete the Workshops (ATE/SB pp. 128–131) and choose a project from the Unit Projects. (ATE/SB p. 132) Then have them choose a book to read from Further Reading. (ATE/SB p. 133)

VOCABULARY

Read these sentences. Use the context to figure out the meaning of the **red** words. Use a dictionary to check your answers. Write each word and its meaning in your notebook.

1. The **archaeologist** dug in the ground and discovered an ancient Egyptian tomb.
2. Fingerprints and other **clues** helped the police find the criminal.
3. The **creature** was an unusual animal with six legs and no eyes.
4. No one knows why dinosaurs **disappeared** millions of years ago.
5. Scientists think that the monster isn't real but a **fantasy**.
6. A church, a temple, and a mosque are three kinds of **sacred** buildings.

LEARN KEY WORDS

archaeologist
clues
creature
disappeared
fantasy
sacred

READING STRATEGY

Distinguishing Fact and Opinion

A **fact** is a statement that someone can prove because there is evidence. It can be checked in such sources as textbooks or encyclopedias. An **opinion** is the statement of a belief that cannot be proved. For example, the statement "The Incas built the city of Machu Picchu in Peru" is a fact because historical evidence proves it is true. However, the statement "Some archaeologists believe that the Incas left Machu Picchu because of smallpox, a deadly disease" is an opinion because it cannot be proved. No one knows for sure why the Incas left Machu Picchu.

How can you distinguish between fact and opinion?

- **For facts:** Ask yourself, "Can this statement be proved?"
- **For opinions:** Look for such words as: *believe, think, feel, might, perhaps.*

93

VOCABULARY

Read the Key Words aloud, and have students repeat them after you. Then read the sentences and have students raise their hands when they hear the Key Word in each sentence. Model for students how to find the context clues in sentence 5: *In this sentence, I read that scientists think that a monster is a fantasy, and "isn't real." The phrase "isn't real" is a context clue that I can use to define the word* fantasy. *It is something that does not exist in real life.* Then have students find the context clues in sentence 1 and explain how to find words in the dictionary. Have students work with partners to complete the activity in their notebooks.

EXTEND THE LESSON

Have students use each Key Word in a sentence of their own.

READING STRATEGY

Read aloud the text for the Reading Strategy with students. Point out that a fact is a statement that can be supported with direct evidence in a text. An opinion is what a person or group believes or feels. It is how someone views or thinks about a subject. Explain to students that an opinion is not wrong; it's just not a statement of fact.

REACHING ALL STUDENTS

LANGUAGE LEVELS

Beginning: Add the Key Words to a word wall, using the following ideas to make the definitions of the Key Words as graphic as possible. Use encyclopedia pictures to define *archaeologist* and *monument.* Show pictures of snakes, lizards, and other animals to define *creature;* pictures of churches and temples to define *sacred;* and pictures of make-believe characters, such as Santa Claus, a dragon, and a unicorn, to define *fantasy.* Then put a paper clip on a table and cover it with a tissue, picking up both to make it look as though the clip *disappeared.* Have students find additional photos and illustrations to add to the word wall. Then have students discuss the words and definitions.

Teach

READING SUMMARY

The selection "Fact or Fiction?" looks at a variety of ancient mysteries, such as why the three Pyramids of Giza are grouped together, and whether mysterious creatures such as the Loch Ness monster or the giant squid really exist.

SCAFFOLDING

Have students listen to the CD/tape as they read silently, following along. Then ask them to take turns reading aloud from the selection.

GUIDED READING

1. What did Robert Bauval discover about the Pyramids of Giza? *(They are in the same position as the stars that make up Orion's Belt.)*
2. Which elements have damaged the Sphinx, hail, wind, or sand? *(Wind and sand have eroded the Sphinx.)*
3. Was Machu Picchu built in Egypt or Peru? *(It was built in Peru.)*

———— *Viewpoint* ————

Invite students to identify and describe what they see in the photographs on these pages. Ask them what mystery is shown in each photograph. *(Why are the pyramids grouped together? How old is the sphinx? Why was Machu Picchu abandoned?)* Ask students to describe any mysterious structures in their countries of origin.

FOCUS ON CONTENT **Science, Social Studies**

As you read, try to distinguish what is a fact and what is an opinion.

Fact or Fiction?

Path to the Stars?

About 4,500 years ago, the **pharaoh** Cheops and his son and grandson built the three Pyramids of Giza in Egypt. These pyramids were tombs, or places to bury the dead. For thousands of years, people didn't understand why these three pyramids were grouped together.

Then Belgian **engineer** Robert Bauval noticed that the shape of the three pyramids was the same as part of a group of stars in the sky called Orion's Belt. The whole group of stars—Orion—was sacred to the Egyptians. When Cheops died, he was buried in the Great Pyramid of Giza. The Egyptians made a shaft—or hole—in this pyramid. The shaft led from Cheops's tomb to the sky and the stars of Orion. Scientists believe that the Egyptians
(1) built this shaft so Cheops could fly from the pyramid to Orion. There, he would become a god.

---

pharaoh, ancient Egyptian ruler
engineer, person who plans how to build machines, roads, etc.

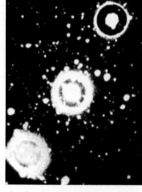

▲ The three stars of Orion's Belt

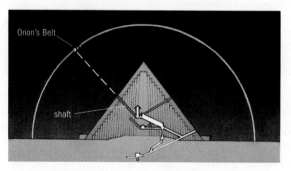

Orion's Belt

shaft

▲ The three Pyramids of Giza from high above

94

The Secret of the Sphinx

How old is the Sphinx? This question is one of the world's great mysteries. For thousands of years, wind and sand have **eroded** the Sphinx. Some archaeologists believe that water also damaged the Sphinx many **centuries** ago. Was the Sphinx once buried at the bottom of the sea? We don't know.

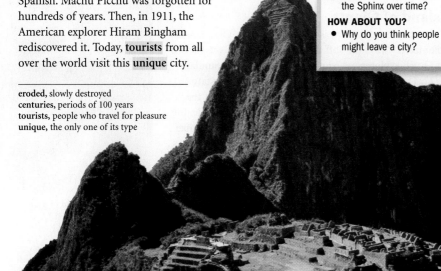

Mysterious Cities

Some ancient cities were abandoned and no one knows why. One of these cities is Machu Picchu, located about 2,440 meters (8,000 ft.) high in the Andes Mountains of Peru. The Incas built Machu Picchu from about 1460 to 1470 C.E. The Incas lived in parts of South America, including what is now Peru. They used stone blocks to build most of the buildings. The blocks fit together perfectly.

In the early 1500s, everyone left the city. No one knows why. Perhaps people died or left because of smallpox, a deadly disease that was brought by the Spanish. Machu Picchu was forgotten for hundreds of years. Then, in 1911, the American explorer Hiram Bingham rediscovered it. Today, **tourists** from all over the world visit this **unique** city.

▲ The Sphinx has the head of a man and the body of a lion.

eroded, slowly destroyed
centuries, periods of 100 years
tourists, people who travel for pleasure
unique, the only one of its type

BEFORE YOU GO ON . . .

1 Why do scientists think the Egyptians made a shaft in the Great Pyramid?

2 What has happened to the Sphinx over time?

HOW ABOUT YOU?
● Why do you think people might leave a city?

Teach

GUIDED READING

1. What are some of the things people believe Stonehenge might have been? *(temple to the sun, calendar, calculator)*
2. What covers much of Easter Island? *(large statues)*
3. What happened to six of the twenty-six people who opened Tutankhamen's tomb in 1922? *(They died within ten years.)*

across the curriculum

MATH   Tell students that the meter has been the official standard unit of measure in the United States since the nineteenth century. However, only in recent years have Americans made an increased effort to use the metric system in their daily lives.

The metric system was developed in Europe in the 1790s so that systems of measurement would become more uniform from country to country. To convert measurements in inches and feet to the metric system, use these guidelines: 1 inch is about 2.5 centimeters. 1 foot equals 30 centimeters. 40 inches (a little more than 1 yard) equal 1 meter. 1,000 meters equal 1 kilometer.

ACTIVITY: Have students solve the following conversion problems:

- If 40 inches equal 1 meter, and 1,000 meters equal 1 kilometer, how many inches would there be in one kilometer?
- A kilometer equals about 3,280 feet. If the Rapa Nui moved the heavy "moai" a distance of 23 kilometers, how far did they move it as measured in feet?

Stonehenge

Stonehenge is a mysterious monument of huge stones in England. Ancient peoples built Stonehenge about 5,000 years ago. No one really knows who these people were or why they built the monument.

Some people believe that Stonehenge was a **temple** to the sun. Other people believe that Stonehenge was a great stone calendar or **calculator**. They think the stones were arranged to measure the sun's movements, such as the summer and winter solstices—the longest and shortest days of the year. Perhaps Stonehenge was created to mark the rise of the sun and moon throughout the centuries. We may never know for sure.

▲ Some stones of Stonehenge came from 480 kilometers (300 mi.) away. How people moved them is a mystery.

Island of Giants

Easter Island is a tiny island in the Pacific Ocean, 3,620 kilometers (2,250 mi.) off the coast of Chile. It was named by Dutch explorers who arrived there on Easter Sunday, 1722. The island is covered with nearly 900 large **statues**, called "moai." Scientists believe they are the gods of the ancient people of Easter Island—the Rapa Nui people. But no one knows for sure. Another mystery is how the Rapa Nui people moved the heavy stones as far as 23 kilometers (14 mi.).

Archaeologists have found wooden tablets with the ancient language of the Rapa Nui people on it. No one knows how to read this language today. So the history of the Rapa Nui people is also a mystery. Only their great stone statues remain to watch over the island.

▲ The average height of a "moai" is 4 meters (13 ft.).

---

temple, holy building
calculator, instrument used to figure out mathematical problems
statues, shapes of people or animals made of stone, metal, or wood

96

SPELLING MINILESSON

Adding *-ing*
Write the following words with *-ing* on the board: *opening, stopping, including.* Say each word, emphasizing and underlining the word ending *-ing.* Above each word, write its root: *open, stop, include.* Ask students which word drops a letter when *-ing* is added. *(include)* State the rule that silent *e* is dropped when adding *-ing.* Ask students which word doubles the last consonant before adding *-ing. (stopping)* Then have students create a three-column chart in their notebooks with the following headings: Add *-ing;* Drop Silent *-e* before Adding *-ing;* Double the Final Consonant before Adding *-ing.* Write the following words related to the selection on the board and ask students to write them in the correct columns in their charts: *carving, rediscovering, believing, abandoning, fitting, swimming.* Then dictate the following words and have students add them to the correct columns in their charts: *playing, sitting, taking, keeping, riding, sitting.* Ask partners to trade notebooks to double-check the spellings. Then have students write sentences using each dictated word.

Curse of the Pharaoh

Tutankhamen was a pharaoh in ancient Egypt. When he died, Tutankhamen was buried in a tomb with gold and other treasures.

In 1922, a group led by British archaeologists Howard Carter and Lord Carnarvon opened the tomb of Tutankhamen. They found many treasures, including a beautiful gold mask. Some people believed that a **message** carved in the tomb wall said, "Death will **slay** with his wings whoever disturbs the peace of the pharaoh." Lord Carnarvon died soon after opening the tomb. According to one story, Carnarvon's dog died at the same time at his home in England. Then, five months after Carnarvon died, his younger brother died suddenly.

According to one report, six of the twenty-six people at the opening of Tutankhamen's tomb died within ten years. However, many other people who were there lived to be very old. Was there really a curse?

▲ Howard Carter and Tutankhamen's mummy

▲ Tutankhamen's mask

2

---

curse, wish that something bad happens to someone
message, information that is sent to someone
slay, kill

BEFORE YOU GO ON . . .

1 What is mysterious about Stonehenge and Easter Island?

2 What is the "curse of the pharaoh"?

HOW ABOUT YOU?
● What are two facts you learned about the pyramids, Stonehenge, or Easter Island? What are two opinions?

97

Have students respond orally or in writing to these questions:
● How do you think people without modern equipment moved the huge blocks of stone that make up Stonehenge 300 miles? *(Possible answer: They dragged them.)*
● Why is "Island of Giants" a good name for the story about Easter Island? *(The island contains many giant statues and stones.)*
● What do you think might be on the wooden tablets written by the Rapa Nui on Easter Island? *(Possible answer: how they lived and why they made the moai)*

MODELING THE READING STRATEGY

Skimming: Ask students why good readers often skim a text before reading it. Draw from students that skimming can help them determine what a text is about and whether it is fiction or nonfiction. Guide students as they skim the text on pages 98 and 99. Discuss with them what the major ideas are on these pages before they read.

———— *Viewpoint* ————

Ask students what the photographs reveal about Stonehenge, the "moai" of Easter Island, and the riches that were found in Tutankhamen's tomb.

REACHING ALL STUDENTS

LANGUAGE LEVELS

Beginning: Pronounce the following words from the text, and have students repeat them several times: *Stonehenge* (stōn • henj), *Rapa Nui* (ră • pə nōō'ē), *Tutankhamen* (tü • tăngk • ä • mən). Then have students discuss and define each word, using the pictures or the words in context as clues.

Advanced: Form three groups of students. Assign a different section of text to each group. Write the following questions on the board: *What is it? What is so mysterious about it?* Have groups answer the questions related to their section of text and report their ideas to the class.

GUIDED READING

1. What is the Loch Ness monster? *(a dinosaur-like creature with two black humps that some say lives in a lake in Scotland)*

2. How big are some of the giant squid that were recently found? *(They had 33-foot-long tentacles.)*

3. What do Bigfoot and Yeti look like, giant bears or giant apes? *(giant apes)*

Viewpoint

Have students describe the creatures shown on these two pages. Encourage them to discuss whether they believe each is real or make-believe.

across the curriculum

SCIENCE Tell students that scientists and archaeologists use evidence to prove or disprove ideas. They test their hypothesis, or idea, and record the results. Ask groups of students to form a hypothesis about the existence of one of the creatures mentioned in the reading. Then challenge them to do an Internet search for evidence to support or refute their hypothesis. Finally, have students write their conclusions and share them with the class.

Terrifying Tentacles

Scientists say we know more about Mars than we do about the mysteries at the bottom of the ocean. Giant octopuses and squid are one of those mysteries. **Octopuses** and **squid** are usually only about 60 to 90 centimeters (2–3 ft.) long. However, there are reports of bigger creatures with tentacles long enough to pull a ship underwater. In 1753, a man in Norway described a huge sea monster "full of arms" that was big enough to crush a large ship. More recently, giant squid have been discovered with tentacles 10 meters (33 ft.) long. Imagine eating **calamari rings** the size of truck tires!

Scary Monsters

Most people believe that dinosaurs disappeared millions of years ago. However, a few dinosaurs may have survived. The famous Loch Ness monster may be a living dinosaur-like reptile called a plesiosaur.

People first reported seeing the Loch Ness monster in April 1933 when a new road was built on the north shore of Loch Ness, a lake in Scotland. A man and woman saw a huge creature with two black **humps** swimming across the lake. Then two more people saw a strange animal crossing the road with a sheep in its mouth. There is now a Loch Ness Investigation Bureau, but most scientists believe that the Loch Ness monster is a fantasy.

---

tentacles, long arm-like parts
octopuses, sea creatures with eight long tentacles
squid, sea creatures with a long body and ten tentacles
calamari rings, sliced squid, often served fried or in a salad
humps, raised parts on the back of an animal

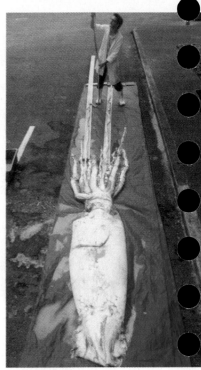

▲ A giant squid caught in the deep ocean off New Zealand. Giant squid live about 550 meters (1,800 ft.) beneath the sea.

This famous photograph of the Loch Ness monster is not authentic. The photographer tied a plastic head to a toy submarine. ▶

98

GRAMMAR MINILESSON

Adjective Placement in Compound Sentences

Recall the definitions of *noun* and *adjective*. Then write the following sentence on the board: *The sailboat was quiet, but the speedboat was loud.* Invite a volunteer to name and underline the adjectives in the sentence *(quiet, loud)* and circle the nouns they describe. *(sailboat, speedboat)*

Explain to students that in compound sentences, an adjective before the comma describes a noun in that part of the sentence, and an adjective after the comma describes a noun in that part of the sentence. Write the following sentences on the board, and have student pairs write the sentences, underline the adjectives, and circle the nouns they describe:

My coat is red, but her coat is blue.

We can go to the comic store, or we can go to the hobby store.

Ask each pair to read aloud a sentence, name the adjectives, and tell which noun each adjective describes.

◀ Bigfoot and Yeti look like giant apes.

Bigfoot and Yeti

There are stories about large ape-like creatures in **various** parts of the world. Different cultures give the creature different names. In the United States, for example, this creature is called Bigfoot or Sasquatch. In Tibet, it is called a yeti.

The first reports of Bigfoot date back to 1811. At that time, a man reported seeing footprints 36 centimeters (14 in.) long. In 1924, another man claimed that Bigfoot had kidnapped him. Each year many people in the United States claim to see Bigfoot. They often report seeing the creature in the forests of the Northwest.

Reports of a huge creature frightened the first European travelers in Tibet. (In Tibet, the word *yeti* means "manlike creature.") In 1951, a Mount Everest explorer found giant footprints in the snow.

Are there really creatures like the yeti and Bigfoot, or are they just stories? Bernard Heuvelmans (1916–1973), a famous **zoologist**, believed that the world is full of creatures still unknown to science. What do you think?

---

various, different
zoologist, scientist who studies animals

BEFORE YOU GO ON . . .

1 Do most scientists believe that the Loch Ness monster is real or a fantasy?

2 In the United States, where is Bigfoot usually seen?

HOW ABOUT YOU?
● Do you believe mysterious animals like the yeti or Loch Ness monster exist? What is your opinion?

99

Have students respond orally or in writing to these questions:
● Which of the creatures discussed on these pages do you believe are real? Why? *(Possible answer: giant squid, because a real one was discovered)*
● In your opinion, why do some people make up stories about fantastic animals? *(Answers will vary.)*

MODELING THE READING STRATEGY

Visualizing: Ask students to discuss why good readers visualize as they read, using adjectives and other descriptive words to create mental pictures. Draw from students that visualizing helps readers understand and enjoy what they read. Invite students to list some of the descriptive words that helped them to visualize the interesting creatures discussed on these two pages.

WEBSITES

For more information, log on to http://www.longman.com/shiningstar for links to other interesting websites about mysterious places and creatures.

REACHING ALL STUDENTS

LANGUAGE LEVELS

Beginning: Provide students with visuals to support additional vocabulary on these two pages, including a globe for *Earth* or *world,* a paper footprint for *footprint,* and pictures or plastic toy models of the following: a dinosaur, an ape, a sheep, and a camel for the word *humps.* Provide photographs for *lake, ocean,* and *snow.* List the vocabulary words on the board, and have students make labels that identify the visuals. Students can consult the visuals as they read or answer questions.

Advanced: Engage students in a debate as to whether any of the creatures described on these pages really exist. Ask students to write their opinion, using two to three details from the article to support it.

Review and Practice

COMPREHENSION

Invite volunteers to read the Comprehension directions with you. Discuss with them the elements of a good quiz, such as clear questions that have only one correct answer. Help students understand that the left column of the organizational chart lists topics to help them compose quiz questions. Then have students copy the chart and write their questions. Have students meet with a partner to ask and answer questions. After students share, have them respond to these questions:

1. Which of the quiz questions are about places? *(the first five)*
2. Which questions are about creatures? *(the last two)*

CRITICAL THINKING

After students complete the chart, have them discuss what they learned. Ask students to respond orally or in writing to these questions:

● What kinds of questions do you have about the mysterious places or creatures? *(Possible answer: Why do so many people believe in monsters?)*
● Which question on your chart do you think is the hardest to answer? Why? Which is the easiest? Why? *(Answers will vary.)*

COMPREHENSION

Reread "Fact or Fiction?" Then copy the chart into your notebook. Make a quiz for your classmates. Write one question in the chart about each of the mysteries. Compare your answers with a partner. How are your answers similar or different?

Mysterious Place or Creature	Question
The Great Pyramid	*Why did the Egyptians build this pyramid?*
Sphinx	*How do some archaeologists believe the Sphinx was damaged?*
Machu Picchu	
Stonehenge	
Easter Island	
Loch Ness monster	
Bigfoot and Yeti	

Work with a partner. Take turns asking and answering your questions.

100

EXTENSION

Copy the chart into your notebook. Choose one of the mysteries from "Fact or Fiction?" In the first column, write your topic and what you already know about it. In the second column, write a question you have about your topic. Then look for the answer to your question in an encyclopedia or other book, or on the Internet. Then write what you learned and how you learned it.

What I Know	What I Would Like to Know	What I Learned	How I Learned It

DISCUSSION

Discuss in pairs or small groups.

1. What do some people believe the Loch Ness monster is? What do you think it is? Why?
2. Which mystery do you think is the most interesting? Why?
3. What other mysteries do you know about? (For example, think about a mystery someone told you, you read about, or you saw in a movie.)
4. Imagine that a city in the United States was abandoned today, and archaeologists rediscovered it 100 years in the future. What clues might help them understand how people live today?
5. Do you think there are creatures in the world today that are unknown to science? Why or why not?

EXTENSION

Call on a volunteer to read the Extension directions. Ask each student to copy the chart into his or her own notebook. Then have students work in pairs to encourage discussion as they complete the chart. Remind students that one of the Reading Strategies they used while reading "Fact or Fiction?" was skimming. Encourage them to skim the selection to find the information they need to fill in the chart.

DISCUSSION

Have students read the questions and discuss them in pairs or small groups. After they have completed their discussion, ask volunteers to share what they learned with the class, giving details from the selection to support their answers.

METACOGNITION

Ask students:

1. How well do you think you understood "Fact or Fiction?" Why do you think so?
2. Did the diagram on page 94 help you to understand why scientists think a shaft was placed in the Great Pyramid? Why or why not?
3. How did the photographs help you to understand the information in the text?

REACHING ALL STUDENTS

LANGUAGE LEVELS

Beginning: As students complete the Extension chart, help beginning students form viable questions for research. Guide them to skim the text for ideas and think of a narrow topic of interest based on the text, such as Bigfoot. Then help them form a question about the topic.

Advanced: Encourage advanced students to check the spelling in the final drafts of their Extension charts. Then ask them to present the information orally to the class. Provide students with criteria they might use to evaluate oral reports, such as appropriate volume. Have them use this criteria to evaluate their presentations.

LEARNING MODALITIES

Auditory: Have an advanced student read aloud additional information about a topic in "Fact or Fiction?". Using an overhead projector, model strategies for listening for information, including taking notes or creating a web. Encourage students to copy and expand on your notes.

Connect

READING SUMMARY

"Truth or Lies?" is a collection of three short stories in which a variety of characters try to get out of trouble by only telling part of the truth. Students are asked to figure out the whole truth and the lie at the end of each story.

SCAFFOLDING

Read aloud the first story, asking students to try to figure out how the character tells the truth without telling the whole truth. Then have students listen to the rest of the selection on the CD/tape.

GUIDED READING

1. What truth did the man speak? *(He picked up a rope on the ground.)*
2. What part of the story did he not reveal? *(The rope was attached to a cow.)*
3. What truth did Helen speak? *(She did not touch one cookie.)*
4. What part of the story did she not reveal? *(She touched and ate all the others.)*

CONNECT TO LITERATURE **Short Stories**

In each of these three stories, the characters tell only part of the truth. As you read, try to figure out what the characters do not say. What is the whole truth? What are lies? Each story ends with a question. If you can't answer it, reread the story and look at the pictures to find the information you need.

Truth or Lies?

George Shannon

Stolen Rope

A man in Trinidad was being led through town on his way to jail. His hands were chained behind his back, and one of his ankles was chained to the officer who was leading him. As the two men neared the **village square**, a former neighbor of the arrested man passed by.

---

truth, what is true; the correct facts
lies, things that are not true
village square, central part of a village

"What have you done that you're in chains and sentenced to jail?"

The chained man sighed. "I picked up a rope I found on the ground."

"You poor man!" said the neighbor. "There's more **injustice** in the **courts** than I realized."

"I know. It's terrible. Please tell them to set me free."

The man being taken to jail had spoken the truth, but he was also far from **innocent.**

What is the truth, the whole truth? And where's the lie?

The Whole Truth ——————

While it was true that the thief was being **punished** for picking up a rope, he was lying by what he did *not* say. The rope he picked up was tied to a cow.

---

injustice, unfairness
courts, places where someone is asked about a crime
innocent, not guilty of doing something wrong
punished, made to suffer because of doing something wrong

102

Tell students that in his *Stories to Solve* series, George Shannon explores folktales from around the world that contain mysteries and other puzzles to solve. His books are recommended as an introduction to multicultural folklore and are true to the cultures from which they are derived. For example, the excerpt from one of his stories, which appears on page 102, is set in Trinidad. Invite students to select other stories by George Shannon to read independently for pleasure. Ask them to keep a record of the places in which the stories are set.

The Cookie Jar

Helen's mother had finished baking a batch of cookies when a neighbor came over and asked for help.

"I'll just be gone a few minutes," said her mother as she put the cookies into the cookie jar. "No snacking while I'm next door. These are for the party tonight."

When Helen's mother returned and checked the cookie jar, there was only one cookie left.

"Helen!" she called as she stomped upstairs. "I told you *not* to eat those cookies I made for the party tonight."

"I didn't touch one," said Helen. ②

"Well, they sure didn't fly away on their own! You can stay in your room till you decide to tell the truth."

What is the truth, the whole truth?
And where's the lie?

The Whole Truth

Helen's exact words, "I didn't touch one," were true. She had not touched *one* cookie, the only one she'd left in the jar uneaten. She had, however, touched—and eaten—all the rest.

---

batch, group of things
on their own, by themselves

BEFORE YOU GO ON . . .

① What reason did the man from Trinidad give for going to jail? Why was he really going to jail?

② What did Helen tell her mother? Did she tell the truth?

HOW ABOUT YOU?

- Do you think the man from Trinidad and Helen deserved to be punished?

103

Have students respond orally or in writing to these questions:

- Why didn't Helen or the man under arrest tell the truth? *(Possible answer: They were trying not to get in trouble for their actions.)*
- What problems did their actions and lies cause? *(Possible answer: Someone could have lost their cow; Helen's mother will have to make more cookies.)*

MODELING THE READING STRATEGY

Distinguishing Fact and Opinion: Recall with students that a fact is a statement that can be supported with direct evidence in a text. An opinion is what a person or group thinks or feels. Ask students how the man's statement about the rope can be proven true or false.

Viewpoint

Tell students that the illustration on page 102 tells the whole story. Ask them to tell the story that the picture shows. Then ask them to study the picture on page 103 and explain how it helps solve the mystery of the missing cookies.

REACHING ALL STUDENTS

LANGUAGE LEVELS

Beginning: Help students analyze the picture on page 102 by asking them to find the rope that is on the ground. Then ask them to find the sentence in the story that tells what the man said about finding a rope. Ask students to follow the rope in the picture and find what it is attached to. Encourage discussion.

Advanced: In advanced students' books, cover "The Whole Truth" boxes with self-adhesive removable notes. Encourage students to use the text and pictures to try to figure out the whole truth. Ask them to share predictions with partners before removing the notes and reading what is in the boxes.

LEARNING MODALITIES

Visual: Invite students to draw a picture that shows what really happened to the cookies in "The Cookie Jar." Ask them to reread the text and study the illustration on page 103 to find details that might reveal what happened. Then invite students to display their drawings and explain their ideas to the class.

T103

School Days

A boy came running into the house for a snack after school and gave his mother a hug.

"How was your day?" asked his mother.

1 The boy grinned. "I got **a hundred** on my math and history tests!"

"That's wonderful," said his mother. "We'll celebrate with a special supper tonight."

It was a delicious meal, but when **report cards** came the next week, the boy's mother discovered there had been nothing to celebrate after all.

2 "How could you get an F in history and a D in math when you didn't miss anything on your tests last week? Did they catch you **cheating**? I certainly hope you weren't telling me lies!"

"Oh, no," answered the boy. "I'd never cheat. And as sure as I didn't cheat, I told you the truth."

His mother **grumbled** and frowned. "Well, something's not what it seems to be. I'm sure of that."

What is the truth, the whole truth?
And where's the lie?

The Whole Truth

The boy had gotten a hundred on his math and history tests. But it was a **combined score** of 100 for both tests—a 60 on the math test and a 40 on the history test.

---

a hundred, 100—a perfect score
report cards, documents giving a student's grades
cheating, doing something that is not honest
grumbled, complained in a quiet but angry way
combined score, total amount

104

About the Author

George Shannon

George Shannon (1952–) has written many books for young people, including *Stories to Solve* and *More Stories to Solve*. Shannon likes writing short, lighthearted stories about serious themes.

BEFORE YOU GO ON . . .

1 What score did the boy say he got on his math and history tests?

2 What grades did he get on his report card?

HOW ABOUT YOU?
- Why do you think the boy lied about his grades?

Link the Readings

Think about the text "Fact or Fiction?" and reread "Truth or Lies?" Then copy the chart into your notebook and complete it. Compare your charts in small groups.

Title of Selection	Type of Text (Genre)	Fiction or Nonfiction	Purpose of Selection	Mystery I Liked Best
"Fact or Fiction?"	*informational text*		*to inform and entertain*	
"Truth or Lies?"		*fiction*		

DISCUSSION

Discuss in pairs or small groups.

1. Look at the chart you made. What two mysteries did you like best? Why?
2. Some mysteries in "Fact or Fiction?" might never be solved. Others might be solved. Choose one mystery that you think might or might not be solved and explain your answer.
3. In "Truth or Lies?" each character tells a half-truth. Find this sentence and discuss why it tells only part of the truth.
4. Imagine you are a group of archaeologists. You must choose a mysterious historical site to study. Which place will you choose? Why?

105

REFLECTION

Have volunteers take turns reading the Reflection directions. Then read the headings on the chart with students and discuss their meanings. Have students skim the selections before they copy and complete the chart. Discuss their finished charts. Then ask:

1. Which text is nonfiction? *("Fact or Fiction?")*
2. What purpose did the author have for writing "Truth or Lies?" *(to entertain)*

DISCUSSION

Read the questions together, and have students discuss them in pairs or small groups. After the discussion, ask groups to report their answers. Encourage beginning students to become involved when they can. For example, for Discussion question 4, beginning students might point to a picture that illustrates the site they have chosen.

COOPERATIVE GROUPING

Pair beginning students with intermediate and advanced students. Ask them to discuss the missing information from the chart and record responses in their notebooks. Ask pairs to discuss and explain their responses.

CRITICAL THINKING

Discuss the mysteries in the selections. Ask students to share which of the mysteries they like best.

REACHING ALL STUDENTS

LANGUAGE LEVELS

Beginning: To help students understand "School Days," discuss the meaning of the idiom "got a hundred on a test." Make a connection with percentages, pointing out that 100% means "everything" or "all," and that 50% means "half." Show a glass 100% full and another 50% full. Then show a paper with everything correct and marked with 100%. Explain to students that this means the same as "a hundred."

Advanced: Invite a group of students to locate the part of the story where the boy in "School Days" was less than truthful. Have them discuss the options the boy had regarding what he would tell his mother. Invite them to present different possible conversations that the boy and his mother could have had, one of which includes the boy being totally truthful.

Connect to Writing

GRAMMAR

Explain that the present progressive is used to express an action that is happening right now. Read the information about the present progressive on page 106 aloud with students, and discuss the examples in the charts. After students have had time to study the picture, invite volunteers to write some of their sentences on the board. Have other students identify the present progressive in the examples. Then have students work independently or in pairs to complete the Practice activity. Students should record the sentences in their notebooks.

SCAFFOLDING

Have students create three-column charts with the following headings: *be* + verb + *-ing;* drop the final *-e* before adding *-ing;* double the final consonant before adding *-ing.* As students find examples of the present progressive in their reading, have them write the words in the correct columns in the chart.

GRAMMAR

The Present Progressive

The **present progressive** describes an action that is happening now. The present progressive uses a form of *be* with a verb + *-ing.*

I **am looking** at a pyramid.	*They* **are visiting** the ancient city.
He **is taking** a picture.	*We* **are swimming** in the lake.
She **is eating** a cookie.	*You* **are telling** the truth.
It **is raining** today.	

Note: When the verb ends in *-e,* drop the *-e* before adding *-ing.*

tak**e**	tak**ing**

Some verbs double the final consonant before adding *-ing.*

swi**m**	swim**ming**

Practice

Look at the picture. In your notebook, write sentences about what the people are doing. Use the present progressive. Here are some phrases to help you.

take a picture	move a stone	visit an ancient city
eat a cookie	drink water	read a map

Example: *A man is taking a picture.*

106

SKILLS FOR WRITING

Using Prepositional Phrases
Some **prepositions** show place—where people or things are located. A **prepositional phrase** is a preposition + a noun or pronoun. You can use prepositional phrases to tell where people or things are.

Prepositions	Prepositional Phrases
under	The dog is *under* the table.
behind	The cow is *behind* it.
next to	The statue is *next to the cookie jar*.
in	The cookies are *in* it.
between	The sun is *between the pyramids*.
near	The man is *near* them.
on	The apples are *on the plate*.

Read this paragraph about the picture on page 106. Then answer the question.

Natalia Dare

At the Pyramids

There are people and animals from all over the world visiting the pyramids. A girl is digging in the sand, a dog is running with a bone in its mouth, and a stork is carrying a baby with its beak. A girl is reading a map, a camel is bathing in a tub, a woman is looking at a bone lying on the sand, and a man is standing behind a palm tree. A man with a surfboard is running, a snake is coming out of a basket in front of a tent called the Sands Hotel, and a camel is wearing sunglasses.

Describe what other people and animals are doing in the picture. Use prepositional phrases and the present progressive.

107

SKILLS FOR WRITING

Have a volunteer read the introductory text about prepositional phrases. Point out that the examples in the chart give information about the picture on page 106. Ask a volunteer to read the list of prepositions in the first column of the chart. Tell students that there are many more prepositions than the ones listed. Then have students take turns reading the sentences in the chart. Ask a volunteer to read the sample paragraph. Have students find the prepositional phrases in the paragraph and ask them to study the picture on page 106. Encourage them to use prepositional phrases as they describe other aspects of the picture.

SCAFFOLDING

As students read the writing sample on page 107, have them find the part of the picture on page 106 that matches the text.

REACHING ALL STUDENTS

LANGUAGE LEVELS

Beginning: The correct use of prepositional phrases is sometimes difficult to master, because different languages use different meanings for doing the same action. For example, in some languages you walk *over* or *under* a door. Support students by modeling the prepositional phrases used to describe the various positions of objects in the illustration on page 106. Have students repeat what you say and then point to what is being described. Then let students describe the positions of people in the illustration. Do not directly correct approximations. Instead, focus on what is said correctly and offer a correct response. For example, if a student were to say "A boy is under a pyramid," you could respond "The boy is on the pyramid." Then have students write a few sentences about the illustration and share them with the class.

WRITING ASSIGNMENT

Descriptive Paragraph

Read the directions together. Remind students to use the present progressive and prepositional phrases in their writing. Then ask students to reread the paragraph on page 107 to locate examples of present progressive verbs and prepositional phrases. List them on the board. Discuss how the present progressive verbs and the prepositional phrases help readers visualize what is taking place.

WRITING STRATEGY

Explain that asking questions is helpful when writing as well as when reading. Have students form groups to study the picture on the page and discuss the answers to the bulleted questions. Have each group create a web to record their ideas. Encourage students to think of other questions they might ask as they look at the picture. Then encourage students to use their webs to help them write a description of the picture.

USING THE EDITING CHECKLIST

Read the Editing Checklist aloud with students. Ask them to reread it with a partner and use the checklist to edit their writing together.

WRITING ASSIGNMENT

Descriptive Paragraph

You will write a description of the picture below, using the present progressive and prepositional phrases.

1. **Read** Reread the paragraph on page 107. How do the prepositional phrases help the reader visualize the people and things in the picture?

> *Writing Strategy: Asking Questions*
>
> Before you describe a picture, ask yourself questions about what you see. The writer of "At the Pyramids" asked herself these questions before writing her description.
>
> - *Who is in the picture?*
> - *Where are they?*
> - *What are they doing?*
>
> Answer these questions when you plan your description.

2. **Write** Write a description of the picture, using the answers to your questions. Use prepositional phrases and the present progressive.

EDITING CHECKLIST

Did you . . .

▶ include prepositional phrases?

▶ use the present progressive correctly?

▶ indent the first sentence in the paragraph?

▶ start each sentence with a capital letter?

▶ end each sentence with a period?

108

PART REVIEW 1

Check Your Knowledge

Language Development

1. What is the difference between a fact and an opinion? Give an example of each.
2. What is a mystery? What do mystery writers do to help readers solve a mystery story?
3. Give examples of three sentences using the present progressive.
4. What do prepositional phrases tell us? Give examples.

Academic Content

1. What new science and social studies vocabulary did you learn in Part 1? What do the words mean?
2. What does an archaeologist do?
3. What is mysterious about the three Pyramids of Giza?
4. What are two mysteries about Easter Island?

▲ An archaeologist works on a dinosaur's jaw.

109

ASSESS

You can assess students' knowledge of the unit in several different ways.

Portfolio: Students can include the answers to Check Your Knowledge in their portfolios.

Traditional: Students can complete the Check Your Knowledge questions as a quiz. After students complete Check Your Knowledge, use the Assessment Package. Students can complete the the Part Test on pages 45–48. For further practice, have students complete the Test Preparation worksheets.

Performance: Have students complete Check Your Knowledge orally with partners as you monitor them to clarify the meaning of each question.

TEST-TAKING TIP

Remind students that they should always raise their hand for help if they do not know the meaning of a word. See the Test Preparation pages in the Assessment Guide for additional test-taking strategies.

METACOGNITION

Invite two advanced students to model the language needed to complete the Check Your Knowledge questions. Then let all students rehearse it.

REACHING ALL STUDENTS

LANGUAGE LEVELS

Beginning: Have beginning students complete Check Your Knowledge in one-on-one conferences with you. Read aloud each question, offering help with word meaning as necessary. Keep anecdotal records of the conferences.

Advanced: Let pairs of advanced students record their Check Your Knowledge answers into a tape recorder. Then have them listen to the tape and improve the wording of their responses. Allow time for them to repeat the activity.

Preteach

OBJECTIVES

Explain to students that in Part 2 they will continue reading about the kinds of mysteries and solutions that they might study in science class. Have students read the list of objectives aloud with you. Pause from time to time and have students paraphrase the objectives. Then ask students to restate the list of things they will learn. Additional practice activities for these objectives can be found in the **Workbook** and **CD-ROM**.

BACKGROUND

Have volunteers read the opening paragraphs aloud. Invite students to talk about detectives they have seen on television. Then have a volunteer read the Make Connections section aloud. Invite students to discuss possible answers. *(Possible answer: Detectives use the tools to see, to hear, to record clues, and to communicate with others.)*

COOPERATIVE GROUPING

Form small groups of students, varying the language proficiency levels of the members. Ask each group to read the Background page and answer the question. Invite students from different groups to share their answers. Ask volunteers to explain their answers.

PART 2 — Prepare to Read

OBJECTIVES

LANGUAGE DEVELOPMENT

Reading:
- Vocabulary building: *Context, dictionary skills*
- Reading strategy: *Compare and contrast*
- Text types: *Mysteries, instructions*
- Literary elements: *Suspense, plot*

Writing:
- Writing strategy: *Flowchart*
- Treasure hunt clues
- Science experiment steps
- Punctuation and capitalization

Listening/Speaking:
- Instructions for science experiments
- Read instructions to an audience
- Support spoken ideas with evidence

Grammar:
- Imperative sentences

Viewing/Representing:
- Diagrams in science experiments

ACADEMIC CONTENT
- Science vocabulary
- Draw conclusions
- Follow steps of science experiments

BACKGROUND

Teenage Detectives includes three short mystery stories. A mystery story contains a problem that has to be solved. The main character or characters gather clues to solve the case. In these stories, the two teenage detectives like to solve mysteries in their neighborhood.

A detective is someone who tries to solve mysteries. For example, a detective tries to find out who has committed a crime. A detective is usually good at asking questions.

Make connections Detectives use special tools to help them with their job. Look at the picture. How do you think the detectives might use these tools?

110

TEACHING GUIDE

PRETEACH	Provide Background	Read and discuss the Background information. Complete the activity. (ATE/SB p. 110)
	Present Concepts	Introduce the Reading Strategy. (ATE/SB p. 111)
TEACH	Monitor Comprehension	Informally monitor comprehension while students read the selection independently or in groups. (ATE/SB pp. 112–117)
	Teach and Practice	Present the Grammar, Usage, and Mechanics. (ATE/SB pp. 124, 125) Complete the Writing activity. (ATE/SB p. 126) Present Grammar, Phonics, and Spelling minilessons. (ATE pp. 112, 114, 116)
CONNECT	Connect to Content	Have students read the informational reading and relate it to the literature. (ATE/SB pp. 120–122)
	Across the Curriculum	Present curriculum links as students read. (ATE pp. 114, 120)
ASSESS	Check Knowledge	Assess students' comprehension by having them complete the Check Your Knowledge section. (ATE/SB p. 127)
	Monitor Progress	Use one or more of the print assessment resources in the Assessment Package.
EXTEND	Integrate Language and Apply Understanding	Have students complete the Workshops (ATE/SB pp. 128–131) and choose a project from the Unit Projects. (ATE/SB p. 132) Then have them choose a book to read from Further Reading. (ATE/SB p. 133)

VOCABULARY

Read these sentences. Use the context to figure out the meaning of the **red** words. Use a dictionary to check your answers. Write each word and its meaning in your notebook.

1. The detective solved the **case** of the stolen treasure.
2. He looked for **evidence**, such as fingerprints, to find the thief.
3. The thief was **guilty** of the crime, and the judge sent him to jail.
4. The "doctor" was a **phony**! She'd never gone to medical school!
5. We had all the information, so the **solution** to the problem was not difficult.
6. The boys are always **up to mischief**, so they are often punished.

LEARN KEY WORDS

case
evidence
guilty
phony
solution
up to mischief

READING STRATEGY

Using a Graphic Organizer to Compare and Contrast

When you **compare**, you find similarities—things that are the same. When you **contrast**, you find differences—things that are different.

Good readers write notes in a chart (such as a Venn diagram) when they need to compare and contrast two or more texts, or something within a text, such as characters. Charts and Venn diagrams help readers to see and remember information. Try using a graphic organizer to compare and contrast the main characters, the settings, the crimes, and the criminals.

"The Case of the Surprise Visitor" — *money stolen*

Both stories — *mystery*

"The Case of the Defaced Sidewalk" — *sidewalk defaced*

111

VOCABULARY

Read the Key Words aloud, and have students repeat them after you. Then read the sentences and have students raise their hands when they hear the Key Word in each sentence. Model for students how to find the context clues in sentence 3: *In this sentence, I read that the thief was guilty. If I'm not sure what the word* guilty *means, the phrase* the judge sent him to jail *can help me to figure it out.* Guilty *must mean that the thief committed the crime; otherwise, the thief would not be going to jail.* Then have students find context clues in the other sentences, and explain how to find words in the dictionary. Have students work with partners to complete the activity in their notebooks.

READING STRATEGY

Ask a volunteer to read the Reading Strategy aloud. Have students tell in their own words what *compare* and *contrast* mean. Then draw a Venn diagram on the board and write *same* in the intersecting section and *different* in the two sections outside of the intersecting area. Ask students to look at the Venn diagram on page 111 to find out how the stories they are about to read compare. *(They are both mysteries.)* Then model how to use a Venn diagram to compare and contrast two familiar stories, such as "Stolen Rope" and "The Cookie Jar" on pages 102 and 103. Have students record the Venn diagram in their notebooks.

REACHING ALL STUDENTS

LANGUAGE LEVELS

Beginning: Read aloud each Key Word and the sentence in which it appears. Work with students to find its meaning in context. Then model how to use guide words to find each word in a dictionary. Explain that clues for "up to mischief" can be found under the word *mischief* in the dictionary.

Advanced: Show students how to create a four-column chart with the following headings: *Words, What I Think It Means, What It Means, Where I Found It.* Then have students copy the chart into their notebooks and use it as they work with partners to figure out the meanings of the Key Words. Have them write the dictionary page on which they find the word in the "Where I Found It" column.

READING SUMMARY

Max and Nina are teenage cousins who have a talent for noticing details that others do not see. They use their talent to find clues and solve mysteries.

SCAFFOLDING

Have students listen to the CD/tape as they read the selection silently to themselves.

MODELING THE READING STRATEGY

Predicting: Remind students that predicting what will happen next in a story will help them to set a purpose for reading. Have students read the first paragraph on page 113. Have students stop reading and describe what they think will happen next.

GUIDED READING

1. Who are the characters in the story? *(Max, a man with a briefcase, Miss Fritz)*
2. What does the tall man do with the envelope? *(He drops it in the mailbox.)*

—Viewpoint—

Have students look at the illustration and make a list of adjectives to describe the setting and characters.

FOCUS ON LITERATURE **Mystery Stories**

As you read the three mystery stories, think about how the stories, the characters, and the settings are similar or different.

Teenage Detectives

Teenage cousins Max and Nina love solving crimes in their town, Harborville. See if you can find the solutions to the following mysterious cases.

112

PHONICS MINILESSON

Digraphs *sh, ph, th*

Say the following sentence aloud: *She phoned Max and told him about the thief.* Have students repeat it. Then write the word *she* on the board and circle the letters *sh*. Say the word, emphasizing the initial sound. Point out that the letters *s* and *h* are not blended, but work together to represent one sound. Have students repeat the following words after you: *shy, shin, ship.* Encourage them to name other words that contain the sound /sh/. Repeat the activity with digraphs *ph* (*phonics, graph, elephant*) and *th.* For *th,* use the words *the* and *thief.* Explain that the letters *th* represent two different sounds in these words, the voiced sound in *the* and the unvoiced sound in *thief.* Then have students look through "The Case of the Surprise Visitor" to find words that contain digraphs *sh, ph,* and *th.* Students can create a three-column chart in their notebooks to record the words they find. Examples include: <u>sh</u>owed, penman<u>sh</u>ip, ca<u>sh</u>ed; <u>ph</u>one, <u>ph</u>ony; <u>th</u>e, <u>th</u>en, <u>th</u>ing, some<u>th</u>ing, <u>th</u>ink, <u>th</u>at. Point out that in *courthouse* the *th* is not a digraph, because the word is actually a compound word made up of the words *court* and *house.*

The Case of the Surprise Visitor

Carol Farley

The clock in the courthouse ahead of Max showed six o'clock. As it began **chiming**, he noticed a tall man with a **briefcase** walking toward him. The man turned around, looked at the clock, and then quickened his steps. He took an envelope out of his briefcase, dropped it in a mailbox, and continued on his way. Max moved faster, too. Miss Fritz, Harborville's oldest music teacher, had invited him for dinner. He didn't want to be late.

"I'm glad you could come," Miss Fritz said. "I've made a lovely salad for us." She **gestured** Max to a chair. "Good thing I prepared ahead. A **surprise** visitor just left."

"Who visited?" Max asked.

"A teacher from Harborville's School for the Deaf. He was totally **deaf** himself, poor man, but he could **read lips** perfectly. He had the loveliest **penmanship** when he wanted to tell me something."

"Why was he here?" Max asked.

LITERARY ELEMENT

Stories with *suspense* make the readers ask themselves, "I wonder what will happen next?" Can you find an example of suspense?

---

chiming, making a sound like a bell
briefcase, case for carrying papers or books
gestured, used hands to tell something
surprise, unexpected
deaf, hearing impaired
read lips, understand a speaker by looking at his or her lips
penmanship, handwriting

"Well, evidently the school **is low on funds**. I was glad to help out. I had just cashed my social security check so I was able to give him five hundred dollars." **①**

"Did he just leave? Was he a tall man with a briefcase?"

"Yes."

"We'd better phone the police. I think that man was a phony. I know for sure he wasn't totally deaf."

How did Max figure it out?

The clock was behind the man as he was walking, so he could not have seen it. He turned around at the sound of the chimes, so he obviously heard them and therefore was not deaf. **②**

"You didn't waste time solving this case," Nina told Max later.

"Just watch me solve another one soon," Max answered.

LITERARY ELEMENT

The *plot* is the sequence of events in a story or novel. Each event results from the previous event and then causes the next event to happen. Most plots involve characters and a conflict.

---

is low on funds, doesn't have much money

BEFORE YOU GO ON . . .

① What does Miss Fritz give the deaf man?

② How does Max figure out the deaf man is a phony?

HOW ABOUT YOU?
- Did you guess that the man was a phony? How?

113

Have students respond orally or in writing to these questions:

- How do you know Miss Fritz did not expect anyone other than Max? *(She called the tall man a surprise visitor.)*
- Why do you think the man wrote things down for Miss Fritz? *(Possible answer: He was pretending to be deaf.)*

LITERARY ELEMENT

Ask a volunteer to read the Literary Element text in the two boxes. Explain that a writer uses suspense by giving the reader small pieces of important information, a little at a time, instead of stating what is happening all at once. This careful use of language keeps the reader engaged in the story. Then explain that a plot is what happens in a story, including the story problem or conflict, the events that lead to solving the problem, and the solution to the problem.

ACTIVE READING

Have students make a four-column chart in their notebooks with the following headings: *Characters, Setting, Crime/Main Events, Ending*. Explain to students that they will use this chart to record information about each of the mystery stories and then use the information to compare the texts.

REACHING ALL STUDENTS

LANGUAGE LEVELS

Beginning: Reread the story with students and record the main events on the board. Form groups of three students. Invite each group to use ideas from the board to create a skit that shows what happened in the story. Have groups share their skits.

Advanced: Ask advanced students to listen as you reread the story. Have students close their books to rely solely on what they hear. Then have students work in pairs and review the text to see what information they missed as you read aloud. Have pairs share the missing information with the class and tell why they think they missed it during your oral reading.

Teach

GUIDED READING

1. What crime has been committed in "The Case of the Defaced Sidewalk"? *(Footprints are left in wet cement.)*
2. Who jumped in the cement in "The Case of the Defaced Sidewalk"? *(Mitzi)*
3. What is the crime in "The Case of the Disappearing Signs"? *(Mrs. Decker's FOR SALE signs are stolen.)*
4. How many people live on Norton Drive? *(Mrs. Stearns is the only person who lives on Norton Drive.)*

——— *Viewpoint* ———

Invite students to study the illustration on page 114 to predict what the crime in the story might be.

across the curriculum

HISTORY Tell students that the Three Musketeers are characters in a historical romance of the same name written by Alexandre Dumas in 1844. They are known for the saying, "All for one and one for all," because they supported one another. Explain that this term is sometimes used to describe good friends who stick together and help one another through good times and bad. Have students research the characters and events on which the story is based and gather three facts to report to the class.

The Case of the Defaced Sidewalk

Carol Farley

One Saturday morning, Nina saw the **three musketeers** in the mall. Jenny, Brittany, and Mitzi called themselves the three musketeers because they were always together.

"I've been shopping for **sandals**," Jenny told Nina. "But I have such a wide foot nothing seems to fit. We've been looking everywhere."

"And it's been slow going," Mitzi added. "On account of Brittany's—"

"I know," Nina said, looking at Brittany. "I heard you **sprained** your ankle in gym yesterday. Does it still hurt a lot?"

"It's okay as long as I move really slowly," Brittany told her. "We're going to get ice cream at the Just Desserts Shop now. Want to join us?"

"Better not. Max is meeting me at home. See you later."

Nina was **taking a shortcut** through Harborville's city park when she saw Mr. Hansen kneeling beside a new sidewalk. The **city maintenance man** frowned as she drew closer.

❶ "Somebody jumped right in the middle here while the cement was still wet," he said, pointing at two narrow footprints

embedded in the concrete. "Now I'll have to rip out this section and redo it. I sure can't leave the sidewalk looking like this!"

"Any idea of who did it?" Nina asked.

"A kid over there on the slide said that three girls named Brittany, Mitzi, and Jenny were the only ones near here. But he doesn't know which one ruined my sidewalk."

"I know who did it," Nina declared.

How did Nina figure it out? ———

The footprints were narrow. Jenny has wide feet. Brittany couldn't have jumped because of her sprained ankle. So Mitzi had to be the guilty one.

"You were able to walk into a quick solution for this case," Max told Nina later. "I sure am glad that I'm on your side."

"I had concrete evidence," Nina answered.

---

defaced, damaged
Three Musketeers, a book about three characters who share adventures
sandals, open shoes worn in warm weather
sprained, hurt but didn't break
taking a shortcut, going a faster way
city maintenance man, man who fixes and cleans things for a city

114

SPELLING MINILESSON

Number Words

Identify what a number word is by pointing out the number words in the two stories. *(page 114: one, two, three)* Then write numerals 1 through 25 on the board. Below the numerals, write the corresponding number words. Draw a line between the numerals 12 and 13, 19 and 20, and 20 and 21 to separate them. Point out that the number words for one through twelve do not follow a spelling pattern. Then ask students what the number words for thirteen through nineteen have in common. *(They end in "teen.")* Have students notice the spelling pattern in twenty-one through twenty-five. *(They each begin with "twenty" and include a hyphen.)* Encourage students to tell you how they think the following number words are written: *forty-eight, sixty-six, fifty-two.* Then erase all the number words from the board, leaving the numerals. Challenge students to write four or five of the number words you erased in their notebooks. Call on volunteers to share their work by writing the number words on the board underneath the correct numerals.

The Case of the Disappearing Signs

Elizabeth Dearl

Nina was eating cold pizza for lunch at Max's house one hot July day. Max's mom, Mrs. Decker, a **real-estate agent**, came in looking warm and weary.

"I'm so **disgusted**," she said. "Remember that old house over on Norton Drive that I **listed**? I put a FOR SALE sign up in the yard early this morning. I just drove by now and it's gone. This is the third sign this month that has disappeared."

"Why would anyone steal a **realtor's signs**?" Nina asked. "What would anybody do with them?"

---

real-estate agent, someone who sells houses
disgusted, upset or angry
listed, advertised; put on a list of items for sale
realtor's signs, signs that advertise a house

"Who knows?" Mrs. Decker poured herself a glass of lemonade. "Probably some kids with nothing better to do. I suppose they could use the signs to build something. They were the wooden ones."

Max nudged Nina. "Want to bike over and see what we can find out?"

"Not much there to see," his mother told him. "Only two houses on that whole street. An old lady—Mrs. Stearns—lives in the house next to the empty one."

"Maybe she saw something," Nina said. "Let's go ask."

Half an hour later, the two were biking toward the end of Norton Drive. A pick-up truck was parked in front of the empty house. A man was standing on the sidewalk looking in all directions.

"Do you kids know anything about this place?" he asked. "I'm from out of town, and my nephew, Paul, has been checking houses for me this past month. He thought I might like the one at the end of Norton Drive, so he let me borrow his truck to drive over here. But I don't know if this is the house he meant. There aren't any signs."

BEFORE YOU GO ON . . .

1 In "The Case of the Defaced Sidewalk," why is Mr. Hansen frowning?

2 In "The Case of the Disappearing Signs," who does Mrs. Decker think stole the signs?

HOW ABOUT YOU?
- Why do you think someone might steal a FOR SALE sign?

115

CRITICAL THINKING

Have students respond orally or in writing to these questions:
- Why wouldn't "The Case of the Defaced Sidewalk" have worked if the girls were shopping for CDs? *(Nina would not have known that Jenny had wide feet.)*
- Without the sign, how could you guess which house on Norton Drive was for sale? *(Possible answer: There were only two houses on the street, and one of them was empty.)*

MODELING THE READING STRATEGY

Using a Graphic Organizer: After students complete the Active Reading chart for "The Case of the Defaced Sidewalk" and "The Case of the Disappearing Signs," ask them to recall the meanings of *compare* and *contrast.* Help students transfer information from their chart to a Venn diagram that compares the two stories. Tell students they will add more information to their charts and Venn diagrams when they finish reading "The Case of the Disappearing Signs."

REACHING ALL STUDENTS

LANGUAGE LEVELS

Beginning: Use real objects, people, pictures, or maps to help define the following words and phrases: *sandals, concrete, city maintenance man, take a short cut, embedded.* Then use pantomime and role-playing to act out the meaning of these terms: *sprained* and *frowned.* Have students use each word in a sentence related to "The Case of the Defaced Sidewalk."

Teach

GUIDED READING

1. Who do Max and Nina interview about the missing signs? *(Mrs. Stearns and Freddie Swanson)*
2. Which two people are using wood that might be the missing signs? How are they using this wood? *(Freddie has a tree house, and Mrs. Stearns has wood in the fireplace.)*
3. What do Nina and Max notice about Freddie's wood? *(The wood in his tree house is gray and weather-beaten.)*

Viewpoint

Have students identify and describe what they see in the illustration. Ask them to look for clues about the weather, eliciting that everyone is dressed for hot weather.

ABOUT THE AUTHORS

Carol Farley has written dozens of books. In addition to mysteries, she has written several folktales, some of which are set in Korea, and several books about women writers.

In the past three years, Elizabeth Dearl has written several successful collections of mystery stories. According to Dearl, "One of the wonderful things about being a writer is that you're able to keep learning, keep stretching, and keep trying new things."

"This house is for sale," Max told him. "My mom is the real-estate agent."

"Great! Then can you tell me her name and company? I'd like to ask about this property. Paul tells me that houses in this part of town sell fast. He says this one has been **on the market** for quite some time. I'm glad I got here before it was sold! I just couldn't get over here any sooner."

As soon as Max gave him the information, the man drove off.

1 Nina stared after the truck. "Know what? His nephew, Paul, might have taken the signs. Maybe he didn't want people to see that the house was for sale until his uncle had a chance to look at it. You can put lots of things in the back of a truck."

Max nodded. "Let's ask Mrs. Stearns if she saw anything this morning."

Mrs. Stearns came to the door as soon as they knocked. She was gray-haired, but she stood straight and tall. "Oh, I think I

---

on the market, for sale

116

---

2 know who might have taken those signs," she told them. "Freddie Swanson. He lives a block away, and he's always up to mischief."

She held the door open as she talked, and Nina peeked inside. She liked the **cozy** living room. The sofa and chairs were velvet-covered **antiques**. Lace doilies covered the end tables. A large painting hung over the intricately carved fireplace mantel, and a cheerful fire **crackled** below.

"I know Freddie," Max said. "And I know where he lives. Let's go see him."

Freddie was putting a lawn mower in the garage when they reached his house. He **mopped his brow** as he talked to them. "Why would I take a dumb old sign?" he asked. "Besides, I've been out here doing yard work all morning."

Nina stared past him at the garage. Her parents could hardly get their car in her garage at home because of all the stuff in it, but this one was **practically bare**. Then she noticed a **crudely built** tree house in the yard. The boards were gray and weather-beaten.

She and Max talked as they biked back to his house. Mrs. Decker was washing the lunch dishes when they ran into the house.

"We think we know who took the signs," Nina told her.

---

cozy, comfortable
antiques, very old, valuable objects
crackled, made popping sounds
mopped his brow, wiped his forehead
practically bare, nearly empty
crudely built, not carefully made

GRAMMAR MINILESSON

Punctuation: Periods and Exclamation Points

Write the following sentences on the board:

> *That dirt bike is for sale.*

> *Wow! I would really like to buy it!*

Have students point out the punctuation marks at the end of each sentence. Ask students to tell what they know about a period, eliciting that it signals the end of a declarative sentence—one that makes a statement. Then identify the exclamation points for students. Explain that exclamation points signal excitement or surprise. They can be used after a word or phrase, such as *Great!* or *Oh no!,* and they can also signal the end of a sentence. Have student pairs find the sentence on page 116 that uses an exclamation mark and read it aloud with excitement. Then have partners take turns writing their own examples of declarative and exclamatory sentences.

T116

CRITICAL THINKING

Have students respond orally or in writing to these questions:

- Why do you think Mrs. Stearns says that Freddie took the signs? *(Possible answer: She wants Max and Nina to go look for the signs somewhere else.)*
- Why might it have been harder for Max and Nina to solve this mystery if it had been winter? *(Possible answer: Burning a fire in winter would have been reasonable.)*

MODELING THE READING STRATEGY

Visualizing: Remind students that when they visualize, they picture in their minds the characters, events, and places in the text. Point out that visualizing can help them use what they already know about a topic to help them understand and enjoy the text. Have students close their eyes as you read the paragraph on page 116 that begins, "She held the door open . . ." When you finish, ask students to describe Mrs. Stearns's living room. Then have students reread the paragraph and point out the adjectives the author uses to help readers visualize the scene.

WEBSITES

For more information, log on to http://www.longman.com/shiningstar for links to other interesting websites about solving mysteries.

About the Authors

Carol Farley

Carol Farley (left) has always loved mysteries. Her first book, *Mystery of the Fog Man*, came from an idea she had in the sixth grade.

Elizabeth Dearl

Elizabeth Dearl (right) is a former Texas police officer. She is the author of several mystery novels.

How did Nina and Max figure it out?

There was no evidence to show that Paul had used his truck to transport the signs. The boards in Freddie's tree house were too old and worn to have been made with the signs. Mrs. Stearns had a fire in her fireplace on a hot July day. She didn't want neighbors moving in next door, so she took the signs and burned them in her fireplace so nobody would know the house was for sale.

"That fire was a **hot tip**," Nina said later as she joined Max and Mrs. Decker for a cold drink of lemonade.

---

hot tip, good clue

BEFORE YOU GO ON . . .

1 Why does Nina think the man's nephew, Paul, might have stolen the signs?

2 What does Mrs. Stearns say to suggest that Freddie stole the signs?

HOW ABOUT YOU?

- Did you guess who stole the signs?

117

REACHING ALL STUDENTS

LANGUAGE LEVELS

Beginning: Write the following phrases on separate pieces of paper: *man drives off in truck, interview with Mrs. Stearns, interview with Freddie, tell Mrs. Decker who stole signs.* Sort the papers in random order, and give each one to a different student. Challenge students to read the phrases and arrange themselves to show the order in which the story events happened. Then have them write a paragraph that places the events in order.

Advanced: Have students imagine they are Max and Nina. Ask student groups to write a letter asking Mrs. Stearns to return the signs. Have students use ideas from the text to explain how they know Mrs. Stearns is guilty, and why they think she should apologize to Freddie and Mrs. Decker.

Review and Practice

COMPREHENSION

Read aloud the introductory paragraph as students follow along. After students copy the chart into their notebooks, have them reread the stories. Then have them work in small groups to complete and discuss the chart. Invite all the groups to compare and contrast their charts. Have students respond to these questions:

1. Which character appears in all three stories? *(Max)*

2. Who is the criminal in each story? *(tall man with briefcase; Mitzi; Mrs. Stearns)*

3. Describe one setting in "The Case of the Disappearing Signs." *(Possible answer: Mrs. Stearns's living room, which has a velvet sofa and a fireplace.)*

CRITICAL THINKING

After students complete the chart, have them use it to respond orally or in writing to these questions:

- Why do you think mystery writers often wait until the end of the story to reveal the criminal? *(Possible answer: They want to build suspense and keep the reader interested.)*

- In your opinion, which story had the most interesting crime and criminal? Why? *(Answers will vary.)*

COMPREHENSION

The three mystery stories that you read are similar in some ways and different in other ways. Reread the stories. Copy the chart into your notebook. Then complete the chart. Work in small groups. Use your charts to discuss similarities and differences in the three cases.

	Main Characters	Setting	Criminal	Description of the Crime
"The Case of the Surprise Visitor"			tall man with a briefcase	
"The Case of the Defaced Sidewalk"				Someone jumped into the wet cement in the sidewalk.
"The Case of the Disappearing Signs"	Max, Nina, Mrs. Decker			

118

Work in pairs. Copy the following story into your notebook. Choose your own words to fill in the blanks. Finish the story in your own words. Make it as funny as you can.

> When we went into the school cafeteria, the cook said, "All the
> _____ and _____ from my kitchen disappeared last night. They
> were on this counter. How did it happen? There were no broken
> windows, and the door was locked."
>
> Just then the cook's _____ dog ran toward us, jumping and
> barking.
>
> "Outside, _____ !" the cook shouted.
>
> We noticed that the dog had a _____ in its mouth.
>
> We left the cafeteria and went to _____. Two students in our
> class, _____ and _____, were sitting on a _____ eating
> _____.
>
> "Where did you get those?" we asked.
>
> _____
>
> _____

Work with another pair of students. Take turns reading your mystery stories aloud. Can you guess each other's solutions to the mystery? How are your mysteries similar? How are they different?

DISCUSSION

Discuss in pairs or small groups.

1. What clue helped Nina figure out that Mrs. Stearns took the signs? What do you think about what Mrs. Stearns did?
2. Think of words to describe Max and Nina. How are they similar? Are you like Max and Nina in any way? If so, how?
3. Which of the three cases was the easiest to solve? Why?

EXTENSION

Have students take turns reading the Extension directions. Then ask them to work in pairs to develop the humorous fill-in-the-blank mystery. Have students discuss the plot and the characters before selecting possible word choices and an ending for the story. Then have pairs work together to complete the second step of the activity.

DISCUSSION

Have students read the questions and discuss them in pairs or small groups. After they have completed their discussion, ask volunteers to report their answers to the class.

METACOGNITION

Ask students:

1. What did you learn by reading these mystery stories?
2. How did making a Venn diagram help you compare the stories?
3. Did the illustrations in each story help you to solve them? Explain.

REACHING ALL STUDENTS

LANGUAGE LEVELS

Beginning: Photocopy the fill-in-the-blank story and number the blanks from 1 to 11. Work with the students to brainstorm ideas for each blank. Write their ideas on the board for them to choose from, numbering the lists to match the blanks in the photocopy. Have students select ideas from the board to complete the sentences.

Advanced: Invite pairs of students to type their fill-in-the-blank stories on a computer for easy text manipulation. Encourage partners to experiment with the words they place in the blanks to make the story as interesting and funny as possible.

LEARNING MODALITIES

Visual: Ask students to visualize what is happening in the fill-in-the-blank mystery. Have students draw a quick sketch for each word or sentence they want to place in the story. Have advanced students assist beginning students in the class as they fill in the words suggested by the pictures.

CONNECT TO CONTENT   Science

*Read the descriptions of two science experiments. Look at how the **materials** and the **method** are organized.*

How To Make a Friend Disappear

Materials

- two chairs
- a small mirror

Method

1. Sit on a chair with a wall to your right. Ask your partner to sit **opposite** you (see the diagram). Your partner should sit very **still**.
2. Hold the bottom of the mirror with your left hand. Put the edge of the mirror against the side of your nose or slightly in front of it. The **reflecting surface** should face the wall. Don't move your head.
3. Turn the mirror so that your right eye sees only the reflection of the wall. Your left eye should look straight ahead at your partner.
4. Move your right hand in front of the wall like you are **erasing** a chalkboard. Watch as parts of your friend's face disappear!

Magicians use this trick to make objects "disappear." They use mirrors to hide the objects from view.

Some people see this effect more easily than others. A few people never see it. You may have to try it several times. Don't **give up**!

give up, stop trying

mirror

materials, things you need
method, instructions; way to do something
opposite, facing; across from
still, without moving
reflecting surface, side of the mirror where you can see yourself
erasing, removing something

120

If you don't see your friend's face disappear, one of your eyes might be stronger than the other. Try the experiment again. This time, change the eye you use to look at the person and the eye you use to look at the wall.

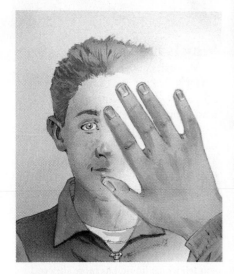

Why Is It So?

Usually, your two eyes see slightly different pictures of the world around you. Your brain combines these two pictures to create a single image.

In this experiment, the mirror lets your eyes see two very different views. One eye looks straight ahead at your partner, while the other eye looks at the wall and your moving hand. Your brain tries to put together a picture that makes sense by choosing parts of both views.

Young Girl or Old Woman?

Your brain works hard to understand the images that you see in the world around you, based on your experiences. Which do you see first—a young girl or an old woman? Once you can see both, your brain can easily switch between one and the other.

BEFORE YOU GO ON . . .

1. What did you need to do this experiment?

2. What new information did you learn about your brain?

HOW ABOUT YOU?
- Did the experiment work easily for you?

121

Have students respond orally or in writing to these questions:
- If this experiment didn't work for you, what do you think you should do differently the next time? *(Answers will vary.)*
- Why is the mirror important to this trick? *(Possible answer: It lets one eye see the partner and the other eye see the wall.)*
- What was the hardest part of doing this trick? *(Answers will vary.)*

MODELING THE READING STRATEGY

Visualizing: Have students recall what good readers do when they visualize. Draw from students that they should use adjectives and other descriptive terms to help them picture what they are reading. Point out that visualizing will help them understand the steps that are necessary to perform a magic trick.

Viewpoint

Focus attention on the two sketches. Ask students to identify what part of the experiment or explanation these illustrations show. Then take a class poll to determine which image the majority of students noticed first, the young girl or the old woman.

REACHING ALL STUDENTS

LANGUAGE LEVELS

Beginning: Ask students to restate the steps to a partner in their own words. Then encourage students to act out the steps as they describe the experiment.

Advanced: Have students demonstrate the trick for the class as if they were teaching it. Ask them to explain the steps in the process and why the trick works. Encourage students to use vocabulary terms in their descriptions.

LEARNING MODALITIES

Kinesthetic: Read aloud the text with students. Then make available the materials for conducting the experiment. Reread the text together as the students actually do the experiment. Model only if necessary.

WATER TRICK

Materials

- a drinking glass
- a **handkerchief**
- a rubber band

Method

1. Fill a glass three-quarters full with water.
2. Place a **damp** handkerchief over the top of the glass.
3. Place a rubber band around the rim of the glass so that it is holding the handkerchief.
4. Push down on the center of the handkerchief until it touches the water. Make sure the rubber band stays around the glass.
5. Keep your fingers pressed on the handkerchief and turn the glass upside down.
6. Pull the handkerchief tight, still keeping the rubber band on, so that the curved shape disappears. The water will remain in the glass.

---

handkerchief, square piece of cloth
damp, a bit wet

Why Is It So?

Molecules at the surface of water attract each other and **clump together**. This is called surface tension. Surface tension prevents the molecules from passing through the small holes of the handkerchief.

At home you can look at different liquids and see how much or how little surface tension they have. Put a drop of water onto a plate and it will form a rounded ball. This is because of surface tension. Put a drop of vinegar onto a plate. Put a drop of oil on a different plate. Can you tell which liquid has more surface tension?

---

molecules, the smallest part into which a substance can be divided without changing its form
clump together, form a group or mass

BEFORE YOU GO ON . . .

1. List the three materials needed for this trick.
2. What prevents the water from going through the handkerchief?

HOW ABOUT YOU?
- Which of the two experiments did you find more interesting? Why?

122

Link the Readings

Review the mystery stories and reread the science experiments. Think about the two kinds of readings as you look at the chart. Then copy the chart into your notebook and complete it. Compare your answers in small groups.

Title of Selection	Type of Text (Genre)	Fiction or Nonfiction	Purpose of Selection	The Mystery
"The Case of the Surprise Visitor"	short story			
"The Case of the Defaced Sidewalk"		fiction		
"The Case of the Disappearing Signs"				
"How to Make a Friend Disappear"	informational text		to explain something about science	
"Water Trick"		nonfiction		Water remains in the glass.

DISCUSSION

Discuss in pairs or small groups.

1. How are the two science experiments similar to a mystery story? How are they different?
2. Would you prefer to be a detective or a scientist? Why?

123

REFLECTION

Explain that scientists and detectives are great observers. They use what they discover to solve mysteries. Have volunteers take turns reading the Reflection directions. Encourage students to apply their own observations and conclusions to the chart. After students complete and discuss their charts, ask:

1. Which readings are mysteries? *("The Case of the Surprise Visitor," "The Case of the Defaced Sidewalk," "The Case of the Disappearing Signs")*
2. Which readings are nonfiction? *("How to Make a Friend Disappear," "Water Trick")*

COOPERATIVE GROUPING

Form small groups, varying the language levels of the students. Ask each group to copy and finish the chart. Tell them to work together to read the items in the chart and discuss how they will complete it. Then ask groups to explain their responses.

DISCUSSION

Ask students to read the questions and discuss them in pairs or small groups. For the first question, you may wish to have students use a Venn diagram to organize their thoughts. After they have completed their discussion, have volunteers share their ideas.

CRITICAL THINKING

Discuss similarities and differences between the work of detectives and scientists. Include the observation skills, tools, and thinking skills used in both professions.

REACHING ALL STUDENTS

LANGUAGE LEVELS

Beginning: Help students answer the second Discussion question by discussing the job requirements of a detective and a scientist, as well as the kinds of problems each might encounter on the job. Provide vocabulary as you discuss both professions. Invite students to use this vocabulary as they answer the question.

Advanced: To help students answer the first Discussion question, review with them the steps of the scientific process: question, hypothesis, materials, experiment, results, conclusion. Invite students to use Key Words and ideas to answer the question.

GRAMMAR

Read aloud the introductory paragraph with students. Point out that an imperative sentence gives an order, an instruction, or a direction. Then ask volunteers to read the sample sentences. Have students identify the verb, end punctuation, and unstated subject in each example. Then have students complete Practice activity 1 on their own and Practice activity 2 with a partner.

SCAFFOLDING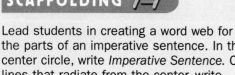

Lead students in creating a word web for the parts of an imperative sentence. In the center circle, write *Imperative Sentence*. On lines that radiate from the center, write *Begins with a Verb; Ends with a Period or Exclamation Point;* and *Unstated You.* Then have students use the web as they look for examples of imperative sentences in Part 2 of the reading selections.

EXTEND THE LESSON

Invite students to look for examples of imperative sentences in recipes and directions for games. Ask students to think of other examples of written text where imperative sentences might be used. *(instructions for putting things together, test directions)*

Connect to Writing

GRAMMAR

Imperatives

An **imperative** gives an instruction, a direction, or an order. In sentences with an imperative, the subject is not stated, but it is understood to be *you*. Imperative sentences end with a period or an exclamation point.

SUBJECT	VERB
(You)	**Follow** the directions.
	Sit on a chair.
	Move your right hand.
	Fill the glass with water.
	Try the experiment again!

Practice

1. Find five imperative sentences in "How to Make a Friend Disappear" and "Water Trick." Write them in your notebook. Underline the imperative verb in each sentence.

2. Now work with a partner. Write five new imperative sentences that tell your partner what to do. Read your sentences to your partner and see if he or she can follow your instructions.

   Example: *Put your hand on your head.*

3. What are the imperative verbs in the cartoon?

PEANUTS reprinted by permission of United Feature Syndicate, Inc.

SKILLS FOR WRITING

Writing Clues

A treasure hunt is a game. In a treasure hunt, you get clues, which are directions you follow to find a hidden treasure or prize. Read these clues. Then answer the questions.

> Jason Preston
>
> Treasure Hunt Clues
>
> Start at the big car.
>
> Walk ten steps between two large trees.
>
> Go into the yellow house.
>
> Walk down the hall.
>
> Turn right and go into the bedroom.
>
> Turn left and walk to the desk.
>
> Look under the desk.
>
> Pick up the box.
>
> Open the box!

1. What verbs are used?
2. What kinds of sentences are used to give the clues?
3. What punctuation marks are used at the end of the sentences?

125

SKILLS FOR WRITING

Have students take turns reading the introductory paragraph and the Treasure Hunt Clues. Point out that the clues here are like directions. Have students use them to answer the questions at the bottom of the page. Let students work in pairs, and encourage use of new grammar terms.

SCAFFOLDING

Review the following types of sentences with students: statements, questions, imperative sentences, and exclamations. Ask students to use their prior knowledge to identify the kind of punctuation that is used with each kind of sentence. Suggest that students create a two-column chart with this information. Display the chart for future reference.

REACHING ALL STUDENTS

LANGUAGE LEVELS

Beginning: Read aloud the list of sample clues for a treasure hunt. Then use the following imperative sentences to help students understand the clues:

> Point to a verb.
> Find an adjective.
> Put your finger on a period.
> Cover a question.
> Show me a question mark.
> Point to an imperative sentence.
> Whisper what the treasure is.

Advanced: Invite students to take turns reading the clues aloud to partners who role-play the directions. After each partner has had the chance to act out the clues, encourage students to write down what they think the treasure is and what led them to this conclusion. Then have them share their responses and their reasoning.

T125

WRITING ASSIGNMENT

Clues for a Treasure Hunt

Read aloud the Writing Assignment directions with students. Have students describe what they will be writing in their own words and then ask them to reread the clues on page 125. Discuss with students why writing a set of clues in the correct order is especially important in a treasure hunt.

WRITING STRATEGY

Have a volunteer read the introductory paragraph and the clues in the flowchart. Ask students to explain why they should fill in the first and the last box before filling in the other boxes. Then model how to make a flowchart, using clues that tell how to get to the school office. After writing the first clue, invite students to help you finish the chart. Then have students work in pairs to create a flowchart in their notebooks that gives clues to their own treasures. Have partners trade papers and visualize themselves completing each step to see if the flowchart makes sense. Before writing their clues, have students review the parts of an imperative sentence. Remind them that their flowchart will help them remember all the clues and write them in order.

USING THE EDITING CHECKLIST

Have pairs work together to read and use the Editing Checklist to revise their writing.

WRITING ASSIGNMENT

Clues for a Treasure Hunt
You will write clues for a treasure hunt in your school.

1. **Read** Reread the clues on page 125. Are the clues easy to understand?

Writing Strategy: Flowchart
A flowchart helps you organize your clues in order. Decide where you want your treasure hunt to begin and write the place in the first box. Decide where you want your treasure hunt to end and write the place in the last box. Then fill in the other boxes. Write clues that tell how to get from the start to the finish. Look at this example:

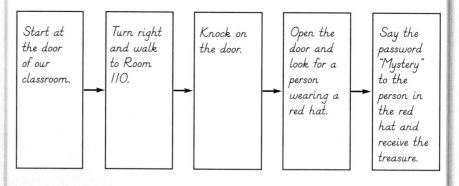

| Start at the door of our classroom. | → | Turn right and walk to Room 110. | → | Knock on the door. | → | Open the door and look for a person wearing a red hat. | → | Say the password "Mystery" to the person in the red hat and receive the treasure. |

---

2. **Make a flowchart** Think of a treasure for your classmates to look for. Then make a flowchart in your notebook, listing each clue.

3. **Write** Write the clues for your treasure hunt. Use imperatives. After your classmates find your treasure, talk about your clues. Are there ways to make the clues easier to understand?

EDITING CHECKLIST

Did you . . .

▶ write clues that are easy to understand?

▶ use imperatives?

▶ use a capital letter at the beginning of each clue?

▶ use a period or exclamation point at the end of each clue?

126

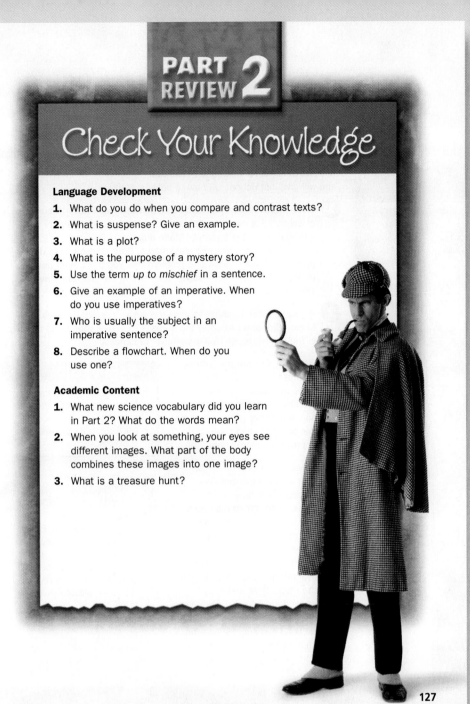

PART REVIEW 2

Check Your Knowledge

Language Development

1. What do you do when you compare and contrast texts?
2. What is suspense? Give an example.
3. What is a plot?
4. What is the purpose of a mystery story?
5. Use the term *up to mischief* in a sentence.
6. Give an example of an imperative. When do you use imperatives?
7. Who is usually the subject in an imperative sentence?
8. Describe a flowchart. When do you use one?

Academic Content

1. What new science vocabulary did you learn in Part 2? What do the words mean?
2. When you look at something, your eyes see different images. What part of the body combines these images into one image?
3. What is a treasure hunt?

127

EXTEND THE LESSON

Have students preview the Put It All Together section on pages 128–131. These end-of-unit pages review and unify concepts, skills, and strategies from the whole unit, with focus on listening, speaking, and writing skills.

LISTENING AND SPEAKING WORKSHOP

Read aloud the task that is presented at the top of the page. Then ask a volunteer to read aloud the first step. Allow time for students to create their lists of problems to solve. Then form small groups. Ask group members to reread step 1 and then read steps 2 through 4. Tell students they will work in their groups to select one problem, make a flowchart of the steps needed to solve it, and practice speaking orally. Encourage students to review how to make a flowchart on page 126. Explain that one speaker from each group will present the problem as others offer support during the presentation.

TEACHING THE TIPS

Speaking Tips: As they practice, have group members who are not speaking serve as the audience to evaluate the presentation.

Listening Tips: Ask a group of students to role-play a scenario in which the Listening Tips are applied.

RESEARCH SKILLS

Nonprint: Encourage students to interview other students or teachers at the school to strengthen their solutions. For example, they might interview a librarian to check if their steps for finding a book are complete.

Put It All Together

OBJECTIVES

Integrate Skills
- Listening/ Speaking: *Instructions to solve a problem*
- Writing: *Instructions for a science experiment*

Investigate Themes
- Projects
- Further reading

LISTENING and SPEAKING WORKSHOP

INSTRUCTIONS TO SOLVE A PROBLEM
You will give instructions on how to solve a problem.

1 **Think about it** Ask yourself: What problems do I have to solve at school? For example, how can I find a book in the library or information on the Internet? Make a list.

Work with two or three classmates. Compare your lists of problems. Then choose one problem that you think most people in your class have. Brainstorm solutions to the problem. Then choose the best solution.

2 **Organize** Work together to write the steps to solve the problem. Make a flowchart to show the steps. Make sure your steps are in the correct order. Use imperative sentences.

3 **Practice** Choose one group member to be your speaker. Have the speaker practice reading the steps to your solution. Other group members can suggest changes to improve the instructions.

4 **Present and evaluate** Have your speaker present your problem and solution to the class. Other group members can help the speaker—for example, by showing the flowchart.

After each speaker finishes, evaluate the presentation. Were the steps clear and easy to understand? What did you like best about the presentation? Do you have suggestions for improvement?

SPEAKING TIPS
- Present each step clearly.
- Pause a few seconds after each step.
- Ask listeners if they have any questions.

LISTENING TIPS
- If you can't hear the speaker, you may say, "Excuse me, could you speak louder, please?"
- If there is something you don't understand, you may say, "Could you please repeat that point?"

128

WRITING WORKSHOP

INSTRUCTIONS FOR A SCIENCE EXPERIMENT

When writing instructions for a science experiment, it is very important to write the steps in the correct order. The writer usually uses imperative sentences that are short and easy to understand.

Good instructions for a science experiment include the following characteristics:

- a list of materials used in the experiment
- clear, simple language to describe the steps
- a correct sequence of steps
- a concluding step that explains what happens in the experiment

You will write instructions for a science experiment. Use the following steps, the model on page 130, and the pictures to help you.

1 **Prewrite** Look at the four pictures of the science experiment on page 131. List the materials that you need to do the experiment.

Study each picture. Make a flowchart to describe what happens in each picture. Use the words in the box under the pictures to complete the flowchart.

WRITING TIPS

- Remember to use imperative sentences to write instructions.
- Use prepositional phrases in the instructions to describe where things are located.
- A science experiment must be done in the correct sequence. Number each step so that the order of your instructions is clear and correct.

129

WRITING WORKSHOP

Instructions for a Science Experiment

Have volunteers take turns reading aloud the introductory text and bulleted list of characteristics. Ask students to tell in their own words what a good set of instructions for an experiment should include. Emphasize the importance of writing the steps in the correct sequence. Additional practice activities can be found in the **Workbook** and **CD-ROM**.

PROCESS WRITING

Before students get started, read aloud the five steps students will follow as they write the science experiment instructions. Then ask a volunteer to read aloud the model. Have students find the materials and steps in the model. Ask students to identify the type of sentences used in the model. *(imperative sentences)* Discuss the order of the sentences and why the order is important. Then focus attention on the pictures and boxed words on page 131. Ask students to describe the pictures and read aloud the words. Clarify the procedure as necessary. Then have students write their instructions for the science experiment.

TEACHING THE TIPS

Writing Tips: Read aloud the tips as a choral reading. Explain that *sequence* means "the order of the steps." After they finish their drafts, have students reread the steps they wrote to see if they are in the correct order.

REACHING ALL STUDENTS

LANGUAGE LEVELS

Beginning: Ask one of the small groups to practice their presentation for you and the beginning students. After each presentation, point out the areas in which the group achieved the objectives. Encourage beginning students to ask questions of the group and to provide additional positive feedback.

Advanced: Encourage students to monitor their understanding of each speaker's presentation and to ask for clarification if needed. Have them determine the purpose for listening and evaluate the solutions offered by each speaker based on their own prior experiences.

Put It All Together

Organization: Before students revise their instructions, explain that *organization* is the plan writers use to present their ideas in the most effective way. When writing instructions, for example, a writer may decide to use numbers or sequence words to indicate a series of steps. Point out that each writer should choose the type of organization that works best for his or her particular topic.

Write the following organizing tips on the board. Tell students to use the tips as they revise their writing.

- Include a title so readers will know what the instructions are for.
- List the materials readers will need to conduct the experiment.
- Use numbers or sequence words such as *first, next,* and *then* so readers can follow the steps in the correct order.
- Make sure to give readers information in the right amount at the right time. Providing too much information at a time may be confusing.
- Write a concluding statement that describes what students can expect to happen after they follow all the steps.

Before you write a first draft of your instructions, read the following model for another experiment. Note the characteristics of clear instructions.

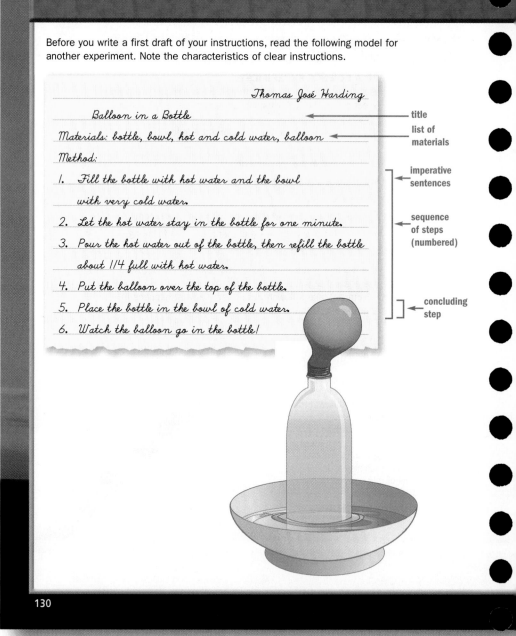

Thomas José Harding

Balloon in a Bottle — title

Materials: bottle, bowl, hot and cold water, balloon — list of materials

Method:

1. Fill the bottle with hot water and the bowl with very cold water.
2. Let the hot water stay in the bottle for one minute.
3. Pour the hot water out of the bottle, then refill the bottle about 1/4 full with hot water.
4. Put the balloon over the top of the bottle.
5. Place the bottle in the bowl of cold water.
6. Watch the balloon go in the bottle!

imperative sentences

sequence of steps (numbered)

concluding step

130

2 **Draft** Use the model and your flowchart to write your instructions for the following science experiment. Use the words in the box.

pour	glass	bottle	salt shaker	sink
salt	olive oil	water	shake	

3 **Edit** Work in pairs. Trade papers and read each other's instructions. Use the questions in the editing checklist to evaluate each other's work.

> **EDITING CHECKLIST**
>
> **Did you . . .**
> ▶ include a title and list of materials?
> ▶ write the steps in the correct order?
> ▶ use imperative sentences?
> ▶ use prepositional phrases?
> ▶ use correct punctuation?

4 **Revise** Revise your instructions. Add information and correct mistakes, if necessary.

5 **Publish** Share your experiment with your teacher and classmates. If possible, perform the experiment.

131

Have students exchange papers and read each other's instructions silently. Then ask them to read the Editing Checklist questions and use them to check each other's work.

ASSESS

Portfolio: Include the science experiment instructions in students' assessment portfolios for comparison with later assignments.

REACHING ALL STUDENTS

LANGUAGE LEVELS

Beginning: Work with students to create instructions for a science experiment. Read aloud each word in the box on page 131, and have students repeat the words. Then make a group flowchart on the board, inviting students to use the words in the box to describe the steps in the pictures. Have students describe each step of the experiment as you write, clarifying approximations orally and in writing. Have students copy the steps.

Advanced: Invite students to present their science experiments to the class. Encourage them to use verbal cuing strategies, such as pauses and exaggerated intonation for key words, and nonverbal cuing strategies, such as gestures and facial expressions.

Unit Projects

EXTEND THE LESSON

Home-School Connection: For Project 3, encourage students to look for a simple science experiment with materials that are readily available at home. Remind them to do the experiment with a family member and to follow the directions carefully to avoid mixing household chemicals that might be harmful. Invite students to record what happened using a picture and a sentence or two.

WEBSITES

For more information, log on to http://www.longman.com/shiningstar for links to other interesting websites.

PROJECTS

Work in pairs or small groups. Choose one of these projects.

1. Create an interesting mystery story about Max and Nina. Give clues to your readers. Then read your story to the class.

2. Choose one of the mysterious places or creatures from "Fact or Fiction?" Draw a picture of the place or creature and write sentences that describe it. Read the description and let your classmates guess what you are describing. Show them the picture when they guess correctly.

3. Find simple science experiments on the Internet, in a textbook, or in a library book. Try one of these experiments at home with a family member and talk about what causes these scientific "mysteries" to happen. Share what you learn with the class.

4. Invite a police detective to your classroom to learn more about how crimes are solved. Prepare a list of questions about detective work before your speaker arrives. Ask the detective to share the tools he or she uses on the job. Also talk about special skills that a detective needs to have.

5. Perform one of the cases from *Teenage Detectives* in a readers theatre. Group members choose their roles. Choose a narrator—someone who tells the parts of the story that the characters don't speak. Practice saying your lines before you perform the story for your classmates. Then perform your scene for the class.

132

Further Reading

To find out more about the theme of this unit, choose from these reading suggestions.

Beastly Tales, Real Encounters with Mysterious Monsters, Malcolm Yorke All around the world people tell stories about seeing mysterious monsters. The storytellers are often accused of making things up. But sometimes a discovery is made that proves them right. Few people believed stories about a manlike ape in Africa, a dragon in Indonesia, or a huge sea monster with long tentacles. However, we now know these creatures really exist!

Rip Van Winkle and The Legend of Sleepy Hollow, Washington Irving One day Rip Van Winkle goes to the mountains with his dog. Who are the strange old men, and why are they there? In *The Legend of Sleepy Hollow*, Ichabod Crane is a teacher who likes ghost stories. Are there really ghosts at Sleepy Hollow, and will Ichabod see one of them?

The Mysterious Island, Jules Verne There are three men, a boy, and a dog in a balloon over the Pacific Ocean, but only two men and the boy arrive on the island. Mysterious things start happening. Are they the only people on the island? Where are the other man and his dog?

Detective Work, John Escott A diamond necklace is stolen from a museum. Everyone who works at the museum might be the thief. But who really took the necklace, and why? Paul, a young student, helps the police find the thief.

Call Me Consuelo, Ofelia Dumas Lachtman Twelve-year-old orphan Consuelo Harburton reluctantly leaves her Mexican-American aunt, uncle, and cousins to live with her American grandmother in Los Angeles. Consuelo struggles with the changes in her life, but she soon becomes involved with solving some mysterious robberies in her new neighborhood.

133

FURTHER READING

- *Beastly Tales, Real Encounters with Mysterious Monsters* and *Rip Van Winkle and The Legend of Sleepy Hollow* are appropriate for beginning students.
- *The Mysterious Island* is appropriate for intermediate students.
- *Detective Work* and *Call Me Consuelo* are appropriate for advanced students.

REACHING ALL STUDENTS

LANGUAGE LEVELS

Beginning: Encourage beginning students to choose one of the following projects, modifying each one as described: For Project 2, have students create a word web in place of the written sentences to describe the picture of a place or creature from "Fact or Fiction?" For Project 4, have students work with advanced partners to prepare a list of questions to ask a police detective.

Advanced: For Project 5, encourage advanced students to perform one of the cases from *Teenage Detectives* and produce a videotape of the production. They can analyze the videotape and make improvements in their production before presenting it to the class. Then have them create a second videotape to compare with the first to chart their progress.

Level 1 Unit 4

Conflict

Make enough duplicate copies of the Letter Home for Unit 4 so that each student has a copy to take home. Show Video Segment 4.

PART 1 TEACHING GUIDE

PRETEACH	Provide Background	• Read and discuss the Part Objectives and Background Information. (SB p. 136; ATE p. T136)
	Present Concepts	• Introduce the Key Words and Reading Strategy. (SB p. 137; ATE p. T137; WB pp. 86–88) • Pronounce the Vocabulary words. (ATE p. T137) • Model how to use context clues to define Key Words. (ATE p. T137)
TEACH	Monitor Comprehension	• Informally monitor comprehension through Guided Reading and Critical Thinking questions. (ATE pp. T138–T149) • Monitor students' comprehension through Critical Thinking, Metacognition, Discussion, and Extension activities. (SB pp. 145, 149; ATE pp. T139, T141, T143–T145, T147, T149)
	Teach and Practice	• Use individually tailored activities for beginning and advanced students. (ATE pp. T135, T137, T139, T141, T143, T145, T147, T149, T151, T153) • Pair beginning, intermediate, and advanced students through Cooperative Grouping activities. (SB pp. 145, 149; ATE pp. T136, T145, T149) • Develop viewing skills using photos and illustrations and present the Viewpoint activities. (ATE pp. T134, T139, T141, T143, T147–T148) • Complete the Vocabulary, Phonics, Grammar, and Spelling lessons. (SB pp. 137, 150; ATE pp. T138, T142, T146, T150; WB pp. 94–95, 98) • Introduce the Writing Strategy and apply students' ability to write a cause-and-effect paragraph using the Writing Model and Writing Assignment. (SB pp. 151–152; ATE pp. T151–T152; WB pp. 96–97; Transparency # 30)
CONNECT	Connect to Literature	• Develop students' ability to analyze characteristics of genres through pairing of selections. (SB pp. 146–148; ATE pp. T146–T148) • Provide students with interactive reading support and practice. (WB pp. 89–93)
	Across the Curriculum	• Develop students' ability to extend the content of the reading selections through extended math, social studies, science, health, and art activities. (ATE pp. T142, T148)
ASSESS	Check Knowledge	• Use the Before You Go On, Check Your Knowledge, Link the Readings, and Review and Practice features to assess students' comprehension of the selection. (SB pp. 139, 141, 143–145, 147, 149, 153; ATE pp. T144–T145, T149, T153)
	Monitor Progress	• Use the Assessment Options, Test-Taking Tip, and the test. (ATE p. T153; AG pp. 53–56)

CONTENT TERMS

Present and elicit definitions of these content-specific terms:

- balance of power
- factory
- overseas
- allies
- assassination
- submarine
- region
- hills
- valleys

T134A

PART 2 TEACHING GUIDE

PRETEACH	**Provide Background**	• Read and discuss the Part Objectives and Background Information. (SB p. 154; ATE p. T154)
	Present Concepts	• Introduce the Key Words and Reading Strategy. (SB p. 155; ATE p. T155; WB pp. 100, 102) • Pronounce the Vocabulary words. (ATE p. T155) • Model how to use context clues to define Key Words. (ATE p. T155)
TEACH	**Monitor Comprehension**	• Informally monitor comprehension through Guided Reading and Critical Thinking questions. (ATE pp. T156–T167) • Monitor students' comprehension through Critical Thinking, Metacognition, Discussion, and Extension activities. (SB pp. 163, 167; ATE pp. T157, T159–T163, T165, T167, T171)
	Teach and Practice	• Use individually tailored activities for beginning and advanced students. (ATE pp. T155, T157, T159, T161, T163, T165, T167, T169, T171, T173, T175, T177) • Pair beginning, intermediate, and advanced students through Cooperative Grouping activities. (SB pp. 163, 167; ATE pp. T154, T163, T167) • Develop viewing skills using photos and illustrations and present the Viewpoint activities. (ATE pp. T156, T159, T161, T165) • Complete the Vocabulary, Phonics, Grammar, and Spelling lessons. (SB pp. 155, 168; ATE pp. T156, T158, T166, T168; WB pp. 108–109, 112) • Introduce the Writing Strategy and apply students' ability to write an eyewitness report using the Writing Model and Writing Assignment. (SB pp. 169–170; ATE pp. T169–T170; WB pp. 110–111; Transparency # 31)
CONNECT	**Connect to Content**	• Develop students' ability to analyze characteristics of genres through pairing of selections. (SB pp. 164–166; ATE pp. T164–T166) • Provide students with interactive reading support and practice. (WB pp. 103–107)
	Across the Curriculum	• Develop students' ability to extend the content of the reading selections through extended math, social studies, science, health, and art activities. (ATE pp. T158, T165)
ASSESS	**Check Knowledge**	• Use the Before You Go On, Check Your Knowledge, Link the Readings, and Review and Practice features to assess students' comprehension of the selection. (SB pp. 157, 159, 161–164, 166, 167; ATE pp. T162, T163, T167, T171)
	Monitor Progress	• Use the Assessment Options, Test-Taking Tip, and the test. (ATE p. T171, AG pp. 57–60)

PUT IT ALL TOGETHER TEACHING GUIDE

EXTEND	**Integrate Skills and Apply Understanding**	• Apply students' ability to present a TV news show using the Listening and Speaking Workshop. (SB p. 172; ATE p. T172) • Apply students' ability to write a history report using the Writing Workshop. (SB pp. 173–175; ATE pp. T173–T175) • Have students complete one or more of the Unit Projects. (SB p. 176; ATE p. T176) • Have students choose a theme-related reading selection from the Further Reading suggestions. (SB p. 177; ATE p. T177)

Suggestions for Newcomers
Unit 4: Conflict

Part 1

Background (p. 136) Discuss *conflict* with the class. Explain that conflict occurs when people, groups, or countries disagree. Discuss some of the conflicts you have experienced, such as arguments with friends or family. How were these conflicts resolved? Ask students what they know about conflict. Ask volunteers to offer examples of conflicts that they know of or have experienced. With the class discuss war and how conflict can escalate into war. Use historical examples that you are familiar with to help explain. Discuss World War I with the class. Ask students what they already know about this war.

Vocabulary (p. 137) Explain that *context clues* are hints within a sentence that can often tell you what a word means. Sometimes context clues simply define the word in a different way. Use the examples on p. 137 to demonstrate context clues. Review each sentence on the board and ask students what context clues help define the vocabulary word. *(allies = "they fought together"; tension = "grew into a conflict")* If necessary, write other examples on the board using these words and similar context. Point out the context clues to the class.

Reading Strategy (p. 137) Explain that a *cause* is something that creates a result, or *effect*. Use examples around the room, or use examples students can easily understand. On the board, write out sentences such as, *Because it rained for three days, floods caused terrible damage; Because he didn't study, John did poorly on the quiz.* Identify and label the cause-and-effect relationship for each one. Ask volunteers to give other examples of cause-and-effect relationships.

World War I (pp. 138–143) Discuss *war* with the class. Explain that wars occur when conflicts escalate and cannot be resolved. Countries turn to violence to resolve the conflict.

Activity 1: Make a timeline on the board to show the major wars the United States has been involved in. Discuss other wars that students know about. Ask when the wars occurred and what countries were involved.

Activity 2: Explain that *chronological order* tells the order in which events occurred. With students make a timeline on the board that traces the major events of World War I. Encourage students to use all resources in this article, including text, photos, maps, and charts; and the background information on p. 136. Have students trace the history of the war, from its back-ground to the signing of the peace treaty.

Activity 3: On the board, make a T-chart to identify cause-and-effect relationships found throughout the article. Have students identify these as they read. Then have volunteers fill in the chart with the different cause-and-effect relationships they found.

Activity 4: Have students reread the section entitled "The 'First Modern War.'" Have students write out cause-and-effect sentences about each new invention. Have the students identify the reason for this invention and how it helped the cause. *(Poison gas was used, so gas masks were invented to protect soldiers.)* Introduce cause-and-effect words and phrases such as *so, because, since,* etc.

Comprehension (p. 144) When students record the facts, make sure they write complete sentences. Have students use a subject and a verb in order to make complete sentences. Students should identify where they found this information in the text. Encourage students not only to identify these facts but also to give supporting evidence in the text, such as, *The United States tried to stay neutral because its citizens were divided about the war.*

Letter Home (p. 146) Have students reread the letter on p. 146. Ask students to identify words or phrases that describe how Frank Earley feels about the war. Ask for volunteers to discuss how they would feel if they were in his shoes.

War Poems (pp. 147–148) Explain that poets use imagery to create images that you can see in your mind. These images help you to picture what the poet is writing about. Explain some examples in the poem, "Can We Forget?" such as *The fever-racked frame and the hideous night* or *All the fierce storms that raged in the wild warfare's wake.* Have students reread the poem. Ask for volunteers to describe what they pictured when reading this poem. Ask what words or phrases helped them imagine what the poet was writing about. Ask students if they can answer the question in the title, "Can We Forget?"

Read the poem "Grass" closely with the class. Ask for volunteers to discuss what they think the poem is about. Have them identify words and phrases that led to this conclusion. Stress that there are no wrong answers.

Grammar: Using *so* as a Conjunction (p. 150) Explain that *conjunctions* join two clauses, or word groups, together. The conjunction *so* is used to demon-strate a cause-and-effect relationship. On the board, use simple examples that students can relate to. Write out two simple cause-and-effect sentences without a conjunction, such as *Tonya missed the bus. She was late to school.* Then have students rewrite these sentences as a compound sentence using the conjunction *so.* Make sure students understand how to use a comma in these sentences. Offer more examples until students understand joining simple sentences with conjunctions. After students complete the activity on p. 150, ask volunteers to write their answers on the board.

Skills for Writing and Writing Assignment (pp. 151–152) Explain that *outlining* is a great way to organize your ideas before you begin writing. Have students create a miniature outline that will organize their ideas for their paragraph. Students should identify an introduction, body, and conclusion. Explain that the introduction should identify the purpose of their paragraph with a clear and concise opening sentence. The body of the paragraph should be background informa-tion and the events that occurred. Encourage students to use the cause-and-effect relationships in the body of the paragraph. The conclusion should sum up the paragraph. Encourage students to turn simple sentences into compound sentences by using conjunctions.

Part 2

Background (p. 154) Explain that a *diary* is a personal journal of your life. In a diary people can record their thoughts and how they feel about their lives and experiences. If you keep a diary, discuss it with the class. Talk about what you write about and why. Discuss how you can go back and reread certain entries to remember how you felt about occur-rences in your own life. Then review the idea of *conflict* with the class. Explain that conflicts occur when people, groups, or countries disagree. The conflict in Yugoslavia caused war to break out. As a result, the country broke up into smaller countries. On the board, list the reasons that may have caused the conflicts in Yugoslavia. You may need to help students get started.

Vocabulary (p. 155) Explain that *context* is how a word is used. Context can help you understand a word's meaning. *Context clues* are hints or other words found in the sentence that can help you understand a word. Review the sen-tences on p. 155 with the class. Identify the context clues in each sentence. For example, *ambulance = "drove, sick and injured"; massacre = "hundreds of people* were killed." Use the vocabulary words in other sentences that use context clues.

Reading Strategy: Analyzing Historical Context (p. 155) Explain that *historical context* gives you a better understanding of what is happening in the story. By understanding the personal context in *Zlata's Diary* you can better understand why Zlata feels the way she does. Before students read the selection, review the background information on p. 154. If possible, show photos or newspaper clippings of the war in Bosnia to help students get a better understanding of the historical context in which Zlata is writing.

From *Zlata's Diary* (pp. 156–161) Explain that *Zlata's Diary* is a *personal narrative*. This type of narrative reveals the author's thoughts and feelings.

Activity 1: Have students pick an entry in *Zlata's Diary*. Have students create a two-column chart labeled "Events" and "Feelings." Have students identify the events that occurred and Zlata's thoughts/feelings in that particular entry. On the board, demonstrate with the first entry to help students get started.

Activity 2: Explain that *imagery* is the use of specific words or phrases that help you picture, or imagine, the story. Have students scan the text to find examples of imagery in this piece. Have volunteers explain what they pictured or imagined. Ask how they felt and whether this use of imagery makes the story clearer or more powerful.

Activity 3: Have students write how they would feel if they were in Zlata's shoes. Encourage students to imagine themselves in this historical context while they write. Ask students to write a short entry—three or four sentences—similar to the entries in *Zlata's Diary*. Ask for volunteers to read their entries to the class.

Comprehension (p. 162) As students complete the exercise on p. 162, make sure they write complete sentences. Review subjects and verbs and how to make complete sentences. Have students read their sentences aloud to practice pronunciation. Encourage them to speak slowly and clearly.

The Physical World: The Balkans (pp. 164–166) Review the difference between *fact* and *fiction*. Then have students identify whether this piece is fact or fiction and why. Teach students how to read the map on p. 165. Ask students to identify cities and capitals in each country. Then have them identify other aspects of the map, such as borders and bodies of water.

Discuss ethnic groups with the class. Identify the different ethnic groups who live in your area or elsewhere in the United States. On the board, make a chart that identifies the different qualities of some of the ethnic groups chosen, such as country of origin, traditions, religion, etc. Try to emphasize the diversity of these ethnic groups.

Grammar: Using Pronoun Referents (p. 168) With the class review that *pronouns* replace nouns. Pronouns are used so you don't have to keep repeating the noun. Explain that a *subject pronoun* is who or what the sentence is about. Explain that an *object pronoun* is who or what receives the action. On the board, use simple examples to demonstrate. Use sentences such as, *I am speaking to you. He bought a new bicycle. It is very nice. You should listen to me.* Have students identify the subject and object pronouns in these examples. Use the students and classroom to pantomime an explanation of singular and plural pronouns, such as, *I am speaking to you. We are in school. She is sitting next to him.*

Skills for Writing and Writing Assignment (pp. 169–170) Explain that *expository writing* explains something. An *eyewitness report* explains something you witnessed firsthand. It is a type of expository writing. Review the five *wh-* questions. Make a chart on the board and ask volunteers to fill in answers using the example. Have students identify *Who, What, Where, When,* and *Why* in the eyewitness report on p. 169.

Explain that *chronological order* is the order in which events occur. Use the chart on p. 170 to further explain chronological order to the class. Introduce sequence words, such as, *first, next, then, last,* etc. Review the pronouns used in the report on p. 169. Have students identify these pronouns as subjects or objects. Be sure the students use past tense when writing their eyewitness report.

Put It All Together

Listening and Speaking Workshop: TV News Show (p. 172) Review the five *wh-* questions with the class. *(who? what? where? when? why?)* Explain that these are the essentials of TV news reporting. Answering these questions will give you the basic facts. If possible, view a broadcast of a local news show. Analyze a story by identifying the *wh-* questions found in the story. Discuss the other elements of the broadcast, such as the role of anchors and reporters, eyewitness accounts, footage, etc. Emphasize how clearly the on-air personalities speak. Before students give their presentations, have them practice speaking slowly and clearly.

Writing Workshop: Report of a Historical Event (pp. 173–175) Use an example to help students create questions for their interview. Choose a person the class will be familiar with, such as a celebrity. Have the class offer questions that they would ask during an interview. Demonstrate how to get more information out of an interview by asking questions that lead to other questions. These questions should demonstrate how to probe deeper in an interview. Make sure students use the past tense when they begin writing their reports.

With the class, review the example provided on p. 174. Make a two-column chart on the board labeled with the five *wh-* questions. Have students identify the *wh-* questions in this example. Then have students identify additional information found in the text that elaborates on the *wh-* questions.

UNIT 4

Conflict

UNIT CONTENT

Part 1 of this unit includes a history selection, "World War I," which will help students understand why this conflict became violent. This article is followed by a letter and two poems about the effects of war.

The second part of the unit includes an excerpt from *Zlata's Diary* by Zlata Filipović. Explain that these diary entries record one girl's experiences during the Bosnian War. It is followed by a social studies article about the Balkans.

—Viewpoint—

Ask students to look at the collage of photos on pages 134–135. Have them describe the illustrations. Then ask students to explain why they think the artist chose these pictures to represent the unit title "Conflict."

WORKSHOP PREVIEW

Listening and Speaking
Students will work together as a team to present a TV news show about recent events in their school or community, or in the world-at-large.

Writing
Students will write a report of a historical event based on an interview with someone who experienced it.

PROJECTS PREVIEW

Projects for this unit include:
- finding or drawing World War I pictures
- visiting a museum with a World War I display
- writing a script for an interview with Lance-Corporal Frank Earley or Zlata Filipović
- finding and sharing a CD of Balkan music
- making a Balkan flag poster
- researching the Balkans on the Internet

TEACHING RESOURCES

Lesson Plans	pp. 45–58
Summaries	pp. 41–48
Graphic Organizers	1–20
Audio Program	CD2/6–9; Cass.2/B
Workbook	pp. 85–112
CD-ROM	Unit 4
Video	Segment 4
Tests	Part Test, pp. 53–60
	Unit Test, pp. 109–117

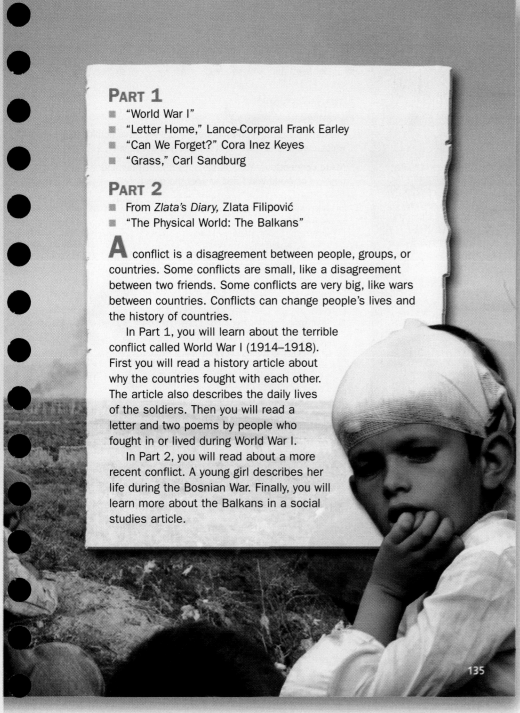

PART 1

- "World War I"
- "Letter Home," Lance-Corporal Frank Earley
- "Can We Forget?" Cora Inez Keyes
- "Grass," Carl Sandburg

PART 2

- From *Zlata's Diary*, Zlata Filipović
- "The Physical World: The Balkans"

A conflict is a disagreement between people, groups, or countries. Some conflicts are small, like a disagreement between two friends. Some conflicts are very big, like wars between countries. Conflicts can change people's lives and the history of countries.

In Part 1, you will learn about the terrible conflict called World War I (1914–1918). First you will read a history article about why the countries fought with each other. The article also describes the daily lives of the soldiers. Then you will read a letter and two poems by people who fought in or lived during World War I.

In Part 2, you will read about a more recent conflict. A young girl describes her life during the Bosnian War. Finally, you will learn more about the Balkans in a social studies article.

135

Read the unit title aloud, and have students repeat it. Discuss with students what *conflict* means. If necessary, explain that a conflict can refer to a physical disagreement, such as a fight between two people. A conflict can also be emotional or psychological, such as deciding whether to tell an adult if a friend is doing something dangerous or dishonest. Ask students:

- to describe conflicts they have faced
- to describe what they think is the best way to resolve a specific conflict
- to tell about world conflicts they've heard about in the news or discussed in their home

QUICK WRITE

Have students list three possible ways to resolve a conflict between two students. One possible scenario might be when one student is accused of copying homework or cheating on a test.

REACHING ALL STUDENTS

LANGUAGE LEVELS

Beginning: Call on volunteers to discuss disagreements they have had with friends. Ask students to describe or act out what the disagreement was about, how they decided to solve the conflict, and how they arrived at this decision.

Advanced: Ask students to list and describe different types of conflicts and their possible solutions in a three-column chart. Write the following headings on the chart: *Conflict, Solution 1, Solution 2.* Encourage students to think of two different solutions for each type of conflict.

LEARNING MODALITIES

Auditory: Form student groups. Encourage students to take turns telling the rest of the group about a conflict they had and how it was resolved.

Preteach

OBJECTIVES

Explain to students that in Part 1 they will be reading about historical events that they might study in history class. Have students take turns reading the list of objectives aloud. If necessary, pause to clarify any difficult words. Encourage students to use the objectives to discuss what they will learn. Additional practice activities for these objectives can be found in the **Workbook** and **CD-ROM.**

BACKGROUND

Have students read the text aloud and study the timeline beneath the map. Ask them what they think the dates on the time-line indicate. *(the year that an event took place)* As student pairs read the timeline, ask them to notice the amount of time that passed between the start of the war and the point at which the United States joined the conflict. *(three years)* Then have pairs answer the questions at the bottom of the page.

COOPERATIVE GROUPING

Pair intermediate and advanced students with beginning students. Ask pairs to read the Background page and discuss the map and timeline together. After answering the questions, have each pair of students meet with another pair to compare answers. Have the groups come to a consensus and share their ideas with the class.

PART 1 — Prepare to Read

OBJECTIVES
LANGUAGE DEVELOPMENT

Reading:
- Vocabulary building: *Context, dictionary skills*
- Reading strategy: *Noting causes and effects*
- Text types: *Social studies article, letter, poems*
- Literary element: *Rhyme*

Writing:
- Cause-and-effect organization
- Cause-and-effect paragraph
- Editing checklist

Listening/Speaking:
- For enjoyment
- Intonation patterns
- Analysis of oral interpretation

Grammar:
- Conjunction *so*

Viewing/Representing:
- Timeline, maps, painting

ACADEMIC CONTENT
- History vocabulary
- Causes and effects of World War I

BACKGROUND

"World War I" is an informational history text. It is nonfiction, which means that it is about real facts and events.

Make connections Work in pairs. Study the map and timeline of World War I and answer the questions.

▲ Europe before World War I

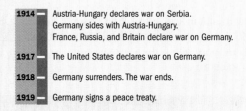

1914 — Austria-Hungary declares war on Serbia. Germany sides with Austria-Hungary. France, Russia, and Britain declare war on Germany.

1917 — The United States declares war on Germany.

1918 — Germany surrenders. The war ends.

1919 — Germany signs a peace treaty.

1. When did World War I begin?
2. When did the United States enter the war?
3. How many years did the war last?

136

TEACHING GUIDE

PRETEACH	**Provide Background**	Read and discuss the Background information. Complete the activity. (ATE/SB p. 136)
	Present Concepts	Introduce the Reading Strategy. (ATE/SB p. 137)
TEACH	**Monitor Comprehension**	Informally monitor comprehension while students read the selection independently or in groups. (ATE/SB pp. 138–149)
	Teach and Practice	Present the Grammar, Usage, and Mechanics. (ATE/SB pp. 150, 151) Complete the Writing activity. (ATE/SB p. 152) Present Grammar, Phonics, and Spelling minilessons. (ATE pp. 138, 142, 146)
CONNECT	**Connect to Literature**	Have students read the literature and relate it to the informational reading. (ATE/SB pp. 146–148)
	Across the Curriculum	Present curriculum links as students read. (ATE pp. 142, 148)
ASSESS	**Check Knowledge**	Assess students' comprehension by having them complete the Check Your Knowledge section. (ATE/SB p. 153)
	Monitor Progress	Use one or more of the print assessment resources in the Assessment Package.
EXTEND	**Integrate Language and Apply Understanding**	Have students complete the Workshops (ATE/SB pp. 172–175) and choose a project from the Unit Projects. (ATE/SB p. 176) Then have them choose a book to read from Further Reading. (ATE/SB p. 177)

VOCABULARY

Read these sentences. Use the context to figure out the meaning of the **red** words. Use a dictionary to check your answers. Write each word and its meaning in your notebook.

1. Britain and France were **allies**, so they fought together against other countries.
2. Britain and France's **enemy** was Germany.
3. Germany knew it could not win the war, so it **surrendered**.
4. The **tension** between the two countries grew into a conflict.
5. A group of **terrorists** hid bombs in the train, frightening the passengers.
6. A **treaty** was signed in 1919, and peace returned to Europe.

LEARN KEY WORDS

allies
enemy
surrendered
tension
terrorists
treaty

READING STRATEGY
Noting Causes and Effects

History texts often have **cause-and-effect organization**. A **cause** is a person, event, or thing that makes something happen. The thing that happens is the **effect**. In a text that has cause-and-effect organization, the writer discusses causes and then shows their effects.

As you read, follow these steps:

- Look for words that show effect, for example, *so*:

  cause   effect
  The two countries couldn't agree, **so** *there was a lot of tension.*

- Look for words that show cause, for example, *because*:

  effect   cause
  Many people lost their homes **because** *the city was bombed.*

Note that sometimes the effect is stated before the cause. Copy the chart into your notebook. Use it to note causes and effects.

Cause	→	Effect
	→	

137

VOCABULARY

Read aloud the Key Words, clearly enunciating each one. Then read each sentence aloud, and have students raise their hands when they hear the Key Words. Model how to use context clues to help students figure out the meanings of any unfamiliar words. For example, *In the first sentence, I read that Britain and France were allies. I'm not sure what the word allies means, but I can use context clues in the sentence to figure it out. It says that they fought together against other countries. So allies must be a synonym for the word friends.* Then demonstrate for students how to use a dictionary to check their answers. Tell students to write each word and its meaning in their notebooks.

READING STRATEGY

Have students read the Reading Strategy text as a choral reading. Point out that history texts are often written using a cause-and-effect organization. This type of text structure explains how or why something happens. Tell students to identify cause-and-effect this way:

1. Look for an event or action that causes, or makes something happen.
2. Pay attention to the effect, or what happens as a result of an event or action.
3. Look for signal words, such as *because, so, due to,* and *as a result.*

Then remind students that sometimes the effect is stated before the cause. Have them copy the chart on page 137 into their notebooks to record cause-and-effect situations as they read.

REACHING ALL STUDENTS

LANGUAGE LEVELS

Beginning: Model a cause-and-effect situation for students. Say, "It's too bright in here." Then walk to the light switch and turn off the light. Ask students why you turned off the light—the cause. *(It was too bright.)* Then ask them what happened as a result—the effect. *(You turned off the light.)* Invite students to demonstrate their own cause-and-effect statements.

Advanced: Write the following words and phrases on the board: *as a result, so, due to, therefore, because, for, this led to, since, hence,* and *thus.* Reread the Vocabulary sentences and tell which ones contain words that signal a cause-and-effect relationship. *(sentences 1 and 3)* Then have students use the Key Words and the words and phrases on the board to write cause-and-effect sentences of their own.

READING SUMMARY

This selection summarizes the events that led to the beginning and end of World War I. It reviews the background to the conflict, lists the countries that made up the Allied Nations and the Central Powers, and describes what life was like in the trenches. In addition, the selection reviews many modern weapons that were used in this armed conflict for the first time.

SCAFFOLDING

Have students read silently as they listen to the selection on the CD/tape. Then read the selection together as a class.

GUIDED READING

1. Which country had bigger and more modern factories, Germany or Britain? *(Germany)*
2. What did Germany want to acquire, more people or more resources? *(more resources)*
3. Whose assassination spurred Austria-Hungary to declare war on Serbia? *(Archduke Franz Ferdinand, the son of the emperor of Austria-Hungary)*
4. What year marked the start of World War I? *(1914)*

FOCUS ON CONTENT — Social Studies

First, preview the article. Then, as you read each paragraph more carefully, look for words such as so *and* because *to find causes and effects. Use the cause-and-effect chart you copied from page 137.*

World War I

Background to the Conflict

At the beginning of the twentieth century, there was a lot of tension among countries in Europe. One reason was the balance of power—that is, no one country wanted another country to have more power than it did. Britain, France, and Germany were competing with each other for **overseas trade**. Britain was worried because Germany had bigger, more modern factories. Germany was worried because France had a lot of power and wealth and **colonies** in Africa. Germany wanted more land and **resources**. Also, Russia and Austria-Hungary were trying to gain more power in the Balkan states in southeast Europe. Because of this tension, the countries formed two powerful **alliances**:

- Britain, France, Russia
- Germany, Austria-Hungary, Italy

By the middle of 1914, Europe was close to war.

▲ A German factory in 1914

overseas trade, the buying and selling of foreign products
colonies, countries or areas that are ruled by other countries
resources, things that create wealth, such as land and energy
alliances, agreements between countries to become allies

138

GRAMMAR MINILESSON

Wh- Questions
Before reading pages 138 and 139, tell students that informational texts often answer questions that begin with *who, what, where, when,* and *why.* Have students preview the text and then generate a list of questions about World War I. Record them on the board and underline *who, what, where, when,* and *why* in each question. After students have completed the reading, have them discuss any answers they found to their questions. Point out that the answers to *who, what,* and *where* are often nouns.

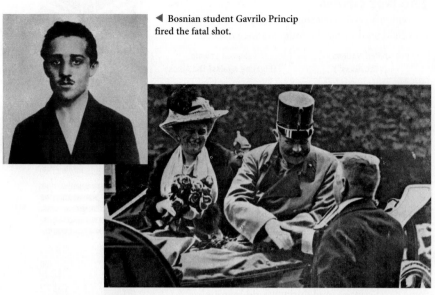

◄ Bosnian student Gavrilo Princip fired the fatal shot.

▲ Archduke Ferdinand and his wife shortly before the assassination

The Assassination

In 1914, Austria-Hungary ruled Bosnia, a small state in the Balkans in eastern Europe. Some people in Serbia, another state in the Balkans, wanted Bosnia to be part of Serbia because many Serbs lived in Bosnia. They wanted to be independent of Austria-Hungary.

Archduke Franz Ferdinand, the son of the **emperor** of Austria-Hungary, visited Sarajevo, the capital of Bosnia. The Serbs in Bosnia were unhappy about the archduke's visit. On June 28, 1914, a Bosnian student, supported by a group of Serbian terrorists, assassinated him. Austria-Hungary declared war on Serbia on July 28. The war quickly spread as other countries defended their allies. By mid-August 1914, most of Europe was at war.

---

assassination, the killing of an important person
emperor, ruler of a country or countries

BEFORE YOU GO ON ...

1. Who ruled Bosnia in 1914? Why did this cause tension?
2. What happened as a result of Archduke Ferdinand's assassination?

HOW ABOUT YOU?
- Do you know about any other assassinations? Discuss.

139

CRITICAL THINKING

Have students respond orally or in writing to these questions:
- Why do you think the Serbians were upset by the visit of Archduke Franz Ferdinand? *(Possible answer: They felt that Bosnia should belong to Serbia.)*
- Do you think war might have been declared even if Archduke Ferdinand had not been assassinated? Why or Why not? *(Possible answer: Yes, because there were so many unresolved conflicts in the area.)*

MODELING THE READING STRATEGY

Noting Causes and Effects: Have students find two cause-and-effect statements on page 138. *(Britain was worried because Germany had bigger, more modern factories. Germany was worried because France had a lot of power and wealth and colonies in Africa.)* Have students copy the statements into their notebooks, underlining the cause and circling the effect.

ACTIVE READING

Have students copy a sequence-of-events chart in their notebooks. After they read pages 138 and 139, model filling out the first box with the assassination of the archduke. Have students complete the chart with other key events of World War I.

Viewpoint

Have students look at the photos on pages 138 and 139. Ask them to use the photos as prompts to state some of the main ideas they read about on these pages.

REACHING ALL STUDENTS

LANGUAGE LEVELS

Beginning: Have students make a two-column chart and label the left column *Country* and the right column *What They Wanted*. Ask students to reread pages 138 and 139 and list all the countries mentioned in the left column. Have them work with a partner to complete the chart, listing in the right column the reason why each country joined the war. Invite them to use their finished chart to write complete sentences based on this model: *Britain wanted more overseas trade.*

Advanced: After students read the first page, discuss with them why Britain and France might have become allies. Have students explain in writing why coming to the aid of Britain would have benefited France, while helping France would have been in Britain's best interest.

GUIDED READING

1. Was Serbia fighting with the Allies or the Central Powers? *(The Allies)*

2. Which country changed sides in 1915? *(Italy)*

3. Why were tanks difficult to destroy? *(They carried big guns, and the metal belts over their wheels made them very difficult to destroy.)*

4. Which invention could protect the wearer from some poisonous gases? *(a gas mask)*

The War Grows

Within a year, many countries had joined in the war. This chart shows how the countries were divided.

Allied Nations ("The Allies")		Central Powers (Fighting against the Allies)
Britain	Australia	Germany
France	New Zealand	Austria-Hungary
Russia	Canada	Bulgaria
Belgium	South Africa	Ottoman Empire (Turkey, etc.)
Portugal	Soldiers from	Italy (changed sides and joined
Greece	French and	the Allies in 1915)
Serbia	British colonies	
Montenegro	in Africa, Asia,	
Romania	the Pacific, and	
	the Caribbean	

The "First Modern War"

World War I is often called the "first modern war" because soldiers used modern weapons for the first time. New **inventions** were created using the latest **technology**. Some new weapons used during World War I were:

Machine guns   These guns, invented by an American, shot many bullets very quickly.

Submarines   These underwater ships shot torpedoes—bombs that are fired underwater.

Poison gas and gas masks   Poison gas caused **choking**, blindness, **blisters**, and sometimes death. Gas masks protected soldiers.

Tanks   These heavy vehicles had big guns and metal belts over their wheels, so they were difficult to attack and destroy.

Periscope rifles   Two mirrors were attached to a rifle, so that when lifted over the top of the trenches, the soldier could see the enemy.

Fighter airplanes   These small planes were armed with machine guns.

---

inventions, completely new things
technology, the knowledge and equipment that is used in the making of machines, etc.
choking, coughing; gasping for breath
blisters, lumps on the skin, filled with liquid, usually caused by burning

140

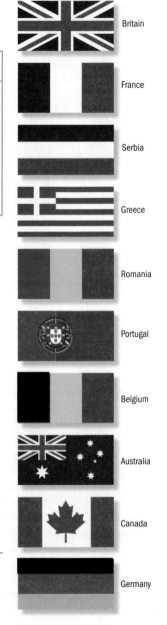

Britain

France

Serbia

Greece

Romania

Portugal

Belgium

Australia

Canada

Germany

MULTICULTURAL NOTE   Tell students that in many parts of the world, young men are required to serve in the armed forces for a certain period of time. Countries that currently require military service include Germany, the Czech Republic, Hungary, Italy, Poland, and Russia. In the United States, young men must register with the government when they turn eighteen years of age. Then, if the need arises, they may be selected for compulsory military service through a process called the draft. Invite students to share what they know about military service in their home countries. Then ask them to discuss the advantages and disadvantages of the draft from the point of view of the government and of the young men who must serve in the armed forces.

◀ Submarine

◀ Gas mask

▲ Fighter airplane

▲ Tank

BEFORE YOU GO ON . . .

1 What were the names of the two groups of countries that were fighting against each other?

2 Why was World War I called the "first modern war"?

HOW ABOUT YOU?
- Have you ever seen any war movies? If so, what weapons were used?

141

Have students respond orally or in writing to these questions:

- If you were a soldier, what do you think the disadvantage to a tank might be? *(Possible answer: It doesn't move very fast.)*
- What do you notice about the chart showing how the countries of the world were divided? *(Possible answer: There were many more Allied Nations than Central Powers.)*

MODELING THE READING STRATEGY

Noting Causes and Effects: Have students find examples of cause-and-effect statements on page 140. Students should look for the words *because* and *so* in the passage. Have students determine what type of question a cause-and-effect statement often answers. *(why)*

Viewpoint

Have students look at the illustrations of the weapons on page 141. Ask them to discuss what it must have been like to use these weapons for the first time.

EXTEND THE LESSON

Have small groups of students research other inventions of the early 1900s. Suggest they look into the fields of medicine, factory equipment, and entertainment. Encourage them to report their findings to the class.

REACHING ALL STUDENTS

LANGUAGE LEVELS

Beginning: Have students focus on the kinds of weapons mentioned in the selection. Ask students to list the words and their definitions in "new word dictionaries." Encourage students to sketch a picture of the item next to the definition. Then have students practice reading the definitions orally.

Advanced: Read aloud the introductory paragraph of the subsection titled "The 'First Modern War.'" Ask students to discuss whether they think the new inventions helped resolve the conflict more quickly than previous weapons might have. Have students explain their ideas in writing.

LEARNING MODALITIES

Visual: Assign each student an Allied or Central Powers country to find in an atlas. Then display a large world map on the wall. Have each student point out where their country was located and identify it as one of the Allied Nations or one of the Central Powers.

T141

Teach

MODELING THE READING STRATEGY

Previewing: Before reading, have volunteers point out the boldface headings that precede each section. Have students read aloud each heading and predict what kind of information they think the section will contain.

GUIDED READING

1. What was one way soldiers protected themselves from the wet conditions? *(They sat on wooden boards called duckboards.)*
2. When did soldiers sleep? *(during the day)*
3. When did the United States enter the war? *(1917)*
4. What happened on June 28, 1919? *(Germany surrendered and signed a peace treaty.)*

across the curriculum

MATH Have students read the chart on page 143. Then ask them what conclusion they can draw from the information on the chart. For example, how severe were U.S. casualties compared to German casualties?

ACTIVITY: Ask students to determine the answers to the following questions:

- What was the total number of soldiers killed in the countries listed on the chart? *(7,101,387)*
- How many more soldiers were lost from France than from Austria-Hungary? *(157,800)*

Life in the Trenches

Soldiers dug trenches for protection from the enemy. The trenches were muddy after it rained, so soldiers put pieces of wood—called duckboards—on the ground to try to stay dry. ❶ The trenches were very hot in the summer and freezing cold in the winter. Rats and lice spread diseases such as trench fever. Soldiers spent about a week in the trenches. Then they went to a rest area where they could wash and change clothes before returning to the trenches.

Most of the fighting was at night, so soldiers often slept during the day. They wrote letters home or kept diaries. Many soldiers were homesick. They had a hard life in the trenches.

The United States Enters the War

From the beginning of the war, President Woodrow Wilson wanted the United States to stay **neutral**. People in the United States were divided about the war. Many U.S. citizens were from European countries, so there was support for both sides. In 1915, Germany announced it would attack all neutral ships headed to Britain. In 1917, Germany announced **unrestricted** submarine warfare. That meant Germany's submarines attacked all foreign **cargo ships** to try to cut **supplies** to Britain. When Germany sank some U.S. ships, President Wilson declared war on Germany and joined the Allies.

---

neutral, not supporting any country or alliance in a conflict
unrestricted, without limits
cargo ships, ships that carry food and other things
supplies, things that people need for daily life

142

◄ The trenches stretched almost 650 kilometers (400 mi.).

▲ U.S. President Woodrow Wilson

PHONICS MINILESSON

Digraphs *wh, ng*

Say the following words aloud: *what, where,* and *wheel.* Explain that the letters *w* and *h* represent the sound students hear at the beginning of these words. (/hw/) Point out that these letters form a digraph, one sound represented by two consonants. Have students repeat the following words: *what, when,* and *why.* Then ask them to name other words that begin with /hw/.

Use the words *sing* and *song* to point out the final *ng* digraph. Then read the following sentences and have students raise their hands when they hear words that contain /hw/ or /ng/:

The trenches were freezing in the winter.
Trenches were long narrow holes in the earth.
When did President Wilson declare war?
Soldiers often slept during the day.
Germany tried to stop supplies from going to Britain.
Where is Hungary?

T142

Germany Surrenders

By 1918, the Allies had stopped supplies from going to Germany, where people were **starving** because there was so little food. By October, the Allies defeated Bulgaria and Turkey. In November, Germany asked the Allies for an **armistice**. They signed an armistice on November 11, 1918. After more than four years, the war finally ended. Germany surrendered and a peace treaty was signed on June 28, 1919.

After the War

With the end of World War I, the map of Europe changed. Some countries, such as Germany, had to give up land. Other countries, such as Greece, gained land. Austria-Hungary and the Ottoman Empire were broken up into separate countries.

More than 65 million soldiers fought in the war, of whom more than half were killed or injured—8 million killed, 2 million dead of illness and diseases, 21 million wounded, and nearly 8 million taken prisoner or missing. More than 6 million **civilians** died, too. People hoped it would be the "war to end all wars," but it wasn't. World War II followed only twenty-one years later.

starving, very hungry
armistice, agreement to stop fighting
civilians, people who aren't in the army or navy

▲ Trenches were long narrow holes in the earth.

Country	Soldiers Killed
Germany	1,773,700
Russia	1,700,000
France	1,357,800
Austria-Hungary	1,200,000
British Empire	908,371
United States	116,516
Serbia	45,000

BEFORE YOU GO ON . . .

1 Why was life in the trenches hard?

2 Which country lost the most soldiers?

HOW ABOUT YOU?
- Why do you think so many civilians died?

143

Have students respond orally or in writing to these questions:

- How do you think writing in their diaries helped soldiers when they were not fighting? *(Possible answer: It helped pass the time and was a way for them to express their feelings.)*
- Why did Germany want to keep supplies from going to Britain? *(Possible answer: If they forced the British people to starve, they would weaken the British army.)*
- Do you think the United States should have remained neutral? Tell why or why not. *(Answers will vary.)*

Viewpoint

Have students look at the pictures of the World War I trenches. Ask them to tell what they think it might be like to spend a week in a trench. Discuss how they think they would pass the time when they weren't fighting or sleeping.

WEBSITES

For more information, log on to http://www.longman.com/shiningstar for links to other interesting websites about World War I.

REACHING ALL STUDENTS

LANGUAGE LEVELS

Beginning: Have student pairs reread pages 142 and 143. Ask each pair to record information from the text that explains why World War I was hard for soldiers and civilians, such as *Soldiers stayed in muddy trenches* or *German people were starving.* Have pairs report their ideas to the class.

Advanced: Have students reread the second sentence at the top of page 142. Ask them to identify the section of the sentence that tells why soldiers put pieces of wood on the ground. Then divide the class into pairs, and have students reread pages 142 and 143 to find two more cause-and-effect statements. Have each pair read their cause-and-effect statements to the class.

Review and Practice

COMPREHENSION

Call on a volunteer to read the Comprehension directions aloud and then review the chart with students. Have them copy the chart into their notebooks and use the selection to write a fact about each country. After discussing the questions beneath the chart, divide students into two groups. Assign each group to represent a country on the chart that participated in World War I. Have each group use the information on their charts as a starting point to present an oral report on their country, explaining why it participated in the conflict. Then have students respond orally or in writing to these questions:

1. Which country or countries were concerned about overseas trade? *(Britain, France, Germany, United States)*

2. Why did terrorists from Serbia assassinate Archduke Franz Ferdinand? *(They did not want to be ruled by his father, the emperor of Austria-Hungary.)*

3. Which country delayed entry into the war until their trading ships were threatened? *(United States)*

CRITICAL THINKING

After students compare the map on page 136 to the map on page 144, have them respond orally or in writing to these questions:

- Which country changed the most as a result of the war? *(Austria-Hungary)*

- Name one country whose size changed very little as a result of the war. *(France)*

COMPREHENSION

Reread the text. Copy the chart into your notebook. Then write a fact about each country. Use key words, such as *allies, enemy,* and *surrendered,* in some of your sentences. Edit your work in pairs.

Country	World War I Fact
Britain	*Britain formed an alliance with France.*
France	
United States	*The United States tried to stay neutral.*
Germany	
Bosnia	
Russia	
Austria-Hungary	

Compare this map to the map on page 136. Which countries gained land after World War I? Which countries lost land? Which countries are new?

▲ Europe after World War I

144

EXTENSION

Reread the text under the heading "Life in the Trenches" on page 142, and look at the picture of the soldiers in the trenches. Imagine that you are a soldier living in the trenches. In your notebook, write a letter home describing your life. What time of year is it? What do you see? What do you hear? What do you do in your free time?

DISCUSSION

Discuss in pairs or small groups.

1. Why did the war end in 1918?

2. Why do countries form alliances with each other?

3. Look at the map on page 144. How do you think the Allies stopped supplies from going to Germany?

4. Look at the cause-and-effect chart you made as you were reading the text. Talk about the causes and effects you wrote on your chart. Are your charts similar to those of your classmates?

5. Look at the painting, *Gassed*. What do you think is happening?

▲ *Gassed*, by American artist John Singer Sargent, painted in 1918–1919

145

EXTENSION

Have students take turns reading the Extension directions aloud. Ask students to identify the recipient of their letter, and to describe the mood that they wish to convey. Invite students to share examples of some of the sensory words they will use to describe their life in the trenches. After students complete their letters, encourage volunteers to read them aloud to the class.

DISCUSSION

Have students work in pairs or small groups and take turns reading the Discussion questions. Remind students to refer to the reading selection to help them answer the questions. As a class, have students share their answers for each question.

METACOGNITION

Ask students:

1. What activities did you find easiest to complete in this part? Which did you find most challenging? What helped you complete the challenging activities?

2. Which helped you more in understanding "World War I," asking questions or using the cause-and-effect chart? Why?

3. How much did you participate in group discussions? What would help you participate more?

REACHING ALL STUDENTS

LANGUAGE LEVELS

Beginning: Have students point to each box of the chart on page 144 as you read aloud the information. Have students identify the headings. Complete the World War I fact about France together, and ask students to tell where they would find the answers in the reading. Then have students complete the rest of the chart.

Advanced: After students write their letters, have them reread them and look for adjectives that describe the people, places, and things that surround them in the trenches. Encourage students to consider the mood they want to convey (e.g., somber, uplifting) and choose adjectives to add to their letter that communicate that mood. Have each student read aloud to the class two sentences he or she improved by adding precise adjectives.

T145

Connect

In this section, you will read a letter and two poems. The letter, written by a young soldier, Frank Earley, describes his experiences in the war. The poems are based on real events and express the poets' feelings about war.

READING SUMMARY

"Letter Home" is an actual letter written by a young soldier who was killed shortly after he wrote it. It is addressed to his father and examines his thoughts on dying. "Can We Forget?" is a poem by Cora Inez Keyes that describes memories associated with war.

SCAFFOLDING

Before students read the letter, read it aloud to them, modulating your voice to express the emotions of a young man reaching out to his father from the trenches. Ask students to read in a manner that reflects the mood of the letter.

GUIDED READING

1. Is the author writing a letter to his sister or his father? *(his father)*
2. What happened to the man the author was talking to? *(He was killed in the last battle.)*
3. What does the soldier in "Can We Forget?" say as he leaves? *(Be brave and don't grieve.)*

ABOUT THE AUTHOR

Frank Earley's collection of letters is stored at the Imperial War Museum. Students can read portions of his letters in the book *1918: Year of Victory* by Malcolm Brown.

Letter Home

Sunday afternoon, 1st September, 1918

My dear Father,

    It is a strange feeling to me but a very real one, that every letter now that I write home to you or to the little sisters may be the last that I shall write or you read. I do not want you to think that I am depressed; indeed on the contrary, I am very cheerful. But out here, in odd moments the realization comes to me of how close death is to us. A week ago I was talking with a man . . . who had been out here for nearly four years, untouched. He was looking forward with certainty to going on leave soon. And now he is dead—killed in a moment during our last advance. Well, it was God's will.

    I say this to you because I hope that you will realize, as I do, the possibility of the like happening to myself. I feel very glad myself that I can look the fact in the face without fear or misgiving. Much as I hope to live through it all for your sakes and my little sisters! I am quite prepared to give my life as so many have done before me. All I can do is put myself in God's hands for him to decide, and you and the little ones pray for me to the Sacred Heart and Our Lady.

    Well, I have not much time left and I must end. With my dear love.

Pray for me.

Your son,

Frank

---

on the contrary, it's the opposite
going on leave, having a rest from fighting
look the fact in the face, deal with the reality
misgiving, doubt
journalist, someone who writes for a newspaper, magazine, television, or radio
wound, an injury, especially made by a knife or bullet

146

About the Author

Frank Earley

Lance-Corporal Frank Earley was a young British **journalist**. His letters to his family were usually full of enthusiasm and excitement. It is only in this very last letter that he showed his more serious and thoughtful side. The next day Frank Earley suffered a serious **wound** to his chest and died hours later. He was nineteen.

SPELLING MINILESSON

Adding *-ed*

Write *want* and *wanted* on the board and call on a volunteer to read the words aloud. Ask students to tell what difference they see and hear in the words. (*Wanted* has *-ed* on the end.) Repeat with *jump* and *jumped*. Point out that when some verbs are written in the simple past, we add *-ed* to the end. The *-ed* can be pronounced /əd/, /d/, or /t/. Write this two-column chart on the board, and have students copy the chart into their notebooks.

Present	Past		Present	Past
return	returned		move	moved
raid	raided		plead	pleaded
ask	asked		trick	tricked

Have students read each word and listen for the *-ed* pronunciation. Then ask students to look for words that end in *-ed* in the Part 1 readings and list them in their notebooks.

War Poems

Can We Forget?

Can I ever forget? Can I ever forget?
Oh, God! Can I ever forget
My soldier boy's smile and the light in his eye,
With the army badge fresh on his sleeve—
The firm clasp of his hand and the warmth of his kiss
As he said, "Dear, be brave and don't grieve"?

Can I ever forget? Can I ever forget?
Oh, God! Can I ever forget
How the wealth of his spirit shone out of his face
When he knew we might see him no more,
While we watched his dear form where he stood on the deck
As the steamer pulled out from the shore?

Can I ever forget? Can I ever forget?
Oh, God! Can I ever forget
The long, weary days in the hospital ward,
The brow knot with pain and the face, wan and white,
The fever-racked frame and the hideous night—
The death at the left and the death at the right—
Oh, God! Can I ever forget?

Can I ever forget? Can I ever forget?
Oh, God! Can I ever forget
All the fierce storms that raged in the wild warfare's wake—
All the ways where my lad did his part—
Or the messages chill over the telegraph line,
Or the cold charge that went through his heart?

Cora Inez Keyes

steamer, ship
ward, patients' room
fever-racked, having a fever, or high temperature, resulting from sickness
fierce, wild
lad, boy

U.S. corporal, 1918 ▶

LITERARY ELEMENT

Sometimes words in a poem *rhyme*. Words that rhyme have the same sound, except for the beginning sound. For example, in "Can We Forget?" the words *sleeve* and *grieve* rhyme. What other words in the poem rhyme?

BEFORE YOU GO ON . . .

1. Why does Frank Earley say that every letter he writes may be the last?
2. What do you think happened to the soldier in the poem? **Answers will vary.**

HOW ABOUT YOU?
• What do you find sad in the letter or poem? Why?

147

CRITICAL THINKING

Have students respond orally or in writing to these questions:
● What is one way you think the author of the letter copes with the knowledge that he may die soon? *(Possible answer: He depends on his religious faith.)*
● How do you think Frank Earley's father felt when he read his son's letter? *(Answers will vary.)*
● Who do you think is speaking in "Can We Forget?" *(Possible answer: a dead soldier's mother)*

MODELING THE READING STRATEGY

Visualizing: Have students read the poem, and ask them to describe the pictures that come to mind as they are reading. Ask students to tell whether the images of the poem make them feel peaceful or uncomfortable.

Viewpoint

Have students look at the illustration on page 147 and brainstorm adjectives that describe the mood of the picture.

LITERARY ELEMENT

Have volunteers read aloud the text in the box. Then have students identify the other rhyming words in the poem. Next, suggest variations on the rhyming words in the first stanza, such as *sleeve/leave*. Have students brainstorm other words that rhyme with words such as *more, shore, white, night, right.*

REACHING ALL STUDENTS

LANGUAGE LEVELS

Beginning: Have students reread "Letter Home" on page 146. Then guide students to scan the text for adjectives that the soldier uses to describe himself and his feelings, such as *strange, not depressed, cheerful, without fear, without misgiving*. Ask students if they think these words truly reflect what the young man is feeling and why they think as they do. Challenge students to write a sentence stating their opinion and their reasons.

Advanced: Have students imagine that they are one of the sisters referred to in "Letter Home." Ask them to write a letter in reply to Frank Earley. Remind students to reread "Letter Home" and use information from Earley's letter in their response. Encourage them to respond to the soldier in a way that will make him feel both comforted and confident.

Connect

READING SUMMARY

In "Grass" by Carl Sandburg, grass is personified as the poet reflects on death as a result of war.

GUIDED READING

1. According to "Grass," where are bodies piled high? *(Austerlitz, Waterloo, Gettysburg, Ypres ['ēprə], Verdun [vərdən'])*

2. What do the passengers ask the conductor after grass has covered the bodies? *(What place is this? Where are we now?)*

ABOUT THE AUTHOR

Carl Sandburg was known for his poems about urban life and rural America. His style featured unrhymed free verse and clear, vivid imagery.

—Viewpoint—

Have students look at the photo of Carl Sandburg. Ask them to discuss what it might have been like to go to war at the age of 20. How might Sandburg's experiences have contributed to his work as a writer?

across the curriculum

HISTORY Have students locate the places mentioned in "Grass" in an atlas. Then have them use an encyclopedia or the Internet to research which war is associated with each place.

T148

Grass

Pile the bodies high at **Austerlitz** and **Waterloo**.
Shovel them under and let me work—
　　　　　　　I am the grass; I cover all.
And pile them high at **Gettysburg**
And pile them high at **Ypres** and **Verdun**.
Shovel them under and let me work.
Two years, ten years, and passengers ask the **conductor**:
　　　　　　　What place is this?
　　　　　　　Where are we now?

　　　　　　　I am the grass.
　　　　　　　Let me work.

　　　　　　　　　　Carl Sandburg

Austerlitz, Waterloo, Gettysburg, Ypres, Verdun, places where battles were fought in different wars
shovel them under, bury them
conductor, the person on a train or bus who sells tickets and announces stops

About the Poet

Carl Sandberg
(1878–1967)

From age thirteen, Sandburg worked at many jobs—milkman, bottle-washer, shoe-shiner, and farmer. He joined the army when he was twenty and fought in the Spanish-American War. After that, he worked his way through college and became a reporter in Chicago.

BEFORE YOU GO ON . . .

1 What does the grass do to the places where battles were fought?

2 What do the last two lines of "Grass" mean?

HOW ABOUT YOU? Answers will vary.

• How does the poem "Grass" make you feel?

148

Link the Readings

REFLECTION

Reread the letter and poems about World War I. Then copy the chart into your notebook and complete it. Compare your answers in small groups.

Title of Selection	Type of Text (Genre)	Purpose of Selection	How I Feel about It
"World War I"	social studies article		
"Letter Home"			
"Can We Forget?"			
"Grass"		to make people think about war and to see it in a different way	

DISCUSSION

Discuss in pairs or small groups.

1. Choose one war poem and read it aloud in pairs or small groups. Then discuss the words that express emotion. What does each part of the poem mean?
2. List five negative effects of war on people's lives. Compare your lists.

149

REFLECTION

Have students take turns reading the Reflection directions. Read the headings on the chart together and discuss their meanings. Have students copy the chart into their notebooks and complete it. As students complete the third column, encourage them to explain their feelings. Have student groups discuss the answers when the charts are complete. Then ask:

1. Which reading selections are meant to express the thoughts and feelings of the author? *("Letter Home," "Grass," "Can We Forget?")*
2. What type of text is "Grass"? *(a poem)*

COOPERATIVE GROUPING

Pair intermediate and advanced students with beginning students. Have pairs read the Reflection activity and complete the chart together. Tell students to refer to the text together, agree on an answer, and then take turns recording their answers. Call on one student in each pair to choose their favorite selection and share with the class how they feel about it.

DISCUSSION

Have students work in pairs or small groups and take turns reading the Discussion questions. As a class, have students share their answers for each question.

CRITICAL THINKING

Discuss the conflicts faced in each of the selections. Ask students to tell in writing how they think war impacts soldiers.

REACHING ALL STUDENTS

LANGUAGE LEVELS

Beginning: Help students understand the use of personification in "Grass" by asking them who is speaking. Point out that personification gives a nonhuman thing human attributes, so that it can speak, feel, and think. Ask students how the grass seems to feel in the poem. Invite students to suggest other things the grass might say and feel.

Advanced: Ask students to discuss how the letter and poems helped them understand more about conflict and conflict resolution. Have students explain which piece they found most informative and which they found more interesting.

Teach

GRAMMAR

Have students read the introductory text aloud. Make sure students understand that a conjunction can link two complete sentences, and show a relationship between two or more ideas. After reading the examples, emphasize that the meaning of the two original statements is not changed when the sentences are joined.

Have students skim "World War I" and write examples of sentences that contain the word *so* in their notebooks, such as *The trenches were muddy after it rained, so soldiers put pieces of wood, called duckboards, on the ground to try to stay dry.* Have them read their sentences aloud, identify the two complete ideas, and tell which is the cause and which is the effect. Then have students complete items 1 to 6 at the bottom of the page.

SCAFFOLDING

Write ____ *so* ____ on the board. Invent a problem with a touch of the ridiculous, such as *There weren't any forks for my spaghetti,* and write the phrase in the first part of the sentence frame. Have a volunteer think of a consequence or a solution, come to the board, and write it in the second part of the frame. Repeat until you have a few examples on the board. Then have students find the portion of each sentence that states the cause *(first)* and the portion that states the effect *(second)*. Invite students to write their own silly sentences and then exchange them with a partner to find the cause and the effect in each sentence.

Connect to Writing

GRAMMAR

Using *so* as a Conjunction

Use the **conjunction so** to connect two sentences to show a result. The first sentence shows the **cause** for something, and the second sentence shows the **effect** or result. Use a comma before *so*.

cause	effect
Rats and lice lived in the trenches. Many of the soldiers got trench fever.	
Rats and lice lived in the trenches, **so** many of the soldiers got trench fever.	

cause	effect
Serbia and Russia were allies. Russia supported Serbia.	
Serbia and Russia were allies, **so** Russia supported Serbia.	

cause	effect
Tanks were heavy vehicles with big guns. They were difficult to destroy.	
Tanks were heavy vehicles with big guns, **so** they were difficult to destroy.	

Practice

Match the cause sentences to the effect sentences. Then write them in your notebook, combining them using *so*. Remember to use commas.

1. Trenches were very muddy.
2. Most fighting was at night.
3. Soldiers wrote letters home.
4. Mustard gas was a dangerous new weapon.
5. Cities and towns were bombed.
6. The Allies stopped supplies from going to Germany.

a. Many civilians died.
b. Soldiers put duckboards on the ground to keep dry.
c. Germany became weaker.
d. Soldiers often slept during the day.
e. Soldiers needed gas masks.
f. Their families knew they were still alive.

150

T150

SKILLS FOR WRITING

Cause-and-Effect Organization in Writing

Sometimes a text is organized in terms of causes and effects. Here are some tips for writing a text with cause-and-effect organization:

- Think about why the event happened. This is the cause. Use the word *because* to show a cause.
- Think about what happened. This is the effect. Use the word *so* to show an effect.

Read this model. Then answer the questions that follow.

Gabrielle Johnson

Friendship

Spreading rumors can cause a friendship to end. There is a girl in my school named Carrie. We used to be really close friends. However, she began to phone my friends and spread bad rumors about me. I got very upset, so I decided to confront her. When I asked her about it, she denied it. That made me even angrier with her. I stopped talking to her because I was so mad at her. Then she tried to be friends with other kids at school. She betrayed them as well, so she ended up friendless. The whole situation made me realize the effect that one small event can have on a friendship.

---

1. What event is discussed in the paragraph?
2. What is the cause? What is the effect?
3. What words show that the writer is using cause and effect?

151

SKILLS FOR WRITING

Read aloud the introductory text, including the bulleted list of tips. Have a volunteer read aloud the sample paragraph. Then point out the sentences in the paragraph that illustrate cause and effect through the use of *so* and *because*. Finally, have students use the paragraph to answer the questions below it.

SCAFFOLDING

Have students brainstorm questions they have about World War I and choose one that starts with the word *why* to research. After students gather enough information to answer the question, have them write a sentence that summarizes their findings. Call on volunteers to read their summarizing statements aloud. Then have students suggest ways to rewrite the sentences using *so* and/or *because*. Finally, have the group decide which portion of each sentence describes the cause and which describes the effect.

REACHING ALL STUDENTS

LANGUAGE LEVELS

Beginning: Tell students that a conjunction is a word that connects two related ideas. Remind them that the conjunction *but* connects two related but contrasting ideas, as in the sentence *He liked to be on time, but he was late for dinner.* The word *so* connects two related ideas that show cause and effect. Invite students to create their own cause-and-effect sentences. Call on volunteers to write them on the board.

Advanced: Have the group choose three recent school events in which they all participated. Have them discuss why the events took place and record their responses on the board. Explain that these statements are the cause. Have students suggest complete cause-and-effect sentences that tell what happened and why. Encourage students to use the words *so* or *because* to connect their phrases.

WRITING ASSIGNMENT

Cause-and-Effect Paragraph

Ask a volunteer to read aloud the text at the top of page 152. Then make a list of the cause-and-effect statements as students reread the paragraph on page 151. Read through the list and have students point out the signal words *so* and *because*. Point out to students that sometimes two ideas are written in consecutive sentences.

WRITING STRATEGY

Explain that a cause-and-effect chart can help establish the order of events and show which events caused others to happen. Model with an example, such as *How would you describe a recent basketball game if you were a sports announcer?* Write students' responses in the chart so that a chain of cause-and-effect events is established. Ask questions about your model, such as *What happened first? Who passed the ball? What happened at the end?* Then ask students to write a paragraph that shows a cause or effect related to a specific event. Remind them to first create a chart in their notebooks to put their thoughts in order.

USING THE EDITING CHECKLIST

Have students read aloud the Editing Checklist. Have them read it again with a partner, and use it to revise their writing. Circulate among the students, offering guidance as needed.

WRITING ASSIGNMENT

Cause-and-Effect Paragraph

You will write a paragraph describing an event and its effects.

1. **Read** Reread the paragraph on page 151. Identify the causes and effects.

> **Writing Strategy: Cause-and-Effect Chart**
>
> Before you write your paragraph, organize your ideas. The writer who wrote the model on page 151 used this chart to organize her ideas. First, the writer wrote the causes and then she listed the effects.
>
> | Cause | | Effect |
> |---|---|---|
> | Carrie spread bad rumors. | ⟶ | I got upset. |
> | Carrie denied it. | ⟶ | I got angrier. |
> | Carrie betrayed other friends. | ⟶ | She ended up friendless. |

2. **Use a cause-and-effect chart** Make a chart in your notebook like the one above.

3. **Write** Use your chart to write your paragraph. Use the words *so* and *because* to show the relationship between causes and effects.

> **EDITING CHECKLIST**
>
> **Did you . . .**
> - simply and clearly describe events?
> - show the relationship between events that cause each other?
> - use *so* and *because* to show cause and effect?
> - use capital letters correctly?
> - use commas and periods correctly?

152

PART REVIEW 1

Check Your Knowledge

Language Development

1. Describe cause-and-effect organization. What are two words that signal this kind of organization in a text?
2. Give an example of rhyme. In what type of text do you often find rhyme?
3. What is a cause-and-effect chart? Why is it helpful to use one?
4. Did the letter and the poems you read have anything in common? If so, what?
5. How do the map and timeline on page 136 help you understand the article "World War I"?

Academic Content

1. What new social studies vocabulary did you learn in Part 1? What do the words mean?
2. Which countries formed alliances in World War I?
3. What two changes in the map of Europe resulted from World War I?

British soldier, World War I ▶

153

ASSESS

You can assess students' knowledge of the unit in several different ways.

Portfolio: Have students write their Check Your Knowledge answers on a separate sheet of paper to include in their portfolios.

Traditional: Students can complete the Check Your Knowledge questions as homework. After students complete Check Your Knowledge, use the Assessment Package. Students can complete the Part Test on pages 53–56. For further practice, have students complete the Test Preparation worksheets.

Performance: Have students complete the Check Your Knowledge questions in groups of three as you monitor their discussions.

TEST-TAKING TIP

Remind students to skim through a test before they begin, planning how much time to spend on each section. Explain that students should plan to spend more time on open-ended questions rather than on "quick" questions such as true/false. See the Test Preparation pages in the Assessment Guide for additional test-taking strategies.

METACOGNITION

Before completing Check Your Knowledge, ask students to look for key words that tell them exactly what the question is all about. Have students determine the key words for question 1. *(two words, signal, cause and effect)* Ask students to restate this question in their own words.

REACHING ALL STUDENTS

LANGUAGE LEVELS

Beginning: Write the following sentences on the board:
- *It was hot outside, so he wanted to go swimming.*
- *He practiced the violin because he wanted to be in the orchestra.*

Read each sentence twice. During the second reading, ask students to identify the cause and effect. Have students say "cause" when they hear the cause, and "effect" when they hear the effect.

Advanced: As a class, read aloud the first cause-and-effect statements on the student chart. Have the class discuss which cause-and-effect signal word would best connect the two ideas to make a cause-and-effect sentence. Support students by writing *because, so, therefore,* and *for* on the board for students to choose from. Record the complete sentences on the board. Have students use conjunctions to connect the remaining cause-and-effect sentences.

OBJECTIVES

Explain that in Part 2, students will be reading about historical events that they might study in social studies class. Read the list of objectives to students as they follow along. Explain the meaning of difficult words. When you have finished, ask students to restate what they will learn in their own words. Additional practice activities for these objectives can be found in the **Workbook** and **CD-ROM**.

BACKGROUND

Have students read the text aloud. Help them understand that the phrase "the former Yugoslavia" refers to the country before it was divided into smaller nations. Ask students to find the information that identifies what percentage of the people living in Yugoslavia represents a specific ethnic group. Have students discuss how this information can help them understand the events of the Bosnian War.

COOPERATIVE GROUPING

Pair intermediate and advanced students with beginning students. Have pairs read the Background text. Then have them study the map and answer the questions. Ask pairs to record their responses in their notebooks.

PART 2 Prepare to Read

OBJECTIVES

LANGUAGE DEVELOPMENT

Reading:
- Vocabulary building: *Context, dictionary skills*
- Reading strategy: *Analyzing historical context*
- Text types: *Diary, social studies article*
- Literary element: *Images*

Writing:
- Retell a story
- Sequence-of-events chart
- Eyewitness report

Listening/Speaking:
- Compare and contrast
- Express opinions and feelings

Grammar:
- Pronoun referents

Viewing/Representing:
- Maps, illustrations, Venn diagram

ACADEMIC CONTENT
- Geography vocabulary
- Historical context of the Bosnian War
- Geography of the Balkans

BACKGROUND

Zlata Filipović, an eleven-year-old Bosnian girl, wrote *Zlata's Diary* in 1992, during the Bosnian War. She lived in Sarajevo, the capital of Bosnia, where some of the worst fighting occurred. She used her diary to write about her experience of day-by-day events.

Make connections The map shows the former Yugoslavia in 1991, just before the Bosnian War. Yugoslavia was a united country for many years. It had always been home to many different groups of people. During the 1980s and 1990s, long-standing conflicts caused war among different groups in Yugoslavia. As a result of the war, Yugoslavia broke up into several smaller countries: Bosnia and Herzegovina, Croatia, Macedonia, Slovenia, and Serbia and Montenegro.

Look at the map and answer the questions.

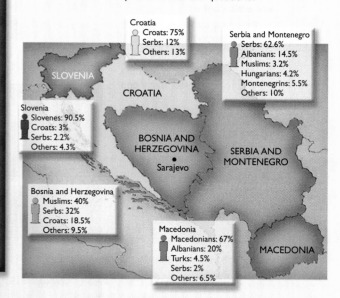

Croatia
- Croats: 75%
- Serbs: 12%
- Others: 13%

Serbia and Montenegro
- Serbs: 62.6%
- Albanians: 14.5%
- Muslims: 3.2%
- Hungarians: 4.2%
- Montenegrins: 5.5%
- Others: 10%

Slovenia
- Slovenes: 90.5%
- Croats: 3%
- Serbs: 2.2%
- Others: 4.3%

Bosnia and Herzegovina
- Muslims: 40%
- Serbs: 32%
- Croats: 18.5%
- Others: 9.5%

Macedonia
- Macedonians: 67%
- Albanians: 20%
- Turks: 4.5%
- Serbs: 2%
- Others: 6.5%

1. How many different groups of people can you see?
2. What might have caused the conflicts in Yugoslavia?

154

TEACHING GUIDE

PRETEACH	Provide Background	Read and discuss the Background information. Complete the activity. (ATE/SB p. 154)
	Present Concepts	Introduce the Reading Strategy. (ATE/SB p. 155)
TEACH	Monitor Comprehension	Informally monitor comprehension while students read the selection independently or in groups. (ATE/SB pp. 156–161)
	Teach and Practice	Present the Grammar, Usage, and Mechanics. (ATE/SB pp. 168, 169) Complete the Writing activity. (ATE/SB p. 170) Present Grammar, Phonics, and Spelling minilessons. (ATE pp. 156, 158, 166)
CONNECT	Connect to Content	Have students read the informational reading and relate it to the literature. (ATE/SB pp. 164–166)
	Across the Curriculum	Present curriculum links as students read. (ATE pp. 158, 165)
ASSESS	Check Knowledge	Assess students' comprehension by having them complete the Check Your Knowledge section. (ATE/SB p. 171)
	Monitor Progress	Use one or more of the print assessment resources in the Assessment Package.
EXTEND	Integrate Language and Apply Understanding	Have students complete the Workshops (ATE/SB pp. 172–175) and choose a project from the Unit Projects. (ATE/SB p. 176) Then have them choose a book to read from Further Reading. (ATE/SB p. 177)

Read these sentences. Use the context to figure out the meanings of the red words. Use a dictionary to check your answers. Write each word and its meaning in your notebook.

1. An ambulance drove the sick and injured people to the hospital.
2. The war killed many people and achieved little. It was madness.
3. Hundreds of people were killed in the massacre.
4. The two presidents must negotiate to end the war between their countries.
5. People were happy when the war was over and there was peace again.
6. War causes a lot of pain and suffering for many people.

LEARN KEY WORDS

- ambulance
- madness
- massacre
- negotiate
- peace
- suffering

VOCABULARY

Clearly pronounce each Key Word. Then read each sentence aloud, and have students raise their hands when they hear the Key Words. Model how to use context clues to help students figure out the meanings of any unfamiliar words. For example, *In the first sentence, I read that an ambulance drove the sick and injured people to the hospital. I'm not sure what an ambulance is, but I know that* drove *is the past tense of* drive. *You can drive a car, so an* ambulance *must be a kind of car that carries sick and injured people.* Then demonstrate for students how to use a dictionary to check their answers. Tell students to write each word and its meaning in their notebooks.

READING STRATEGY

Analyzing Historical Context

When we read a personal narrative, such as a diary, knowing what is happening in the background—its **historical context**—can make the text more understandable and meaningful. Historical contexts may include the political or cultural changes happening at a particular time. If the historical context is a war, this will explain some of the mood of the personal narrative and the emotions that the writer is expressing.

As you read, think about these questions:

- What is happening at the time and place where the writer is?
- What is the writer's reaction to what is happening?

READING STRATEGY

Explain to students that determining the historical context of a selection is a bit like identifying the setting. It includes the political and cultural changes that were taking place in the setting where the story occurs. Suggest that students skim the text for clues about the historical context in which *Zlata's Diary* was written. Have students discuss what information would be helpful for them to know in order to understand the mood and cultural climate of the time. Emphasize that if the text deals with a period of conflict or war, it would help the reader to know who was involved and why there was a conflict.

155

REACHING ALL STUDENTS

LANGUAGE LEVELS

Beginning: Have students look at an atlas page that shows either the former Yugoslavia or its present-day political boundaries. Explain that, beginning in 1991, several of the republics that comprised Yugoslavia broke away to become independent nations, spurring ethnic violence and civil wars that still continue. Have students tell what they know about other civil wars, including the one they read about in Part 1.

Advanced: Explain that when the former Yugoslavia was a single country, the people did not share the same culture, language, or religion. When the region split into independent countries, the resources were also divided, and some countries still faced serious cultural differences. Economic hardship and cultural conflict left these countries unstable. Have students use the map on page 154 to identify the countries and discuss factors that might make Slovenia stable and Bosnia and Herzegovina unstable.

Zlata Filipović was a fifth-grader living in Sarajevo when it came under attack during the Bosnian War in 1992. She describes the experience in her diary.

SCAFFOLDING

Have students read silently as they listen to *Zlata's Diary* on the CD/tape. Ask them to listen for information that answers the *wh-* questions: *who* was involved, *what* happened, *when* did it happen, *where* did it happen, and *why* did it happen. Have students write their answers in a "*wh-* words" web.

GUIDED READING

1. Where is Zlata living, in Sarajevo or Dubrovnik? *(Sarajevo)*
2. Why have Zlata's old friends moved to Dubrovnik? *(The war has stopped there.)*
3. Why is Mirna at her grandparents' house? *(Her apartment was shelled.)*

———————*Viewpoint*———————

Ask students to look at the photos on pages 156 and 157. Discuss how the use of photographs helps to reinforce the genre of nonfiction, connect the reader to the author, and strengthen the author's voice.

FOCUS ON LITERATURE · **Diary**

As you read, think about the events that Zlata describes. How does knowing something about the historical context—in this case, war—help you to understand what Zlata is experiencing? Does it help you understand the mood?

from ZLATA'S DIARY

When Zlata Filipović wrote her diary, she was eleven years old and living in Sarajevo. The people of Sarajevo, including Zlata's family and friends, were caught in the middle of a war. Zlata calls her diary "Mimmy."

Saturday, May 23, 1992

Dear Mimmy,

I'm not writing to you about me anymore. I'm writing to you about war, death, injuries, **shells**, sadness and **sorrow**. Almost all my friends have left. Even if they were here, who knows whether we'd be able to see one another. The phones aren't working, we couldn't even talk to one another. Vanja and Andrej have gone to join Srdjan in Dubrovnik. The war has stopped there. They're lucky. I was so unhappy because of that war in Dubrovnik. I never dreamed it would move to Sarajevo. . . .

I now spend all my time with Bojana and Maja. They're my best friends now. Bojana is a year-and-a-half older than me, she's finished seventh grade and we have a lot in common. Maja is in her last year of school. She's much older than I am, but she's wonderful. I'm lucky to have them, otherwise I'd be all alone among the **grown-ups**.

▲ "I will try to get through this with your support, Mimmy. . . ."

shells, bombs
sorrow, sadness
grown-ups, adults

156

On the news they reported the death of Silva Rizvanbegović, a doctor at the **Emergency Clinic**, who's Mommy's friend. She was in an ambulance. They were driving a wounded man to get him help. Lots of people Mommy and Daddy know have been killed. Oh, God, what is happening here???

Love, Zlata

Tuesday, May 26, 1992

Dear Mimmy,

I keep thinking about Mirna; May 13 was her birthday. I would love to see her so much. I keep asking Mommy and Daddy to take me to her. She left Mojmilo with her mother and father to go to her grandparents' place. Their apartment was shelled and they had to leave it.

▲ In the beginning, the arrival of the blue berets (United Nations peacekeepers) brought hope.

There's no shooting, the past few days have been quiet. I asked Daddy to take me to Mirna's because I made her a little birthday present. I miss her. I wish I could see her.

I was such a **nag** that Daddy decided to take me to her. We went there, but the downstairs door was locked. We couldn't call out to them and I came home feeling **disappointed**. The present is waiting for her, so am I. I suppose we'll see each other.

Love, Zlata

Emergency Clinic, place to go for emergency medical attention
nag, someone who asks for something again and again
disappointed, sad because you expected something different

BEFORE YOU GO ON . . .

1 What happens to Silva in the ambulance?
2 Why is Zlata disappointed when she visits Mirna?

HOW ABOUT YOU?
● What do you think will happen next?

157

Have students respond orally or in writing to these questions:
● Why do you think Zlata writes such sad letters? *(Possible answer: Her life is full of sad events.)*
● In what ways do you think it helps Zlata to have friends who are older than she is nearby? *(Possible answer: They keep her from being too lonely and help look after her.)*

MODELING THE READING STRATEGY

Analyzing Historical Context: Have students create a two-column chart in their notebooks, labeled *Changes* and *Zlata's Reaction.* Students can use the chart to record information about the historical context of *Zlata's Diary* as they read. For example, on page 156, Zlata states that the phones aren't working as a result of the war. Ask how this makes Zlata feel. *(sad, lonely, isolated)* Have students discuss how realizing that this has taken place as a result of the war adds to their understanding of Zlata's feelings.

ACTIVE READING

Have students create a simple word web in their notebooks. Then have them write *Zlata* in the center circle. As students read the excerpts from *Zlata's Diary,* have them write, on lines that radiate from the center circle, the names of characters Zlata mentions, and any important information she gives about these characters.

REACHING ALL STUDENTS

LANGUAGE LEVELS

Beginning: Have students use information in the photographs and the diary entries to discuss what daily life is like for Zlata. Use the information to create a web, with the center circle labeled *Life in Sarajevo.* Draw details from students, such as *shelling, soldiers in the streets, fences preventing travel, no phones.* Add the details to the web.

Advanced: After students read pages 156 and 157, have them discuss the importance of Zlata's friends, particularly at such a difficult time in their lives. Encourage students to offer generalizations about what Zlata and her friends mean to one another, how they support and help one another, and how they give one another hope. Write the generalizations on the board for students to copy into their notebooks.

GUIDED READING

1. How does Zlata see some of the shelling? *(It's shown on TV.)*
2. Where does Zlata's father decide to look for her mother, at her parents' house or the hospital? *(the hospital)*
3. What does Zlata's father intend to do with the furniture, burn it or repair it? Why? *(burn it; They need a way to keep warm since they are without electricity and gas.)*

LITERARY ELEMENT

Ask a volunteer to read the Literary Element text aloud. Explain that a writer uses images to help the reader visualize details. Strong images can help make the author's writing vivid and clear.

across the curriculum

CIVICS   Tell students that one way to solve conflicts is for both sides to sit down and talk about their differences. By talking, a solution that everyone can agree upon can sometimes be reached. Have students use an electronic or print thesaurus to look up synonyms for the following words: *negotiate, compromise, solution.* Ask students to list in their notebooks three synonyms for each word.

Wednesday, May 27, 1992

Dear Mimmy,

SLAUGHTER! MASSACRE! HORROR! CRIME! BLOOD! SCREAMS! TEARS! DESPAIR!

That's what Vaso Miskin Street looks like today. Two shells exploded in the street and one in the market. Mommy was nearby at the time. She ran to Grandma and Granddad's. Daddy and I **were beside ourselves** because she hadn't come home. I saw some of it on TV but still can't believe what I actually saw. It's unbelievable. **I've got a lump in my throat** and a **knot in my tummy**. HORRIBLE! They're taking the wounded to the hospital. It's a **madhouse**. We kept going to the window hoping to see Mommy, but she wasn't back. They released a list of the dead and wounded. Daddy and I were

❶ **tearing our hair out**. We didn't know what had happened to her. Was she alive? At 4:00 Daddy decided to go and check the hospital. He got dressed, and I got ready to go to the Bobars', so as not to stay home alone. I looked out the window one more time and . . . I SAW MOMMY RUNNING ACROSS THE BRIDGE. As she came into the house she started shaking and crying. Through her tears she told us how she had seen **dismembered bodies**. All the neighbors came because they had been afraid for her. Thank God, Mommy is with us. Thank God.

A HORRIBLE DAY. UNFORGETTABLE. HORRIBLE! HORRIBLE!

Your Zlata

---

were beside ourselves, were very worried
I've got a lump in my throat, I feel like crying
knot in my tummy, bad feeling about something
madhouse, a place where everyone seems crazy
tearing our hair out, feeling very worried
dismembered bodies, bodies with no arms or legs

158

LITERARY ELEMENT

Images are words or phrases that create pictures in the reader's mind. Writers use images to describe how things look, feel, sound, smell, and taste. What images does Zlata use to describe the conflict in Sarajevo?

▲ An injured woman is taken to the hospital.

PHONICS MINILESSON

Digraphs *ch, tch*

Say the words *watch, catch,* and *hatch,* emphasizing the final sound /ch/. Write the words on the board and circle the letters *tch.* Point out that the letters *tch* represent the sound they hear at the end of these words. Then say the words *change, children, chew,* and *such.* Have students repeat the words after you. Write the words on the board and call on volunteers to circle the letters *ch* in each one. Point out that these words also contain the sound /ch/, but the sound is represented by the letters *ch.* Ask students to repeat the following words and listen for the sound /ch/: *much, batch, childhood, fetch, chin, choice, itch, cheerful.* Then have students find other words that contain the sound /ch/ in the story. *(each, check, checking, cheerful, childhood)*

Thursday, October 1, 1992

Dear Mimmy,

Spring has been and gone, summer has been and gone, and now it's autumn. October has started. And the war is still on. The days are getting shorter and colder. Soon we'll move the stove upstairs to the apartment. But how will we keep warm? God, is anyone thinking of us here in Sarajevo? Are we going to start winter without electricity, water or gas, and with a war going on?

The **"kids"** are negotiating. Will they finally negotiate something? Are they thinking about us when they negotiate, or are they just trying to **outwit** each other, and leave us to our fate?

Daddy has been checking the attic and cellar for wood. It looks to me as though part of the furniture is going to **wind up** in the stove if this keeps up until winter. It seems that nobody is thinking of us, that this madness is going to go on and on. We have no choice, we have to rely on ourselves, to take care of ourselves and find a way to fight off the oncoming winter.

Mommy came home from work in a state of shock today. Two of her **colleagues** came from Grbavica. It really is true that people are being **expelled** from there. There's no sign of Mommy's and Nedo's relatives or of Lalo. Nedo is going **berserk**.

Your Zlata

---

the **"kids,"** Zlata's slang for the politicians
outwit, be more clever than someone; trick
wind up, end up; finally be
colleagues, people you work with
expelled, forced to leave
berserk, crazy

▲ Cooking is quite an achievement without electricity.

BEFORE YOU GO ON . . .

1. How do Zlata and her father feel after the massacre on Vaso Miskin Street? Why?
2. What is the "madness" that Zlata refers to?

HOW ABOUT YOU? Answers will vary.
- What would you do if you were in Zlata's family?

159

Have students respond orally or in writing to these questions:

- Why didn't Zlata and her father immediately go out and look for Zlata's mother? *(Possible answers: They wanted to be home if she arrived or tried to contact them; it was too dangerous to go out in the streets.)*
- Why do you think people call the politicians "the kids"? *(Possible answer: The people felt the politicians were behaving like selfish children.)*
- In what way does Zlata feel betrayed by the political leadership? *(She thinks they don't care about the people they govern.)*

MODELING THE READING STRATEGY

Visualizing: Have students close their eyes and picture in their mind the details of Zlata's home as you read aloud the diary entry on page 159. When you have finished, ask students to describe what they pictured and identify any descriptive words that helped them visualize.

—————Viewpoint—————

Have students look at the photo on page 158. Ask them to imagine what Zlata is feeling as she watches scenes like this on the television.

REACHING ALL STUDENTS

LANGUAGE LEVELS

Beginning: Draw on the board the first box in a vertical sequence diagram. Have volunteers read the May 27 diary entry, stopping after every three or four sentences to have the group paraphrase the text. Record their summaries in the event boxes, adding boxes one at a time. Use arrows to show progression from one event to another.

Advanced: Have students make a two-column chart in their notebooks to show causes and effects. Have them label the left column *Why It Happened* and the right column *What Happened*. Then have students reread the diary entry on page 159 and use the information to fill in the chart. Students may have to make inferences to identify cause and effect situations that are not directly stated in the text.

GUIDED READING

1. How many years has Zlata been studying music? *(five years)*

2. How are Zlata's parents passing the time? *(reading)*

3. What is one way that Zlata's mother has changed physically from the war? *(Possible answers: She's lost weight; she has wrinkles.)*

EXTEND THE LESSON

Have students listen to recordings of the works of Czerny, Bach, Mozart, or Chopin. Ask them to describe the mood each piece of music creates and discuss how they think recordings like this may have helped Zlata to forget her troubles.

Monday, December 28, 1992

Dear Mimmy,

I've been **walking my feet off** these past few days.

1 I'm at home today. I had my first piano lesson. My teacher and I kissed and hugged, we hadn't seen each other since March. Then we moved on to **Czerny, Bach, Mozart, and Chopin**, to the étude, the invention, the sonata and the "piece." It's not going to be easy. But I'm not going to school now and **I'll give it my all**. It makes me happy. Mimmy, I'm now in my fifth year of music.

You know, Mimmy, we've had no water or electricity **for ages**. When I go out and when there's no shooting it's as if the war were over, but this business with the electricity and water, this darkness, this winter, **the shortage of** wood and food, brings me **back to earth** and then I realize that the war is still on. Why? Why on earth don't those "kids" come to some agreement? They really are playing games. And it's us they're playing with.

As I sit writing to you, my dear Mimmy, I look over at Mommy and Daddy. They are reading. They lift their eyes from the page and think about something. What are they thinking about? About the book they are reading

▲ Zlata gets water for her family.

---

walking my feet off, walking a lot
Czerny, Bach, Mozart, and Chopin, composers who wrote piano music
I'll give it my all, I'll do my best
for ages, for a long time
the shortage of, not enough
back to earth, not dreaming; in reality

160

Explain that countries on almost every continent have experienced civil war. Use a world map and point out countries that have experienced this kind of internal conflict, such as Vietnam, Somalia, Nicaragua, El Salvador, and the United States. Explain that civil war often occurs when groups of people within one country have different philosophies about human rights or an economic situation. Have groups of students choose a nation you pointed out on the world map. Ask each group to research that nation's civil war and present three facts about it to the class.

or are they trying to put together the **scattered** pieces of this war puzzle? I think it must be the **latter**. Somehow they look even sadder to me in the light of the oil lamp (we have no more wax candles, so we make our own oil lamps). I look at Daddy. He really has lost a lot of weight. The scales say twenty-five kilos, but looking at him I think it must be more. I think even his glasses are too big for him. Mommy has lost weight too. She's shrunk somehow, the war has given her **wrinkles**. God, what is this war doing to my parents? They don't look like my old Mommy and Daddy anymore. Will this ever stop? Will our suffering stop so that my parents can be what they used to be—cheerful, smiling, nice-looking?

This stupid war is destroying my childhood, it's destroying my parents' lives. WHY? STOP THE WAR! PEACE! I NEED PEACE!

I'm going to play a game of cards with them!

Love from your Zlata

---

scattered, in many different places
latter, the second of two things mentioned
wrinkles, lines in the face

About the Author

Zlata Filipović

In December 1993, Zlata Filipović escaped to Paris, where she began to study at the International School. Her diary has been translated into more than twenty languages.

With the money from her book, Zlata helped to start a charity for victims of the Bosnian War. Zlata was awarded the Special Child of Courage Award.

BEFORE YOU GO ON . . .

1 What has Zlata started studying again?
2 Why is Zlata worried about her parents?

HOW ABOUT YOU?
- If you met Zlata, what questions would you ask her?

▲ Sarajevo

161

CRITICAL THINKING

Have students respond orally or in writing to these questions:
- If you were Zlata, how would you try to help your parents? *(Answers will vary.)*
- How does Zlata's diary help you understand the Bosnian conflict? *(Possible answer: It explains what it was like to live through it.)*

MODELING THE READING STRATEGY

Distinguishing Fact and Opinion: Remind students that a fact is a statement that can be supported and proven true. An opinion is what a person or group believes or feels. As students read, encourage them to try to distinguish between facts and opinions in the text.

Viewpoint

Have students look at the older-looking Zlata. Ask students how Zlata has "grown up" since the the war.

WEBSITES

For more information, log on to http://www.longman.com/shiningstar for links to other interesting websites about the Balkan conflict.

ABOUT THE AUTHOR

Zlata Filopović wrote her diary from September 1991 to October 1993.

REACHING ALL STUDENTS

LANGUAGE LEVELS

Beginning: Have students read the last diary entry. Ask students to look for examples that detail ways the war is "destroying [Zlata's] childhood . . . destroying [her] parents' lives" and list their ideas in their notebooks. Have students read their lists and discuss which effects of the war would be most difficult for them.

Advanced: Point out that Zlata begins the entry on page 160 feeling upbeat as she writes about starting to play piano again. Have students use their notebooks to write about how Zlata keeps her spirits up and what kinds of events make her feel sad. Then have students share their ideas with the group.

LEARNING MODALITIES

Kinesthetic: Divide the class into small groups, and have them choose one day from *Zlata's Diary* to role-play. Have students reread the day together, divide up the characters among the members of the group, and practice acting out the events of that day. Have students present a completed skit to the class.

Review and Practice

COMPREHENSION

Ask a volunteer to read the Comprehension directions to the class. Read aloud each date from the diary, and have students find that date in the reading. Ask them to skim the entry to refresh their memory and then discuss which event of the day they might write about in their notebook.

After students complete the activity and share what they have written in pairs or small groups, have them respond to these questions:

1. How could you find out what key events happened if you weren't sure? *(You could refer back to the reading.)*

2. How many months passed between the first and last entry? *(seven months)*

CRITICAL THINKING

Have students respond orally or in writing to these questions:

● Why do you think it might have been good for Zlata to keep a diary? *(Possible answer: It was a healthy way for her to express her fear and anger about the war.)*

● When you read each entry, how did you decide which events were important? *(Possible answer: Zlata wrote a lot of details about the event.)*

COMPREHENSION

Reread the excerpts from *Zlata's Diary*. Write the five dates she writes about in your notebook. Then write something important that happened on each of these days. Compare what you write in pairs or small groups.

Saturday, May 23, 1992
Zlata tells Mimmy that she will now write to her about the war instead of herself.

Tuesday, May 26, 1992

Wednesday, May 27, 1992

Thursday, October 1, 1992

Monday, December 28, 1992

162

EXTENSION

How is Zlata similar to you? How is she different? Copy the diagram into your notebook and complete it. Then compare your diagrams in pairs.

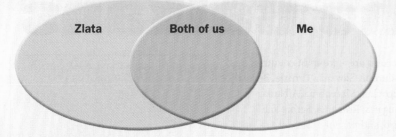

Zlata   Both of us   Me

DISCUSSION

Discuss in pairs or small groups.

1. What is the worst day of the war for Zlata? Why?
2. What kind of emotions does Zlata express in her diary?
3. Describe Zlata. What kind of person is she? Do you admire her?
4. Talk about what was happening around Zlata. How would you have felt if you were she?
5. What are some images that you remember after reading Zlata's diary entries?

◀ Zlata writes at her desk, as the sound of guns echoes from the hills.

163

EXTENSION

Have students look at the Venn diagram and read the directions together. Discuss with students how the completed Venn diagram will illustrate the similarities between Zlata and each student in the class. Then have them identify the heading of each circle. Invite students to work in pairs to complete the Venn diagram in their notebooks.

DISCUSSION

Have students work in pairs or small groups to read and answer the Discussion questions. Encourage students to return to the reading to answer any challenging questions. As a class, have students share their answers.

METACOGNITION

Ask students:

1. How does the Venn diagram help you organize and remember information?
2. How did analyzing the historical context help you better understand the mood of the selection?
3. How did the diary format help you understand the order in which events occurred?

REACHING ALL STUDENTS

LANGUAGE LEVELS

Beginning: Complete the Comprehension activity as a class. On the board, write each diary entry date horizontally from left to right as in a flowchart. Form five student groups and assign each group a different date. Have the groups complete the activity for their date. Then have them write their ideas on the board under the date. Have members from each group explain why they chose these events.

Advanced: For the Comprehension activity, point out that the dates are in chronological order and correspond to the diary entry dates. Have students find each date in the reading and examine each entry. Call on volunteers to relate some of the key events of the day. Then have students complete the chart.

Connect

READING SUMMARY

This nonfiction article discusses how geography influenced cultural development in the Balkans. In addition, it explains how land features may contribute to the ongoing conflict.

MODELING THE READING STRATEGY

Previewing: Remind students that identifying the visual aids on a page is an important part of previewing a text. It can help them determine what kind of information they will find in the text. Have students find and describe the visual aid on page 164.

SCAFFOLDING

Listen to the CD/tape with students as they follow along in their books. Then read the selection together. Ask students to find each place they read about on the first map on page 164.

GUIDED READING

1. What does the word *Balkan* mean, "slow and serene" or "mountains"? *("mountains")*
2. The Balkans form a land bridge between which two areas? *(Europe and Asia)*
3. Why are the Balkans called "the powder keg of Europe"? *(Many wars have started there.)*

 CONNECT TO CONTENT **Social Studies**

This is an informational text about the geography of the Balkans. Is it fiction or nonfiction? As you read about the different places, try to find them on the map.

The Physical World: The Balkans

The Balkans are a group of countries in southeast Europe. Slovenia, Croatia, Bosnia and Herzegovina, Macedonia, Albania, Greece, Bulgaria, Romania, Serbia and Montenegro, and part of Turkey are all in the Balkans.

The word *Balkans* comes from an old Turkish word that means "mountains." The Balkans is a good name for the area because it has so many mountains.

The Balkans form a land bridge between Europe and Asia. Since ancient times, this area has been the border between the empires of the East and the West. People from different **ethnic** groups traveled through the region and settled in the hills and valleys of the region. The mountains made it difficult for the different groups of people to **interact** with each other. Therefore, many different languages, cultures, and customs developed. These differences have led to many conflicts in the area. The Balkans are often called "the **powder keg**" of Europe" because many wars have started there.

ethnic, cultural
interact, communicate; do things together
powder keg, something that is ready to blow up at any time

164

▲ The western Balkans are in southeast Europe.

BEFORE YOU GO ON . . .

1 Why are there many different languages, cultures, and customs in the Balkan region?

2 Look at the map on page 165. What is the longest river? What is the highest mountain?

HOW ABOUT YOU?
● How are the Balkans similar to where you live? How are they different?

0 50 100 miles
0 50 100 kilometers

AUSTRIA

THINGS TO LOOK FOR ON THIS MAP

Longest river: Sava, Slovenia/Croatia/Bosnia and Herzegovina/Serbia; 938 km (583 mi.)

Highest point: Triglav, Slovenia; 2,864 km (9,395 ft.)

Largest lake: L. Scutari, Montenegro/Albania, maximum size 531 sq. km (205 sq. mi.)

HUNGARY

ROMANIA

Mura R.
Drava R.
Maribor
Triglav
Kranj
Velenje
Ptuj
Celje
Varazdin
Koprivnica
Nova Gorica
SLOVENIA
Ljubljana
Bjelovar
Zagreb
Virovitica
Subotica
Kanjiza
Sombor
Backa Topola
Koper
Karlovac
Sisak
Osijek
Apatin
Vojvodina
Rijeka
CROATIA
Nova
Dakovo
Vukovar
Zrenjanin
Pula
Ogulin
Gradiska
Slavonski Brod
Novi Sad
Vrsac
Bosanska
Gospić
Bihać
Prijedor
Gradiska
Modrica
Gracanica
Pancevo
Danube
Zadar
Banja Luka
Doboj
Belgrade
Smederevo
Pozarevac
Kljuc
BOSNIA and
Tuzla
Sabac
Loznica
Velika Plana
Knin
Jajce
Zenica
Zvornik
Valjevo
Arandelovac
HERZEGOVINA
Srebrenica
Kolubara
Livno
Visoko
Sarajevo
Cacak
Kragujevac
Zajecar
Sibenik
Konjic
Priboj
Krusevac
Kraljevo
DINARIC
Foca
SERBIA and
Nis
Aleksinac
DALMATIA
Mostar
MONTENEGRO
BALKAN MTS.
Split
L. Zlatar
Novi Pazar
Leskovac
ALPS
Metković
Bijelo Polje
Kosovska
Pristina
Trebinje
Niksić
Ivangrad
Mitrovica
BULGARIA
Dubrovnik
Podgorica
Peć
Gnjilane
L. Scutari
Kosovo
Urosevac
ADRIATIC SEA
NORTH ALBANIAN ALPS
Prizren
Kumanovo
Bar
Shkod r
Skopje
Kocani
Drin R.
Tetovo
Gostivar
Veles
Stip
Kicevo
MACEDONIA
Strumica
Tirana
Kavadarci
Vardar
ITALY
Durr s
Prilep
Shkumbin R.
Elbasan
L. Ohrid
Ohrid
Bitola
ALBANIA
L. Prespa
Fier
Berat
Korc
GREECE
Vlor
Vijose R.

▲ The western Balkans

165

CRITICAL THINKING

Have students respond orally or in writing to these questions:

● How do the mountains make it difficult for people to interact with one another? *(Possible answer: People can't cross mountains easily, so they're less likely to leave their area to interact with others.)*

● Do you think "powder keg" is a good term for this area? *(Possible answer: Yes. A powder keg and the political situation in the Balkans are both unstable and can easily explode.)*

————*Viewpoint*————

Have students look at the map on page 164. Ask how the map helps them to visualize the information on the page. Then have students use the map on page 165 to find the countries listed in the text.

across the curriculum

GEOGRAPHY Tell students that a scale can help them measure the distance between two places on a map. Point out the scale in the map on page 165. Show students how to place the edge of a piece of paper at 0 on the map scale and copy the scale onto the edge of their paper. Then demonstrate how students can use their paper to estimate the distances between two or more places on the map. Invite students to share their findings.

REACHING ALL STUDENTS

LANGUAGE LEVELS

Beginning: On the board, list the geographical features shown on the relief map. Discuss with students how these features might have prevented people from exchanging language, customs, and ideas.

Advanced: Encourage students to study the relief maps and search for information in the text to discuss similarities and differences between two or more Balkan countries.

LEARNING MODALITIES

Visual: Have students create a poster that illustrates the history and culture of a country in the Balkans. Have them use the information on pages 164 and 165 as well as any additional information they find on the Internet or in an encyclopedia or trade book. Have students describe their posters and answer any questions.

T165

Connect

GUIDED READING

1. In what way is the Balkan region a land of many contrasts? *(Possible answer: It has old and modern cities.)*
2. Which city in the photos is shown as an ancient city, Sarajevo or Dubrovnik? *(Dubrovnik)*

The two main religions in the Balkans are Christianity and Islam. The people of the Balkans speak many different languages: Albanian, Greek, Serbian, Croatian, Hungarian, Macedonian, Turkish, Slovenian, Bulgarian, and Romanian.

The Balkan region is a land of many contrasts. It has ancient and modern cities, beautiful mountains and rivers, as well as the scars of war, as these photos show.

▼ Danube River, Serbia

Dubrovnik, Croatia ▶

Sarajevo, the capital of Bosnia and Herzegovina ▶

BEFORE YOU GO ON . . .

1. What geographic features do you see in the photos?
2. What are some signs of war in the photos?

HOW ABOUT YOU? Answers will vary.
● Which photo interests you the most? Why?

166

SPELLING MINILESSON

Adding -es

Write these words on the board:

means	travels	flows
reaches	fixes	wishes
tries	worries	flies

Have students read aloud the words in each line and identify any similarities between them. *(All the verbs in the first line end with -s; all the verbs in the second line end with -es; all the verbs in the third line end with -ies.)* Tell students that there are different rules for spelling verbs in the simple present. Point out that -s is added to most verbs. Then review the following rules:

● If a verb ends with the letters -ch, -sh, -s, -x, or -z, add -es.
● If a verb ends in a consonant + -y, change the -y to -i and add -es.

Have students look for words that end in -es in any piece of literature they have available and list the words in their notebooks.

Link the Readings

Reread the text on the Balkans and think about the excerpts from *Zlata's Diary.* Copy the chart into your notebook and complete it.

Title of Selection	Type of Text (Genre)	Fiction or Nonfiction	Purpose of Selection	What I Learned
From *Zlata's Diary*		*nonfiction*		
"The Physical World: The Balkans"			*to inform*	

DISCUSSION

Discuss in pairs or small groups.

1. How does Zlata feel about war? How do you feel about it?
2. What do you find most interesting about the Balkans?
3. Does learning about the geography of the Balkans help you understand the region's history? Explain.
4. Which reading did you enjoy more? Why?

A worker repairs a building in Sarajevo. ▶

167

REFLECTION

Read the Reflection directions aloud with students and discuss the chart headings. After rereading "The Physical World: The Balkans," ask students to copy the chart into their notebooks and complete it. Have them discuss their answers when the charts are complete. Then ask students:

1. What is the purpose of *Zlata's Diary*? *(to record facts about the Bosnian War and their effect on a group of people)*
2. What type of text is "The Physical World: The Balkans"? *(informational)*

COOPERATIVE GROUPING

Pair intermediate and advanced students with beginning students. Have pairs read the Reflection activity and complete the chart together.

DISCUSSION

Have students read the questions and discuss their answers. Point out that many of the questions ask them to examine their feelings. Tell students to try visualizing themselves in the situation to help them answer the question.

CRITICAL THINKING

Discuss the conflicts described in both reading selections. Have students think about how people were affected by these conflicts and then write a paragraph about the value of using nonviolent methods to solve problems.

REACHING ALL STUDENTS

LANGUAGE LEVELS

Beginning: To help students remember the difference between fiction and nonfiction, tell them that the text in nonfiction books is comprised of facts that can be supported. Fiction is comprised of events that never happened or could never happen in real life. Have students identify both selections as fiction or nonfiction. *(Both are nonfiction.)* Then have students complete this section of the chart.

Advanced: Review the Reflection chart together. Have students discuss which columns in the chart list facts, such as *Fiction or Nonfiction,* and which list opinions, such as *What I Learned.* Then have students complete the chart.

GRAMMAR

Read aloud the definition of pronoun referents to students. Make sure they understand that a pronoun takes the place of a noun without changing the meaning, and that the position of the noun in a sentence helps determine the correct pronoun to use. Emphasize the boldface noun and its pronoun in the examples. Then have students complete the Practice exercises, checking them with a partner.

SCAFFOLDING

Have students help you write each pronoun from the chart at the top of page 168 on a separate index card. Then ask students to write the names of people or things that could correspond to each pronoun on index cards, such as *Alma and Ava* for *they* or *them.* Put a piece of tape on the back of each card. Write several sentence frames on the board. For example, ____ *gave the ball to* ____. ____ *dropped* ____. Give noun cards to students, and have volunteers place noun cards in the first sentence frame. Display the pronoun cards, and have the class discuss which pronouns would correctly complete the second sentence frame. Call on volunteers to place their pronoun cards in the frame.

GRAMMAR

Using Pronoun Referents

Pronouns replace and refer to nouns. There are two types of pronouns: **subject pronouns** and **object pronouns**.

	Subject Pronouns	Object Pronouns
Singular	I, you, he, she, it	me, you, him, her, it
Plural	we, you, they	us, you, them

Subject pronouns replace nouns that are subjects. In this sentence, *It* refers to *Balkans*.

> subject ◄————————► subject
> **Balkans** is a Turkish word. **It** means "mountains."

Object pronouns replace nouns that come after the verb. In this sentence, *it* refers to *a diary*.

> object ◄————————► object
> Zlata wrote a **diary**. Many people have read **it**.

A **singular pronoun** (*he, she, it*) refers to a singular noun. A **plural pronoun** (*them*) refers to a plural noun.

Practice

Copy these sentences into your notebook. Draw an arrow from each underlined pronoun to the noun that it refers to. Then check your answers in pairs.

1. The mountains are beautiful. <u>They</u> are steep and rocky.
2. Zlata wrote her diary in Croatian. People have translated <u>it</u> into many languages.
3. Do you know my brother? <u>He</u> goes to your school.
4. Please write to Marta and Silva. Tell <u>them</u> to come.
5. Alana Jost is a doctor. <u>She</u> works in the hospital.
6. The bomb did not explode. Soldiers removed <u>it</u>.

SKILLS FOR WRITING

Writing Eyewitness Reports

An eyewitness report is a type of expository writing. It explains something from the point of view—or "eyes"—of someone who witnessed, or saw, something happen. A good eyewitness report:

- answers the five *wh-* questions: *Who* was involved? *What* happened? *When* did it happen? *Where* did it happen? and *Why* did it happen?
- uses sequence words to show the order in which things happened
- uses interesting details to help readers visualize
- uses pronouns to replace some nouns

Read this eyewitness report. Then answer the questions that follow.

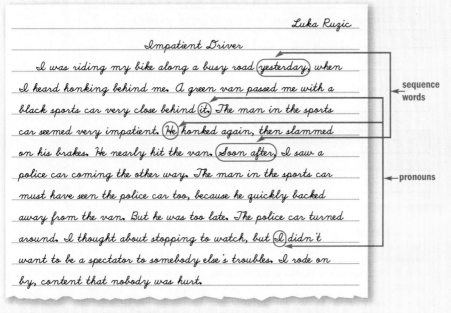

Luka Ruzic

Impatient Driver

I was riding my bike along a busy road (yesterday) when I heard honking behind me. A green van passed me with a black sports car very close behind (it.) The man in the sports car seemed very impatient. (He) honked again, then slammed on his brakes. He nearly hit the van. (Soon after,) I saw a police car coming the other way. The man in the sports car must have seen the police car too, because he quickly backed away from the van. But he was too late. The police car turned around. I thought about stopping to watch, but (I) didn't want to be a spectator to somebody else's troubles. I rode on by, content that nobody was hurt.

← sequence words

← pronouns

1. What event does the writer describe? Who was involved in this event?
2. When did the event happen? Where did it happen? Why did it happen?
3. Find a sentence with a subject pronoun. What noun does it refer to?

169

SKILLS FOR WRITING

Read aloud the introductory text. Have students take turns reading and paraphrasing the bulleted descriptors and the sample eyewitness report. Point out how all of the sentences in the report tell about the same event. Review the eyewitness report descriptors, and have students find examples of each one in the sample report. Then have students use the report to answer the questions at the bottom of the page.

SCAFFOLDING

Have students work in pairs. Have one student read an eyewitness descriptor from the bulleted list while the partner finds an example of it in *Zlata's Diary*. Have pairs take turns reading and searching. Invite students to share their examples with the class.

REACHING ALL STUDENTS

LANGUAGE LEVELS

Beginning: After students read aloud the list of descriptors on page 169, review the use of sequence words. Ask them to think of examples, such as *then* and *soon after*. List their responses on the board. Have students copy the list of sequence words into their notebooks. Encourage them to refer to the list when writing their eyewitness report.

Advanced: After reading the eyewitness report descriptors and the student sample, have students brainstorm words or phrases that might be added to the report to help readers visualize the event. If students have trouble, provide a few examples, such as *A green van swept past me so fast I nearly lost control of my bike.*

Teach

Eyewitness Report

Read the task description, and have students identify what they will be writing. Have students reread the eyewitness report on page 169, taking notice of words that express time and chronological order. Call on volunteers to list the words on the board. *(yesterday, then, soon after)* Point out how these words give the reader a sense of how quickly or slowly the events occurred.

WRITING STRATEGY

Have a volunteer read the definition of a sequence-of-events chart aloud. Explain that using a sequence chart can help them place events in the correct time order. Have students describe a recent sporting event or show that most students have seen. Demonstrate how to write what happened in appropriate places on a sequence chart using transitional clue words. Then ask students to write an eyewitness report about a real or imaginary event. Remind them to create a sequence chart in their notebooks to help put the events in order.

USING THE EDITING CHECKLIST

Have students read the Editing Checklist and use it to revise their writing. Remind students to look for one item on the checklist at a time.

WRITING ASSIGNMENT

Eyewitness Report

You will write an eyewitness report about a real or imaginary event.

1. Read Reread the eyewitness report on page 169. Note how all the sentences describe the past.

> ### Writing Strategy: Sequence-of-Events Chart
> A sequence-of-events chart helps you describe events in chronological order.
> The writer of the eyewitness report on page 169 prepared this chart.
>
> | I was riding my bike along a busy road. |
>
> ↓
>
> | A green van passed me with a black sports car very close behind it. |
>
> ↓
>
> | A black sports car slammed on its brakes and nearly hit the van. |
>
> ↓
>
> | I saw a police car coming the other way. |
>
> ↓
>
> | The police car turned around. |
>
> ↓
>
> | I rode on by, content that nobody was hurt. |

2. Make a sequence-of-events chart Choose a real or imaginary event. Make a chart for your eyewitness report in your notebook. Complete the chart, showing the events in chronological order.

3. Write Use your chart to write an eyewitness report in the simple past.

EDITING CHECKLIST

Did you . . .

▶ answer the five *wh-* questions: *Who? What? When? Where?* and *Why?*

▶ describe events in chronological order?

▶ use interesting details?

▶ use pronouns correctly?

170

Check Your Knowledge

Language Development

1. Why is it important to analyze the historical context when reading some texts?

2. What five *wh-* questions do you answer in an eyewitness report?

3. How can a sequence-of-events chart help you write an eyewitness report?

4. Make up two sentences, one with a subject pronoun and one with an object pronoun.

5. How do maps help you understand the article "The Physical World: The Balkans"?

Academic Content

1. What new social studies vocabulary did you learn in Part 2? What do the words mean?

2. What are two effects of war that Zlata describes in her diary?

3. Name three countries in the Balkans. What are some of the geographical features of the Balkans?

▲ Montenegro

171

You can assess students' knowledge of the unit in several different ways.

Portfolio: Students can answer the Check Your Knowledge questions as a homework assignment and then place it in their portfolios.

Traditional: Students can complete the Check Your Knowledge questions in preparation for the test. After students complete Check Your Knowledge, use the Assessment Package. Students can complete the Part Test on pages 57–60. For further practice, have students complete the Test Preparation worksheets.

Performance: Ask students to answer the Check Your Knowledge questions during a one-on-one conference with you to demonstrate their understanding.

TEST-TAKING TIP

Tell students that it is not necessary to reread the whole passage to answer some questions. Instead, students can skim the text looking for key words from the question. See the Test Preparation pages in the Assessment Guide for additional test-taking strategies.

METACOGNITION

Remind students to look carefully at any visual aids that accompany nonfiction text. Point out that these graphics sometimes contain information not found in the text. Have students find three examples of visual aids in the selections and explain what kind of information they add to the text.

REACHING ALL STUDENTS

LANGUAGE LEVELS

Beginning: To help students choose an event to write about, form student groups. Write the following questions on the board: *What are some exciting or interesting events that you know about? Who was there? When did it happen? What happened? Where did it take place?* Invite groups to take time to talk about these events. Then guide students within each group to narrow down their ideas and choose one event about which to write an eyewitness report.

Advanced: Have students act out the events from their sequence-of-events chart. Help students see that when they create a sequence-of-events chart, it is important to list things in the order they happened, or the report will be difficult to write and difficult for the reader to understand.

Put It All Together

Put It All Together

EXTEND THE LESSON

Have students preview the Put It All Together section on pages 172–175. These end-of-unit pages review and consolidate concepts, skills, and strategies from both parts of the unit, with an emphasis on listening, speaking, and writing skills.

LISTENING AND SPEAKING WORKSHOP

Divide the class into small groups. Ask each group to discuss recent events at school, locally, or in the world, and agree on two or three events as the subjects for a TV news show. Have groups complete the activities on page 172 after discussing the assignment as a class. Provide opportunities for students to practice their presentation with their group and then present it to the whole class. Before groups make their final presentations, encourage them to discuss and create visuals that best support their news stories. Encourage the class to provide appropriate feedback.

TEACHING THE TIPS

Speaking Tips: Read the Speaking Tips with students. Then show video clips of reporters. Ask students to describe what they see and hear and tell how they will use this information to present their reports.

Listening Tips: Have students read the Listening Tips on page 172. Before working in groups, remind students that much of their group time will be spent listening to others. Tell students to use the Listening Tips to determine the speaker's main idea.

RESEARCH SKILLS

Print: If students choose to focus on local or world events in their news report, have them use the Internet to research background information and the historical context of their subject.

OBJECTIVES

Integrate Skills
- Listening/ Speaking: *TV news show*
- Writing: *Report of a historical event*

Investigate Themes
- Projects
- Further reading

LISTENING and SPEAKING WORKSHOP

TV NEWS SHOW
You will present a TV news show. Report on events at your school, in your town, or in the world.

1 **Think about it** What kind of information do TV news shows include? Make a list of interesting recent events at your school, in your town, or in the world. What news would you like to tell others about?

Work in small groups. Compare your lists. Choose two or three events to use in a TV news show.

2 **Organize** Choose one person to be the news anchor (the main person who reads the news on TV). The other group members can be TV reporters. The news anchor introduces a reporter and tells what the report is about. Next, the reporter gives the eyewitness report. Then the anchor introduces the next reporter.

3 **Practice** Watch some TV news shows to help you plan what to say and how to say it. Practice your news show with your group. Try to do the whole show without stopping. Use pictures or maps to illustrate what you are reporting.

4 **Present and evaluate** Present your news show to the class. If possible, videotape your show. After each group finishes, evaluate the presentation. Discuss what made the news show interesting and enjoyable. Do you have suggestions for improvement?

SPEAKING TIPS
- Speak slowly and clearly.
- Use notes, pictures, and maps to help you remember and explain the event clearly.
- Use words that help the audience visualize the event.

LISTENING TIPS
- Listen for answers to the five *wh-* questions: *Who? What? When? Where? Why?* The answers to these questions give the speaker's main ideas in each report.
- Listen for supporting details and reasons. Ask yourself, "Did the speaker explain why these ideas are important?"

172

WRITING WORKSHOP

REPORT OF A HISTORICAL EVENT

A history report is a type of expository writing. It explains an important historical event. Like a news report, it answers the five *wh-* questions.

A good report includes the following characteristics:

- an interesting introduction that tells what the report is about
- information that answers *Who? What? When? Where? Why?*
- chronological organization
- a conclusion that summarizes the most important information

You will interview someone who has lived through a historical event, such as World War II, the Vietnam War, the Gulf War, a hurricane, a tornado, or an earthquake. Write a report based on the interview. Use the following steps and the model report to help you.

1 Prewrite Make a list of questions to ask in your interview. Use your questions to help you choose your topic. Be sure your topic isn't too big. For example, if you are writing about a war, ask questions about a single event or time period.

Organize your list of questions into groups. Did you include the five *wh-* questions? Interview the person. During the interview, take notes on the answers.

> ### WRITING TIPS
>
> - When you write facts, make sure that your information is accurate. If you are not sure, check additional sources.
> - Don't copy information from a book; use your own words. Be sure to cite your sources.
> - When you describe a past event, focus on the most important details and interesting facts.

◄ A tornado

173

WRITING WORKSHOP

Report of a Historical Event

Tell students that they will be writing a history report based on an interview with someone who witnessed a historical event. Remind them to check the Grammar and Writing pages in Parts 1 and 2 of the unit to review strategies and view examples. Additional practice activities can be found in the **Workbook** and **CD-ROM.**

PROCESS WRITING

Read the Writing Workshop aloud as students follow along. Then have a volunteer read the sample history report on page 174 aloud. Discuss components of the report by asking the following questions: *What is this report about? If the author got her information from the interview, what* wh- *questions might she have asked?* Record the *wh-* questions on the board. Then have students make a list of the questions they will ask, using the examples on the board for ideas. After students conduct their interviews and take notes, have them write their history reports.

TEACHING THE TIPS

Writing Tips: Read aloud the Writing Tips with students. After students finish their drafts, have them read their report. Ask: *Have you verified that all your facts are correct? Did you write the information in your own words?* Provide time for students to research any additional facts they need to clarify the information in their reports.

REACHING ALL STUDENTS

LANGUAGE LEVELS

Beginning: Before assigning roles for the TV news show, list each role on the board. Have students discuss the responsibilities of specific jobs and list them under each job title. Then have each student choose a role. Review responsibilities with each student during the practice sessions.

Advanced: Have students search the Internet for examples of news articles and reports. Encourage students to share the examples with the class. Have students complete the Listening and Speaking activity and then discuss how the student TV news shows were similar to and different from their examples.

Put It All Together

CREATING BETTER WRITERS

Ideas and Content: Read aloud the sample report and the call-outs in the right-hand margin with students. Discuss the information that the writer includes to make her topic interesting to readers. Then have students list the five *wh-* questions that the writer addresses in the body of her report. Finally, have students identify the important information that is summarized in the last paragraph.

Before students revise their writing, explain that all of the *ideas and content* that they include contribute to their report. Point out that the main idea should be clearly presented. Details should convey what is really important about the topic and should hold the reader's interest.

Write the following organizing tips on the board. Tell students to use the tips as they revise their writing.

- Be sure your topic is narrow enough to allow your writing to stay clear and focused. Discussing a border dispute between Ecuador and Peru is better than writing a report on "The History of Ecuador and Peru."

- Use details that not only support the main idea but also surprise readers and make your writing fun to read.

- Check that any research you have presented to support your main idea is correct.

Before you write a first draft of your report, read the model. The student interviewed her mother, who assisted the president of the Peace Committee during the signing of the Ecuador-Peru Border Peace Treaty in 1998.

Cami Troya

From Conflict to Peace

On October 26, 1998, the presidents of Ecuador and Peru met in Brasilia, Brazil, to sign a peace treaty. The treaty ended a fifty-year-old conflict between Ecuador and Peru. The cause of the dispute was an unclear border between Ecuador and Peru. As a result of the unclear border, citizens of both countries did not know who owned land at the border.

The treaty stated that Ecuador was to be given one square mile of Peruvian territory named Tiwintza. This small piece of hilly land in the Amazon jungle was important to the people of Ecuador. During the last border war in 1995, Ecuadorian troops had defeated the stronger Peruvian army on this land.

In spite of their disagreements, Ecuador and Peru rediscovered a common historical artifact. This artifact was the spondylus shell. A long time ago, it was used as a form of currency by both Ecuador and Peru. The shell became a symbol of peace, and also a symbol of the new, positive relationship between the two countries.

The writer begins with an interesting introduction.

The conclusion summarizes important information.

174

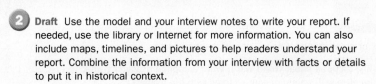

2 **Draft** Use the model and your interview notes to write your report. If needed, use the library or Internet for more information. You can also include maps, timelines, and pictures to help readers understand your report. Combine the information from your interview with facts or details to put it in historical context.

3 **Edit** Work in pairs. Trade papers and read each other's reports. Use the questions in the editing checklist to evaluate each other's work.

> ### EDITING CHECKLIST
> **Did you . . .**
> ▶ answer the five *wh-* questions?
> ▶ use simple past verbs?
> ▶ use pronouns correctly?
> ▶ write complete sentences with correct punctuation?

4 **Revise** Revise your report. Add information and correct mistakes, if necessary.

5 **Publish** Share your report with your teacher and classmates.

Spondylus shell ▶

175

Have students work in pairs. Ask partners to read each other's reports and use the checklist to suggest revisions. Then have students revise and publish their drafts.

ASSESS

Portfolio: Include the history report in students' assessment portfolios for comparison with later assignments.

REACHING ALL STUDENTS

LANGUAGE LEVELS

Beginning: As students work on step 2 of their writing assignment, have them meet with partners to discuss the kinds of visuals they might like to add to their report. Show students examples of visuals that are suited for history reports, and ask them to discuss which would work best with their topic.

Advanced: After students have completed their first draft, have them work with a partner. Ask pairs to read each other's work and look for clue words that reveal the time order of events. If the partner cannot find at least three such words, have the writer go back and add words that indicate chronological order.

Unit Projects

EXTEND THE LESSON

Home–School Connection: For Project 2, encourage students to watch the World War I movie with an adult who can explain historical references and provide needed commentary.

WEBSITES

For more information, log on to http://www.longman.com/shiningstar for links to other interesting websites.

PROJECTS

Work in pairs or small groups. Choose one of these projects.

1. Draw or find pictures about World War I. Write a caption explaining what the picture shows. Then share your pictures with the class.

2. Visit a museum with a World War I display or watch a movie about World War I. Then share what you learned with your class.

3. Reread Lance-Corporal Frank Earley's letter or Zlata's diary entries. Write a script for an interview with one of them. Ask and answer *wh-* questions. Then perform the dialogue for the class.

4. Find tapes or CDs of folk music from the Balkan countries at the library. Share the music with your class.

5. Make a poster that shows the flags of countries in the Balkans. Look for them in encyclopedias or on the Internet. At the bottom of the poster, design a flag for *all* the Balkan countries. Then display your flag in the classroom.

6. Find an Internet site about the Balkans. With your teacher's help, connect your class with a class in a Balkan city like Sarajevo. Become pen pals and share information about your two countries.

A poster made by the
U.S. government in 1917 ▶

176

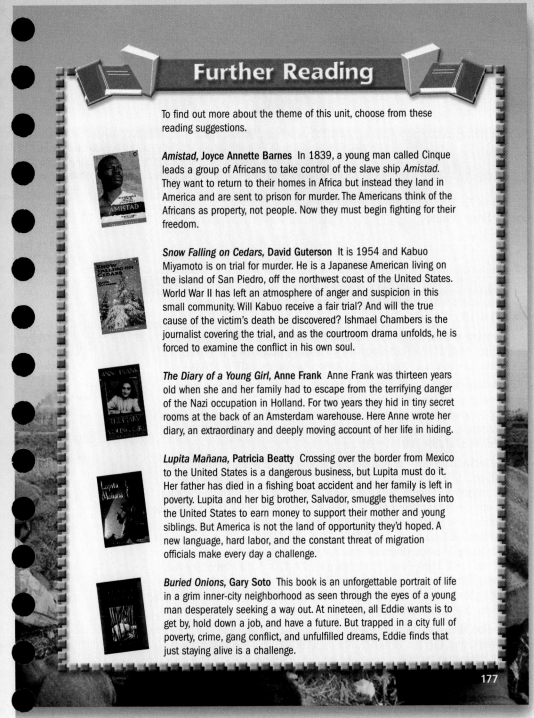

Further Reading

To find out more about the theme of this unit, choose from these reading suggestions.

Amistad, **Joyce Annette Barnes** In 1839, a young man called Cinque leads a group of Africans to take control of the slave ship *Amistad.* They want to return to their homes in Africa but instead they land in America and are sent to prison for murder. The Americans think of the Africans as property, not people. Now they must begin fighting for their freedom.

Snow Falling on Cedars, **David Guterson** It is 1954 and Kabuo Miyamoto is on trial for murder. He is a Japanese American living on the island of San Piedro, off the northwest coast of the United States. World War II has left an atmosphere of anger and suspicion in this small community. Will Kabuo receive a fair trial? And will the true cause of the victim's death be discovered? Ishmael Chambers is the journalist covering the trial, and as the courtroom drama unfolds, he is forced to examine the conflict in his own soul.

The Diary of a Young Girl, **Anne Frank** Anne Frank was thirteen years old when she and her family had to escape from the terrifying danger of the Nazi occupation in Holland. For two years they hid in tiny secret rooms at the back of an Amsterdam warehouse. Here Anne wrote her diary, an extraordinary and deeply moving account of her life in hiding.

Lupita Mañana, **Patricia Beatty** Crossing over the border from Mexico to the United States is a dangerous business, but Lupita must do it. Her father has died in a fishing boat accident and her family is left in poverty. Lupita and her big brother, Salvador, smuggle themselves into the United States to earn money to support their mother and young siblings. But America is not the land of opportunity they'd hoped. A new language, hard labor, and the constant threat of migration officials make every day a challenge.

Buried Onions, **Gary Soto** This book is an unforgettable portrait of life in a grim inner-city neighborhood as seen through the eyes of a young man desperately seeking a way out. At nineteen, all Eddie wants is to get by, hold down a job, and have a future. But trapped in a city full of poverty, crime, gang conflict, and unfulfilled dreams, Eddie finds that just staying alive is a challenge.

177

FURTHER READING

- *Amistad* and *Snow Falling on Cedars* are appropriate for beginning students.
- *The Diary of a Young Girl* is appropriate for intermediate students.
- *Lupita Mañana* and *Buried Onions* are appropriate for advanced students.

REACHING ALL STUDENTS

LANGUAGE LEVELS

Beginning: Tell students who decide to complete Project 5 that many elements of a national flag have specific meanings. For example, each star in the American flag represents one of the fifty states. Have students discuss the ideas they want to communicate in their all-Balkan flag, and then have them choose colors and symbols that represent those ideas.

Advanced: For Project 3, have students write interview questions for Earley or Zlata that are appropriate to the settings and characters. Remind students that Earley is a soldier in World War I, and Zlata is an eleven-year-old girl in war-torn Sarajevo in 1992. Encourage students to work with a partner to discuss whether the questions fit the characters and settings.

Level 1 Unit 5

We Can Be Heroes

Make enough duplicate copies of the Letter Home for Unit 5 so that each student has a copy to take home. Show Video Segment 5.

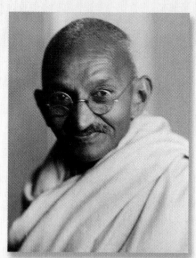

PART 1 TEACHING GUIDE

PRETEACH	Provide Background	• Read and discuss the Part Objectives and Background Information. (SB p. 180; ATE p. T180)
	Present Concepts	• Introduce the Key Words and Reading Strategy. (SB p. 181; ATE p. T181; WB pp. 114, 116) • Pronounce the Vocabulary words. (ATE p. T181) • Model how to use context clues to define Key Words. (ATE p. T181)
TEACH	Monitor Comprehension	• Informally monitor comprehension through Guided Reading and Critical Thinking questions. (ATE pp. T182-193) • Monitor students' comprehension through Critical Thinking, Metacognition, Discussion, and Extension activities. (SB pp. 189, 193; ATE pp. T179, T183, T185, T187, T189, T191, T193)
	Teach and Practice	• Use individually tailored activities for beginning and advanced students. (ATE pp. T179, T181, T183, T185, T187, T189, T191, T193, T195, T197) • Pair beginning, intermediate, and advanced students through Cooperative Grouping activities. (SB pp. 189, 193; ATE pp. T180, T189, T193) • Develop viewing skills using photos and illustrations and present the Viewpoint activities. (ATE pp. T178, T182, T185–T186, T191–T192) • Complete the Vocabulary, Phonics, Grammar, and Spelling lessons. (SB pp. 181, 194; ATE pp. T182, T184, T186, T194; WB pp. 122–123, 126) • Introduce the Writing Strategy and apply students' ability to write a biography using the Writing Model and Writing Assignment. (SB pp. 195–196; ATE pp. T195–196; WB pp. 124–125; Transparency # 33)
CONNECT	Connect to Literature	• Develop students' ability to analyze characteristics of genres through pairing of selections. (SB pp. 190–192; ATE pp. T190-T192) • Provide students with interactive reading support and practice. (WB pp. 117–121)
	Across the Curriculum	• Develop students' ability to extend the content of the reading selections through extended math, social studies, science, health, and art activities. (ATE pp. T184, T187)
ASSESS	Check Knowledge	• Use the Before You Go On, Check Your Knowledge, Link the Readings, and Review and Practice features to assess students' comprehension of the selection. (SB pp. 183, 185, 187, 188-189, 191, 193; ATE pp. T188–T189, T193)
	Monitor Progress	• Use the Assessment Options, Test-Taking Tip, and the test. (ATE p. T197; AG pp. 61-64)

CONTENT TERMS

Present and elicit definitions of these content-specific terms:

• patriot	• industrialist	• apartheid	• poverty
• colonists	• abolish	• volunteer	• fascist
• democratic	• sketch	• atomic bomb	

PART 2 TEACHING GUIDE

PRETEACH	**Provide Background**	• Read and discuss the Part Objectives and Background Information. (SB p. 198; ATE p. T198)
	Present Concepts	• Introduce the Key Words and Reading Strategy. (SB p. 199; ATE p. T199; WB pp. 128, 130) • Pronounce the Vocabulary words. (ATE p. T199) • Model how to use context clues to define Key Words. (ATE p. T199)
TEACH	**Monitor Comprehension**	• Informally monitor comprehension through Guided Reading and Critical Thinking questions. (ATE pp. T200-T211) • Monitor students' comprehension through Critical Thinking, Metacognition, Discussion, and Extension activities. (SB pp. 207, 211; ATE pp. T201, T203, T205-T207, T209, T211, T215)
	Teach and Practice	• Use individually tailored activities for beginning and advanced students. (ATE pp. T199, T201, T203, T205, T207, T209, T211, T213, T215, T217, T219, T221) • Pair beginning, intermediate, and advanced students through Cooperative Grouping activities. (SB pp. 207, 211; ATE pp. T198, T207, T211) • Develop viewing skills using photos and illustrations and present the Viewpoint activities. (ATE pp. T200, T202, T209) • Complete the Vocabulary, Phonics, Grammar, and Spelling lessons. (SB pp. 199, 212; ATE pp. T202, T210, T212; WB pp. 136-137, 140) • Introduce the Writing Strategy and apply students' ability to write a persuasive essay using the Writing Model and Writing Assignment. (SB pp. 213-214; ATE pp. T213-T214; WB pp. 138-139; Transparency # 34)
CONNECT	**Connect to Content**	• Develop students' ability to analyze characteristics of genres through pairing of selections. (SB pp. 208-210; ATE pp. T208-T210) • Provide students with interactive reading support and practice. (WB pp. 131-135)
	Across the Curriculum	• Develop students' ability to extend the content of the reading selections through extended math, social studies, science, health, and art activities. (ATE pp. T200, T208)
ASSESS	**Check Knowledge**	• Use the Before You Go On, Check Your Knowledge, Link the Readings, and Review and Practice features to assess students' comprehension of the selection. (SB pp. 201, 203, 205, 206-207, 209-211; ATE pp.T206-T207, T211, T215)
	Monitor Progress	• Use the Assessment Options, Test-Taking Tip, and the test. (ATE p. T215, AG pp. 65-68)

PUT IT ALL TOGETHER TEACHING GUIDE

EXTEND	**Integrate Skills and Apply Understanding**	• Apply students' ability to give a persuasive speech using the Listening and Speaking Workshop. (SB p. 216; ATE p. T216) • Apply students' ability to write a letter to the editor using the Writing Workshop. (SB pp. 217-219; ATE pp. T217-T219) • Have students complete one or more of the Unit Projects. (SB p. 220; ATE p. T220) • Have students choose a theme-related reading selection from the Further Reading suggestions. (SB p. 221; ATE p. T221)

Unit 5: We Can Be Heroes

Part 1

Background (p. 180) Discuss *heroes* with the class. Ask what types of heroes they are familiar with. Then begin a class discussion on what makes a hero. Explore ideas about who can be a hero and why. For each photograph on p. 180, ask for volunteers to describe what is happening. Then ask why each person is heroic. You may need to build a scenario around each photo in order to help clarify.

Vocabulary (p. 181) Explain that *context* can help you understand a word's meaning. Context is how the word is used in a sentence. *Context clues* are hints or other words found in the sentence that can help you understand a word. Review the sentences on p. 181 with the class. Identify the context clues in each sentence. For example, *beliefs* = "ideas and values"; *imprisoned* = "years in jail."* Use the vocabulary words in other sentences that have context clues. Have students use their dictionaries to identify the correct definition for each vocabulary word.

Reading Strategy: Making Inferences (p. 181) Explain to students that *making inferences* is guessing what the writer is saying by identifying clues in the text or by applying what you know from your own experience. Pantomime different activities and have students infer what is happening. For instance, stretch and yawn. Students should be able to guess that you are tired. Put on a jacket, close it up, and pretend to shiver. Students should be able to guess that you are cold. Stress that you are not telling the students that you are cold or tired, but they are applying their own experience to infer that you are cold or tired. Then propose different situations for students. For example, *If I saw Miguel loading skis and ski boots into his car, what can I guess, or infer? (Miguel is going skiing.)*

Heroes: Yesterday and Today
(pp. 182–187) Explain that a *biography* tells about a person's life. A biography uses facts to explain important events and occurrences in a person's life. Use the "Joan of Arc" section to review different aspects of biography, such as dates, events, personal information, etc. Ask students to identify the major information in Joan of Arc's biography.

Activity 1: Discuss *inspiration* with the class. Explain what inspires you. Then ask students what inspires them. After reading each biographical piece have students identify what inspired the people in the selection.

Activity 2: Have students give a brief description of someone who inspires them, someone they consider to be a hero. Begin by discussing some of the heroes in your life. Explain that these heroes could be anybody—parents, teachers, an older sibling—anyone they look up to for inspiration.

Activity 3: Tell students to choose a biography they like and give a short presentation to the class. Have students work with partners or in small groups. Students should begin with an introduction to the biography and then review the major events and information about their subject.

Activity 4: Discuss heroes who live in your area. Explain that the sections "Doctor Without Borders" and "New York City Firefighters" discuss everyday heroes. Ask students to identify people like doctors and community workers and discuss how they help the people they serve.

Comprehension (p. 188) Explain that *goals* are things you set out to do. Each of the individuals in these biographies had specific goals. Explain that *obstacles* are things that stand in the way of achieving your goals. Give examples of goals and obstacles in your life. Choose examples students can relate to, such as doing well on a big test, practicing for a big game, or finishing school. In order to complete the chart on p. 188, have students break down the material by identifying three specific things. First, have students identify what goals each individual had. Then have students identify what obstacles the people overcame in order to achieve their goals. Finally, have students identify what these individuals accomplished by achieving their goals.

Wind Beneath My Wings (p. 190) If possible, play the song for the class so students can listen along. Then have students try to identify what the song is about. Ask, *Who might this song be about?* Emphasize that there are no wrong answers.

Sebastião Salgado (p. 191) Have students look at Salgado's photograph *Ethiopia* on p. 191. Ask students to write down how this photo makes them feel. What do they see? Why? Then discuss why they think Salgado takes these pictures. Is he a hero? Why or why not?

Leaves of Grass (p. 192) Explain that the poet uses *imagery* to help you "see" what he is writing about. Ask students to describe the images they see in their mind when they read the poem. Then ask, *Why does the poet use imagery? Does imagery make the poem easier to understand?*

Grammar: The Passive Voice (p. 194) Explain *active* and *passive* in plain terms for students. In the active voice, the sub-ject *performs* the action; in the passive voice, the subject *receives* the action. Give examples of the active voice, such as, *Donna answered the question; My dog destroyed my new shoes.* Then give examples of the passive voice, such as, *The question was answered by Donna; My new shoes were destroyed by my dog.* Explain that the verb *be + past participle* is used in the passive voice. Have students identify the *be* verbs in the examples you give them.

Skills for Writing and Writing Assignment (pp. 194–195) Explain that *chronological order* is the order in which events occur. To clarify, use an example such as the events in your day. List them in chronological order on the board. Then use the example timeline on p. 196 to walk students through the biographical essay on p. 195. Explain how the timeline can be used as a guide to put the biographical information in chronological order. After students have chosen a subject for their biography, have them make lists of facts about the person they chose. Then have the students choose which facts and events are most important to their biography. After students have created their timeline, have them create an introductory sentence that explains why the person they chose is a hero to them. Explain that this would be a great way to begin their biography.

Part 2

Background (p. 198) Discuss *theater* with the class. Explain that theater brings stories to life by using a script, a stage, performers, and props. Often, written stories can be interpreted for the stage. These stories, like *The Diary of Anne Frank,* can be turned into theatrical pieces. Discuss theater experiences you have had, such as participating in a play or seeing a performance. Ask the class to discuss theater experiences they have had. Then discuss *historical context* with the class. Explain that historical context helps you understand the story better because you know what is happening in the characters' world. Discuss the situation for Jewish people in Europe during World War II. Make sure students understand the historical context in which *The Diary of Anne Frank* was written.

Vocabulary (p. 199) Explain that *context* can help you understand a word's meaning. *Context clues* are hints or other words found in the sentence that can help you understand a word. Review the sentences on p. 199 with the class. Identify the context clues in each sentence. For example, *destination* = "The family left Germany"; *forbidden* = "They had to go to special Jewish schools." Try to use these vocabulary words in other sentences that contain context clues.

Reading Strategy: Visualizing (p. 199) Explain that *visualizing* helps you picture what the author is trying to tell you. By paying close attention to the author's descriptive detail, you can create pictures in your mind. Give a short, simple piece as an example. Show the class a story that uses vivid narration to help them visualize. (You might use a children's magazine from your school library.) Read the story aloud to the class and ask the students to visualize. Then explain that *stage direction* is part of a script. It tells the actors what to do and how to act. Reading a script gives the reader a chance to visualize the action that would occur on stage.

From *The Diary of Anne Frank: The Play* (pp. 200–205) Remind students that a *personal narrative* is a story about something that happened to you. The opening to this piece (pp. 200–201) is written in a personal-narrative style. Ask students how they can identify this part of the selection as a personal narrative. *(It uses words like I, me, us, we, etc.).* Review the historical context so students understand this introduction.

Activity 1: Reread the opening voiceover with the class. Explain that the narrator is telling the story from her own point of view. Have students identify how Anne felt. As they answer, have students point out examples from the text.

Activity 2: Break the class into small groups to perform parts of this piece. Emphasize that students should concentrate on speaking slowly and clearly to pronounce their lines correctly.

Activity 3: Remind students that a Venn diagram compares and contrasts two things. Have students create a Venn diagram to explore the similarities and differences between themselves and Anne Frank. Make sure students use all elements of the piece, including the opening personal narrative, the script, and the family photos.

Comprehension (p. 206) Remind students that *chronological order* tells the reader the order in which events happened. Use something simple to help explain chronological order, like the events in your day. Write these events

on the board and number them to make it easier for students to understand. Then have students give a brief chronological description of events in their days. For example, *got dressed, cleaned room, made breakfast,* etc. Before students work with partners to complete the exercise, introduce chronological order words like *first, after, next, then,* and *last.*

Heroic Art (pp. 208–210) Before students read "Heroic Art" have them look at Picasso's *Guernica.* Have students write two or three sentences that describe what they see and how they feel about the painting. Then have students read the piece and learn about the historical context of the painting. Ask students if knowing the historical context changed their ideas about the painting.

Grammar: Comparative and Superlative Adjectives (p. 212) Remind students that *adjectives* are words that describe nouns. Explain that *comparative adjectives* compare two nouns. Give examples that compare things in the classroom. For example, compare your desk to a student's, or compare the height of two students. After you demonstrate with several examples, ask for volunteers to use comparative adjectives to describe other objects around the classroom. Use the same activities to explain *superlative adjectives.* Continue using examples from around the classroom to demonstrate the different forms of one-syllable, two-syllable, and irregular adjectives.

Skills for Writing and Writing Assignment (pp. 213–214) Emphasize that students should clearly identify the purpose of their review in the first sentence. Make sure they state the name of the book, movie, or TV show and give a basic summary of their review. Have students list three main points that they would like to discuss in their review. These should be ordered in a way that indicates which points are most important. The T-chart should be filled out with *main ideas* that tell why they did or did not enjoy the book, movie, or TV show they chose. Have students add *supporting details* to each of these main ideas. Explain that these details support and reinforce the main ideas. Use the review on p. 213 to demonstrate how supporting details are used to support main ideas.

Put It All Together

Listening and Speaking Workshop: Speech (p. 216) Choose an existing after-school program to model with students. Have students identify the purpose of the after-school program. Also have students identify what the programs accomplishes as well as, who is involved, where it takes place, how much money it costs, what resources are needed, etc. Use this model to write a clear and concise letter that uses all of the information to persuade someone that the program is necessary. Have each group, choose someone to write down all the information the group comes up with.

Writing Workshop: Letter to the Editor (pp. 217–219) Bring in a sample letter to the editor taken from a local newspaper. If possible, use one that discusses a topic students are familiar with. Review the letter with students. Have them identify the main idea and supporting details of the letter. Is it persuasive? How does the writer support his or her argument? Ask the students to offer ideas as to how they could improve the letter.

Have students make a simple outline to help them get organized before they write their letter. Make sure they create an introduction to their argument, supporting details that use evidence to support the main idea, and a conclusion that reviews their arguments in a clear and concise manner. Also review the proper format for letter writing.

UNIT CONTENT

The first part of this unit includes the nonfiction selection "Heroes: Yesterday and Today." In addition, students will read the lyrics to the popular song "Wind Beneath My Wings" and a nonfiction article about photographer Sebastião Salgado. The unit concludes with an excerpt from Walt Whitman's *Leaves of Grass*. Each selection helps readers better understand the challenges and rewards of being a hero.

The second part of the unit includes an excerpt from the play *The Diary of Anne Frank,* which is based on the book *Anne Frank: The Diary of a Young Girl.* Anne Frank wrote her diary in Amsterdam, Holland, between 1943 and 1945 while hiding from the Nazis during World War II. This unit culminates with a nonfiction article about paintings that depict war and peace.

—Viewpoint—

Have students examine the art on the unit opener spread. Encourage them to discuss what the people in the photographs have in common, and how their actions and beliefs relate to the idea of being a hero. Have them explain how bravery and the quest for survival influence the actions of heroes.

UNIT 5

We Can Be Heroes

178

WORKSHOP PREVIEW

Listening and Speaking
Students will present a persuasive speech about an after-school program.

Writing
Students will write a persuasive letter to the editor of the school newspaper, presenting an idea that they think will help the school.

PROJECTS PREVIEW

Projects for this unit include:
- reading and reporting about a hero
- choosing and evaluating famous photographs
- performing a readers theatre
- painting a picture that expresses strong feelings
- making a scrapbook with stories about heroic people
- making a thank-you card for a local hero

TEACHING RESOURCES

Lesson Plans	pp. 59–72
Summaries	pp. 49–56
Graphic Organizers	1–20
Audio Program	CD3/1–5; Cass.3/A
Workbook	pp. 113–140
CD-ROM	Unit 5
Video	Segment 5
Tests	Part Test, pp. 61–68
	Unit Test, pp. 119–127

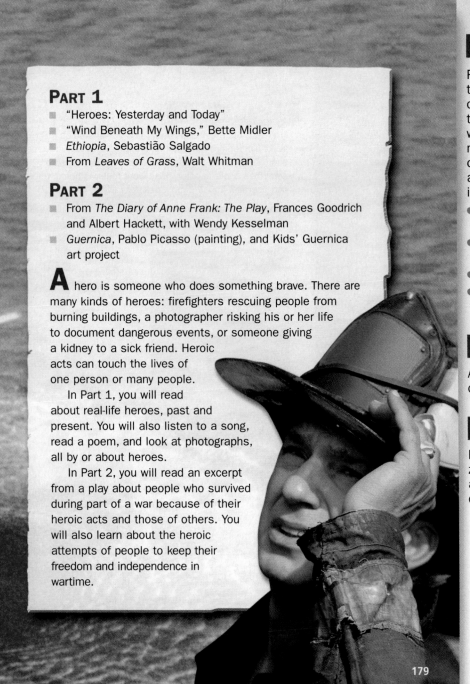

PART 1
- "Heroes: Yesterday and Today"
- "Wind Beneath My Wings," Bette Midler
- *Ethiopia*, Sebastião Salgado
- From *Leaves of Grass*, Walt Whitman

PART 2
- From *The Diary of Anne Frank: The Play*, Frances Goodrich and Albert Hackett, with Wendy Kesselman
- *Guernica*, Pablo Picasso (painting), and Kids' Guernica art project

A hero is someone who does something brave. There are many kinds of heroes: firefighters rescuing people from burning buildings, a photographer risking his or her life to document dangerous events, or someone giving a kidney to a sick friend. Heroic acts can touch the lives of one person or many people.

In Part 1, you will read about real-life heroes, past and present. You will also listen to a song, read a poem, and look at photographs, all by or about heroes.

In Part 2, you will read an excerpt from a play about people who survived during part of a war because of their heroic acts and those of others. You will also learn about the heroic attempts of people to keep their freedom and independence in wartime.

179

DISCUSS THE THEME

Read or ask a student volunteer to read the unit title, "We Can Be Heroes." Ask students to discuss what the word *hero* means to them. Point out that heroes are people who do something brave. It can be a dramatic deed, such as saving someone's life, or it can be a simple act of kindness, such as going out of your way to help someone in need. Ask students:

- to name heroes they have heard or read about in the news
- to identify any heroes they know personally
- to describe heroic things they have done
- to discuss what it takes to be a hero

QUICK WRITE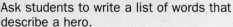

Ask students to write a list of words that describe a hero.

EXTEND THE LESSON

Have students find newspaper and magazine pictures to make a group collage about heroes. Encourage discussion of the completed artwork.

REACHING ALL STUDENTS

LANGUAGE LEVELS

Beginning: Show students an illustration of a popular comic book hero, such as Superman or Wonder Woman, and have them tell what they know about the character. Ask students, *Is this character good or bad? What makes this comic book character a hero?* Explain that real people, everyday citizens, can be heroes as well. Have a volunteer reread the first paragraph on page 179. Guide students to see the traits common to both comic book heroes and real-life heroes, such as selflessness, bravery, and a strong belief in what is right.

Advanced: Have partners take turns reading aloud page 179. Draw a three-column chart on the board with the following headings: *Heroes, Part 1, Part 2.* Invite volunteers to come to the board and, in the correct column, write a phrase or sentence that identifies one piece of information they learned from the text.

OBJECTIVES

Explain to students that in Part 1 they will be reading about heroes that they might study in history or civics class. Have volunteers take turns reading the list of objectives aloud. If necessary, explain any unfamiliar terms such as *text types* or *passive voice*. Tell students that they will learn more about these topics as they work through the unit. Additional practice activities for these objectives can be found in the **Workbook** and **CD-ROM**.

BACKGROUND

Ask students to read the Background text and look at the photographs. Use the questions beneath the photographs as the basis for a discussion. Draw from students that these people are heroes because they are doing courageous things to help others. Encourage students to suggest other ways people can be heroes, such as helping a lost pet find its owners.

COOPERATIVE GROUPING

Form four student groups. Assign a different photo from page 180 to each group. Have groups discuss their photos by answering these questions: *Who is the hero in this picture? Who is he or she helping? Would you do this? Why or why not?* Have groups share their ideas with the class.

PART 1

Prepare to Read

OBJECTIVES

LANGUAGE DEVELOPMENT

Reading:
- Vocabulary building: *Context, dictionary skills*
- Reading strategy: *Making inferences*
- Text types: *Biography, song, poem*

Writing:
- Using a timeline
- Biography
- Self-evaluation
- Editing checklist

Listening/Speaking:
- Appreciation: *Song, poem*
- Sharing experiences

Grammar:
- Passive voice
- Time phrases

Viewing/Representing:
- Photographs, paintings
- Interpreting photographs

ACADEMIC CONTENT
- Social studies vocabulary
- Heroes in history

BACKGROUND

"Heroes: Yesterday and Today" is a social studies article. It gives biographical information about several heroic women and men who are well known in history. The text also describes some people whose work requires heroic effort and courage. These people risk their lives every day.

Make connections Look at the pictures and answer the questions.

1. What is happening in each picture?
2. Why is each person heroic?
3. What are some other ways that people can be heroic?

180

TEACHING GUIDE

PRETEACH	Provide Background	Read and discuss the Background information. Complete the activity. (ATE/SB p. 180)
	Present Concepts	Introduce the Reading Strategy. (ATE/SB p. 181)
TEACH	Monitor Comprehension	Informally monitor comprehension while students read the selection independently or in groups. (ATE/SB pp. 182–193)
	Teach and Practice	Present the Grammar, Usage, and Mechanics. (ATE/SB pp. 194, 195) Complete the Writing activity. (ATE/SB p. 196) Present Grammar, Phonics, and Spelling minilessons. (ATE pp. 182, 184, 186)
CONNECT	Connect to Literature	Have students read the literature and relate it to the informational reading. (ATE/SB pp. 190–192)
	Across the Curriculum	Present curriculum links as students read. (ATE pp. 184, 187)
ASSESS	Check Knowledge	Assess students' comprehension by having them complete the Check Your Knowledge section. (ATE/SB p. 197)
	Monitor Progress	Use one or more of the print assessment resources in the Assessment Package.
EXTEND	Integrate Language and Apply Understanding	Have students complete the Workshops (ATE/SB pp. 216–219) and choose a project from the Unit Projects. (ATE/SB p. 220) Then have them choose a book to read from Further Reading. (ATE/SB p. 221)

VOCABULARY

Read these sentences. Use the context to figure out the meaning of the red words. Use a dictionary to check your answers. Write each word and its meaning in your notebook.

1. Nelson Mandela lived by his **beliefs**. Because of his refusal to abandon these ideas and values, he went to jail.
2. Mandela is internationally famous because of his brave **deeds**. He took these actions to help his people.
3. Some heroes, such as Mandela, Gandhi, and Joan of Arc, have been **imprisoned** and have spent years in jail.
4. Gandhi taught people how to show their objection to something through **passive resistance**, or nonviolent confrontation.
5. Benito Juárez was interested in **social justice**, especially the rights of native peoples.
6. People all get along better if they have greater **tolerance** for others. We have to accept other people's right to be different from us.

LEARN KEY WORDS

- beliefs
- deeds
- imprisoned
- passive resistance
- social justice
- tolerance

READING STRATEGY

Making Inferences

Fill in details, or "complete the picture" of what you are reading, by **making inferences**—combining the information in the text with your own knowledge and experience. When you make inferences, you make logical guesses and assumptions.

For example, read this sentence:

When the firefighter saw the burning house, she ran in without hesitating.

You can make the inference, or infer, that the firefighter is brave and ready to risk her life, although this is not stated in the sentence.

Making inferences whenever you read will help you understand more.

181

VOCABULARY

Read aloud the Key Words, asking students to repeat each one. Then read each sentence, and have students raise their hands when they hear the Key Word. Model how students can use other words in the sentence to help them find the meaning of the Key Word. For example, *In sentence 3, I read that some heroes have been imprisoned and have spent years in jail. I'm not sure what the word* imprisoned *means, but I know that* jail *is a synonym for the word* prison. *So to be imprisoned must mean to be sent to prison, or jail.* After students write definitions for each Key Word in their notebooks, ask them to compare definitions with a partner and make corrections where necessary.

READING STRATEGY

Have a volunteer read the strategy information aloud. Explain to students that making inferences is also called "reading between the lines," because you use story clues and what you already know to figure out information that is not directly stated in the text. Have students discuss inferences they have made in their everyday lives. For example, *I figured out which team was winning the baseball game by noticing that the Hawks were giving high-fives. People give high-fives when they are happy.*

REACHING ALL STUDENTS

LANGUAGE LEVELS

Beginning: Display the opening sentence from "Heroes: Yesterday and Today" on page 182: *Joan of Arc was a famous French patriot.* Then model how to make inferences about Joan of Arc's role: *I know that patriots from the American Revolution fought for U.S. independence. I can infer that Joan of Arc fought for French independence.* Then guide students to make inferences about Florence Nightingale's dedication with this sentence: *Florence Nightingale often visited the soldiers at night.*

Advanced: Have student pairs reread Vocabulary sentence 4. Ask pairs to make an inference about Gandhi's personality based on the sentence content and what they already know about nonviolent confrontation. Have pairs share their ideas.

T181

Teach

READING SUMMARY

This biographical selection offers information about the heroic deeds of both individuals and groups from around the world.

SCAFFOLDING

Have students listen to the CD/tape as they read the selection silently, following along. Then ask them to take turns reading paragraphs from the selection aloud in small groups.

GUIDED READING

1. Which army did Joan of Arc lead? *(the French army)*

2. Why was Florence Nightingale called "The Lady with the Lamp"? *(She often visited soldiers late at night, carrying a lamp.)*

3. Was Benito Juárez the first Zapotec Indian to become president of Mexico or a man who protected Jewish workers from the Nazis? *(the first Zapotec president of Mexico)*

4. What product did the factory managed by Oskar Schindler make? *(weapons)*

Viewpoint

Ask students to study the portraits of the heroes on pages 182 and 183. Ask them to make inferences about each person's personality, based on what students observe in the picture and what they already know.

FOCUS ON CONTENT

Social Studies

As you read, think about what you already know about these people. Then think about the new information you learn. What inferences can you make about each person or group based on what the writer tells you?

Heroes: Yesterday and Today

Joan of Arc

Joan of Arc (1412–1431) was a famous French **patriot**. Joan was a very religious child. When she was thirteen, she believed she heard God's voice telling her to help her country and fight the English, who occupied northern France.

Seventeen-year-old Joan led the French army against the English. Later, the English captured and imprisoned her. She was **burned at the stake** in 1431 when she was only nineteen. Joan of Arc was named a saint in 1920 for her heroic deeds.

Florence Nightingale

Florence Nightingale (1820–1910) came from a wealthy English family. Against her parents' wishes, she became a nurse.

In 1853, she became **superintendent** of a hospital for women in London. In 1854, Britain, France, and Turkey fought against Russia in the Crimean War. Nightingale volunteered to go to Turkey to help. She took thirty-eight nurses with her. They helped many wounded soldiers recover. Nightingale often visited the soldiers at night, carrying a lamp. Soldiers called her "The Lady with the Lamp."

When Nightingale returned to England, she started a school for nurses. The school still exists today.

---

patriot, a person who is very loyal to his or her country
burned at the stake, put to death by tying to a post and burning
superintendent, manager; chief

182

▲ Joan of Arc never learned to read or write, but she was considered to be a great army leader.

▲ Florence Nightingale worked for many long hours to help the sick and dying men.

PHONICS MINILESSON

Digraphs *wr, kn*

Read this sentence aloud, emphasizing the underlined words: *Joan of Arc did not <u>know</u> how to read and <u>write</u>.* Write the words *know* and *write* on the board, and have students repeat the words after you. Point to the word *know*. Ask students what sound they hear at the beginning of the word. *(/n/)* Circle the first two letters in the word. Point out that the letter *k* is silent. Repeat the activity with the word *write*.

Then have students write *kn* and *wr* on separate index cards. Say the following words, and ask students to hold up the card with the letters that represent the beginning sound in each word: *knock, wring, knuckle, wrist, knight, knot, wrap.*

Benito Juárez

Benito Juárez (1806–1872) is a national hero in Mexico. He was the son of poor Zapotec Indian farmers in the state of Oaxaca, Mexico. At age thirteen he couldn't read, write, or speak Spanish. He trained to become a priest, but later he decided to become a lawyer. As a young man, he became interested in social justice, especially the rights of native peoples. He was very popular among the native Indian population, and in 1847 he was elected governor of Oaxaca.

In 1861, Juárez became the first Zapotec Indian president of Mexico. He improved education. For the first time, it was possible for every child to go to school. He stopped the French from colonizing Mexico. His many reforms made Mexico a fairer, more modern society.

▲ Benito Juárez fought for the rights of native peoples.

Oskar Schindler

Oskar Schindler (1908–1974) was a rich German **industrialist**. During World War II, he managed a factory in Krakow, Poland. The factory made weapons for the German army. Krakow's 50,000 Jews had to live in a ghetto—a poor and crowded part of the city. Schindler saw the **brutality** of the Nazi soldiers. He said, "No thinking person could fail to see what would happen. I was now resolved to do everything in my power to **defeat** the system."

Schindler hired Jewish workers in his factory. He protected them when the Nazis tried to send them to **concentration camps**. By the end of the war he had saved about 1,300 Jews.

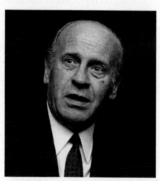

▲ Oskar Schindler's courageous deeds saved lives.

---

industrialist, owner or manager of a factory or industrial company
brutality, cruelty; viciousness
defeat, conquer; overcome
concentration camps, places where the Nazis killed Jews and other people in World War II

BEFORE YOU GO ON . . .

1. Why was Joan of Arc imprisoned?
2. What did Benito Juárez make it possible for all children to do?

HOW ABOUT YOU?
- Which person do you think is the most heroic? Why?

183

CRITICAL THINKING

Have students respond orally or in writing to these questions:
- Why do you think Joan of Arc could not read or write? *(Possible answer: European women were often not allowed to attend school in the 1400s.)*
- Do you think it would be difficult to be the president of a country, like Benito Juárez? Why or why not? *(Answers will vary.)*
- Which hero do you think had the most dangerous task? Why? *(Answers will vary.)*

MODELING THE READING STRATEGY

Making Inferences: Remind students that when they make inferences, they fill in details about what they are reading by combining text information with what they already know. Write the following sentence from page 183 on the board: *Krakow's 50,000 Jews had to live in a ghetto—a poor and crowded part of the city.* Have students make an inference about Jewish life in Krakow based on the text and what they know about the Nazi policy toward Jews during World War II. *(Life in the Jewish ghetto in Krakow was miserable because of crowded living conditions and cruel treatment from the Nazis.)*

ACTIVE READING

Have students make a three-column chart with the following headings: *Ideas from the Text, What I Knew, Inference I Made.* Then ask students to add more inferences to the chart as they continue to read the selection.

REACHING ALL STUDENTS

LANGUAGE LEVELS

Beginning: Form four student groups. Assign a different biography from pages 182 and 183 to each group. Meet with each group to discuss making a word web about the hero described in their biography, with details about the person's life drawn from the text. Have groups share their webs with the class.

Advanced: Ask students to reread the text on pages 182 and 183. Form student pairs and have them use their Active Reading graphic organizers to record one inference about each biography subject. Have pairs share their ideas with the class.

LEARNING MODALITIES

Visual: Invite students to focus on the visuals of the heroes on these pages and compare the paintings on page 182 with the photographs on page 183. Encourage discussion by asking students what kinds of different information they can get from paintings and photographs.

Teach

GUIDED READING

1. What American leader did Gandhi influence? *(Martin Luther King Jr.)*
2. At what age did Mother Teresa become a nun? *(eighteen)*
3. What award did Mother Teresa win? *(the Nobel Peace Prize)*
4. According to Mandela, what kind of democratic and free society did he cherish? *(one in which all persons live together in harmony and with equal opportunities)*
5. When was apartheid abolished? *(1994)*

across the curriculum

HISTORY The Nobel Prize has been awarded since December 10, 1901, the fifth anniversary of the death of Alfred Bernhard Nobel, a Swedish chemist. It was Nobel who established the fund that contributes money for the awards. Prizes are usually awarded annually to chemists, physicians, writers, economists, and others who make significant contributions to the people of the world. The Nobel committee also awards a peace prize each year to the person who has done the most to promote peace and understanding around the world. Have students look up "Nobel Prize" in an encyclopedia or on the Internet and compile a list of recipients in a class chart or timeline.

Mohandas Gandhi

Mohandas Gandhi (1869–1948) was born in Porbandar, India. At that time, India was a British colony. Gandhi went to England in 1888 and studied law. He returned to India and worked as a lawyer in Bombay (Mumbai).

In 1893, Gandhi traveled to South Africa. At that time, the government of South Africa had a system of **apartheid**. A group of white South Africans attacked Gandhi and beat him. After this experience, he encouraged people to practice passive resistance against the South African authorities and apartheid. Gandhi went to prison many times for his beliefs.

After he returned to India in 1915, Gandhi became a leader in India's struggle for independence. He became the  international symbol of nonviolent protest. He believed in religious tolerance. In 1947, he negotiated an end to 190 years of British rule in India. Then, in 1948, Gandhi was assassinated by someone who didn't agree with his beliefs.

Gandhi **inspired** nonviolent movements everywhere. In the United States, his ideas about passive resistance influenced Martin Luther King Jr., when he became a leader of the Civil Rights movement in the 1950s and 1960s.

▲ Gandhi was imprisoned many times because of his beliefs.

Mother Teresa

Mother Teresa (1910–1997) was born in a part of Albania that is now in Macedonia. At age eighteen, she became a nun. She went to India in 1929. For the next twenty years, she worked as a teacher at the convent school in Calcutta. In September 1946, she "heard a voice from God." The voice told her to help poor people. She moved into one of the poorest parts of the city to teach and nurse the poor. She also set up a home for **lepers**. Mother Teresa traveled the world to talk about the terrible problems of poverty. In 1979, she won the Nobel Peace Prize.

▲ Mother Teresa with two sight-impaired children

---

apartheid, a system in which different races in a country are separated
inspired, caused; created
lepers, people with leprosy, a skin disease

184

SPELLING MINILESSON

Silent Letters *wr, kn*

Remind students that when the letter *w* is followed by the letter *r* at the beginning of some words, the letters are represented by the sound /r/; the *w* is silent, as in the word *wrong*. Also, when the letter *k* is followed by the letter *n*, the letters are represented by the sound /n/; the *k* is silent, as in the word *knife*.

Write the words *wrong* and *knife* on the board and underline the letters *wr* and *kn* respectively. Have students read each word aloud. Then dictate the following words for students to spell, using each in a sentence to help define it: *write, wrote, wrist, wrong, wreck, know, knee, knock, knot.* Have students record each word and then trade papers with partners to check the spellings. Have volunteers write the correct spellings on the board.

Nelson Mandela

Nelson Mandela (1918–) is considered a great hero of the twentieth century. His country, South Africa, was ruled by a white government made up of **descendants** of English and Dutch colonists. South Africans lived under a system of apartheid. Blacks had few rights and opportunities compared to whites.

Mandela refused to accept the suffering and injustice. He became a lawyer and joined the African National Congress (ANC) to fight for his people's rights. The government **banned** the ANC. Mandela continued to travel and speak against the government. In 1962, the government arrested him and sent him to prison, where he spent the next twenty-eight years.

Mandela said, "During my lifetime I have dedicated myself to the struggle of the African people. I have fought against white domination, and I have fought against black domination. I have cherished the ideal of a democratic and free society in which all persons live together in harmony and with equal opportunities."

In February 1990, he was finally freed from prison. The people of South Africa **abolished** apartheid in 1994, and they elected Mandela as president of South Africa.

Mandela retired in 1999 at age eighty. He is still considered a heroic figure. However, Mandela doesn't agree. He once said, "I was . . . an ordinary man who had become a leader because of extraordinary **circumstances**."

---

descendants, grandchildren, great-grandchildren, etc.
banned, made illegal
abolished, got rid of; eliminated
circumstances, events; situations

▲ Nelson Mandela speaks to people around the world.

BEFORE YOU GO ON . . .

1. What were some of Mohandas Gandhi's beliefs?
2. Why is Nelson Mandela a hero?

HOW ABOUT YOU?
- What questions would you like to ask Mohandas Gandhi, Mother Teresa, and Nelson Mandela?

185

CRITICAL THINKING

Have students respond orally or in writing to these questions:
- What are some ways that two or more heroes on these pages are alike? *(Possible answers: Gandhi and Mother Teresa worked in India; Gandhi and Mandela were lawyers; All believed they should help others.)*
- What do you think Gandhi and Mandela might say to each other if they met? Why? *(Answers will vary.)*

MODELING THE READING STRATEGY

Compare and Contrast: As students read pages 184 and 185, encourage them to compare and contrast the lives and accomplishments of the heroes described in the selection. Guide them to organize their comparison with categories such as these: countries, type of work, risks taken, honors received. If necessary, remind students that when they compare, they analyze how two things are alike. When they contrast, they analyze how two things are different.

Viewpoint

Have students look closely at the portraits on these two pages. Ask students to describe what they can tell about the person's personality and lifestyle based on his or her picture.

REACHING ALL STUDENTS

LANGUAGE LEVELS

Beginning: Display a world map. Reread pages 184 and 185 with students, and have volunteers take turns reading aloud. As each new place is mentioned, invite a volunteer to point to the place on the map and name it.

Advanced: Form student pairs. Have each partner secretly choose a person from pages 184 and 185 to describe. Ask each student to give his or her partner three clues about the person's identity while the partner tries to guess who is being described. Have students give more than three clues as necessary.

Teach

MODELING THE READING STRATEGY

Previewing and Predicting: Before reading, remind students that they will better understand the selection if they preview the text features and predict what the text will be about. Have them read the headings and picture captions. Then ask students to write and share predictions about the kind of information they will find on pages 186–187.

GUIDED READING

1. Is Doctors Without Borders an international organization or an organization from one country? *(an international organization)*
2. Who started Doctors Without Borders? *(a small group of French doctors)*
3. Why did the firefighters go into the burning buildings on September 11, 2001? *(to try to save people)*
4. How many people escaped from the World Trade Center on September 11? *(about 25,000)*

—Viewpoint—

Ask students to describe how the heroes in the photographs on these pages are helping others. Discuss the risks involved in being a firefighter or a "doctor without borders."

Doctors Without Borders

Doctors Without Borders is an international organization whose members believe that every person in every country has the right to medical care. It helps victims of war, diseases (such as AIDS), and natural and man-made disasters. A small group of French doctors started Doctors Without Borders (*Médecins Sans Frontières*) in 1971. Each year, more than 2,500 volunteer doctors, nurses, and administrators from eighteen countries provide medical aid in more than eighty countries. They provide health care, perform surgery, organize nutrition and sanitation programs, train local medical staff, and provide mental health care.

Doctors Without Borders works with the United Nations, governments, and the media to tell the world about their patients' suffering and concerns. For example, Doctors Without Borders volunteers told the media about the atrocities they saw in Chechnya, Angola, and Kosovo.

Doctors Without Borders won the Nobel Peace Prize in 1999. Accepting the award, one of the founders, Bernard Kouchner, said, "I'm deeply moved, and I'm thinking of all the people who died without aid, of all those who died waiting for someone to knock on their door."

▲ Nearly one-third of Angola's children—an average of 420 children every day—die before their fifth birthday of starvation or disease, as a result of the 27-year civil war.

borders, official lines that separate two countries
disasters, horrible events that cause great damage and death
administrators, people who manage businesses or organizations
nutrition, nourishment; eating healthful foods
sanitation, hygiene; cleanliness
atrocities, extremely violent actions
founders, people who start organizations or companies

▲ A doctor helps a child in a refugee camp in Somalia.

186

GRAMMAR MINILESSON

Capitalization

Have students make a poster about capitalization for their own reference. Remind students that there are additional rules for capitalization, but these rules are relevant to this reading.

Capitalize . . .

1. the first word in a sentence (*The fires caused the buildings to collapse.*)
2. a person's name (*Bernard Kouchner*)
3. a person's title (*Mayor Rudolph Giuliani*)
4. the names of places, such as buildings, countries, and cities (*Pentagon, India, New York City*)
5. the month (*September 11, 2001*)
6. the names of organizations (*Doctors Without Borders*)
7. the first word and important words in book or story titles (*"Heroes: Yesterday and Today"*)

Have students find additional examples in the reading selection that follow these rules.

T186

New York City Firefighters

On September 11, 2001, **hijackers** flew planes into the World Trade Center in New York City and the Pentagon outside of Washington, D.C. The planes **exploded**, and the buildings caught on fire.

At the World Trade Center, hundreds of New York City firefighters and other emergency workers ran into the burning buildings to try to save people. The fires caused the buildings to collapse. Three hundred forty-three firefighters and twenty-three police officers died. Nearly 3,000 people died in the disaster, but about 25,000 people escaped. The rescue workers saved many lives.

At a memorial ceremony for one of the firefighters, former New York City Mayor Rudolph Giuliani called September 11 the New York Fire Department's "darkest day and finest hour."

---

hijackers, people who illegally take control of an airplane
exploded, burst into fire and small pieces; blew up

▲ Firefighters search for survivors in the ruins of the World Trade Center.

BEFORE YOU GO ON . . .

1. What does Doctors Without Borders try to tell the world?
2. What buildings were hit by hijacked airplanes on September 11, 2001?

HOW ABOUT YOU?
- How do you think the name Doctors Without Borders describes the group's main belief?

187

Review and Practice

COMPREHENSION

Ask a volunteer to read the Comprehension directions as students follow along. Then read aloud the list of heroes, and invite a student to read the example about the fire-fighters. Have students copy the chart into their notebooks and complete it. When they are finished, invite students to share a three-minute discussion about their favorite hero. Then take a class poll of favorite heroes and use the results to create a bar graph with the information. Have students respond to these questions:

1. Based on what you have written in your chart, what are some general qualities that all these heroes share? *(Possible answers: bravery, determination)*

2. Which of these heroes do you admire most? Why? *(Answers will vary.)*

CRITICAL THINKING

After students complete the chart, have them respond orally or in writing to these questions.

● Which two heroes seem to be the most alike? Why? *(Answers will vary.)*

● Why do you think these people took such big risks? *(Possible answer: They believed in what they were doing.)*

COMPREHENSION

Reread "Heroes: Yesterday and Today." Copy the chart into your notebook. Write at least one sentence about each person or group that tells why you think they are heroic. Use what you already know about being a hero, and facts you learned in the text. Try to use some of these words: *beliefs, deeds, imprisoned, passive resistance, social justice, tolerance.*

Heroes	Why Are They Heroic?
Joan of Arc	
Florence Nightingale	
Benito Juárez	
Oskar Schindler	
Mohandas Gandhi	
Mother Teresa	
Nelson Mandela	
Doctors Without Borders	
New York City firefighters on September 11, 2001	*The firefighters tried to rescue people from the World Trade Center. They knew it was dangerous. They were probably afraid, but they did their jobs anyway.*

188

EXTENSION

Think about someone you believe is heroic. Write three sentences telling about the person (or group).

DISCUSSION

Discuss in pairs or small groups.

1. Which heroes spent time in prison because of their beliefs? Why?
2. Some heroes die for their beliefs. Find an example in the text, and explain.
3. Gandhi believed that passive resistance is a good way to protest against something that is unjust, or wrong. Do you agree with him? Why or why not?
4. Which of the heroes from the text would you like to meet? Why?

189

EXTENSION

Read aloud the Extension directions. Have each student choose a heroic person or group. Then ask students to discuss these questions with a partner before answering them in their notebooks: *Why do you think this person or group is heroic? What beliefs does this person or group have? What risks does this person or group take? How does this person or group show courage?*

DISCUSSION

Have students read the questions and discuss them in pairs or small groups. After they have completed their discussion, have each pair or group answer question 4 by writing a short poem about one of the heroes in this selection that they would most like to meet.

METACOGNITION

Ask students:

1. What inferences did you make about "Heroes: Yesterday and Today"? What information in the text helped you to make those inferences?
2. What reading strategies would you use the next time you had to read a social studies article? Why?
3. Would you like to read more about the heroes in this article? Why or why not? Where would you look to find other material about the people covered in this unit?

REACHING ALL STUDENTS

LANGUAGE LEVELS

Beginning: For Discussion question 4, have students draw a picture of themselves meeting a hero from the text. Invite students to point to features in their illustration as they answer question 4.

Advanced: Help students answer the third Discussion question by writing a Pros and Cons chart on the board. Ask students to name pros and cons regarding passive resistance. Record their ideas on the board, and have students reread them before answering the question.

Connect

As you read this section, think about how the work of singers, photographers, and poets can influence the way we see and experience the world.

READING SUMMARY

The lyrics of "Wind Beneath My Wings" describe how one person inspired and helped another without asking for recognition. *Ethiopia* is a photograph taken in 1984 by award-winning photographer Sebastião Salgado.

SCAFFOLDING

Invite students to share their knowledge of Bette Midler or some of the songs she has sung, including "Wind Beneath My Wings." Then have students listen to the CD/tape as they read the words of the song.

GUIDED READING

1. Who was the one with all the glory, the singer or her hero? *(the singer)*
2. According to the singer, what can he/she do with the help of "the wind beneath my wings"? *(fly higher than an eagle)*
3. When did Sebastião Salgado take the photograph on page 191? *(1984)*

ABOUT THE SONGWRITERS

The song "Wind Beneath My Wings" was written in 1982 by Jeff Silbar and Larry Henley. One day when Silbar and Henley were discussing song ideas, Silbar spotted the title "Wind Beneath My Wings" on Henley's notepad and loved the concept. Recorded by Bette Midler for the soundtrack to the movie *Beaches,* the song won a Grammy Award in 1989 for "Song of the Year."

Wind Beneath My Wings

It must have been cold there in my shadow,
To never have sunlight on your face.
You were content to let me shine,
   that's your way.
You always walked a step behind.

So I was the one with all the glory,
While you were the one with all the strain.
A beautiful face without a name for so long.
A beautiful smile to hide the pain.

Chorus
Did you ever know that you're my hero,
And everything I would like to be?
I can fly higher than an eagle,
For you are the wind beneath my wings.

It might have appeared to go unnoticed,
But I've got it all here in my heart.
I want you to know I know the truth,
   of course I know it.
I would be nothing without you.

Fly, fly, fly high against the sky,
So high I almost touch the sky.
Thank you, thank you,
Thank God for you, the wind beneath my wings.

190

About the Artist

Bette Midler

Entertainer, environmentalist, and singer, Bette Midler was born in 1945. After studying drama at the University of Hawaii, she worked as a film extra and made her stage debut in New York City in 1966. In 1974, she won a Grammy Award for her album *The Divine Miss M,* and a Tony Award for her Broadway show of the same title. Midler is the founder of the New York Restoration Project. In June 2002, she received the Parks and Preservation Award for her commitment and generosity to New York's parks and historic sites.

 Ethiopia, the setting for the photograph on page 191, is a country in northeastern Africa. Much of Ethiopia is covered with rugged mountains, with lowland deserts surrounding the plateau region. Agriculture in this region is a very important part of the country's economy. Beginning in the late 1970s, Ethiopia experienced a series of droughts that lowered agricultural production. A prolonged drought between 1984 and 1986, coupled with civil war, resulted in widespread famine across the nation. At one point, the government forcibly relocated about 600,000 northern Ethiopians to the south, creating an even greater shortage of food and resources. During the 1980s, approximately one million Ethiopians died from starvation. Have student groups research Ethiopian culture. Ask groups to report three interesting facts about the topic.

◀ *Ethiopia*, by Sebastião Salgado, 1984

Sebastião Salgado

Sebastião Salgado was once a successful economist. Then, on a trip to Africa in 1973, he decided to become a photographer. For many years he bravely photographed wars and other crises for news agencies. In the 1980s, he worked with Doctors Without Borders in the Sahel region of Africa during a major **drought** and **famine**. Concerned about the millions of refugees, migrants and dispossessed, Salgado has photographed in thirty-nine countries, such as India, Pakistan, Sudan, Congo, Ethiopia, and Angola. Why? "My photographs . . . give the person who does not have the opportunity to go there the possibility to look. . . ."

Salgado's photographs show people's courage and dignity as they struggle to achieve basic human rights. Today, he is one of the world's most respected photographers. He has published ten books and won many awards.

---

drought, a time when no rain falls and the land becomes very dry
famine, grave shortage of food; starvation

2

▲ Sebastião Salgado was born in Brazil and now lives in France.

BEFORE YOU GO ON . . .

1 What does "You are the wind beneath my wings" mean? Answers will vary.

2 In what ways is Salgado heroic?

HOW ABOUT YOU?
- Would you rather be a musician or a photographer? Explain.

191

CRITICAL THINKING

Have students respond orally or in writing to these questions:

● Do you believe the message in "Wind Beneath My Wings"? Why or why not? *(Answers will vary.)*

● Why do you think Salgado's photograph was chosen to depict heroes? *(Possible answers: Anyone who survives during a famine and fights for his or her life is a hero. Salgado was a hero for taking risks and bringing the plight of others to the attention of the world.)*

MODELING THE READING STRATEGY

Making Inferences: Have students read the first two sentences on page 191. Ask them to use what they know about heroes, what they see in the photograph, and what they learned from the text to make an inference to answer this question: *Why do you think Salgado, a successful economist, would become a photographer?*

Viewpoint

Ask students to study the photograph by Salgado on this page. Discuss with them any feelings the photograph evokes, and whether or not this was Salgado's intention when he took the picture.

ABOUT THE PHOTOGRAPHER

Brazilian photographer Sebastião Salgado has published ten books and won numerous awards in Europe and the Americas.

REACHING ALL STUDENTS

LANGUAGE LEVELS

Beginning: Have students listen to a recording of Bette Midler singing "Wind Beneath My Wings." If students wish, they can sing along during a subsequent replaying of the song. After discussing the song's meaning, ask students whether they prefer listening to the song or reading the lyrics. Have them explain their opinion.

Advanced: Form four student groups. Assign a different verse of the song to each group. Ask group members to summarize the verse in their own words. Have one student from each group record notes. Then have each group share their summaries.

LEARNING MODALITIES

Visual: Have each student draw a picture to illustrate the lyrics of "Wind Beneath My Wings." Have them share, compare, and discuss their illustrations in small groups.

Connect

Written over one hundred years ago, Walt Whitman's poem is eerily contemporary in its story about a fallen firefighter who is rescued by his comrades.

GUIDED READING

1. Who is telling the story in the poem? *(a fallen firefighter)*
2. What does the firefighter hear, shouts or sirens? *(shouts from comrades)*
3. What did the comrades lift away? *(beams)*

Viewpoint

Ask students to study the photograph and describe what they see. Ask them to explain why this photograph was paired with the poem and how it ties into the unit theme, "We Can Be Heroes."

ABOUT THE POET

Walt Whitman was born in West Hills, New York, and spent much of his life in the surrounding region, although he also spent time along the Mississippi River and Great Lakes. He loved opera and claimed that it helped him write *Leaves of Grass*.

---

from
Leaves of Grass

1 I am the **mashed** fireman, with breast-bone broken . . .
  tumbling walls buried me in their **debris**—
Heat and smoke, I respired . . . I heard the yelling
  shouts of my **comrades**—
I heard the distant click of their picks and shovels.
2 They have cleared the **beams** away . . . they **tenderly**
  lift me forth.

Walt Whitman

---

mashed, injured
debris, broken pieces
comrades, fellow workers and friends
beams, long heavy pieces of wood or metal used in building houses
tenderly, gently

© Thomas E. Franklin/The Bergen County Record/CORBIS Saba

◀ New York firefighters raise the American flag among the ruins of the World Trade Center.

192

About the Poet

Walt Whitman

Walt Whitman (1819–1892) was born in West Hills, New York. He is considered one of the greatest American poets. His poems celebrate the dignity and freedom of the ordinary person. His book *Leaves of Grass* is one of the most famous collections of poems in American literature.

BEFORE YOU GO ON . . .

1 What happened to the firefighter in the poem?
2 How do the firefighters treat their injured comrade?

HOW ABOUT YOU?
• Why do you think the firefighters are raising the flag in the photo?

Link the Readings

REFLECTION

In Part 1, you read several texts and looked at a photograph about heroes. Review the texts and photograph. Then copy the chart into your notebook and complete it.

Title of Selection	Type of Text (Genre)	Fiction or Nonfiction	Purpose of Selection
"Heroes: Yesterday and Today"	biographies		
"Wind Beneath My Wings," Bette Midler			to entertain
Ethiopia, Sebastião Salgado			to inform
From *Leaves of Grass*, Walt Whitman			

DISCUSSION

Discuss in pairs or small groups.

1. What are some qualities of heroes?
2. Can you think of a time when you had to be extra strong? What did you do? Were you surprised that you had that strength?
3. Talk about a hero that you know or have heard about. Tell why this person is heroic. Then write a few sentences in your notebook that describe your hero.

193

REFLECTION

Have a volunteer read the Reflection directions. Ask a student to read the titles on the chart aloud. Then discuss the answers already in the chart. Remind students that different genres, including poems, songs, and photo essays have different characteristics. After students complete the charts in their notebooks, ask:

1. What genre is "Wind Beneath My Wings"? *(song)*
2. Is "Heroes: Yesterday and Today" fiction or nonfiction? *(nonfiction)*

COOPERATIVE GROUPING

Pair intermediate and advanced students with beginning students. Ask each pair to complete the chart together, having each student record the answers in his or her own notebook. Later, invite each pair to share at least one answer.

DISCUSSION

Have students read and discuss the questions in pairs or small groups. Then ask each group or pair to choose one question and create a poster to accompany their answer. Have pairs share their posters and answers with the class.

CRITICAL THINKING

Ask student groups to choose one hero from the selections in the text that they think most closely illustrates the ideas in Bette Midler's song. Have them name the person and explain their ideas in two or three sentences.

REACHING ALL STUDENTS

LANGUAGE LEVELS

Beginning: Copy the Reflection chart on the board. Then work with students to look back at the selections and determine what information should go into the chart. Complete the chart together, writing the ideas on the board. Then have students copy the completed chart into their notebooks.

Advanced: Form student pairs to discuss the last column of the Reflection chart. Ask pairs to go back to the text and choose the very best example for each selection. Encourage pairs to discuss their choices, providing support for their opinions.

GRAMMAR

Have volunteers take turns reading each example in the Grammar lesson aloud. Point out that the passive voice generally uses a form of *be* before the verb, such as *am, are, is, was, were.* Identify an example of the passive voice in the text, such as the caption for the photograph of Gandhi on page 184. Ask students to find and write on the board other examples of passive sentences from the selections. Have them write a matching active-voice sentence beside each one. Then have students complete the Practice exercises.

SCAFFOLDING

Model how to complete the first Practice sentence. Explain that to make it passive, you need to include a form of *be,* in this case, *was.* Write on the board *Joan of Arc was burned at the stake when she was nineteen years old.* Then have students complete the remaining sentences.

Connect to Writing

GRAMMAR

The Passive Voice

Verbs in sentences are in either the **active voice** or the **passive voice**.

active voice	passive voice
Schindler **hired** Jewish workers.	Jewish workers **were hired** by Schindler.

Use a form of *be* + past participle of the verb to form the passive voice.

Thousands of people **were saved** by the firefighters.

Use the active voice to focus on the *performer* of an action.

performer   action
Police officers **rescued** people from the collapsed buildings.

Use the passive voice to focus on the *receiver* of an action.

receiver   action
Many people **were rescued** from the collapsed buildings.

Use a *by* phrase to tell who or what performed the action. Use the *by* phrase only when it is important to know who performed the action.

Martin Luther King Jr. was influenced **by Gandhi**.

When it is not important to know who performed the action, the *by* phrase is not necessary.

Many soldiers **were wounded**.

Practice

Complete the sentences in your notebook. Use the passive forms of the verbs in parentheses. Remember to use *by* when necessary.

1. Joan of Arc _____ (burn) at the stake when she was nineteen years old.
2. More than 1,300 Jewish workers _____ (save) Oskar Schindler.
3. Benito Juárez _____ (elect) governor of Oaxaca in 1847.
4. The refugees _____ (help) Doctors Without Borders.

194

SKILLS FOR WRITING

Using Time Phrases to Write a Biography

In a biography, a writer usually tells events in chronological order. Writers use time phrases to show chronology and to tell when things happened. Here are some examples:

yesterday	the next day	on September 11, 2001	in 1948
at age eighty	last night	during the summer	

Read the biography below. Then discuss the questions.

> *A. J. Seidner*
>
> *Michael Jordan: Basketball Hero*
>
> Michael Jordan was born on February 17, 1963. During his youth, Jordan enjoyed playing baseball, basketball, and football. At age fifteen, however, he was cut from the high school basketball team. But in the following years, his playing greatly improved.
>
> Jordan was chosen to play on the U.S. Men's Olympic Team in 1984. Two months after the Olympics, he played his first season with the Chicago Bulls. He led the Bulls to three World Championships. In 1995, after a one-year retirement from the NBA, he returned, and one year later, he led the Bulls to their fourth Championship title. In 2002, he joined the Washington Wizards, continuing his legendary performances.
>
> Michael Jordan is truly an American hero. He shows that all dreams can be realized and that persistence is the key to victory.

1. What time phrases does the writer use to tell when the events happened?
2. Where does the writer use the active voice? What does this show?
3. Where does the writer use the passive voice? What does this show?

195

SKILLS FOR WRITING

Ask a volunteer to read the introductory text. Then have other students read the examples of time phrases that follow. Challenge students to use each example in another sentence. Then call on a volunteer to read the student writing sample on page 195 aloud. Guide students to answer the questions below the biography.

SCAFFOLDING

Ask student pairs to find time phrases—words that tell "when"—in the reading selections. Then ask students to share what they found. Examples include: *In 1854, Britain, France, and Turkey fought against Russia in the Crimean War* and *As a young man, he became interested in social justice. . . .*

REACHING ALL STUDENTS

LANGUAGE LEVELS

Beginning: Have students copy the student writing sample on page 195 in their notebooks. Guide students to circle the time phrases in the biography and tell how they know each is a time phrase.

Advanced: Write the following time phrases on the board:

> *Yesterday,*
> *In fifth grade,*
> *Tomorrow,*
> *At age three,*

Ask each student to write a sentence about himself or herself using each time phrase. Have students share their sentences with the class.

WRITING ASSIGNMENT

Biography

Ask a volunteer to read the first sentence aloud and identify the writing task. Direct students to reread the biography of Michael Jordan on page 195. Then give them a few minutes to think of someone they consider to be a hero.

WRITING STRATEGY

Have students read the information about using a timeline and then study the sample timeline about Michael Jordan. Discuss the questions as a group. Then draw a timeline on the board. Model how to create a timeline by recording information about yourself. Have students create their own timelines by following step 2. When students have finished, tell them to use the information from their timelines to write a short biography about their hero. Remind students to use time phrases in their biography.

USING THE EDITING CHECKLIST

Have student pairs look over the Editing Checklist together and use it to revise their biographies.

WRITING ASSIGNMENT

Biography

You will write a biography of someone that you consider to be a hero.

1. **Read** Reread the biography on page 195. Then think of someone you admire and you consider to be a hero. It can be someone you know or someone you've read about.

> ### Writing Strategy: Timeline
>
> Biographies usually tell events in chronological order. A timeline can help you organize ideas for your biography. Look at the timeline that the writer created for a biography of Michael Jordan.
>
> | 1963 | 1984 | 1994 | 1995 | 2002 |
> |------|------|------|------|------|
> | born | played in Olympics; played with Chicago Bulls | retired from NBA | returned to NBA | played with Washington Wizards |
>
> 1. What does each point on the timeline show?
> 2. Did the writer include the most important events? Would you add or subtract anything?

2. **Make a timeline** Make a timeline of your hero's life in your notebook. Write some important events and the years they happened. Begin with your hero's birth or with an important event early in his or her life. When you finish, exchange timelines with a partner. Discuss your timelines, and choose the most important events to write about.

3. **Write** Use your timeline to write a short biography of your hero. Remember to use the active and passive voices. Use time phrases to show the order of events and tell when things happened.

EDITING CHECKLIST

Did you . . .

▶ include the most important events?
▶ use time phrases to show the order of events and when things happened?
▶ use the active and passive voices?
▶ use correct punctuation?

196

PART REVIEW 1

Check Your Knowledge

Language Development

1. Describe the reading strategy of making inferences.
2. What is a biography? Is it fiction or nonfiction? Explain.
3. How are a poem and a song similar? How are they different?
4. How can a timeline help you write a biography?
5. What is the passive voice? How is it different from the active voice? Give one example of a sentence using the passive voice.
6. What is a time phrase? Why do writers use time phrases?
7. Choose one of the photographs in Part 1 and describe it. Why do you think it is included in a unit about heroes and heroic acts?

Academic Content

1. What new social studies vocabulary did you learn in Part 1? What do the words mean?
2. Why is Florence Nightingale called "The Lady with the Lamp"?
3. What do Gandhi and Mandela have in common?

Florence Nightingale ▶

197

ASSESS

You can assess students' knowledge of the unit in several different ways.

Portfolio: Students can include the answers to the Check Your Knowledge questions and their biographies in their portfolios.

Traditional: Students can complete the Check Your Knowledge questions as a pretest. After students complete Check Your Knowledge, use the Assessment Package. Students can complete the Part Test on pages 61–64. For further practice, have students complete the Test Preparation worksheets.

Performance: Use six of the Check Your Knowledge questions for a student "game show." Form two teams. Write six of the seven Language Development questions on separate slips of paper. Have each team choose three questions, one at a time, alternating between teams. Students work with their team to answer the questions.

TEST-TAKING TIP

Remind students to use context clues to answer word-meaning questions. Students should find the word in the passage and then read the sentence that contains the word as well as the sentences around it. See the Test Preparation pages in the Assessment Guide for additional test-taking strategies.

METACOGNITION

Have pairs of students practice using the following terms in sentences: *making inferences, biography, timeline, passive voice, active voice, time phrase.*

REACHING ALL STUDENTS

LANGUAGE LEVELS

Beginning: As students complete step 2 of the Writing Assignment, have them share their timeline with a partner. Have pairs work together to revise the timeline and add time phrases to help organize ideas sequentially.

Advanced: Before completing the timeline for the Writing Assignment, invite students to research their selected heroes in the library. Encourage them to add details from their research to the timelines.

OBJECTIVES

Explain to students that in Part 2 they will be reading about people and ideas that they might study in history or art class. Read the list of objectives, encouraging students to join in. Emphasize italicized words, such as *Visualizing* and *Recognizing and analyzing setting,* and identify the base words. *(visualize, recognize, analyze)* Ask students to paraphrase what they think they will learn in this part of the unit. Additional practice activities for these objectives can be found in the **Workbook** and **CD-ROM.**

BACKGROUND

Ask students to read the introductory text. Have students discuss plays they have seen, telling about elements explained in the text. Then have a volunteer read the Make Connections section. Ask students to study the diagram of the attic where the Frank family hid. Read aloud and discuss each question.

COOPERATIVE GROUPING

After discussing the Background section as a class, assign a different question on page 198 to each of two groups. Have each group prepare an oral presentation to answer the question. Encourage groups to create visuals that might make their presentation more effective, such as an abstract painting that expresses their feeling about hiding or a poster showing items they would miss from the outside world.

PART 2 — Prepare to Read

OBJECTIVES

LANGUAGE DEVELOPMENT

Reading:
- Vocabulary building: *Context, dictionary skills*
- Reading strategy: *Visualizing*
- Text types: *Play, social studies article*
- Literary element: *Recognizing and analyzing setting*

Writing:
- Book or movie review
- Self-evaluation
- Editorial checklist

Listening/Speaking:
- Retelling a story
- Comparing and contrasting

Grammar:
- Comparative and superlative adjectives

Viewing/Representing:
- Interpreting paintings

ACADEMIC CONTENT
- Social studies vocabulary
- World War II
- Spanish Civil War

BACKGROUND

The play, *The Diary of Anne Frank*, is based on the book *Anne Frank: The Diary of a Young Girl.* Anne Frank wrote her diary in Amsterdam, Holland, between 1943 and 1945 while hiding from the Nazis during World War II.

People who write plays are called playwrights. Actors usually perform plays for an audience. The script of a play has dialogue and stage directions. The dialogue is the words the actors speak. The stage directions are the words in parentheses in the script. They tell how the actors should look, move, and speak.

Make connections Anne Frank and her family hid in secret rooms, called the annex, for over two years. They had to be very quiet during the day so no one would hear them. They couldn't leave the annex. They depended on Mr. Frank's work colleagues to bring them food and other necessities. These people heroically risked their lives to help the family.

Look at the pictures of the hiding place. Then answer the questions.

▲ The secret annex was at the back of Mr. Frank's office building.

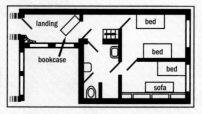

1. Imagine you had to live here for two years with six other people. How would you feel?
2. What would you miss the most about the outside world?

198

TEACHING GUIDE

PRETEACH	Provide Background	Read and discuss the Background information. Complete the activity. (ATE/SB p. 198)
	Present Concepts	Introduce the Reading Strategy. (ATE/SB p. 199)
TEACH	Monitor Comprehension	Informally monitor comprehension while students read the selection independently or in groups. (ATE/SB pp. 200–205)
	Teach and Practice	Present the Grammar, Usage, and Mechanics. (ATE/SB pp. 212, 213) Complete the Writing activity. (ATE/SB p. 214) Present Grammar, Phonics, and Spelling minilessons. (ATE pp. 202, 210, 212)
CONNECT	Connect to Content	Have students read the informational reading and relate it to the literature. (ATE/SB pp. 208–210)
	Across the Curriculum	Present curriculum links as students read. (ATE pp. 200, 208)
ASSESS	Check Knowledge	Assess students' comprehension by having them complete the Check Your Knowledge section. (ATE/SB p. 215)
	Monitor Progress	Use one or more of the print assessment resources in the Assessment Package.
EXTEND	Integrate Language and Apply Understanding	Have students complete the Workshops (ATE/SB pp. 216–219) and choose a project from the Unit Projects. (ATE/SB p. 220) Then have them choose a book to read from Further Reading. (ATE/SB p. 221)

VOCABULARY

Read these sentences. Use the context to figure out the meaning of the red words. Use a dictionary to check your answers. Write each word and its meaning in your notebook.

1. The family left Germany—their **destination** was Holland.
2. Jewish children were **forbidden** to go to school with non-Jewish children. They had to go to special Jewish schools.
3. Many Jews had to **go into hiding** to escape the Nazis.
4. Her **identity** was secret. No one knew who she was.
5. Anne's diary gives the **impression** that she was older than she really was.
6. If people didn't obey the Nazis' **regulations**, they were punished.

LEARN KEY WORDS

destination
forbidden
go into hiding
identity
impression
regulations

READING STRATEGY

Visualizing

Visualizing means getting mental images, or pictures in your mind, from a text. You learned about this reading strategy in Unit 2, when you read an excerpt from the novel *A Boat to Nowhere*.

When reading a play, use the stage directions to help you visualize the action, the characters, and the surroundings, or setting. Stage directions are usually in parentheses. For example:

(She looks down the steps where Peter van Daan, a shy, awkward boy of sixteen, wearing a heavy coat with the conspicuous yellow star, waits nervously. He is carrying a cat in a basket.)

One of the rooms in the annex ▼

199

VOCABULARY

Form six groups of students, assigning each group a different Key Word. Have groups present their word or phrase to the other students, explaining the term in their own words. Then have students read aloud the sentences and use context clues to record the definitions of each Key Word in their notebooks.

READING STRATEGY

Review the concept of *visualizing* with students. Remind them that when they visualize as they read they use descriptive details from the text as well as their own prior knowledge to picture characters, settings, and story events. Ask students to copy the sample stage directions in their notebooks and work with partners to underline descriptive words that helped them visualize the text.

REACHING ALL STUDENTS

LANGUAGE LEVELS

Beginning: Ask students to close their eyes as you reread the sample stage directions in the Reading Strategy box. Then have them draw a picture of what they visualized. Tell students to compare their drawings with a partner and discuss similarities and differences. Ask pairs to share with the class how their pictures reflect what they visualized.

Advanced: Discuss the Reading Strategy with students. Reread the sample stage directions, inviting students to imagine they are set designers who will create a set design based on these directions. Have each student visualize what the set would look like and meet with partners to come up with a definite plan. Have student pairs share their ideas.

READING SUMMARY

In this excerpt from the play *The Diary of Anne Frank,* Anne and her family take refuge in a secret annex to hide from the Germans who are occupying Holland.

SCAFFOLDING

Ask students to listen to the CD/tape of this selection as they read it silently.

GUIDED READING

1. In what country do the Franks live? *(Holland)*
2. What does Anne have to wear after the Dutch surrender? *(a yellow star)*
3. Where is the the secret annex? *(at the back of Anne's father's office building)*

──────── *Viewpoint* ────────

Ask students to identify and describe what they see in the photograph on this page. Have them explain why they think Anne kept a diary.

across the curriculum

GEOGRAPHY Have students find Germany and Holland on a world map or globe. Ask students to describe the locations of the countries in relation to each other and in relation to the United States. Provide students with vocabulary, such as *north, south, east,* and *west.*

FOCUS ON LITERATURE ▸ **Play** ●

As you read this excerpt from the play, try to visualize the action, characters, and setting. Use the stage directions to help you.

from The Diary of Anne Frank
The Play

Frances Goodrich and Albert Hackett, with Wendy Kesselman

On June 12th, 1942, Anne Frank received a diary for her thirteenth birthday. A few weeks later, on July 6th, the family was forced to move into the secret annex. They lived there for two years with the van Pels family (Anne calls them the van Daans in her diary) and another Jewish man. Mr. Frank's former work colleagues, Mr. Kraler and Miep Gies, helped the families survive.

ANNE: *(Voiceover)* July sixth, 1942. A few days ago, Father began to talk about going into hiding. He said it would be very hard for us to live **cut off** from the rest of the world. He sounded so serious I felt scared. "Don't worry, Anneke. We'll take care of everything. Just enjoy your **carefree** life while you can." *(She pauses.)*
     Carefree? I was born in Frankfurt on June twelfth, 1929. Because we're Jewish, my father **emigrated**

---

cut off, separated
carefree, without worries
emigrated, left one's own country to live in another

▲ Anne Frank and her diary

200

to Holland in 1933. He started a business, manufacturing products used to make jam. But Hitler **invaded** Holland on May tenth, 1940, a month before my eleventh birthday. Five days later the Dutch surrendered, the Germans arrived—and the trouble started for the Jews. *(A pause.)*

Father was forced to give up his business. We couldn't use streetcars, couldn't go to the theater or movies anymore, couldn't be out on the *street* after 9 P.M., couldn't even sit in our own gardens! We had to turn in our bicycles; no beaches, no swimming pools, no libraries—we couldn't even walk on the sunny side of the streets! My sister Margot and I had to go to a Jewish school. Our identity cards were stamped with a big black "J". And . . . we had to wear the yellow star. But somehow life went on. Until yesterday, when a call-up notice came from the **SS**. Margot was ordered to report for work in Germany, to the **Westerbork transit camp**. A call-up: Everyone knows what that means! *(She pauses.)*

At five-thirty this morning, we closed the door of our apartment behind us—ten days earlier than my parents had planned. My cat was the only living creature I said goodbye to. The unmade beds, the breakfast things on the table all created the impression we'd left in a hurry. *(A pause.)*

And our destination? We walked two and a half miles in the pouring rain all the way to . . . Father's office building! Our hiding place, the "Secret Annex," is right behind it upstairs. Even though the Germans forced Father out, he still runs the office with Mr. Kraler and Miep, who've agreed to help us while we're in hiding. *(As Mr. Frank pulls a large **tarpaulin** off the kitchen table, he sees a rat move across the floor. Mrs. Frank shrieks.)*

---

invaded, entered a place using military force
SS, high-ranking members of the Nazi Party
Westerbork transit camp, a place in Holland where people were put on trains to the concentration camps
tarpaulin, a piece of material used to cover and protect an object

---

LITERARY ELEMENT

The *setting* is the time and place of the action in a story or play. To recognize, or identify, the setting, ask yourself when and where the story takes place.

When analyzing, or thinking about, the setting, consider all the details the writer gives about the time and place.

1

---

2 **BEFORE YOU GO ON . . .**

1 Why do the Franks go into hiding?
2 Who helps them?

HOW ABOUT YOU?

- Imagine you have to go into hiding. What would you take with you?

201

CRITICAL THINKING

Have students respond orally or in writing to these questions:

- Do you think it's fair to stop a group of people from doing things such as using streetcars or going to the movies? Why or why not? *(Answers will vary.)*
- Why do you think the Frank family wanted it to look as though they left in a hurry? *(Possible answer: They did not want the Nazis to look for them.)*

MODELING THE READING STRATEGY

Visualizing: Have students reread the stage direction at the bottom of page 201. Encourage them to identify any descriptive words that help them visualize the scene.

LITERARY ELEMENT

Read aloud the Literary Element text as students follow along silently. Explain that most setting information in a play appears in parentheses as stage directions, but sometimes information is included in the dialogue. Read the last two paragraphs on page 201 aloud, asking students to think about the setting. Then have them describe the setting in their own words.

ACTIVE READING

Have students create a word web in their notebooks. Have students write *What I See* in the center circle and descriptions of the setting, characters, and costumes on lines extending from the circle. Have students add to the web as they read.

Teach

GUIDED READING

1. What kind of pet does Peter bring with him? *(a cat)*
2. How does Anne feel about living with another family in such close quarters? *(She thinks it will be an adventure—like being on vacation in some strange pension.)*
3. Who first notices that Peter is anxious? *(Mr. Frank)*

―――――― *Viewpoint* ――――――

Have students look closely at the photographs on page 203. Ask them to identify and describe what they see. Have them discuss what they learned from the pictures about Anne and her family that they did not know before.

MRS. FRANK: A rat!

MR. FRANK: Shhh! *(Quickly he motions her to be quiet, as Miep comes up the steps.)*

MR. FRANK: Ah, Miep!

MIEP: Mr. Frank. Thank God you arrived safely.

ANNE: Miep!

MIEP: Anne. Margot. *(As Margot and Mrs. Frank slowly sit up.)* Mrs. Frank, you must be exhausted. If only we'd known we would have had it all ready for you.

MR. FRANK: You've done too much already, Miep. Besides, it's good for us to keep busy. As you see, Anne's my little helper.

MIEP: I can see that. *(She looks down the steps where Peter van Daan, a shy, awkward boy of sixteen, wearing a heavy coat with the **conspicuous** yellow star, waits nervously. He is carrying a cat in a basket.)* Peter—come in!

MR. FRANK: *(Quickly coming forward.)* Peter. The first to arrive. *(Shaking his hand.)* Welcome, Peter. Peter van Daan, children.

ANNE: *(Rushing toward him.)* Welcome to the Annex!

MR. FRANK: Peter—Margot, Anne. You already know Mrs. Frank.

PETER: *(Solemnly shaking hands with Mrs. Frank.)* Mrs. Frank.

MRS. FRANK: Forgive me, Peter. I'm not quite myself. But I'm so glad you'll be with us.

---

conspicuous, very easy to notice
solemnly, seriously or sadly

202

MARGOT: I am too.

ANNE: *(Looking down at the basket.)* A cat! *(Turning to Margot.)* He has a cat!

PETER: *(Self-conscious.)* A black one.

ANNE: We have a cat too. I wanted to bring her but . . . *(Glancing at her mother.)* I know our neighbors will take care of her till we come back. I don't know what I'll do without her. But it'll be great having a cat here. Won't it, **Pim**? Won't it be fantastic?

MRS. FRANK: Anne dear, don't get so excited. Peter doesn't know you yet.

ANNE: *(Laughing.)* He'll get to know me soon though. It's going to be so much fun having people around. A whole other family. Won't it, Margot?

MARGOT: Yes.

① **ANNE:** *(Skipping around the room.)* Like being on vacation in some strange **pension** or something. An adventure—**romantic** and dangerous at the same time!

MR. FRANK: *(Watching Peter's **anxious** face.)* What is it, Peter?

② **PETER:** My parents. They were right behind me, one street away.

MR. FRANK: *(Laying his hand on Peter's shoulder.)* They'll be here.

PETER: You don't think they were . . .

MRS. FRANK: Don't worry, Peter. *(Smiling.)* You're just like me.

---

self-conscious, shy; awkward
Pim, Anne's nickname for her father
pension, a hotel or boarding house
romantic, emotional and dreamlike
anxious, worried

PHONICS MINILESSON

r-controlled Vowels

Write the following words on the board, underlining the *r*-controlled vowel in each word: *start, person, third, hurt, short.* Say each word as you point to it, and ask students to repeat it. Point to each *r*-controlled vowel and say the sound it represents. (/är/, /er/, /er/, /er/, /ôr/) Ask students to repeat each vowel sound.

Have students draw a five-column chart in their notebooks with the following headings: *ar, er, ir, ur, or.* Then have students find *r*-controlled vowels on page 202 of the text, in magazines, or in newspapers and record them in the appropriate columns on the chart. Form small groups for students to practice saying the words in their charts. Examples from the selection include: *Margot, star; nervously, her, were; first; for, forward, turning.*

T202

▲ Margot (left) and Anne

The Frank family ▶

▲ Peter

▲ The entrance to the annex, hidden by a bookcase

Anne at school ▶

BEFORE YOU GO ON . . .

1 How does Anne feel about hiding in the annex?

2 Why is Peter anxious about his parents?

HOW ABOUT YOU?
● Is Anne like you in any way? If so, how?

203

Have students respond orally or in writing to these questions:

● In a similar situation, do you think most people would feel excited like Anne or anxious like Mrs. Frank and Peter? Explain your answer. *(Answers will vary.)*

● How do you think Peter meant to complete the sentence "You don't think they were . . . "? Why? *(Possible answer: " . . . captured by the Nazis?" That would have been a Jew's greatest fear in a country that was occupied by the Germans.)*

MODELING THE READING STRATEGY

Making Inferences: Remind students that when they make inferences, they use text information as well as their own prior knowledge to figure out information that is not directly stated in the text. Have students make an inference by asking why they think Anne gets so excited when she sees that Peter has brought a cat with him. *(Anne is glad because she had to leave her own cat behind; a cat will scare away the rats.)*

REACHING ALL STUDENTS

LANGUAGE LEVELS

Beginning: Help define the following new vocabulary by pantomiming the meaning of each word: *solemnly, self-conscious, anxious.* Ask students to describe what they see. Say each word, and have students repeat it. Then distribute pictures to help define the word *pension.* Have students share other words that mean the same thing as pension *(inn, hotel),* and call on volunteers to write the words on the board.

Advanced: Tell students to create a three-column chart. In the first column, ask them to list any new words they encounter on these two pages. Then have them work with partners to try and figure out the meaning of each word. In the second column of the chart, have them write what they think each word means. In the third column, ask them to write the dictionary definition and page number on which they find the word.

Teach

GUIDED READING

1. Why did it take Peter's parents such a long time to get to the hiding place? *(They had to go the long way to avoid the police.)*
2. Who is helping the Franks, Mr. and Mrs. van Daan or Mr. Kraler and Miep? *(Mr. Kraler and Miep)*
3. What is the last thing Mr. Kraler gives to the Franks and the van Daans before he leaves them in the annex? *(a radio)*

MODELING THE READING STRATEGY

Analyzing Historical Context: Remind students that knowledge of historical events can help them to read and understand historical fiction. Guide student groups to research the rise of the Nazis in Germany and their policies toward the Jews. Have groups find and share with the class three facts that they think will help them better understand the dangers Anne and her family faced during the war.

ANNE: Mother's always jumping at every little thing. *(Peeking into Peter's basket.)* What's its name?

PETER: *(Self-conscious.)* Mouschi.

ANNE: *(To the cat.)* Mouschi! Mouschi. I love cats. *(To Peter.)* Where'd you go to school?

PETER: They set up a **technical school** in someone's house, once we were forbidden—

ANNE: *(Breaking in.)* I had to switch from my Montessori school to the Jewish Lyceum.

PETER: I know. I saw you there.

ANNE: You did? *(Mr. Kraler hurries up the stairs with Mr. and Mrs. van Daan. Mrs. van Daan is wearing a fur coat and carrying an umbrella and a large hat box. Mr. van Daan carries a **satchel** and his briefcase. All three are out of breath.)*

MR. FRANK: *(To Peter, smiling.)* See— what did I tell you? Now we're all here.

MR. KRALER: *(Obviously shaken.)* Just in time. We had to take the long way around—there were too many **Green Police** on the streets. *(Mr. van Daan breaks open a package of cigarettes, nervously starts smoking.)*

MR. FRANK: *(Shaking hands with the van Daans.)* Welcome, Mrs. van Daan. Mr. van Daan. You know my wife, of course, and the children. *(Mrs. Frank, Margot, and Anne shake hands with the van Daans.)*

MR. KRALER: We must hurry. The workmen will be here in half an hour.

MR. FRANK: Such trouble we're causing you, Mr. Kraler, after all you and Miep have done. And now we arrive early!

MR. KRALER: You couldn't let your daughter be taken away, Mr. Frank.

MIEP: Please don't worry. We will do everything we can to help you. Now I must run and get your **ration books**.

MRS. VAN DAAN: Wait—if they see our names on ration books, they'll know we're here, won't they?

MIEP: Trust me—your names won't be on them. I'll be up later. If you make a list every day, I'll try to get what you want. And every Saturday I can bring five library books. *(She hurries out.)*

MR. FRANK: Thank you, Miep.

ANNE: Five! I know what my five are going to be.

MRS. FRANK: Anne, remember, there are seven of us.

ANNE: I know, Mother.

MARGOT: *(Troubled.)* It's **illegal**, then, the ration books? We've never done anything illegal.

MR. VAN DAAN: I don't think we'll be living exactly according to regulations here. *(The **carillon** is heard playing the quarter hour before eight.)*

ANNE: Listen. The Westertoren!

---

technical school, a school that teaches auto mechanics, machine repair, and other skills
satchel, a small bag for carrying clothing, books, etc.
Green Police, Dutch police who supported the Nazis

ration books, booklets of coupons that allow people to buy food during wartime
illegal, not allowed by law
carillon, bells on a clock tower

MRS. FRANK: How will I ever get used to that clock?

ANNE: Oh, I love it!

MR. KRALER: Miep or I will be here every day to see you. I've hidden a **buzzer** to signal you when we come up, and tomorrow I'll have that bookcase placed in front of your door. Oh, and one last thing . . . the radio . . . *(He points to a small radio hidden beneath a sheet.)*

ANNE: *(Bounding over to the radio.)* A radio! Fantastic!

MRS. VAN DAAN: A radio. Thank God.

MR. VAN DAAN: How did you get it? We had to turn ours in months ago.

MR. FRANK: Thank you, Mr. Kraler. For everything. *(Mr. Kraler turns to go, as Anne drops a batch of silverware.)*

MR. KRALER: *(To Mr. Frank.)* Oh . . . you'll tell them about the noise?

MR. FRANK: I'll tell them.

MRS. FRANK: *(Following Mr. Kraler to the top of the stairs.)* How *can* we thank you really? How can we ever—

MR. KRALER: I never thought I'd live to see the day a man like Mr. Frank would have to go into hiding. *(He hurries out, as she stands still, watching him.)*

***

On August 4, 1944, the secret annex was raided by the Security Police. Anne and the seven others in hiding were arrested. They were transported to Auschwitz concentration camp. After a month there, Anne and Margot were sent to Bergen-Belsen concentration

---

buzzer, a small device that makes a loud noise

camp, where they both got typhus, a deadly disease. They died within a short time of each other in March 1945, only a few weeks before the camp was liberated by the British. Only Anne's father Otto Frank survived. In 1947, he published Anne's diary.

About the Authors

Frances Goodrich and Albert Hackett

Frances Goodrich and Albert Hackett wrote the screenplays for some of Hollywood's most famous movies. *The Diary of Anne Frank*, written in 1955, was perhaps their greatest achievement. Wendy Kesselman's version, based on an expanded and unedited version of the original diary, portrays a more realistic Anne.

BEFORE YOU GO ON . . .

1 How will Miep and Mr. Kraler signal that they are coming up to the annex?

2 Why do you think Anne is so excited about the radio? **Answers will vary.**

HOW ABOUT YOU?
- Do you like Anne? Why or why not?

205

COMPREHENSION

Have a volunteer read the Comprehension directions and the first answer in the list of story events aloud. Then ask students to reread the selection with partners. Encourage each pair to discuss the remaining events on page 206 before placing them in chronological order. Ask students to record the list in their notebooks and write a number before each sentence to indicate chronological order. Then have students respond to these questions:

1. What happens just after the Dutch surrender to Hitler? *(The Jews in Holland are forced to wear yellow stars.)*

2. To what location did the Franks walk two and a half miles? *(the secret annex)*

3. Who arrives to live in the annex just after the Franks? *(Peter and his parents)*

CRITICAL THINKING

After students have placed the list of story events in chronological order, have them think about the acts of the Nazis. Ask them to respond orally or in writing to these questions:

- Which two events listed in the Comprehension activity demonstrate people being kind to one another? *(welcoming Peter, offering to bring library books)*

- Which two events reflect actions that were unkind? *(Hitler invading Holland, Jews being forced to wear a yellow star)*

Review and Practice

COMPREHENSION

Reread the excerpt from *The Diary of Anne Frank*. Number the events in chronological order. Remember that some of these events took place before the two families moved into the annex.

_____ The Frank family welcomes Peter.

_____ Jews in Holland are forced to wear a yellow star.

_____ Anne sees the cat Mouschi for the first time.

_____ The Frank family walks two and a half miles in the pouring rain.

___1___ Hitler invades Holland, and the Dutch surrender.

_____ Miep offers to bring library books to the families.

Now use your list to retell the story to a partner.

◀ Anne's diary

206

EXTENSION

1. The excerpt from *The Diary of Anne Frank* describes the first day of life in hiding for the two families. What did you visualize as you read? Draw a picture of what you visualized and share it with the class.

2. Visualize yourself in the Secret Annex, hiding with the two families. How do you feel after a year? Copy the chart into your notebook. Make a list of things that are difficult for you. For example, think about things you can't do because you are hiding. Make another list of things you have learned. Share your ideas with a partner. How are your lists similar and different?

What Is Difficult	What I've Learned

DISCUSSION

Discuss in pairs or small groups.

1. When the Germans invaded Holland, how did life change for Anne and her family?

2. What are some things that Miep and Mr. Kraler have to worry about?

3. What do you think life was like in the annex after a year? Do you think Anne was still happy? Why or why not?

207

EXTENSION

Read the first item aloud, allowing time for students to draw and discuss their illustrations. Then have a student read aloud the second item. Ask students to discuss the questions in small groups or with partners. Then focus students' attention on the T-chart and provide an example for each column. *(What Is Difficult: being quiet all the time; What I've Learned: People need freedom to be happy.)* Have students complete the charts before sharing them with a partner.

DISCUSSION

Have students read the questions and discuss them in pairs or small groups. After they have completed their discussion, ask groups to report their answers to the class.

METACOGNITION

Ask students:

1. Did you like reading a play more or less than reading a story or article? Why?

2. What did you do when you found unfamiliar words in the play? What other strategies could you use to figure out their meanings?

3. How well did you participate in the group activities? What would help you participate more?

REACHING ALL STUDENTS

LANGUAGE LEVELS

Beginning: Offer support in completing the Extension activity by asking leading questions as students discuss item 2, such as *Do you think the families felt free or trapped in the annex? Why might a child feel unhappy in an attic after a year?* Then work with students to create a single T-chart with their ideas about what it would be like to be in the annex for a year. Record the chart on the board and have students copy it into their notebooks.

Advanced: Encourage students to write their Extension chart responses in complete sentences and check their spelling by looking up difficult words in a dictionary. After they have shared their charts with a partner, encourage students to discuss their ideas with a small group of advanced students and add additional ideas to their charts.

Connect

READING SUMMARY

Pablo Picasso painted *Guernica* to show the horror and chaos of war. A reproduction of this painting with informative text is followed by *Hiroshima,* a painting created by children affiliated with Kids' Guernica, an international art project that works to create peace.

SCAFFOLDING

Have students listen to the CD/tape of this selection as they read it silently.

GUIDED READING

1. Who ordered planes to bomb Guernica, Picasso or Franco? *(Franco)*
2. On what date did Nazi planes bomb Guernica? *(April 26, 1937)*
3. What did Pablo Picasso do after he saw photographs of Guernica? *(He painted the mural* Guernica.)*

across the curriculum

ART Have students identify the colors Picasso used to paint *Guernica.* Ask students what colors the artist saw in the newspaper photographs. Point out that Picasso could have chosen any colors to create his work, but he chose colors that closely match the black-and-white photographs. Invite students to create their own monochromatic illustrations of an event they have read about in a newspaper or seen on TV.

CONNECT TO CONTENT **Art, Social Studies**

This is an informational text. It tells about the Spanish Civil War, and about some ways that war inspires artists. Is it fiction or nonfiction?
Does Pablo Picasso's Guernica *tell you how he feels about war? Can you tell from the painting* Hiroshima *how the students feel about war and peace?*

Heroic Art

Guernica

During the Spanish Civil War (1936–1939), Spain was a divided country. A large group of Spaniards hated General Franco, Spain's fascist **dictator**. This group was called the Resistance. The Resistance wanted to defeat Franco's government, but Franco was a powerful leader. Franco was supported by Hitler (the leader of Nazi Germany) and Mussolini (the leader of fascist Italy). The Resistance made Franco very angry.

At this time, Guernica, a town in northern Spain, had a population of 7,000. Guernica was independent and democratic. On April 26, 1937, Franco ordered Nazi planes to bomb the town. It was 4:00 P.M. on a busy market day. About 1,650 innocent people were killed and 889 were injured.

---

dictator, a ruler who has complete power over a country

Pablo Picasso ▶

Picasso's symbols
the bull = the brutality of war
the horse = the people
the electric light = an all-seeing God
the flower = hope

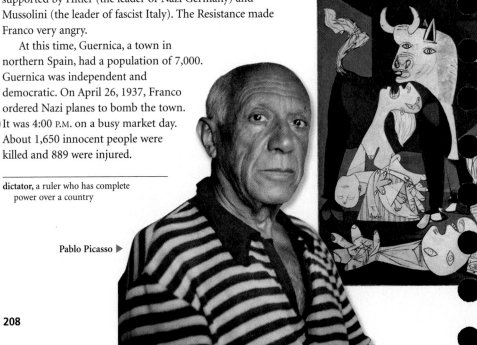

208

MULTICULTURAL NOTE Explain to students that *Guernica* has made its home throughout the world. It was first hung in the Spanish Pavilion of the Paris International Exposition in 1937 in Paris, France. The mural was later placed on extended loan at New York City's Museum of Modern Art from 1939 until 1981. In 1981, the mural made its way to the Prado Museum in Madrid, Spain. In 1992, it moved across town to Madrid's new museum of twentieth-century art, the Reina Sofia Art Center. Have student groups choose a location that once held or currently holds *Guernica,* and do research to find out three facts about the location. Have groups report their findings to the class.

Pablo Picasso

Picasso (1881–1973) was one of the most important artists of the twentieth century. He was born in Spain and moved to Paris when he was twenty-three.

After the bombing of Guernica, Picasso was shocked by the black-and-white photographs he saw in the newspapers. He quickly sketched the first images for a mural. *Guernica* shows the horror and **chaos** of war.

Picasso wrote this **prose-poem** about the bombing of Guernica.

> . . . *cries of children cries of women cries of birds cries of flowers cries of timbers and of stones cries of bricks cries of furniture of beds of chains of curtains of pots and of papers cries of odors which claw at one another cries of smoke pricking the shoulder of cries . . .*

---

chaos, confusion
prose-poem, descriptive writing that is similar to poetry

BEFORE YOU GO ON . . .

1 What happened to the town of Guernica?

2 How did Picasso feel about war? *Answers will vary.*

HOW ABOUT YOU?

• How does the painting *Guernica* make you feel?

▲ Pablo Picasso painted *Guernica* in 1937. It is a powerful statement about war.

209

CRITICAL THINKING

Have students respond orally or in writing to these questions:

● Do you like *Guernica*? Why or why not? *(Answers will vary.)*

● Why do you think Picasso included an image of a mother and dead child in the mural? *(Possible answer: to express his outrage over the many innocent people who died in the attack)*

MODELING THE READING STRATEGY

Analyzing Historical Context: Remind students that having a better understanding of the historical events that influenced the creation of a work of art can help them to appreciate it. Have volunteers work in a small group to research the events that led to the Spanish Civil War. Have them report their findings to the class.

Viewpoint

Focus students' attention on the painting. Ask students to describe what they see, including a bull, a dying horse, a fallen warrior, and a woman trapped in a burning building. Discuss why the painting is a powerful statement against war.

REACHING ALL STUDENTS

LANGUAGE LEVELS

Beginning: Reread Picasso's poem on page 209 aloud. Ask students to visualize as they listen. Then ask them whether or not flowers, timbers, and stones can cry as Picasso has described. Have them explain why they think the artist used these images. Help students understand that the artist is attempting to show that everything is in pain as a result of the attack.

Advanced: Form student groups. Challenge each group to think of a way to perform the prose-poem on page 209 so that it evokes strong images and feelings on the part of each listener. Students can use role playing, visuals, or sound effects as they read. Be sure students take turns reading. Invite students to perform their renditions for the class.

Connect

GUIDED READING

1. About how many children have participated in Kids' Guernica? *(more than 500)*
2. What tragic event took place in Hiroshima when the United States was at war with Japan? *(The United States dropped an atomic bomb on the city in 1945, and Hiroshima was completely destroyed.)*
3. Why did Japanese children create the mural *Hiroshima*? *(to remember the people who died in 1945 and to express their hope for peace)*

▲ *Hiroshima*, by students participating in the Kids' Guernica art project

Kids' Guernica

1 Kids' Guernica is an international art project for peace. In 1995, Yasuda Tadashi started the project in Kyoto, Japan. Using the Internet, Tadashi organized schools around the world to participate in the project. His idea was for children in different parts of the world to create peace paintings on huge **canvases** the same size as Pablo Picasso's *Guernica*. Children participate in workshops in their schools and create their paintings. So far, more than 500 children from schools in Cambodia, Sri Lanka, Chile, Nepal, India, Algeria, Germany, the United States, Australia, China, Canada, France, Italy, and other countries have participated. Their paintings express powerful messages of peace.

In 1945, the United States dropped an **atomic bomb** on the city of Hiroshima, Japan, ending World War II. The city was completely destroyed. In 1999, forty-one students from four elementary schools in Hiroshima participated in the Kids' Guernica art project. These schools are all located in the area where the bomb exploded. The students created their mural in memory of the 140,000 people who died and to express their hope for peace in the future.

---

canvases, strong cloths on which artists paint pictures
atomic bomb, a weapon that causes a huge explosion and kills many people

BEFORE YOU GO ON . . .

1 What is the Kids' Guernica art project?

2 What message do you think the painting *Hiroshima* expresses about war and peace?

HOW ABOUT YOU? Answers will vary.
• Would you like to participate in Kids' Guernica? If so, what would you paint?

GRAMMAR MINILESSON

Comparatives and Superlatives

Write the chart below on the board. Explain that some adverbs are used to tell how or in what manner something happens in comparison to something else. The *comparative* form of an adverb is used to compare two items, and the *superlative* form is used to compare three or more items.

	Comparative (2 items)	Superlative (3 or more items)
One-Syllable Adverbs:	adverb + -er	the adverb + -est
-ly Adverbs:	more + adverb + -ly	the most + adverb + -ly

Write the following sentences on the board, and have students identify the adverbs.

Picasso worked <u>harder</u> than many artists.
Some say he worked <u>the hardest</u> of all.
Picasso finished some paintings <u>more quickly</u> than others.
He completed one painting the <u>most quickly</u> of all.

Link the Readings

Reread "Heroic Art" and think about the excerpt from *The Diary of Anne Frank*. Copy the chart into your notebook and complete it.

Title of Selection	Type of Text (Genre)	Fiction or Nonfiction	Purpose of Selection	Heroic Act
From *The Diary of Anne Frank*				
"Heroic Art"	informational text			defending one's beliefs; giving one's life for a cause

DISCUSSION

Discuss in pairs or small groups.

1. Study the paintings on pages 208–210. What words or expressions describe these two pictures? Make two lists comparing the paintings. Share your lists with the class.

2. Imagine that Anne Frank made a painting after two years in the annex. What are some things you think she would put in her painting?

3. Review the list of Picasso's symbols on page 208. Do you see any symbols in *Hiroshima*, on page 210? Can you think of other symbols that artists use in their work?

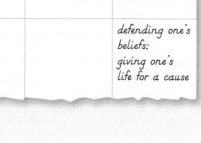

211

REFLECTION

Have a volunteer read the Reflection directions. Read the headings in the chart aloud and discuss them with students. When they have completed the chart, have students compare their answers with a partner. Then ask:

1. Which selection is a play? (*The Diary of Anne Frank*)
2. What is the purpose of "Heroic Art"? (*to inform*)

COOPERATIVE GROUPING

Form two student groups. Have each group use the completed chart to deliver an oral presentation on one of the two reading selections. Encourage groups to add details that support why they placed specific information in the chart.

DISCUSSION

Have students read and discuss the questions in pairs or small groups. Then have each group or student pair choose one question to answer visually. For question 1, for example, students might create a poster of their word lists. Have students share their visuals with the class.

CRITICAL THINKING

Discuss the impact of war on the people who live in the countries where they are fought. Ask students to discuss what happens to people physically, emotionally, and financially. Then have them write their responses in paragraph form.

REACHING ALL STUDENTS

LANGUAGE LEVELS

Beginning: Guide students to complete the Fiction or Nonfiction section of the Reflection chart. Explain to students that although Anne Frank was a real person, the play includes dialogue and situations that may or may not have happened in real life. Guide students to the conclusion that the play is historical fiction and write the words in the chart. Then discuss how "Heroic Art" contains facts that can be proven and is nonfiction. Write the word in the chart.

Advanced: Have students take turns rereading each paragraph in "Heroic Art" aloud. Then have students copy the Reflection chart into their notebooks. Complete the chart together, inviting volunteers to offer examples and explanations.

Connect to Writing

GRAMMAR

Have volunteers take turns reading the definitions and the examples of comparative and superlative adjectives aloud. Explain that comparative adjectives are used to compare two people, places, things, or ideas. Superlative adjectives are used to compare three or more of these things. Have students reread the examples of comparative and superlative adjectives in the two boxes at the top of the page. Call on volunteers to give additional examples for each category.

Before completing the Practice exercises, have students find and circle examples of comparative and superlative adjectives in newspaper advertisements. Invite students to write some examples on the board in a two-column chart labeled *Comparative* and *Superlative*.

SCAFFOLDING

Model how to use comparative and superlative adjectives by holding up a pen and a piece of chalk. Say, *The pen is longer than the chalk.* Then hold up a pencil, a piece of chalk, and a pen. Say, *The pencil is the longest of all.* Give one or two more examples and have students write the sentences in their notebooks to use as models.

GRAMMAR

Comparative and Superlative Adjectives

Use **comparative adjectives** to compare two things.

> Margot is **older than** Anne.
> Paris is **more famous than** Guernica.

Use **superlative adjectives** to compare three or more things.

> Peter is **the oldest** of all three children.
> Paris is **the most famous** city in France.

Make the comparative/superlative forms of one-syllable adjectives like this:

Adjective	Comparative	Superlative
old	old**er than**	**the** old**est**
young	young**er than**	**the** young**est**

Make the comparative/superlative forms of adjectives of two or more syllables like this:

Adjective	Comparative	Superlative
famous	**more** famous **than**	**the most** famous
heroic	**more** heroic **than**	**the most** heroic

Some adjectives have irregular comparative and superlative forms.

Adjective	Comparative	Superlative
good	**better than**	**the best**
bad	**worse than**	**the worst**

Practice

Complete the sentences in your notebook. Use comparative or superlative adjectives.

1. Anne Frank was _____ person in the annex. (young)
2. Anne's diary is _____ book ever written by a young girl. (famous)
3. The annex was _____ room in the house. (small)
4. Margot was _____ Anne. (tall)

212

SPELLING MINILESSON

Changing to *i* to Add *-er* and *-est*

Write *easy, easier,* and *easiest* on the board. Explain that to form the comparative of words that end in *y*, you change the *y* to *i* and add *-er*. Point out that to form the superlative of words that end in *y*, you change the *y* to *i* and add *-est*. Have students circle *-ier* and *-iest* in the examples on the board. Then write *funny* on the board, and invite volunteers to write the comparative and superlative forms of the word. Next, write the following words on the board: *happy, healthy, friendly, pretty.* Ask students to copy the words and write the comparative and superlative forms in their notebooks.

SKILLS FOR WRITING

Writing Reviews

A review is a type of persuasive writing. A review gives the writer's opinion about a movie, a book, a play, or an exhibition. A review includes:

- the writer's opinion: does he or she like or dislike the work?
- examples that support the opinion: what was good or bad?
- the writer's recommendation: does he or she suggest that you see or read the work?

Read the review. Then discuss the questions that follow.

Adam Chodoff

Billy Stargate and the Space Heroes: The Movie

The movie *Billy Stargate and the Space Heroes* was not as good as the book, though it did have its fun parts. First of all, the movie was more fast-paced than the book because many scenes were cut out. For example, the movie didn't include many of the scenes in which Billy is investigated by the space police. In the book, these scenes helped to create the mood for the story. However, the movie's outer space scenes were more exciting than the ones in the book. The wonderful special effects made them extremely exciting. Overall, I thought the book was better than the movie. It's not the greatest movie I've seen, but it's fun.

1. What is the writer's opinion of the work?
2. What reasons does he give to support his opinion?
3. Where does the writer use comparative or superlative adjectives? What do they compare?

213

Have volunteers read the definition of a review. Then ask a volunteer to read the sample review aloud. Point out that the review is based on the student's opinion. Have students write *fact* and *opinion* on separate index cards. Then write several sentences on the chalkboard, such as *I think* Scooby Doo *is the worst movie of all time* and *Freddie Prinze Jr. starred in* Scooby Doo. As you read each sentence aloud, have students identify it as a fact or an opinion by holding up the appropriate index card. Point out clues for opinion statements, such as *I think* and *In my opinion*. Have students look again at the sample review and find a clear statement of the writer's opinion, facts to support the opinion, and the writer's recommendation. Then have students use the paragraph to answer the questions at the bottom of the page.

SCAFFOLDING

Model how to distinguish fact from opinion in the review. Find an opinion, and write it on the board. Identify a statement that supports the opinion. Then find a fact and tell how it might be proven true.

REACHING ALL STUDENTS

LANGUAGE LEVELS

Beginning: Read aloud the sample review as students follow along. Help students analyze the paragraph based on the three characteristics of a review: a clear statement of the writer's opinion, facts and examples to support the opinion, and the writer's recommendation. Ask students to locate the comparative and superlative adjectives in the review and list them in their notebooks. Guide students to use this information to answer the questions below the sample review.

Advanced: Have students read the review silently. Then invite them to form a group to discuss the review based on the three characteristics described at the top of the page as well as the questions that follow the review. Have students list in their notebooks any comparative and superlative adjectives they find. Ask each group to share their opinion of the review and tell how it met the criteria described at the top of the page.

Teach

WRITING ASSIGNMENT

Review

Have students read aloud the writing task as a class. Guide them to reread the movie review on page 213 and note how the writer used comparative and superlative adjectives.

WRITING STRATEGY

Read aloud the information about Making a T-Chart. Then call on a volunteer to read aloud the T-chart that the writer created for his movie review. Ask students to choose a book, movie, or TV show to review. Guide students to follow the directions to make a T-chart for the subject they chose. Then ask students to write a review based on the information in their T-charts. Remind them to state their opinions clearly, to provide facts that support them, and to use comparative and superlative adjectives in their reviews.

USING THE EDITING CHECKLIST

Form student pairs. Have pairs look over the Editing Checklist together and use it to edit their writing together. Monitor students and offer guidance if necessary.

WRITING ASSIGNMENT

Review

You will write a one-paragraph review of a book, movie, or TV show.

1. Read Reread the movie review on page 213. Note how the writer used comparative and superlative adjectives.

Writing Strategy: T-Chart

Before you write your review, think about what you liked and didn't like about the movie, book, or TV show. One way to do this is to make a T-chart.

Look at the T-chart that the writer created for his review of *Billy Stargate and the Space Heroes* on page 213.

What I Liked	What I Didn't Like
Movie was more fast-paced than the book.	Movie was less interesting than the book.
Special effects made parts of movie more exciting than the book.	Some important parts were left out. Some of the story's mood was lost.

---

2. Make a T-chart Make a T-chart in your notebook. On one side of the T-chart, list what you liked about the movie, book, or TV show. On the other side, list what you didn't like about it. Look at the number of ideas in each list. The list with the most ideas tells you whether you liked or didn't like the movie, book, or TV show.

3. Write Use your T-chart to write your review. In the first sentence, give your opinion—whether you liked it or not. Then write your ideas supporting your opinion. End your review by recommending the movie, book, or TV show, or not, to your readers.

EDITING CHECKLIST

Did you . . .

▶ include the name of the book, movie, or TV show in your title?

▶ indent the first line of the paragraph?

▶ state your opinion clearly?

▶ give reasons that support your opinion?

▶ use comparative or superlative adjectives correctly?

▶ use correct punctuation?

214

Check Your Knowledge

Language Development

1. How do you use visualizing when you read a play? When you read a novel?

2. What is setting? Give an example.

3. What is an example of a comparative adjective? When do you use this form of adjective?

4. What is an example of a superlative adjective? When do you use this form of adjective?

5. What kind of things do you think about when you interpret a painting? Give an example, using one of the paintings in Part 2.

6. How can a T-chart help you write a review?

Academic Content

1. What new social studies vocabulary did you learn in Part 2? What do the words mean?

2. What do you know about the Spanish Civil War? Who was the Spanish dictator at the time?

3. What happened in the town of Guernica? Why did Pablo Picasso paint *Guernica*?

4. What is the Kids' Guernica art project? What do the children's paintings express?

215

ASSESS

You can assess students' knowledge of the unit in several different ways.

Portfolio: Students can include the answers to the Check Your Knowledge questions and their reviews in their portfolios.

Traditional: Students can complete the Check Your Knowledge questions as a practice test. After students complete Check Your Knowledge, use the Assessment Package. Students can complete the Part Test on pages 65–68. For further practice, have students complete the Test Preparation worksheets.

Performance: Have students complete Check Your Knowledge. Ask students to exchange papers with a partner and edit each other's answers before presenting them to you in a private conference.

TEST-TAKING TIP

Remind students to check all their answers before turning in a test. If they finish a test before the allotted time is up, they should skim the questions and their answers to check for any mistakes. See the Test Preparation pages in the Assessment Guide for additional test-taking strategies.

METACOGNITION

Have students scan Check Your Knowledge to find the key terms they will need to use or understand for a formal test. Encourage them to review the terms with partners.

REACHING ALL STUDENTS

LANGUAGE LEVELS

Beginning: Model your own T-chart on the board. Use *What I Liked* and *What I Didn't Like* as the column headings. List your opinions about a book, movie, or TV show. Then lead students in creating a group T-chart about a book, movie, or TV show they have all experienced. Guide them in writing a group review based on their ideas.

Advanced: Invite students to give persuasive speeches based on the reviews they wrote. Their goal is to convince the audience to read or not read or watch or not watch the reviewed item. Encourage the audience to listen for persuasive techniques and to distinguish between the speaker's opinion and facts.

Put It All Together

EXTEND THE LESSON

Have students preview the Put It All Together section on pages 216–219. These end-of-unit pages review and consolidate concepts, skills, and strategies from both parts of the unit. Special emphasis is given to listening, speaking, and writing skills.

LISTENING AND SPEAKING WORKSHOP

Have students read the description of the speech they will give. Then call on volunteers to paraphrase what they will be doing in the workshop. Encourage discussion of different ways people in the selections were persuasive. Then read each step of the process with students, answering questions and clarifying the assignment. Have students individually brainstorm a list of possible after-school programs. Then form groups, varying the language levels, to complete steps 2 through 4.

TEACHING THE TIPS

Speaking Tips: Ask volunteers to read aloud the three tips. Model how to make note cards for use as prompts during a speech. Tell students to number the note cards so they stay in order during the presentation.

Listening Tip: Ask a volunteer to read the tip aloud. Encourage students to use the tip to generate criteria for evaluating the presentations, such as *presents reasonable arguments; presents facts as well as opinions; answers questions I had.*

RESEARCH SKILLS

Print: Remind students that they want to use vivid verbs and words that convey excitement in order to entice audience members and convince them to join their after-school club. Suggest that students use a thesaurus to replace any bland, nondescriptive words in their speeches.

T216

OBJECTIVES

Investigate Skills
- Listening/ Speaking: *Speech*
- Writing: *Letter to the editor*

Investigate Themes
- Projects
- Further reading

LISTENING and SPEAKING WORKSHOP

SPEECH

You will give a persuasive speech about an after-school program to improve your school.

1 **Think about it** What kinds of after-school programs would help students at your school? Make a list of possible programs. Work in small groups. Discuss your lists. Which programs would help the greatest number of students? Choose one.

2 **Organize** Work together to write a speech about your after-school program. In the speech, include the name of your program, the main purpose for it, and the reasons that it would be good for the school. Choose a group speaker to give the speech to the class.

3 **Practice** Listen carefully to your group speaker as he or she practices the speech. Give the speaker ideas to make the speech better.

4 **Present and evaluate** Give your group's speech to the class. After each speaker finishes, evaluate the speech. Were the speaker's arguments persuasive? Vote to decide which after-school program is the best. Consider presenting the idea to your principal or your parent-teacher group.

SPEAKING TIPS

- Write important ideas of your speech on note cards. Write just a few words in big letters on each card. Use the cards to help you remember your main ideas.
- Speak clearly and slowly. You might use gestures to emphasize important ideas.
- End your speech by restating the main purpose of your after-school program.

LISTENING TIP

When people want to persuade you to do something, they often give only arguments that support their position or point of view. As you listen to a speech, think about the opposite point of view. Then draw your own conclusions.

216

WRITING WORKSHOP

LETTER TO THE EDITOR

People write letters to a newspaper editor to express their opinions. Sometimes a letter to the editor includes an idea for solving a problem or improving something in the community. The writer uses arguments to persuade the reader of his or her opinion and idea.

A good letter to the editor includes the following:

- an opening paragraph with a clear statement of the writer's opinion
- reasons or arguments that support the writer's opinion, presented in a clear, organized way
- a concluding paragraph that restates the writer's opinion in a different way

You will write a persuasive letter to the editor of your school newspaper. Use the following steps and the model on page 218 to help you.

1 Prewrite Think about some ways to improve your school. What changes would make your school a better place? Make a list of ideas.

Look at your list. Next to each idea, write how it would make your school better. For example, who would be helped by the idea or change? Then review your ideas, and choose one idea to write about in a letter to the editor.

Make a T-chart. Over the left column write *For*, and over the right column write *Against*. In the *For* column, give arguments that support your idea. In the *Against* column, give arguments that don't support your idea.

> #### WRITING TIP
>
> Transition words connect ideas and make your arguments more persuasive. Look at how these transition words are used:
> - *In addition,* some of the bike racks are broken.
> - *Besides* being good exercise, bike riding is fun.
> - *Futhermore,* bikes do not cause air pollution like buses and cars.
> - *Another* argument in favor of more bike racks is safety.

217

Put It All Together

CREATING BETTER WRITERS

Word Choice: Have volunteers read aloud the call-outs in the right-hand margin. Ask students to identify the opinion presented by the writer in the first paragraph. Then have students identify and list each supporting argument that the writer uses to support this opinion. Finally, discuss with students how the writer strengthens her argument by restating her opinion in a different way in the concluding paragraph.

Before students revise their letters to the editor, point out that good *word choice* can help readers to really understand the writer's feelings and point of view.

Write the following tips on the board. Tell students to use the tips as they revise their writing to make sure they have used just the right word to express their opinions to the editor.

- Use nouns that clearly describe or relate your feelings about a person, place, or thing. (*air pollution* instead of *fumes,* as in the writing sample)
- Choose verbs that show exactly what is happening. (*complain* instead of *say,* as in the sample)
- Look for words that you repeat again and again and try to find synonyms to use instead.

Before you write a first draft of your letter, read the following model. Notice the characteristics of a letter to the editor.

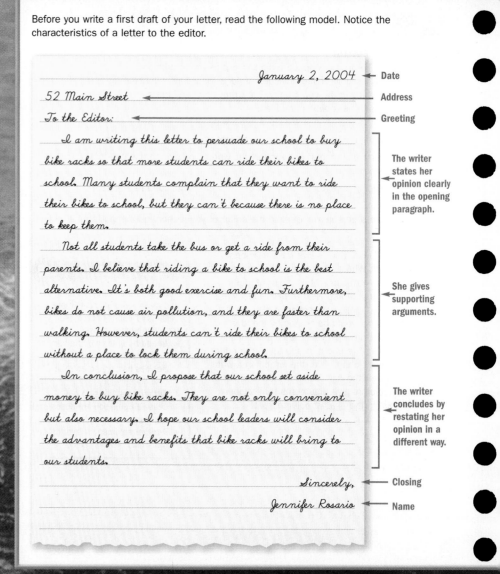

January 2, 2004 ← Date

52 Main Street ← Address

To the Editor: ← Greeting

    I am writing this letter to persuade our school to buy bike racks so that more students can ride their bikes to school. Many students complain that they want to ride their bikes to school, but they can't because there is no place to keep them.

    Not all students take the bus or get a ride from their parents. I believe that riding a bike to school is the best alternative. It's both good exercise and fun. Furthermore, bikes do not cause air pollution, and they are faster than walking. However, students can't ride their bikes to school without a place to lock them during school.

    In conclusion, I propose that our school set aside money to buy bike racks. They are not only convenient but also necessary. I hope our school leaders will consider the advantages and benefits that bike racks will bring to our students.

Sincerely, ← Closing

Jennifer Rosario ← Name

The writer states her opinion clearly in the opening paragraph.

She gives supporting arguments.

The writer concludes by restating her opinion in a different way.

218

2 **Draft** Use your T-chart and the model to write your letter to the editor. Use your supporting arguments to persuade readers to agree with your idea.

3 **Edit** Work in pairs. Trade papers and read each other's letters. Use the questions in the editing checklist to evaluate each other's work.

EDITING CHECKLIST

Did you . . .

▸ state your opinion clearly in the first paragraph?

▸ include arguments that support your opinion?

▸ use comparative and superlative adjectives correctly?

▸ use transition words at the beginning of some sentences?

▸ restate your opinion in the last sentence?

▸ use correct form for writing a letter to the editor?

4 **Revise** Revise your letter. Add information and correct mistakes if necessary.

5 **Publish** You may want to send your letter to the school newspaper. If your school doesn't have one, create a class newspaper on a computer. Include as many letters as you can.

219

USING THE EDITING CHECKLIST

Have students exchange papers. Ask them to read each other's persuasive letters silently before reading and using the checklist.

ASSESS

Portfolio: Include the persuasive letters in students' assessment portfolios for comparison with later assignments.

REACHING ALL STUDENTS

LANGUAGE LEVELS

Beginning: Lead students in interactive writing. Together, create a list of ideas that will help the school. After students vote for one of these ideas, make a T-chart on the board on which they can list arguments that support the selected idea and arguments that do not support it. Then have them use the T-chart for ideas as you write the first draft of a group letter on the board. Have them edit the letter as a group using the Editing Checklist. Help them revise and publish the letter.

Advanced: Have students read their first drafts to a partner. Ask partners to determine the writer's perspective and the persuasive techniques in the letter. Have partners decide how they can make the writing stronger by clarifying opinions, supporting arguments, and choosing words that evoke strong feelings from readers.

Unit Projects

EXTEND THE LESSON

Home-School Connection: For Project 5, encourage students to include any printed captions that accompany the photographs they collect. If there are no captions or they prefer an alternative, students can label each photograph with the name and deed of the hero or heroes pictured.

WEBSITES

For more information, log on to http://www.longman.com/shiningstar for links to other interesting websites.

PROJECTS

Work in pairs or small groups. Choose one of these projects.

1. Find biographies of different heroes in the library or on the Internet. Choose a person from the past or the present and read about his or her life. Give an oral report about your hero to the class.

2. Find some books about or photographs of famous photographers in the library or on the Internet. For example, some famous American photographers are Margaret Bourke-White, Dorothea Lange, Walker Evans, and Gordon Parks. Choose a photographer and look at his or her work. Choose one or two photographs that you really like. Show the photographs to the class, and explain why you like them.

3. Do a readers theatre. Take the full script of *The Diary of Anne Frank: The Play* out of the library. Let group members choose the characters they want to be. Practice reading the play together several times. Help each other get the words just right. Then present your readers theatre to the class.

▲ Anne with Mr. Frank in the play, *The Diary of Anne Frank.*

4. Think about how Picasso expressed strong feelings in his painting *Guernica*. Choose a person, place, or thing that you feel strongly about. Paint or draw a picture that expresses your feelings about your subject. Share your picture with the class.

5. With a family member, look through newspapers or magazines for pictures of heroes. Make a scrapbook that contains the stories of a few people that you think are heroic. Share your scrapbook with your class.

6. Make a thank-you card for a hero in your community. Tell the person how you feel about his or her heroic deed. Ask your teacher to help you find the person's address so that you can mail your card.

220

Further Reading

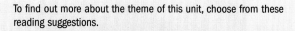

To find out more about the theme of this unit, choose from these reading suggestions.

Free At Last, The Story of Martin Luther King Jr., **Angela Bull** This is a biography of civil rights leader Martin Luther King Jr., who encouraged nonviolent protest to fulfill his dream of an America where people would be judged by "the content of their character, not by the color of their skin."

Joan of Arc, **Angela Bull** Learn more about the amazing story of a young peasant girl in the fifteenth century who believed that she was being directed by the voices of saints to lead the French to freedom in battle against the occupying English.

The Red Badge of Courage, **Stephen Crane** This classic tale of the American Civil War follows the fortunes of a proud young soldier, Henry Fleming, who quickly learns that there is much more to war than adventure and bravery.

The Barefoot Book of Heroic Children, **Rebecca Hazel** Is it possible for children to make a difference in the world? What children have influenced the course of history and what can we learn about them? This book brings together the stories of some of the most amazing young people in history, and gives inspiring accounts of their optimism and ideals in the face of great suffering and hardship.

We'll Never Forget You, Roberto Clemente, **Trudie Engel** Roberto Clemente was an unforgettable baseball hero. When he was growing up in Puerto Rico, his family didn't have enough money to buy baseballs or baseball bats. So he learned to play by hitting tin cans with a broomstick. Later, he became one of the greatest hitters in the history of the game.

221

FURTHER READING

- *Free at Last: The Story of Martin Luther King Jr.* and *Joan of Arc* are appropriate for beginning students.
- *The Red Badge of Courage* is appropriate for intermediate students.
- *The Barefoot Book of Heroic Children* and *We'll Never Forget You, Roberto Clemente* are appropriate for advanced students.

REACHING ALL STUDENTS

LANGUAGE LEVELS

Beginning: Encourage students to choose one of the following Projects, modifying each one as described. For Project 1, have students create a word web in place of or to prepare for the oral report about a hero. For Project 3, have students work with advanced partners to practice for the readers theatre.

Advanced: For Project 4, students can write a poem about the topic of their picture as Picasso did for *Guernica.* As students share their pictures with the class, have them read the poems.

Look Into the Future

Make enough duplicate copies of the Letter Home for Unit 6 so that each student has a copy to take home. Show Video Segment 6.

PART 1 TEACHING GUIDE

PRETEACH	**Provide Background**	• Read and discuss the Part Objectives and Background Information. (SB p. 224; ATE p. T224)
	Present Concepts	• Introduce the Key Words and Reading Strategy. (SB p. 225; ATE p. T225; WB pp. 142, 144) • Pronounce the Vocabulary words. (ATE p. T225) • Model how to use context clues to define Key Words. (ATE p. T225)
TEACH	**Monitor Comprehension**	• Informally monitor comprehension through Guided Reading and Critical Thinking questions. (ATE pp. T226-237) • Monitor students' comprehension through Critical Thinking, Metacognition, Discussion, and Extension activities. (SB pp. 233, 237; ATE pp. T227, T229, T231–T233, T235, T237)
	Teach and Practice	• Use individually tailored activities for beginning and advanced students. (ATE pp. T223, T225, T227, T229, T231, T233, T235, T237, T239, T241) • Pair beginning, intermediate, and advanced students through Cooperative Grouping activities. (SB pp. 233, 237; ATE pp. T224, T233, T237) • Develop viewing skills using photos and illustrations and present the Viewpoint activities. (ATE pp. T222, T226, T228, T231, T235) • Complete the Vocabulary, Phonics, Grammar, and Spelling lessons. (SB pp. 225, 238; ATE pp. T230, T236, T238, T240; WB pp. 150–151, 154) • Introduce the Writing Strategy and apply students' ability to write a note card using the Writing Model and Writing Assignment. (SB pp. 239–240; ATE pp. T239-T240; WB pp. 152–153; Transparency # 36)
CONNECT	**Connect to Literature**	• Develop students' ability to analyze characteristics of genres through pairing of selections. (SB pp. 234–236; ATE pp. T234-T236) • Provide students with interactive reading support and practice. (WB pp. 145-149)
	Across the Curriculum	• Develop students' ability to extend the content of the reading selections through extended math, social studies, science, health, and art activities. (ATE pp. T230, T234)
ASSESS	**Check Knowledge**	• Use the Before You Go On, Check Your Knowledge, Link the Readings, and Review and Practice features to assess students' comprehension of the selection. (SB pp. 227, 229, 231, 232-233, 235, 237, 241; ATE pp. T232-T233, T237, T241)
	Monitor Progress	• Use the Assessment Options, Test-Taking Tip, and the test. (ATE p. T241 AG pp. 69-72)

CONTENT TERMS

Present and elicit definitions of these content-specific terms:

• population	• convenient	• satellites	• hypersonic
• explore	• genes	• traits	• inherit

PART 2 TEACHING GUIDE

PRETEACH	**Provide Background**	• Read and discuss the Part Objectives and Background Information. (SB p. 242; ATE p. T242)
	Present Concepts	• Introduce the Key Words and Reading Strategy. (SB p. 243; ATE p. T243; WB pp. 156, 158) • Pronounce the Vocabulary words. (ATE p. T243) • Model how to use context clues to define Key Words. (ATE p. T243)
TEACH	**Monitor Comprehension**	• Informally monitor comprehension through Guided Reading and Critical Thinking questions. (ATE pp. T244–T255) • Monitor students' comprehension through Critical Thinking, Metacognition, Discussion, and Extension activities. (SB pp. 251, 255; ATE pp. T245, T247, T249–T251, T253, T255, T259)
	Teach and Practice	• Use individually tailored activities for beginning and advanced students. (ATE pp. T243, T245, T247, T249, T251, T253, T255, T257, T259, T261, T263, T265) • Pair beginning, intermediate, and advanced students through Cooperative Grouping activities. (SB pp. 251, 255; ATE pp. T242, T251, T255) • Develop viewing skills using photos and illustrations and present the Viewpoint activities. (ATE pp. T245–T246, T248, T253) • Complete the Vocabulary, Phonics, Grammar, and Spelling lessons. (SB pp. 243, 256; ATE pp. T244, T248, T254, T256; WB pp. 164–165, 168) • Introduce the Writing Strategy and apply students' ability to write a sentence outline using the Writing Model and Writing Assignment. (SB pp. 257–258; ATE pp. T257–T258 WB pp. 166–167; Transparency # 37)
CONNECT	**Connect to Content**	• Develop students' ability to analyze characteristics of genres through pairing of selections. (SB pp. 252–254; ATE pp. T252–T254) • Provide students with interactive reading support and practice. (WB pp. 159–163)
	Across the Curriculum	• Develop students' ability to extend the content of the reading selections through extended math, social studies, science, health, and art activities. (ATE pp. T248, T252)
ASSESS	**Check Knowledge**	• Use the Before You Go On, Check Your Knowledge, Link the Readings, and Review and Practice features to assess students' comprehension of the selection. (SB pp. 245, 247, 249–251 253, 255, 259; ATE pp. T250–T251, T255, T259)
	Monitor Progress	• Use the Assessment Options, Test-Taking Tip, and the test. (ATE p. T259, AG pp. 73–76)

PUT IT ALL TOGETHER TEACHING GUIDE

EXTEND	**Integrate Skills and Apply Understanding**	• Apply students' ability to give a presentation using the Listening and Speaking Workshop. (SB p. 260; ATE p. T260) • Apply students' ability to write a research report using the Writing Workshop. (SB pp. 261–262; ATE pp. T261–T262) • Have students complete one or more of the Unit Projects. (SB p. 264; ATE p. T264) • Have students choose a theme-related reading selection from the Further Reading suggestions. (SB p. 265; ATE p. T265)

Unit 6: Look Into the Future

Part 1

Background (p. 224) Explain that the *future* is what is yet to happen. Discuss things that might happen in your future. Begin with the immediate future, such as after class. Then move on to things in the distant future. Ask for volunteers to do the same. Discuss some of the things that have changed dramatically over the last 100 years, such as technology, medicine, transportation, etc. Then ask students to predict what will be different in the future. Stress that there are no wrong answers.

Vocabulary (p. 225) Explain that *context* can help you understand a word's meaning. *Context clues* are the words that come before or after an unknown word or phrase that can help determine its meaning. Review the sentences on p. 225 with the class. Identify the context clues in each sentence. For example, *population* = "millions of people"; *traffic jams* = "too many cars on the road."* Use the vocabulary words in other sentences that use context clues. Have students check their dictionaries to identify the correct definition for each vocabulary word.

Reading Strategy: Summarizing (p. 225) Explain that *summarizing* reviews the main points of a text. Use a short, simple piece as an example, such as an encyclopedia entry that breaks down the information clearly. Review each paragraph with students. Have students identify the *main idea* and *supporting details* in each paragraph. Write these on the board. Then have students use these sentences to write one or two sentences that summarize the entire encyclopedia entry. As the students read the selection "Life in the Future," have them write down one sentence that summarizes each subhead.

Life in the Future (pp. 226–231) Explain that this is an informational text. This selection uses *facts,* or things that can be proved. The text also uses *predictions,* or educated guesses based on facts. Have students identify the facts used in the section "The Growing World." Then use the section "Cars of the Future" to have students differentiate between fact and prediction.

Activity 1: With the class discuss what life was like 100 years ago. Then discuss things that have changed over the last century, such as technology, transportation, etc. Make a chart on the board to compare life then and now.

Activity 2: Have students identify the problem and solution in each category. Explain that a *problem* is a situation that presents a challenge. Explain that

a *solution* is something that can fix the problem. In each of the sections, have students identify the problem and solution the author discusses.

Activity 3: Review the *multiple sources* used in this text, such as text, charts, illustrations, timelines, etc. Have students identify how and why these things help them better understand the text.

Activity 4: With the class review the timeline of inventions on p. 226. Have students make their own predictions about the future. As an assignment, tell students to think of something that may be invented in the future. Have them write a few sentences about this invention. Make sure they explain what it is and how it can help civilization. Use examples from the selection to help them.

Comprehension (p. 232) Review with students that *summarizing* is describing the main ideas of a text. Stress that students should write complete-sentence summaries. Review that a complete sentence must have a *subject* and a *verb*. Explain that the subject tells who or what the sentence is about. The verb describes the action. Identify the subject and verb in the sample sentence on p. 232.

Interview with an Astronaut: Dan Bursch (pp. 234–236) To help students understand the context of this text, explain that the United States and Russia were not always friends. Have each student write down two or three things they learned about space travel from reading this selection. Make sure they write complete sentences. Ask for volunteers to share their sentences with the class.

Have students write a list of questions they would ask an astronaut if given the chance. Then have students work in pairs to role-play an interview. Students can compile a list of questions that they would ask someone who will be traveling into space. Have students write questions such as, *What do you hope to accomplish in space? How long would you like to stay? What will you bring with you?* Ask for volunteers to give a presentation about their make-believe interview.

Grammar: Using *will* for the Future (p. 238) Explain that the word *will* tells something that is going to happen in the future. It is used to predict. Give examples using classroom activities, such as, *I will open the window; I will sit at my desk.* Pantomime to clarify. Use a similar exercise to demonstrate the use of the negative *will not.* Ask for volunteers to demonstrate things or give sentences using *will* and *will not.* Before doing the

exercise on p. 238, demonstrate with simple sentences on the board. Have students turn sentences into predictions about the future using the positive and negative forms of the word will. Use students as the subject of the examples, such as, *Angela will not go to a movie tonight; Miguel will do well on the quiz.*

Skills for Writing and Writing Assignment (pp. 239–240) Explain that *taking notes* is a way to prepare for writing. It helps to organize the information the writer has found about a subject. Demonstrate with a small informational text, such as an encyclopedia entry. With the class demonstrate taking notes from this informational text. If possible, try to use more than one source in order to demonstrate the importance of cross-referencing. Begin by writing down the title of the piece as well as information such as author, publisher, date, etc. Discuss the dangers of *plagiarizing.* Demonstrate how to avoid plagiarizing by taking the information you have found and explaining it in your own words.

Part 2

Background (p. 242) Discuss *science fiction* with the class. Explain that *fiction* is a story that is made up; the characters are not real and the events did not take place. Explain that science fiction uses elements of science in fictional stories. Start a discussion about science fiction stories students may be familiar with, such as *Star Wars.* On the board, list the elements that make this a work of science fiction. Point out that science fiction often tries to predict what life will be like in the future. Before beginning the exercise on p. 242, have students think about future advancements by discussing what things were like 100 years ago. Then have them "look into the future" to guess what these things will be like 100 years from now. Stress that this is a creative exercise and there are no wrong answers.

Vocabulary (p. 243) Pictures can help students understand the meanings of key words such as *mechanical* or *streamlined.* Have students develop dictionary skills by instructing them to look up these words in a dictionary. Explain that many words have several entries. Point out that context clues can help students pick the best entry for each word used in context. Remind them that context clues are words that come before or after an unknown word or phrase. Review the sentences on p. 243 with the class. Identify the context clues in each sentence. For example, *revolutionary* = "it changed the way people lived."

Reading Strategy: Reading for Enjoyment (p. 243) Explain that *purpose* is the reason you do something. People read textbooks for instruction. They read the newspaper for information. Sometimes people read stories just because they are enjoyable. Some stories can take you on an adventure, or on a visit to a faraway land. This is reading for enjoyment. Discuss what else you do for enjoyment—go to movies, play sports, etc. Discuss some books you have read for enjoyment that students may be familiar with, such as *Charlotte's Web*. Ask students what books they have read for enjoyment and why they enjoyed them.

From *The Time Warp Trio: 2095* (pp. 244–249) As students read the excerpt from *The Time Warp Trio: 2095*, have them write down what elements of the story make it a work of science fiction. What do the people look like? The city? What futuristic things do the people use?

Activity 1: Explain that dialogue identifies what people are saying in a story. On the board, write several examples from the text. Then demonstrate the proper punctuation when writing dialogue.

Activity 2: Explain that the *narrator* is the person telling the story. A *first-person narrative* is the story told through the eyes of one person. Have the students identify who the narrator is in this story. Then ask what clues reveal that this is a first-person narrative.

Activity 3: Remind students that when events in a story are presented in chronological order, they are given in the order in which they took place. Review the story with the class. On the board, ask students to list the chronological order of events in this story.

Comprehension (p. 250) As students complete the exercise on p. 250, make sure they write complete sentences. Review subjects and verbs and how to write complete sentences. If possible, have students write a short and concise paragraph about what they liked or didn't like about this selection. Ask for volunteers to read their paragraphs aloud to practice pronunciation. Encourage them to speak slowly and clearly.

DNA, Genes, and Traits (pp. 252–254) Explain that science is the study of the natural world. This is a science article that supplies facts, or things that can be proved. Have students identify several facts about DNA. Then have them identify several facts about how DNA can be used. Have students make a small family tree that includes their grandparents. Have them identify what traits they have inherited from their parents and grandparents. Use yourself as an example. Then apply this to the previous selection. How do genetics work in *The Time Warp Trio: 2095? (The girls look very similar to the three boys.)*

Grammar: Using *be going to* to form the Future (p. 256) Introduce the forms of the verb *to be. (am, is, are, was, were)* These are helping verbs that precede a main verb. Use the examples on p. 256 to demonstrate the verb *be* as a helping verb. Explain the difference between using *be going to* + a verb and using *will*. Using *be going to* + a verb explains something that is going to happen. Using the word *will* predicts or guesses what will happen based on what you already know. Use simple examples to demonstrate the difference, such as, *Adam is going to see a movie; Adam will do well on the test.* Clarify the difference between *is* and *are*. Explain that the verb *is* is used to demonstrate the singular. The verb *are* is used the demonstrate the plural. Use examples to clarify.

Skills for Writing and Writing Assignment (pp. 257–258) Explain that *outlining* is a great way to organize your notes before you begin writing. An outline is like a skeleton for an essay. On the board, make a simple outline that demonstrates this concept. Begin with an introduction, three paragraphs, and a conclusion. Stress that students should be able to write from this outline. Remind students that a *main idea* is what the paragraph is about; it is what you are trying to say. Each paragraph should have a main idea. The *supporting details* back up, or support, the main idea by supplying evidence or reasons. Use the example on p. 257 to demonstrate how the notes break down into two main ideas, *Building the Skycar M400* and *What the Skycar will do*. Then show how the supporting details support the main idea.

Put It All Together

Listening and Speaking Workshop: Presentation (p. 260) Use photographs of inventions or other technology, such as computers and calculators, and discuss them with the class. Have students identify possible reasons why these things were invented. Then have students identify how these inventions changed everyday life. Write the answers on the board. As students break into groups, have them think about what they need in their everyday lives. Get them to think of an invention that would make something easier, better, or more efficient. Then have students practice making a presentation on one of the inventions you discussed with the class. Make sure they develop clear ideas as to why this thing was invented and how it changed everyday life. Have them present to the class.

Writing Workshop: Research Report (pp. 261–263) Use a short informational text, such as an encyclopedia entry, to demonstrate taking notes from a source. Walk through the text and identify the main idea and supporting details. Use a second source as a cross reference. Have students add additional information to their notes from this second source. Then use the notes to put together a clear essay about the subject.

Preview the Unit

UNIT CONTENT

Explain to students that the first part of this unit opens with an informative reading selection about inventions and advances that people are developing for the future. Invite students to describe inventions they would like to see in their own lifetimes. Then tell students that this selection is linked to an interview with an astronaut who has lived and worked on the International Space Station.

Next, tell students that in Part 2 they will enjoy an excerpt from the science fiction novel *The Time Warp Trio: 2095,* in which three young friends travel into the future. Explain that this reading is paired with a science article about DNA. The article describes how families from generation to generation are similar in eye and hair color and other ways.

—*Viewpoint*—

Ask students to look at the selection of photos on the unit opener. Ask volunteers to name each image on the pages and tell which photo they think best represents their own visions of the future. Have students give reasons for their answers.

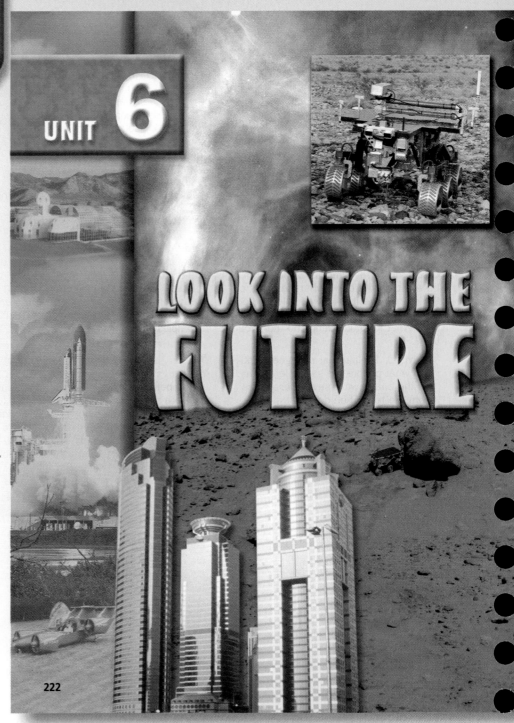

UNIT 6

LOOK INTO THE FUTURE

222

WORKSHOP PREVIEW

Listening and Speaking
Students will deliver a report on an invention that will help students in the future.

Writing
Students will write a three-paragraph research report.

PROJECTS PREVIEW

Projects for this unit include:
● writing a science fiction story
● creating a visual aid for an invention
● painting a picture of people, places, or things in the future
● discussing inherited family traits
● interviewing a forensic scientist
● creating a futuristic comic strip

TEACHING RESOURCES

Lesson Plans	pp. 73–86
Summaries	pp. 57–64
Graphic Organizers	1–20
Audio Program	CD3/6–9; Cass.3/A&B
Workbook	pp. 141–168
CD-ROM	Unit 6
Video	Segment 6
Tests	Part Test, pp. 69–76
	Unit Test, pp. 129–137

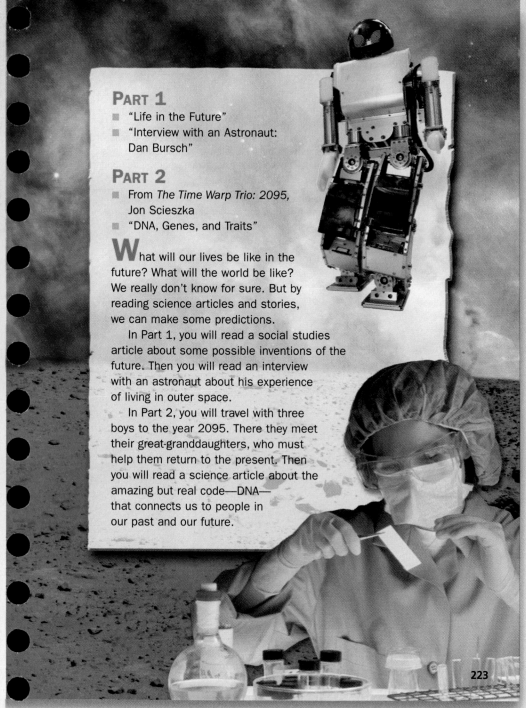

PART 1

- "Life in the Future"
- "Interview with an Astronaut: Dan Bursch"

PART 2

- From *The Time Warp Trio: 2095*, Jon Scieszka
- "DNA, Genes, and Traits"

What will our lives be like in the future? What will the world be like? We really don't know for sure. But by reading science articles and stories, we can make some predictions.

In Part 1, you will read a social studies article about some possible inventions of the future. Then you will read an interview with an astronaut about his experience of living in outer space.

In Part 2, you will travel with three boys to the year 2095. There they meet their great-granddaughters, who must help them return to the present. Then you will read a science article about the amazing but real code—DNA— that connects us to people in our past and our future.

223

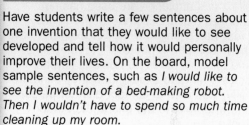

OBJECTIVES

Explain to students that in Part 1 they will be reading about topics that they might study in a social studies or science class. Read aloud the list of objectives, encouraging students to read along with you. Pause to explain the meaning of any difficult words. Ask students to restate the list of things they will learn. Additional practice activities for these objectives can be found in the **Workbook** and **CD-ROM**.

BACKGROUND

Have a volunteer read the introductory text aloud. Have others paraphrase the information. Then direct students to look at each photo and identify what it shows. Tell students that the way telephones, automobiles, and airplanes are used has not changed much, but what they look like today has changed a lot. For example, have them look at the photo of the telephone and notice there is no numeric keypad. Ask students to explain how they think the caller was able to contact another person and what part of the phone the person spoke into.

COOPERATIVE GROUPING

Pair intermediate and advanced students with beginning students. Have pairs read the Background page and answer the questions together. Ask pairs to share and compare their answers.

PART 1

OBJECTIVES

LANGUAGE DEVELOPMENT

Reading:
- Vocabulary building: *Context, dictionary skills*
- Reading strategy: *Summarizing*
- Make observations about text
- Text types: *Social studies article, interview*

Writing:
- Subtopic web
- Taking notes
- Research report

Listening/Speaking:
- Compare and contrast
- Ask for and give information

Grammar:
- Future: *Will*

Viewing/Representing:
- Timeline
- Future images and inventions

ACADEMIC CONTENT
- Social studies vocabulary
- Life in the future
- Comparison of Earth and Mars

Prepare to Read

BACKGROUND

"Life in the Future" is a social studies article. It tells what some scientists think life will be like in the future. It is nonfiction—it uses facts to describe what will be happening years from now.

Make connections Look at these pictures of a telephone, a car, some children, and an airplane from the past. Then answer the questions.

1. Compare the telephone, car, clothes, and airplane with those of today. How are they similar? How are they different?
2. How do you think telephones, cars, clothes, and airplanes will be different in the future?

224

TEACHING GUIDE

PRETEACH	Provide Background	Read and discuss the Background information. Complete the activity. (ATE/SB p. 224)
	Present Concepts	Introduce the Reading Strategy. (ATE/SB p. 225)
TEACH	Monitor Comprehension	Informally monitor comprehension while students read the selection independently or in groups. (ATE/SB pp. 226–237)
	Teach and Practice	Present the Grammar, Usage, and Mechanics. (ATE/SB pp. 238, 239) Complete the Writing activity. (ATE/SB p. 240) Present Grammar, Phonics, and Spelling minilessons. (ATE pp. 230, 236, 240)
CONNECT	Connect to Literature	Have students read the literature and relate it to the informational reading. (ATE/SB pp. 234–236)
	Across the Curriculum	Present curriculum links as students read. (ATE pp. 230, 234)
ASSESS	Check Knowledge	Assess students' comprehension by having them complete the Check Your Knowledge section. (ATE/SB p. 241)
	Monitor Progress	Use one or more of the print assessment resources in the Assessment Package.
EXTEND	Integrate Language and Apply Understanding	Have students complete the Workshops (ATE/SB pp. 260–263) and choose a project from the Unit Projects. (ATE/SB p. 264) Then have them choose a book to read from Further Reading. (ATE/SB p. 265)

VOCABULARY

Read these sentences. Use the context to figure out the meaning of the red words. Use a dictionary to check your answers. Write each word and its meaning in your notebook.

1. Doctors sometimes use **artificial** hearts to replace diseased hearts.
2. Outer space is sometimes called a **frontier** because we know so little about it.
3. Cars are no longer made one at a time—they are **mass produced**.
4. The **population** of Earth will increase greatly. There will be billions more people in the next 100 years.
5. Human beings won't need to do dangerous work in the future because **robots** will do the work.
6. **Traffic jams** are the result of too many cars on the road.

LEARN KEY WORDS

artificial
frontier
mass produced
population
robots
traffic jams

READING STRATEGY

Summarizing

Summarizing helps you remember important information in a text. It also helps you check to see if you understand what you are reading.

When you summarize, you retell the text's main ideas. A summary is always much shorter than the text. When you write a summary, use some words from the text and some of your own words. As you choose the information you want to summarize, keep in mind your reason for reading the text.

Before you summarize, ask yourself these questions:

- What happened?
- What are the main ideas?

225

VOCABULARY

Pronounce each of the Key Words. After you say a word, have students point to it and repeat it. Then read each sentence, and have students raise their hands when they hear the Key Word. Model how students can use other words in the sentence to help them find the meaning of the Key Word. For example, *In sentence 4, I read that the population on Earth will increase greatly, and within 100 years there will be billions more people on Earth. Population must mean "the total number of people in a place."* Then demonstrate for students how to use a dictionary to check their answers. Tell students to write each word and its meaning in their notebooks.

READING STRATEGY

Have students read the Reading Strategy. Point out that summarizing is a strategy that students do *after* they read a passage. Explain that in order to summarize what they read, students must identify the most important ideas or events in a selection and then restate those ideas in order. Point out that when summarizing nonfiction, students should include only the main ideas. Explain that when summarizing the plot of a story, they should say what the characters' goals were, how they tried to reach their goals, and what the outcome was.

REACHING ALL STUDENTS

LANGUAGE LEVELS

Beginning: Use each vocabulary word in a new sentence for students. Have them clap their hands when they hear the vocabulary word. Then have each student select one vocabulary word and use it in a sentence.

Advanced: List the following Key Words on the board: *artificial, frontier, mass produced, population, robots,* and *traffic jams.* Have students work with a partner to use an online or traditional thesaurus to search for synonyms and related words. Ask students to make a word web for each of the Key Words and list synonyms for the words on the branches. Then have students use the vocabulary words in sentences of their own.

Teach

READING SUMMARY

This informational article looks at the inventions and research that will affect the future of the ever-expanding human population. The article explores future cities and methods of transportation. It also describes new frontiers, such as colonies on Mars.

SCAFFOLDING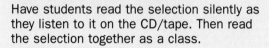

Have students read the selection silently as they listen to it on the CD/tape. Then read the selection together as a class.

GUIDED READING

1. Which will probably happen first, robotic pets or underground cities? *(robotic pets)*
2. Why is the world's population of humans expanding at such a fast rate? *(The birth rate is higher than the death rate.)*
3. What do scientists predict the world's population will be in the year 2100? *(11 billion)*

—————Viewpoint—————

Have students look at the timeline and discuss the predictions for the future. Invite students to share their opinions about whether the predictions—the events and the time in the future at which they will occur—are reasonable.

FOCUS ON CONTENT

Science, Social Studies

Preview and skim the text and set your purpose for reading. Then, as you read more carefully, write a sentence or two after each section summarizing the main ideas of that section.

Life in the Future

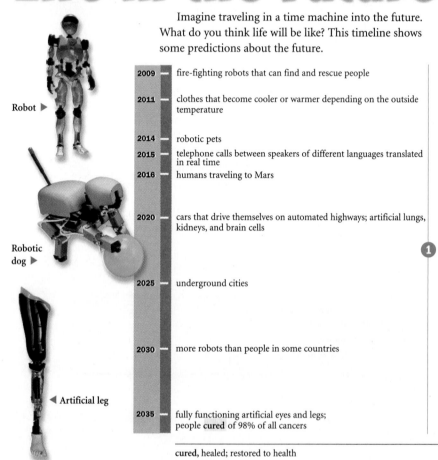

Imagine traveling in a time machine into the future. What do you think life will be like? This timeline shows some predictions about the future.

2009	fire-fighting robots that can find and rescue people
2011	clothes that become cooler or warmer depending on the outside temperature
2014	robotic pets
2015	telephone calls between speakers of different languages translated in real time
2016	humans traveling to Mars
2020	cars that drive themselves on automated highways; artificial lungs, kidneys, and brain cells
2025	underground cities
2030	more robots than people in some countries
2035	fully functioning artificial eyes and legs; people **cured** of 98% of all cancers

Robot ▶

Robotic dog ▶

◀ Artificial leg

cured, healed; restored to health

226

T226

The Growing World

The world's population is growing very fast. In 1800, the population was about 1 billion. Now it is over 6 billion. One reason for this fast growth is that the birth rate is higher than the death rate. That is, there are more people being born than there are people dying. Also, medical advances and better living conditions help people live longer. Scientists predict that in the year 2100, the population will be 11 billion.

Population in billions

▲ Bar graph showing world population growth

Future Cities

As the population grows, it will be necessary to rebuild existing cities and build new ones. Some apartment buildings will be like small cities.

Architects have created a model for an apartment building in Tokyo. It will be 840 meters (2,750 ft.) high and will have 180 floors. A population of 50,000 will be able to live there. High-speed **elevators** will carry eighty people at a time. The building will have stores, restaurants, and cinemas. People won't ever have to leave!

◀ Model for an apartment building in Toyko

elevators, machines in a building that carry people from one floor to another

BEFORE YOU GO ON . . .

1 Look at the timeline. What new inventions do experts predict?

2 What do they predict the population will be in 2050?

HOW ABOUT YOU?
● What new inventions do you want to have in the future?

227

CRITICAL THINKING

Have students respond orally or in writing to these questions:
● What would be an advantage of, or a good reason for, having everything you need in the building where you live? What would be a disadvantage? *(Possible answers: less traffic, less distance to travel for services, time saved; fewer chances to meet new people, feeling homebound)*
● Look at the timeline. What will be happening when you graduate from college? When you turn 30? 50? *(Possible answers: Clothes adapt to temperature. Cars drive themselves. Cancer is cured.)*

MODELING THE READING STRATEGY

Summarizing: After students finish reading page 227, have them identify the most important ideas on the page. List their responses on the board. Have students put the ideas in chronological, or time, order. Then model how to read the ordered list as a summary, adding sequencing words (such as *first, next,* and *then*) to connect the ideas.

ACTIVE READING

In their notebooks, have students draw a two-column chart with the headings *Problem* and *Solution*. As students read, guide them to write about problems of the future and the related invention or solution to that problem. Provide an example. Under *Problem* write: *Population is growing too fast.* Under *Solution* write: *New apartment building will house 50,000 people.* Have students add to the chart as they read.

REACHING ALL STUDENTS

LANGUAGE LEVELS

Beginning: Ask students to reread the section "The Growing World" and find four reasons why the population is growing. In their notebooks, have them rewrite the reasons in their own words. Then have each student choose one of the reasons and write why they think it contributes the most to the increasing population. Allow time for each student to read aloud his or her explanations.

Advanced: Have students reread the section on future cities. Then ask students to discuss what features the apartment building would need in order for it to be a satisfying place for them to live. Have students consider what activities in their lives they find important and to imagine how those activities could be built into an enormous building.

Cars of the Future

As more people own cars, the roads become more crowded. This causes more traffic jams and more accidents. The cost of traffic jams in the United States is about $78 billion per year—4.5 billion hours of travel time plus 26 billion liters (7 billion gal.) of fuel wasted sitting in traffic.

Car manufacturers are always looking for ways to make cars safer, faster, and more convenient. In the future, there may be automated highways. On these highways, cars will **steer** themselves. They will go faster and brake by themselves. Cars will have computers that pick up signals from **magnets** in the road.

What about flying cars? Flying cars may fill the skies in the future. Paul Moller has spent forty years and millions of dollars developing his Skycar. He is now close to completing the first successful flying car, the Skycar M400. Computers and satellites will control it. The Skycar will cost about $1 million. Once it is mass produced, however, the price could be as low as $60,000.

▲ An artist's idea of transport in the future

steer, guide
magnets, pieces of iron that attract other pieces of iron

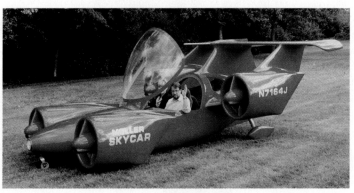

◄ Skycar M400 will be able to reach a speed of 560 kilometers (350 mi.) per hour.

228

Tell students that over 55 percent of oil used in the United States comes from foreign resources, and the amount of oil imported from other countries continues to grow. Europe imports 52 percent of its oil; Japan imports 98 percent of its oil. Two-thirds of the world's oil supply is in the Middle East, with Saudi Arabia being the world's largest oil producer.

In order to reduce the dependency on foreign oil and decrease air pollution, a new generation of automobiles is being designed. In the near future, people will have the option of buying mass-produced electric, hybrid, and fuel-cell cars. Japanese engineers are refining the fuel-cell car with production set for 2003. One prototype of the fuel-cell car can go 700 miles on twenty dollars worth of fuel.

Encourage students to use library and Internet resources to research the future of automobiles and other forms of transportation. Have students discuss the advantages and disadvantages of each type of innovative car or new mode of transportation.

▲ The X-43A will be the first plane to reach hypersonic speeds using an air-breathing engine.

Hypersonic Planes

The National Aeronautics and Space Administration (NASA) is developing a hypersonic plane. A hypersonic plane will be able to fly five times faster than the speed of sound, and it will be able fly to outer space. NASA produced a $185 million **prototype** plane in April 2001. But it doesn't expect to use the hypersonic plane for space travel until about 2020.

The X-43A prototype plane looks like a flying surfboard. It is thin and has a wingspan of 1.5 meters (5 ft.). It is 3.6 meters (12 ft.) long and weighs 1,270 kilograms (2,800 lbs). A working version of the X-43A will be about 60 meters (200 ft.) long.

prototype, the first model

BEFORE YOU GO ON . . .

1 Give an example of what a car of the future will do.

2 What is a hypersonic plane?

HOW ABOUT YOU?
- Do you think a flying car is a good idea? Why or why not?

229

CRITICAL THINKING

Have students respond orally or in writing to these questions:
- What kind of person do you think Paul Moller is? Explain your answer. *(Possible answers: intelligent, determined, wealthy; Moller has spent a lot of money and years working on his project.)*
- Would you buy a flying car if you could afford one? Why or why not? *(Answers will vary.)*
- What advantage does a hypersonic plane have over a rocket? *(Possible answer: A plane is much easier to land.)*

MODELING THE READING STRATEGY

Summarizing: Have students reread the sections on pages 228–229 and stop after each section to ask:
- What is the topic of this section?
- What is the main idea of each paragraph?

Then have students write a brief summary of the pages and read it aloud to the class.

EXTEND THE LESSON

Have students design and illustrate a car of the future. Ask them to label the features of the car. Then have students develop a sales pitch or commercial to sell the car. Encourage students to present their commercials to classmates.

REACHING ALL STUDENTS

LANGUAGE LEVELS

Beginning: Ask students to name some of the improvements predicted for cars of the future, such as self-braking and flying cars. Have students discuss other improvements they think should be made to cars to make them safer, faster, and more convenient.

Advanced: Have students reread the section on flying cars and brainstorm the advantages of having a flying car. List their responses on the board. Then have students discuss what problems might develop as a result of this invention. Prompt students to consider noise pollution, safety issues, and costs. Ask students to debate the advantages and disadvantages of flying cars.

GUIDED READING

1. Who was the Italian artist who designed flying machines in the fifteenth century? *(Leonardo da Vinci)*
2. How will people living on Mars be protected from poisonous air? *(They will live inside a giant dome.)*
3. Which is a gas in Earth's atmosphere—oxygen, arsenic, or borax? *(oxygen)*

across the curriculum

MATH Tell students that a chart presents information using numbers and/or words that are arranged in columns or rows. Explain that columns present information vertically. They usually have headings or labels. Rows present information horizontally. Point out that to read a chart, students should first note the heading and then read each row from left to right. Tell students that charts can make information easily accessible so that students don't have to review a number of sentences or paragraphs.

ACTIVITY: Have students study the chart on page 231. Ask students to discuss and agree on answers for the following questions:

● Which planet has the lower average temperature? *(Mars)*
● How much longer is a Mars year than an Earth year? *(321.75 days)*
● How much longer is a Mars day than an Earth day? *(41 minutes)*

Jetpacks

People have always dreamed of flying. In the fifteenth century, the Italian artist Leonardo da Vinci drew many designs of flying machines. But a personal flying machine—or jetpack—has proved to be one of the most difficult inventions.

Jetpacks have appeared in such movies as *The Rocketeer, Spy Kids,* and *Minority Report.* A "rocket man" flew into the opening ceremony of the 1984 summer Olympics in Los Angeles. Jetpacks today can fly for only a short time. In the future, they will fly longer and go faster.

The most successful jetpack prototype is the SoloTrek Exo-Skeletor Flying Vehicle (XFV). The XFV uses propellers to lift you off the ground. Once in the air, you can **zip** over treetops at 130 kilometers (80 mi.) per hour for 240 kilometers (150 mi.) before **refueling**.

▲ Leonardo da Vinci designed flying machines in the 1400s.

---

zip, move very fast
refueling, refilling with fuel

▲ The SoloTrek Exo-Skeletor Flying Vehicle (XFV) can climb as high as 3,000 meters (10,000 ft.). ▶

230

PHONICS MINILESSON

Diphthongs: *ou, ow, oy, oi*

Model the vowel sound /ou/ represented by the letters *ou* and *ow*. Have students repeat the sound after you. Then read the following words from the selection: <u>ground</u>, dreamed, <u>crowded</u>, cars, <u>about</u>, <u>throughout</u>, <u>now</u>, five, <u>sound</u>. Ask students to raise their hands when they hear the sound /ou/ in a word.

Repeat the modeling and listening activity for the sound /oi/ represented by the letters *oi* and *oy*. Use the following words from the selection as examples: <u>poisonous</u>, travel, <u>soil</u>, small. Have students find and read aloud other words in this selection or in magazines that have the diphthongs *ou, ow, oi,* and *oy*. Encourage students to choose one word with each diphthong and write a sentence for each word.

New Frontiers

Throughout history, humans have loved to explore. Today, we have explored most of our planet. There are few new lands to explore. But there are new worlds, new planets, and new **galaxies**.

▲ An artist's idea of a colony on Mars

In the future, perhaps we will **colonize** other planets. The most likely planet will be Mars. NASA scientists have already sent probes—spacecraft without people—to explore Mars. But when will people be able to go there? Astronauts could travel to Mars by about 2015. But it will be a difficult task! It will take six months to reach Mars. (It takes only three days to reach the moon.) And Mars is not a friendly **environment**. Mars probably once had liquid water, but now it is a cold, rocky desert. It has the largest volcano in the solar system and the deepest canyons. Dust storms can cover the whole planet. There is no breathable **oxygen**.

For people to live on Mars, the cities will have to be protected from the **poisonous** air. Giant **domes** will have to be built to control the atmosphere. All food will have to be grown inside the domed cities.

Earth–Mars Comparison

	Earth	Mars
Average distance from sun	150 million kilometers (93 million mi.)	228 million kilometers (142 million mi.)
Length of year	365.25 days	687 Earth days
Length of day	23 hours 56 minutes	24 hours 37 minutes
Temperature	average 14°C (57°F)	average –63°C (–81°F)
Atmosphere	nitrogen, oxygen, argon, others	mostly carbon dioxide, some water vapor
Number of moons	1	2

---

galaxies, very large groups of stars
colonize, set up human communities
environment, the land, water, and air
oxygen, a gas in the air that all plants and animals need in order to live
poisonous, deadly
domes, round roofs

BEFORE YOU GO ON . . .

1. What is an example of a new frontier that humans can explore?
2. Look at the Earth–Mars Comparison chart. Which planet is farther away from the sun? Which planet has only one moon?

HOW ABOUT YOU?
- Would you like to travel to Mars? Why or why not?

231

Review

COMPREHENSION

Call on a volunteer to read and study the directions and chart on page 232. After students copy the chart into their notebooks, remind them how to read the chart both across and down. Point out the column headings (Section, Summary) and the six rows with section titles.

Remind students to make each summary one sentence long and to use one of the key words listed in the directions in each sentence. Have students work in pairs to complete the Summary column. When everyone has finished, have volunteers take turns reading their summary for each section. Then have students respond to these questions:

1. What can you do if you cannot remember the main ideas in a section? (You can skim or reread the section.)

2. Which vocabulary word was used in the section about the growing world? (population)

3. In which section will you find traffic jams? ("Cars of the Future")

CRITICAL THINKING

After students complete the chart, have them compare the different sections of the reading. Then have them respond orally or in writing to these questions:

- Why do you think the sections of the chart are listed in this order? (Possible answer: The chart reflects the order in which the information is presented.)
- Why might people have to travel to Mars? (Possible answer: Earth might become too crowded.)

Review and Practice

COMPREHENSION

Reread "Life in the Future." Copy the chart into your notebook. Write a one-sentence summary of each section. Try to use the key words—*artificial, frontier, mass produced, population, robots,* and *traffic jams*—in your summary.

Section	Summary
The Growing World	*Scientists predict that the world population will grow to 11 billion by the year 2100.*
Future Cities	
Cars of the Future	
Hypersonic Planes	
Jetpacks	
New Frontiers	

Now use your summary to tell a partner about "Life in the Future."

232

EXTENSION

1. Pretend that you are living in the future. Write a paragraph about what a typical day is like for you. Where do you live? How do you get around? What kind of clothes do you wear? You can use some of the inventions described in "Life in the Future," or you can create your own inventions. Exchange your paragraph with a partner. How are your future lives similar and different?

2. What are some jobs you think robots will have in the future? Make a list.

DISCUSSION

Discuss in pairs or small groups.

1. Why would people have to live in giant domes on Mars?

2. What would you like about living on the 180th floor of an apartment building? What wouldn't you like about it?

3. Would you rather live 100 years in the future or 100 years in the past? Why?

4. Do you think robots should do some jobs that people now do? Why or why not?

An artist's idea of a space colony of the future, where 10,000 people will live and work ▶

233

EXTENSION

Have students take turns reading aloud the Extension exercises. Invite students to brainstorm ideas for each question before they begin to write. Encourage students to work in pairs and to ask their partners questions about their "Life in the Future." After students complete their paragraph and list, have volunteers read them aloud for the class.

DISCUSSION

Invite volunteers to read the questions aloud. Then have other students take turns paraphrasing each question to make sure everyone understands what they are being asked. Before students begin, model how to answer question 3, choosing either the present or the past. For example, *I would like to live 100 years ago, because I am interested in history and want to know more about life in the early 1900s.* Encourage students to take notes as you talk and use them as a springboard for their own ideas.

METACOGNITION

Ask students:

1. How did filling in a summary chart help you understand each section of the reading better?

2. How did the section entitled "New Frontiers" help you imagine what life on Mars might be like?

3. How did the illustrations in this reading help you visualize the future?

REACHING ALL STUDENTS

LANGUAGE LEVELS

Beginning: Have students find three main ideas in the Future Cities section. Write the ideas on the board, and discuss them. Have students decide which one best summarizes the section. Ask them to summarize the idea in a sentence, using their own words, and copy the sentence into the chart. Repeat the activity for each section.

Advanced: Have students work in small groups to read aloud the paragraphs they wrote for the Extension exercise. Tell groups to select a paragraph and turn it into a play. Ask groups to create characters and dialogue. They can also make futuristic props. When groups are ready, have them perform their dramatizations.

LEARNING MODALITIES

Visual: Have students create a poster showing an invention for a futuristic item they think the world needs. Have students include on the poster why we need this item and how it works. Then have students present the poster to the class. Allow time for students to answer questions about their posters from their classmates.

Connect

READING SUMMARY

This article records an on-line interview between a group of students and astronaut Dan Bursch who has lived and worked on a space shuttle and the International Space Station.

SCAFFOLDING

Have students name any famous astronauts they have heard or read about or may have seen in popular movies such as *Apollo 13*. Ask students to describe how life in a space station is probably different from life on Earth. Then have students listen to the selection on CD/tape as they read silently.

GUIDED READING

1. What does Dan Bursch do before a flight that will last up to six months? *(He selects a menu of the food he will eat.)*

2. How long does it take to get used to not feeling gravity? *(a day or two)*

3. What can the astronauts see when there are no clouds? *(lights from Earth's cities)*

across the curriculum

HEALTH   Tell students that space travelers can experience dramatic loss of bone density, a weakening of the heart and other muscles, and serious levels of exposure to radiation. Have students use on-line or library resources to research what scientists are doing to combat these problems and maintain astronauts' health while in space. Encourage students to share their findings with the class.

CONNECT TO LITERATURE   Interview

In this section, you will read an interview. In an interview, one person—the interviewer (or, in this case, interviewers)—asks questions, and another person answers. For this interview, students used the Internet to ask an astronaut about his work. As you read, think about the main topics that the students ask about.

Interview with an Astronaut: Dan Bursch

Dan Bursch has made three space flights and has been in space for 746 hours. He lived on the International Space Station from December 5, 2001 until June 19, 2002. Before this expedition, he chatted online with some students on www.discovery.com.

▲ Dan Bursch

Dan Bursch: I would just like to say welcome to everyone tonight. Thank you for spending your Sunday evening with me. . . .

Cody: I am ten years old, and I would like to know what the food is like. I would also like for you to trade me just one day in the space station and you can go to my school.

Dan Bursch: Well, thanks, Cody. Food is very important for us up in space, as it is here on Earth. In fact, one of the things that I will be starting tomorrow . . . is food tasting. We are **selecting** our menu for the four- to six-month flight that I will have in space. What is different about my next mission on the space station is that we will have a mixture of American and Russian food, so that will certainly make it different. . . . Perhaps I can come to your school someday and perhaps in fifteen years or so you can go to space!

Gary TX: What kind of work do you do when you are at the space station?

Dan Bursch: We have a crew of three—myself, Carl Walz (another American astronaut), and Yuri. He is a Russian **cosmonaut**. He will be our **commander**. We divide up the work because there is a lot of work to be done. . . .

---

selecting, choosing
cosmonaut, Russian word for astronaut
commander, leader

---

chatted, talked informally

234

▲ The International Space Station

Galileo Guest: How do the astronauts deal with the effects of zero gravity on the space station?

Dan Bursch: Learning to work in space without feeling gravity is always a challenge.... Getting used to not feeling gravity usually takes a day or two.

International: What is it like working with scientists and other astronauts from all around the world? Do you all **get along**? Do you have fun?

Dan Bursch: This job is particularly interesting just because of that fact.... In the astronaut office, the range of different kinds of people is pretty wide.... But we all share one common goal, and that is to fly and live and work in space.... ❷

Hollifeld: Can you see the lights of the world's cities from space?

get along, act friendly

Dan Bursch: Yes. We spend half of our time while **in orbit** on the dark side of the planet. If there is a thin cloud layer, you see kind of a glow like from a lampshade that dampens the light a little bit. But when it is clear—when there are no clouds—the lights are **spectacular**....

Venus: What is the first time you go into space like? Is it hard to learn to use the tools or get used to things **floating around**?

---

in orbit, circling around Earth
spectacular, wonderful and exciting
floating around, moving around freely in the air

BEFORE YOU GO ON . . .

❶ What is different about the menu on this trip?

❷ What is a common goal for Bursch and the people he works with?

HOW ABOUT YOU?
• Would you like to live and work on the space station? Why or why not?

235

CRITICAL THINKING

Have students respond orally or in writing to these questions:
• What kinds of foods would you choose for a six-month flight into space? *(Answers will vary.)*
• Why would it be important for all the astronauts to get along while they are working? *(Possible answer: They have to live in a very small space with one another for a long time.)*

MODELING THE READING STRATEGY

Making Inferences: Remind students that when they make inferences, they fill in details about what they are reading by combining text information with what they already know. Read aloud Bursch's response to the student whose Internet handle is International, on page 235. Ask students to make an inference about how Bursch feels about the people he works with. *(He enjoys the fact that people can come from so many different backgrounds and parts of the world, and still share the same dream.)*

———————————*Viewpoint*———————

Have students look at the photo on page 235. Ask students to discuss why the author chose a photo of the space station instead of an illustration. How does the photo help the reader understand that the space station is not something in the future, but rather is something that exists right now?

REACHING ALL STUDENTS

LANGUAGE LEVELS

Beginning: Point out to students that many of the students interviewing Dan Bursch have on-line nicknames, called Internet handles. Help students find examples of on-line handles, such as *International, Venus,* and *AstroBob.* Then have students work in pairs to read the interview aloud. Ask one student in each pair to read the interviewers' questions while the other student reads Bursch's responses. Switch assignments and repeat.

Advanced: Have students find the word *cosmonaut* on page 234. Ask them to use context clues to figure out the word's meaning. Have students look up *cosmonaut* in the dictionary. Link the word's meaning to its etymology. Say, *Cosmonaut comes from the Greek words* kosmos, *meaning "beautiful, orderly universe," and* naut, *meaning "sailor."* Ask students to explain how a cosmonaut is like a sailor.

Connect

GUIDED READING

1. Why do the astronauts use Velcro? *(to strap things down so they don't float off in zero gravity)*
2. How do astronauts communicate with friends and family from the space station? *(They use e-mail.)*
3. What does Dan Bursch say is the most important thing to come out of the space station project? *(Former enemies are working together to build a large and complex structure in space.)*

Dan Bursch: I remember my first flight in 1993 on [the space shuttle] *Discovery*. . . . At lift-off, there is a lot of vibration and a lot of noise, and eight-and-a-half minutes later you are in orbit. When the engines turn off, instantly everything floats. . . . You have to make sure that you either strap something down or use **Velcro** because you will probably lose it otherwise.

Fun 2 Travl: What are the **entertainment options** available to you during your **down time** on the space station?

Dan Bursch: We will have movies that we will be able to play in orbit. . . . People will try to bring up a **hobby** such as reading. . . . We do have e-mail. Most of our down time will be spent sending e-mails to our families and friends.

Jurgen: What kind of personal items will you take with you from Earth?

Dan Bursch: The most popular personal item is probably pictures of our families. Other things may include perhaps a special **memento**, either from a parent or a grandparent. But the most popular personal items are pictures. And usually ones that include some scene or the background of what it is like back on Earth.

Velcro, a material made of two special pieces of cloth, used for fastening clothes, shoes, etc.
entertainment options, things to do for fun
down time, free time
hobby, something people do for pleasure during free time
memento, an item that helps you remember something or someone; a souvenir

AstroBob: Do you think that at some point ordinary people will get to go to the space station? Or will it always be **reserved for** scientists?

Dan Bursch: I think that is certainly a goal that we should try to reach. If it will be in my lifetime, I don't know. . . . When airplanes first came out, they were reserved at first for just the very **daring** or risk takers. And now anybody can fly on an airplane. So, I don't think it is a question of IF the opportunity will come . . . it is simply a matter of WHEN.

Sandy Fay: What kinds of things do they hope the space station will be good for once it is completed?

Dan Bursch: . . . I see the biggest challenge and the biggest thing that we are learning is two former enemies learning how to work together and build such a large and **complex** structure in space. And not just two former enemies, but all of the over one dozen countries that are working together. . . .

Discovery.com: Thank you, Dan, for chatting with us tonight.

---

reserved for, set aside for
daring, brave
complex, not simple; complicated

BEFORE YOU GO ON . . .

1. What do astronauts bring with them to remind them of home?
2. For Dan Bursch, what is the biggest challenge of the space station?

HOW ABOUT YOU?
- What question would you like to ask Dan Bursch?

236

SPELLING MINILESSON

Spelling Diphthong Sounds /ou/ and /oi/

Explain to students that there is more than one way to spell the sounds /ou/ and /oi/. Create a two-column chart on the board with the following headings: /ou/*ou*; /ou/*ow*; /oi/*oi*; /oi/*oy*.

Write the following words on the board: *south, foil, now, soy, town, joy, ground*. Read the words aloud, emphasizing the vowel sound in each one. Have students repeat them and then list the words in the appropriate columns on the board.

Ask students to look for words with these spelling patterns in the reading selection and list them in their notebooks. Examples include *without, around, cloud, noise, down, background, point, out*. Then have students create song lyrics about living in outer space using these words or words with similar spelling patterns. Ask them to write the song lyrics in their notebooks.

Link the Readings

Reread "Interview with an Astronaut." Then copy the chart into your notebook and complete it.

Title of Selection	Type of Text (Genre)	Fiction or Nonfiction	Purpose of Selection	How Travel Will Be Different in the Future
"Life in the Future"		*nonfiction*		
"Interview with an Astronaut: Dan Bursch"	*interview*			*Ordinary people will fly in space shuttles.*

DISCUSSION

Discuss in pairs or small groups.

1. Imagine you are going to the International Space Station. What personal items will you take with you?
2. Do you think humans will be able to live in space for a long time? Why or why not?
3. Dan Bursch talks about the challenges of living on the space station, such as choosing food, dealing with gravity, and working with others. What do you think would be your biggest challenge? Why?

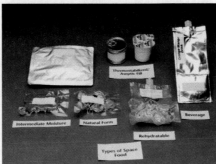

▲ Space food

237

REFLECTION

Direct students to look at the chart on page 237. Read the headings of the chart together and discuss their meanings. Be sure students know that *Purpose of Selection* means why the text was written. Then have students copy the chart into their notebooks and complete it. Have students discuss their answers. Then ask:

1. What type of text is "Life in the Future"? *(informational article)*
2. What is the purpose of "Interview with an Astronaut: Dan Bursch"? *(to inform)*

COOPERATIVE GROUPING

Have intermediate and advanced students work in small groups with beginning students to complete the Reflection chart. Groups should refer to the text, agree on answers, take turns recording answers, and then share their answers with the class.

DISCUSSION

Have students read the questions and discuss their answers. Point out that there is more than one correct answer for each question. Explain that students must draw on their own feelings, experiences, and opinions to answer the questions.

CRITICAL THINKING

Read this sentence from "Life in the Future": *Throughout history, humans have loved to explore.* Have small groups of students write a few sentences in support of this statement, using what they learned in Part 1.

REACHING ALL STUDENTS

LANGUAGE LEVELS

Beginning: To answer the first Discussion question, ask students to complete sentences orally, such as *I will take _____ with me to the International Space Station.* Encourage students to tell why the items they have chosen are important to them. Invite students to compare and contrast the items they have chosen with those of their classmates.

Advanced: For the third Discussion question, have students look up the word *challenge* in a dictionary and select the meaning that best fits its usage on page 236. Then ask students to paraphrase the meaning they have selected. Have students take turns sharing their definitions orally. Encourage students to discuss any differences in their definitions.

GRAMMAR

Have a volunteer read the grammar skill explanation and the example sentences as others follow along in the text. Make sure students understand that the word *will* is used to make predictions about the future. *Will* precedes the base form of the verb. Explain that the words *will* and *will not* are often contracted in speech and informal writing, but not in formal writing.

Have students scan the text of "Life in the Future" and "Interview with an Astronaut: Dan Bursch" and find examples of sentences containing the word *will*. Have them write the sentences in their notebooks and circle each base verb. Then have students complete the Practice activity.

SCAFFOLDING

Write each word in the following sentence on a separate index card: *Motorcycles have jet engines.* Give each of four students a card and have the students arrange themselves so that they form a sentence. Point out that the sentence is talking about the present, or right now. Next, write the word *will* on a fifth card. Give the *will* card to another student and have that person move between the students who are holding the words *Motorcycles* and *have.* Ask students to tell when motorcycles will have jet engines. *(in the future)* Repeat with a new sentence that contains a plural subject and a verb in the simple present. Then have students form sentences using the word *will.*

GRAMMAR

Using *will* for the Future

Use *will* + **base form of the verb** to talk about the future. When you make predictions about the future, you use *will*.

> Astronauts **will fly** to Mars by the end of the century.
> Cars **will drive** themselves on automated highways.
> The population **will grow** to 11 billion by 2100.

Note that *will* is usually contracted to *'ll* in speaking and informal writing. Do not use contractions in formal writing.

> We**'ll build** a space station in ten years.

The contracted form of *will* + *not* is **won't**.

> They probably **won't find** life on Mars.

Practice

Write sentences in your notebook. Use the words below to make predictions about the future.

Example: People (live) on space stations.
　　　　　People will live on space stations.

1. Fire-fighting robots (rescue) people.
2. In 2050 the population (be) 10 billion.
3. Humans (travel) to Mars.
4. Medical discoveries (help) people live longer.
5. Apartment buildings (have) 180 floors.
6. High-speed elevators (carry) eighty people at a time.
7. Cars (steer) themselves on automated highways.
8. Car manufacturers (make) safer, faster cars.
9. The price (be) $60,000.
10. People (fly) with jetpacks.

238

SKILLS FOR WRITING

Writing Notes for a Research Report

A research report gives detailed information about a topic. A writer can find facts about the topic in reference books, magazines, newspapers, and on the Internet. These are called sources. It is important to keep the facts from your sources organized. Before writers start writing a research report, they often organize facts by taking notes about each piece of information they find.

Here is an example of a note card for a research report on future transport. It is about one subtopic, or smaller topic, that the writer wants to include in the report.

NOTE-TAKING TIPS

- Use one note card for each subtopic.
- Summarize facts with your own words or phrases. Don't copy facts word for word from the source.
- For each note, record the source (the Internet, a book, a magazine, etc.). If the source is from the Internet, record the website address. If the source is a book, record the title, author, publisher, place and date of publication, and page number. For example, *Future*, by Michael Tambini, Dorling Kindersley, New York, 1998, p. 44.

Skycar M400

- *Paul Moller is developing a flying car called Skycar M400.*
- *Computers will control the car.*
- *Moller thinks Skycar will be the first mass-produced flying car.*
- *The first Skycar will cost about $1 million.*
- *Moller thinks it will cost about $60,000 to mass produce his car.*

Source: www.moller.com/skycar/

1. What subtopic is this note card about?
2. What source did the writer use for the notes on this card?
3. Where does the writer list the source?

239

Teach

WRITING ASSIGNMENT

Notes

Have a volunteer read aloud the introductory sentence and step 1. Then have students work in pairs and reread each section in the article "Life in the Future" to find ideas on topics related to the future that interest them. Ask students to state the ideas from the article that interest them or any other topics about future life they would like to explore. List the topics on the board. Have students suggest possible subtopics for the topics.

WRITING STRATEGY

Have students copy the subtopic web into their notebooks, leaving the circles blank for their own ideas. Help students choose a main topic and make a list of a number of subtopics. Refer them to the list on the board if they have difficulty. When students have a list of subtopics, ask them to narrow it to two and add them to the web. Give students time to research their subtopics. Suggest that they use Internet and library sources. Have students use cards to take notes. Remind them to start a new card for each subtopic and to follow the format shown in the sample note card on page 239.

USING THE EDITING CHECKLIST

Have students read aloud the Editing Checklist. Ask them to read it again with a partner, and use it to revise their notes. Tell students to find each item listed in the checklist on their note cards.

WRITING ASSIGNMENT

Notes

You will research and take notes on a topic about the future that interests you.

1. **Read** Reread the note card on page 239. Then think of a topic you would like to write about, such as the growing population, future cities, future transport (cars, planes, and jetpacks), or future exploration.

Writing Strategy: Subtopic Web

After you choose a topic to research, you need to decide what subtopics you want to take notes on. Write your topic in the middle of a page and then brainstorm smaller topics that are related to your topic. Look at this subtopic web about future transport.

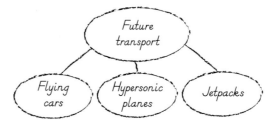

Narrow your ideas down to two subtopics. As you look at different sources, see which subtopics have the most information written about them. Choose two of these subtopics to write about.

1. Can you think of any other subtopics about future transport?
2. What sources can you check to get information about future transport?

2. **Make a subtopic web** Once you decide on a topic, make a subtopic web in your notebook. List as many subtopics as you can. Then narrow your list down to two or three subtopics.

3. **Write** Write one note card for each subtopic. Use only nonfiction sources that tell facts about your subtopics. Remember the rules for writing note cards.

EDITING CHECKLIST
Did you . . .
▶ look for facts about at least two subtopics?
▶ use your own words in your notes?
▶ record the source on each note card?

240

GRAMMAR MINILESSON

Word Order in Questions

To help students understand English word order in a question, write on the board:

(Question word) + helping verb + subject + main verb + (rest of sentence)

| Where | will | people | live | in the future? |
| Will | they | live | on Mars? |

Explain that questions usually have a helping verb, followed by a subject and a main verb. Point out that questions often begin with question words such as *who, what, where, when, why,* or *how.* Read aloud sentence 1 and identify each part: the question word *Where,* the helping verb *will,* the subject *people,* and the main verb *live.* Read aloud sentence 2. Elicit that this sentence has no question word but has the same word order. Next, have students write two questions for Dan Bursch. Tell them to use the helping verb *will* in both questions and to include a question word in one question. Students can then exchange questions with a partner and identify the helping verb, subject, and main verb in their partner's questions.

T240

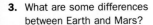

PART REVIEW 1

Check Your Knowledge

Language Development

1. Why do you summarize a text? Describe how you summarize.
2. Why do writers take notes?
3. What is a research report?
4. What is a subtopic? A subtopic web?
5. What are two sources of information that you can use when you are writing a research report?
6. Make three predictions about the future, using *will*.

Academic Content

1. What new social studies vocabulary did you learn in Part 1? What do the words mean?
2. What can a hypersonic plane do that a regular airplane cannot?
3. What are some differences between Earth and Mars?

241

ASSESS

You can assess students' knowledge of the unit in several different ways.

Portfolio: Have students include their note cards and subtopic web in their portfolios.

Traditional: Students can complete the Check Your Knowledge questions as a quiz. After students complete Check Your Knowledge, use the Assessment Package. Students can complete the Part Test on pages 69–72. For further practice, have students complete the Test Preparation worksheets.

Performance: Ask students to work in small groups to answer the Check Your Knowledge questions. Have students compare how their answers are alike and different from others in their group.

TEST-TAKING TIP

Tell students that when they read a multiple-choice question that asks them to identify the correct meaning of an unfamiliar word, they should think of other words with the same root word or ask themselves if they know a similar word in their first language. Tell them to use similar words to decode the meaning of the new word. See the Test Preparation pages in the Assessment Guide for additional test-taking strategies.

METACOGNITION

Tell students to read for signal words that indicate what kind of answer the question requires. Words such as *summarize* and *predict* appear often in test questions and students should feel comfortable knowing how to answer such questions.

REACHING ALL STUDENTS

LANGUAGE LEVELS

Beginning: Draw a subtopic web on the board. Write *Our Class* in the main circle. Then have students brainstorm related subtopics. Elicit that if there are only two to three subtopics, the information is more focused. This makes the writing both informative and interesting to the reader. Have students narrow their choices and add two subtopics to the circles on the board.

Advanced: Have students brainstorm a list of possible resources to use when writing a research report. Ask them to discuss the advantages and disadvantages of using each type of resource. Explain that some resources are better for certain topics than others. For example, when searching for information on new inventions, students should look in a source that includes recent information, such as a current science article on the Internet.

Preteach

OBJECTIVES

Tell students that in Part 2 they will be reading about experiences and topics that they might study in science class. Have volunteers take turns reading the list of objectives aloud. Explain any unfamiliar words. Have volunteers paraphrase each objective. Additional practice activities for these objectives can be found in the **Workbook** and **CD-ROM.**

BACKGROUND

Have students read page 242 silently and then aloud as a choral reading. Ask students to describe what they see in the picture. Then have them form small groups to discuss the chart entries. Encourage groups to make notes as they discuss how people and things may look in the future. Then have groups write complete sentences to fill in the chart. Have groups read aloud their answers.

COOPERATIVE GROUPING

Form four student groups. Have each group choose a different topic from the chart. Have groups create a Venn diagram on chart paper to compare their topic as it looks today with what they think it will look like in the future. Have groups share their Venn diagrams with the class.

PART 2 Prepare to Read

OBJECTIVES
LANGUAGE DEVELOPMENT

Reading:
- Vocabulary building: *Context, dictionary skills*
- Reading strategy: *Reading for enjoyment*
- Text types: *Novel, science article*
- Literary element: *Dialogue*

Writing:
- Sentence outline
- Research report

Listening/Speaking:
- Listen to a report
- Present a report

Grammar:
- Future: *be going to*

Viewing/Representing:
- Inherited traits

ACADEMIC CONTENT
- Science vocabulary
- DNA, genes, and traits
- Make predictions about life in the future

BACKGROUND

The Time Warp Trio: 2095 is a science fiction story about traveling into the future. Science fiction combines elements of fiction and fantasy with scientific fact. Most science fiction stories are set in the future. In this excerpt, the characters travel into the future, to the year 2095.

Make connections Pretend that you are able to travel 100 years into the future. Copy this chart into your notebook. Fill in the blanks with predictions of how people, places, and things will look.

People, Places, or Things	What They Will Look Like in the Future
My home	
My school	
My town	
My family	

▲ An artist's idea of a city of the future

242

TEACHING GUIDE

PRETEACH	Provide Background	Read and discuss the Background information. Complete the activity. (ATE/SB p. 242)
	Present Concepts	Introduce the Reading Strategy. (ATE/SB p. 243)
TEACH	Monitor Comprehension	Informally monitor comprehension while students read the selection independently or in groups. (ATE/SB pp. 244–255)
	Teach and Practice	Present the Grammar, Usage, and Mechanics. (ATE/SB pp. 256, 257) Complete the Writing activity. (ATE/SB p. 258) Present Grammar, Phonics, and Spelling minilessons. (ATE pp. 244, 248, 254)
CONNECT	Connect to Content	Have students read the informational reading and relate it to the literature. (ATE/SB pp. 252–254)
	Across the Curriculum	Present curriculum links as students read. (ATE pp. 248, 252)
ASSESS	Check Knowledge	Assess students' comprehension by having them complete the Check Your Knowledge section. (ATE/SB p. 259)
	Monitor Progress	Use one or more of the print assessment resources in the Assessment Package.
EXTEND	Integrate Language and Apply Understanding	Have students complete the Workshops (ATE/SB pp. 260–263) and choose a project from the Unit Projects. (ATE/SB p. 264) Then have them choose a book to read from Further Reading. (ATE/SB p. 265)

LEARN KEY WORDS

mechanical
plastic
revolutionary
stories
streamlined
transported

VOCABULARY

Read these sentences. Use the context to figure out the meaning of the red words. Use a dictionary to check your answers. Write each word and its meaning in your notebook.

1. The **mechanical** sidewalk moves people quickly from place to place.
2. Her **plastic** raincoat kept her dry in the rain.
3. The new invention was **revolutionary**—it changed the way that people lived.
4. The tall buildings had 200 **stories**! We couldn't see the top.
5. Cars of the future will be smaller, faster, and more **streamlined** than cars of the past.
6. They pressed the numbers and were **transported** 100 years into the future.

READING STRATEGY

Reading for Enjoyment

Sometimes you read for information. Other times you read just for fun or entertainment. When your purpose for reading is to enjoy, you want to be entertained by the characters, the setting, and the pictures that go with the text. People often read novels to be entertained.

Think about how the words and pictures in this excerpt make you want to read more.

243

VOCABULARY

Clearly enunciate each of the Key Words. Then read each sentence aloud, and have students raise their hands when they hear the Key Words. Model how to use context clues to help students figure out the meanings of any unfamiliar words. For example, *In the first sentence, I read that a mechanical sidewalk moves people from place to place. The people aren't walking, so a machine must be moving them. The word* mechanical *must be describing a type of machine. I assume that a* mechanical *sidewalk must be a machine-operated tool that moves people along automatically.* Then demonstrate for students how to use a dictionary to check their answers. Tell students to write each word and its meaning in their notebooks.

READING STRATEGY

Have students read the Reading Strategy. Point out that reading for enjoyment still involves thinking about what one is reading. Discuss as a class how reading for enjoyment can help readers improve their ability to read for information. For example, when you read for fun, you may learn new words and ideas that you may see again in nonfiction texts. Remind students to pay attention to how the characters, setting, and pictures increase their enjoyment of the excerpt.

REACHING ALL STUDENTS

LANGUAGE LEVELS

Beginning: Have each student choose a Key Word that seems most unclear. Record students' choices on the board and circle the two words most often mentioned. Work together as a class to investigate more about the meanings of these two words. Resources may include interviewing other teachers, looking up information on the Internet, or using a reference text such as a dictionary, thesaurus, or synonym finder.

Advanced: After students record the Key Words and meanings in their notebooks, have them work in pairs to write each word in an original sentence. Have pairs share one or two sentences with the group.

READING SUMMARY

Three friends find themselves in the future, where they meet three girls who are their own great-granddaughters.

SCAFFOLDING

Have students listen to the selection on CD/tape as they follow along in their books. Then have students read the first two pages aloud, alternating paragraphs. After reading, ask students to name the main characters and describe the setting of the story. Then have students take turns reading the remainder of the selection aloud.

GUIDED READING

1. What did Uncle Joe give young Joe? (The Book, *a time-travel guide*)
2. How are people floating, with wings or antigravity disks? *(They have antigravity disks.)*
3. What does skin look like in the future? *(Skin can be any color and have patterns.)*
4. What do the three friends see when they look up above Central Park? *(layers of anitgravity cars and lines of people)*

LITERARY ELEMENT

Have a volunteer read the Literary Element text. Then have volunteers find examples of dialogue on page 245 and read them aloud. Write the sentences on the board. Have students circle the exact words of the speaker in each example.

FOCUS ON LITERATURE Novel

Read this science fiction novel excerpt for your enjoyment. Are the characters, the setting, and the story entertaining? Why or why not?

from

THE TIME WARP TRIO: 2095

Jon Scieszka

244

GRAMMAR MINILESSON

Punctuation: Comma

Explain that commas tell readers when to pause, and they help make a sentence's meaning clear. Discuss the following examples of different kinds of comma use:

- in a compound sentence before the conjunction: *A tidal wave of people came flooding in, and we were right in its path.*
- in a series or list: *There were people with green skin, blue skin, purple skin, orange, striped, plaid, dotted, and you-name-it skin.*
- after an interjection: *"Hey, you're right."*
- in dialogue to separate the spoken words from the part of the sentence that tells who is speaking and how: *"Look closely," said Sam.*

Form small groups of students. Have groups scan this and other selections to find examples of each kind of comma use. Ask groups to write and read aloud their samples to the class, explaining how the comma is used in each sentence.

Sam, Fred, and Joe are a trio, or three friends. They are visiting the American Museum of Natural History in New York City in the year 1995. Joe, the narrator, has The Book, a time-travel guide given to him by his Uncle Joe. Without meaning to, Joe does something that transports him and his two friends into the year 2095. As this excerpt begins, the trio is running away from a security robot called SellBot.

We jumped over the twitching SellBot and ran down a **flight of stairs**. We had almost made it to the lobby, when the sound of a buzzer filled the halls.

The museum doors opened. A **tidal wave of people** came flooding in, and we were right in its path.

We dodged the first bunch of teenagers. They had corkscrew, spike, and Mohawk hair in every color you can think of. But the most amazing thing was that no one was touching the ground.

"They're flying. People in the future have figured out how to fly," said Sam.

A solid river of people flowed past us. An old man in an aluminum suit. A woman with leopard-patterned skin. A class in shiny school uniforms. Everyone was floating about a foot above the floor.

"How do they do that?" I said.

LITERARY ELEMENT

Dialogue is what characters say to each other. The words in quotation marks (" ") tell the exact words of the characters.

flight of stairs, steps from one floor to the next
tidal wave of people, a large crowd of people

"Look closely," said Sam. "Everyone has a small disk with a green triangle and a red square."

"Hey, you're right," I said.

"I'm always right," said Sam. "That is obviously the **antigravity disk** that kid was talking about. Now let's get out of here before another SellBot **tracks us down**."

Fred grabbed my belt. Sam grabbed Fred's belt. And we fought our way outside. We stopped at the statue of Teddy Roosevelt sitting on his horse looking out over Central Park. We stood and looked out with him.

"Wow," said Fred. "I see it but I don't believe it."

The sidewalk was full of floating people of every shape and color. There were people with green skin, blue skin, purple skin, orange, striped, plaid, dotted, and **you-name-it skin**. The street was packed three high and three deep with floating bullet-shaped things that must have been antigravity cars. And all around the trees of Central Park, towering buildings spread up and out like gigantic mechanical trees taller than the clouds.

---

antigravity disk, a small item that fights the force of gravity, allowing one to float above the ground
tracks us down, finds us
you-name-it skin, every kind of skin

BEFORE YOU GO ON . . .

1 Where are the boys transported?

2 What is New York like in the future?

HOW ABOUT YOU?
- Imagine that you could travel to any time period. Which would you choose?

245

CRITICAL THINKING

Have students respond orally or in writing to these questions:
- Would you be afraid if you were one of the boys in the story? Why or why not? *(Answers will vary.)*
- Which of the boys do you like best so far? Why? *(Possible answer: Sam, because he is self-confident.)*
- How do you think you would have reacted to seeing the New York City of the future? *(Possible answer: I would have been excited by the floating people and cars.)*

MODELING THE READING STRATEGY

Reading for Enjoyment: Have students reread the page and pick out the passage or scene they most enjoyed. Ask, *How did this passage make you want to read more of the story?*

ACTIVE READING

Draw on the board a web with six spokes. End each spoke with one of the following questions: *What happened? When did it happen? How did it happen? Why did it happen? Who was involved in the event? Where did it happen?* Have students copy the event map in their notebooks. For every two pages of the story, have students complete the event map by answering the questions.

Viewpoint

Have students look at the illustration on page 244 and explain how the drawing describes what life might be like in the New York City of the future.

Teach

GUIDED READING

1. What made the building door open? *(The door recognized the girl's voice.)*
2. What is Vitagorp? *(a food of the future)*
3. Where does the note tell the girls to meet their great-grandfathers? *(under Teddy Roosevelt's statue at the Museum of Natural History)*

Viewpoint

Have students look at the illustration on page 246 and discuss how the picture helps the reader understand this scene in the story. Ask, *What do the people in this picture have in common? (Possible answers: antigravity disks; the girls resemble the boys.)*

Layers and layers of antigravity cars and lines of people snaked around a hundred stories above us. New York was bigger, busier, and noisier than ever. . . .

* * *

Now wearing antigravity disks, the boys fly through the streets of New York, still chased by the SellBot and three futuristic girls who look strangely familiar. Uncle Joe has appeared out of nowhere to help. The girls catch up, and Joe is surprised to see that one of the girls looks very much like his sister.

"Come on," said the girl who looked like my sister. "Follow us."

Sam looked at Fred. Fred looked at me. I looked at Uncle Joe.

"Do we have any choice?" I asked.

We **took off** and followed the girls around the buildings, over crowds of crazily colored people, past streamlined **pods** and more talking, blinking, singing 3-D ads, until I had no idea where we were.

We finally stopped in front of a building too tall to believe.

"Here's my house," said the **lead girl**.

Fred, Sam, and I looked up and up and up at the building that disappeared in the clouds.

The girl led us through a triangle door that opened at her voice. She put her hand over a blinking red handprint on the wall. And in five seconds we were all transported to a room that must have been five miles above New York City.

---

took off, left quickly
pods, long vehicles
lead girl, girl at the front of the others

246

The girls flopped down on cushions. "This is my room," said the girl who looked like my sister.

We stood nervously in one corner.

"So you're not **killer time cops**?" I said.

The three girls looked at me like I was crazy.

"Of course not," said one.

"Whatever gave you that idea?" said another.

Then we all started asking questions.

---

killer time cops, secret police who catch time travelers

Explain that the boys visit the American Museum of Natural History in New York City, which contains a treasure trove of scientific and cultural exhibits from around the world. You may wish to show students the museum's website as you explain the kinds of exhibits and performances the museum features. Tell students that the museum has featured exhibits on the history of American baseball and the life of Albert Einstein, a performance of a ceremony by an Eastern Siberian Yakut shaman from Asia, a display of featherwork from the Amazon region of South America, and a replica of the Dzanga-Sangha rainforest in central Africa. Write the following questions on the board and ask student groups to read them, discuss them, and write a sentence to answer each one: *Why do you think museums like this are popular? What values or interests do these exhibits reveal? If you were a curator (museum exhibit planner), what exhibits would you include in a museum? What is a famous museum from your native country? What kinds of exhibits does it feature?*

"Who are you guys?"

"How did you know we'd be at the museum?"

"Do you have anything to eat?"

The girls laughed. The one who led us there pushed a green dot on a small table. A bowl of something looking like dried green dog food appeared with a pile of liquid filled plastic balls.

"Here's some **Vitagorp and Unicola**," said the girl who looked like my sister. "Now let me try to explain things from the beginning."

We copied the girls and sucked on the plastic ball things the same way they did. Fred ate a handful of the green dog food.

"I'm Joanie. This is Samantha. That's Frieda."

"But everybody calls me Freddi," said the girl with the baseball hat.

"And we have these names," Joanie continued, "because we were named after our great-grandfathers—Joe, Sam, and Fred."

"Or in other words—you," said Samantha.

Everything suddenly made sense. That's why they looked so much like us.

"Of course," said Uncle Joe, dusting off his **top hat**. "Your great-grandkids have to ❶ make sure you get back to 1995. Otherwise you won't have kids. Then your kids won't have kids. Then your kids' kids won't have—"

_____

Vitagorp and Unicola, imaginary food and drink of the future
top hat, tall black hat

"Us," said Samantha. "Your great-grandkids. And we knew you would be at the ❷ museum because you wrote us a note." Samantha handed me a yellowed sheet of paper that had been sealed in plastic. It was our Museum Worksheet from 1995. On the back was a note in my handwriting that said:

Girls,
Meet us under Teddy Roosevelt's statue at the Museum of Natural History, September 28, 2095.
Sincerely,
Joe, Sam, Fred

"How did you get our worksheet from 1995?" asked Sam.

"I got it from my mom," said Joanie. "And she got it from her mom."

"But we didn't write that," I said.

"You will," said Samantha, "if we can get you back to 1995."

BEFORE YOU GO ON . . .

❶ Who are the three girls?

❷ How do the girls know the boys will be at the museum?

HOW ABOUT YOU?

• Imagine you are Joe. How do you feel at this point in the story?

247

Teach

1. Who pitched for the Yankees? *(Fred's daughter)*

2. Does Samantha compare the discovery of the antigravity disks to the discovery of the telephone or the discovery of penicillin? *(the telephone)*

3. Who are some of the people that the girls have visited? *(cavewomen, Ann the Pirate, Calamity Jane, Cleopatra)*

4. What does Uncle Joe's Time Warp Watch look like, a wristwatch or a pocket watch? *(a pocket watch)*

——————Viewpoint——————

Have students look at the picture of Uncle Joe holding the pocket watch on page 249. Have students discuss why they think the author chose to include the pocket watch in the picture. Ask, *Why would the author pick this scene to illustrate? How does it help you understand the story?*

across the curriculum

HISTORY Form two student groups. Assign Calamity Jane to one group and Cleopatra to the other. Ask each group to research the famous woman from history and record five to ten facts about her. Have the groups present their facts to the class using complete sentences. Instruct them to explain why they think the girls in the story might have wanted to meet the famous women they researched.

"Saved by our own great-grandkids with a note we haven't written yet?" said Sam. "I told you something like this was going to happen. Now we're probably going to **blow up**."

"Wow," said Fred, eating more Vitagorp. "Our own great-grandkids. So what team is that on your hat? I've never seen that **logo**."

"That's the **Yankees**," said Freddi. "They changed it when Grandma was **pitching**."

"Your grandma? Fred's daughter?" I said. "A pitcher for the Yankees?"

"Not just a pitcher. She was a great pitcher," said Freddi. "2.79 lifetime ERA, 275 wins, 3 no-hitters, and the Cy Young award in '37."*

"Forget your granny's **stats**," said Sam. "We could be genius inventors back in 1995 if we could reconstruct these **levitation devices**."

"What did he just say?" asked Freddi.

"He wants to know how the antigravity disks work," said Samantha. "A truly amazing discovery. More surprising than Charles Goodyear's accidental discovery of vulcanized rubber. More revolutionary than Alexander Graham Bell's first telephone. But all I can tell you is that the antigravity power

* This information shows that Fred's future daughter is a great baseball player. This is especially interesting because there are no women players in professional baseball today.

---

blow up, explode and die
logo, brand name or label
Yankees, New York baseball team
pitching, throwing a ball to a batter
stats, short for statistics—facts about a certain subject
levitation devices, machines that let you float off the ground

248

---

comes from the chemical BHT. And it was discovered in a breakfast accident."

"What's a breakfast accident?" said Sam. "A **head-on collision** with a bowl of cornflakes? And who found out BHT could make things fly?"

"You did," said Samantha. "That's why we can't tell you more. You know the Time Warp Info-Speed Limit posted in *The Book*. Anyone traveling through time with too much information from another time blows up."

Sam's eyes nearly **bugged out** of his head. "I knew it. Don't tell me another word."

"Hey, wait a minute," I said. "Where did you say that info-speed limit was?"

Samantha looked at me like I was an insect.

"In *The Book*, of course."

"How do you know about *The Book*?"

"I got it for my birthday last year," said Joanie.

"And since then we've been all over time," said Freddi. "We've met cavewomen, Ann the Pirate, **Calamity Jane**. . . ."

"And don't forget **Cleopatra** and the underground cities of Venus," said Samantha.

"But if you have *The Book*, that means we're saved," said Sam.

---

head-on collision, a violent crash
bugged out, popped out
Calamity Jane, American frontier woman from the 1800s famous for her unconventional behavior and courage
Cleopatra, ancient Egyptian queen

PHONICS MINILESSON

Schwa

Say the word *about*. Tap out the two syllables in *about* to enable students to hear that the accent falls on the second syllable and that the first syllable is unstressed. Tell students that in some words, the vowel sound in the unstressed syllable is weak, and this weaker vowel sound is known as the schwa sound. Have students listen for the sound of the vowel in the first syllable as you say *about* again. Ask them to repeat the word after you.

Provide other examples using the schwa sound for the vowels *a, e, i, o,* and *u*. Have students repeat each word after you: *alike, given, imagine, observe, succeed*. Then have student pairs find and write other words from the selection that have the schwa sound, such as *woman, about, above, around, disappeared, opened, hundred, happen, discovery, telephone, aluminum, mechanical, color, seconds, Venus, futuristic*.

Samantha gave Sam her look. "If you remember the Time Warpers' Tips, you know nothing can be in two places at once. Of course our *Book* disappeared as soon as your *Book* appeared."

"So now we have to help you get *The Book* back to the past," said Freddi, "so we can have it in the future."

"Of course," said Sam.

"We knew that," said Fred.

"Uh, right . . ." I said, trying to talk my way out of this mess. "We knew that would happen, but we uh . . ." I looked around at Sam, Fred, Samantha, Freddi, and Joanie. Then I **spotted** Uncle Joe. "We thought we could really learn some tricks about finding *The Book* from Uncle Joe!"

Uncle Joe looked up from something he was **fiddling with** in his lap. "*The Book*? Oh, I never could get it to work the way your mother did. That's why I gave it to you for your birthday."

"Oh, great," said Sam. "We're **doomed**."

---

spotted, saw
fiddling with, playing with
doomed, in a hopeless situation

"But that's also why I put this together." Uncle Joe held up the thing he had been fiddling with in his lap. It was an old-fashioned pocket watch. "My Time Warp Watch."

"We're saved!" yelled Sam.

BEFORE YOU GO ON . . .

1. Which character discovered the antigravity disk, but doesn't know it?
2. What will happen to the boys if they learn too much information while visiting the future?

HOW ABOUT YOU?

- Imagine you are able to travel through time. Who would you take with you? Why?

249

CRITICAL THINKING

Have students respond orally or in writing to these questions:

- Which character seems to enjoy time travel the most? Why? *(Possible answer: Sam, because he has so many questions.)*
- This selection is part of a novel. What do you think will happen next? How do you think the novel ends? *(Answers will vary.)*

MODELING THE READING STRATEGY

Reading for Enjoyment: Remind students that authors use descriptive words, pictures, and dialogue to help readers enjoy and understand a story. Read aloud pages 248 and 249. After reading, ask students to write a review of the story for someone who is trying to find a book to read for pleasure.

ABOUT THE AUTHOR

Jon Scieszka was born in 1956 in Flint, Michigan. He had a choice between attending medical school and art school; he chose art school. Before becoming a writer, he taught first and second grade. His first published book was *The True Story of the Three Little Pigs by A. Wolf.*

WEBSITES

For more information, log on to http://www.longman.com/shiningstar for links to other interesting websites about the future.

REACHING ALL STUDENTS

LANGUAGE LEVELS

Beginning: After reading pages 248 and 249, have student pairs work together to write a plot summary of what happened on the pages. Prompt students with questions such as, *What did the characters want? How did they try to achieve their goals? What was the outcome?* Invite pairs to read aloud their plot summaries.

Advanced: Form groups of seven students. Ask each student to choose a different character from the story: Uncle Joe, Fred, Joe, Sam, Joanie, Samantha, Freddi. Guide groups to role-play the conversation and events on pages 248 and 249. Invite groups to practice and then perform for the class.

LEARNING MODALITIES

Auditory: Have each student secretly choose a main character from the story. Have students, one at a time, speak as the character and reveal information about him or her. Ask the rest of the class to listen and then guess which character the student is portraying.

Review and Practice

COMPREHENSION

COMPREHENSION

Have a volunteer read the Comprehension directions. Read aloud each heading on the chart. Have students discuss what they liked about each element before they write a sentence in the *What I Enjoyed* column.

Have students respond to these questions and work in small groups to compare responses:

1. What can you do if you cannot recall all the pictures? *(You can go back to the story and look at them again.)*

2. What are some of the details about everyday life in the future that you can recall? *(Possible answers: flying cars, robots, antigravity disks, huge apartment buildings, voice-activated doors)*

CRITICAL THINKING

After students complete the chart, have them pick the element of the story they found the most entertaining. Then have them write a paragraph explaining their choice and giving examples that tell why they found that part to be entertaining. Ask students to compare their responses with other students. Then ask:

● What makes the characters entertaining to you? *(Answers will vary.)*

● Why are the pictures enjoyable to you? *(Possible answer: The pictures help me imagine what the future will look like.)*

Reread the excerpt from *The Time Warp Trio: 2095.* Then copy the chart into your notebook and complete it. In the right column, write sentences telling what you enjoyed in the story.

	What I Enjoyed
Characters	
Pictures	
Setting	
Details about Everyday Life in the Future	

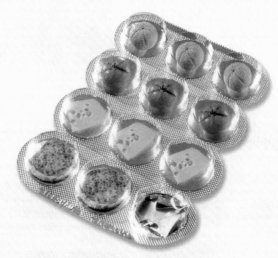

▲ How future food may look

250

EXTENSION

1. The girls offer the boys Vitagorp and Unicola. Make up your own food of the future. What does it look and smell like? What is its name?

2. Create an advertisement for a food or another product for 2095. Draw a picture of the product and write a description of it.

3. Make a TV commercial for your product. Practice your commercial and perform it for the class.

DISCUSSION

Discuss in pairs or small groups.

1. What do you think was the best part of time travel for Sam, Fred, and Joe? What was the worst part?

2. How did the dialogue in the excerpt from *The Time Warp Trio: 2095* help you understand the characters?

3. Reread the definition of "science fiction" on page 242. Can you find some fiction, some fantasy, and some scientific fact in *The Time Warp Trio: 2095*? Explain.

An artist's idea of a city of the future ▶

251

EXTENSION

Have three volunteers read the steps for the Extension activity. Form student groups to complete each step. Point out that students will need to use persuasive and descriptive language in their advertisements and commercials. Allow groups time to practice their product commercials. Then videotape them as they preform their advertisements for the class.

DISCUSSION

Have students work in pairs or small groups to complete the Discussion questions. Encourage students to return to the reading to answer any challenging questions. Have students share their answers for each question with the class.

METACOGNITION

Ask students:

1. What did you do to remember how the characters are related?

2. How can pictures help you better understand the story?

3. How did you use the defined terms and the note at the bottom of page 248 to help you understand what was happening in the story?

REACHING ALL STUDENTS

LANGUAGE LEVELS

Beginning: Before completing the Comprehension chart, have students discuss the topic in each row with a partner. Have pairs narrow down each answer to one collective idea and then complete the chart.

Advanced: After students complete their Comprehension chart, have them use the chart information to help them write a magazine advertisement for the book *The Time Warp Trio: 2095*. Tell students that the purpose of their advertisement is to persuade people to buy the book. Suggest that students look at newspaper ads for books and movies to get ideas for their advertisements.

CONNECT TO CONTENT Science

This is a science article. You will read facts about DNA—the "building blocks" of all forms of life. The purpose of this article is to give information about DNA. After each section, stop and summarize what you read.

DNA, Genes, and Traits

What Is DNA?

Every form of life is put together and controlled by a chemical "recipe," or code, called DNA (**d**eoxyribo**n**ucleic **a**cid). DNA is found in cells—very small parts of humans, animals, and plants. DNA contains genes. Genes on DNA look something like a supermarket **bar code**. The white lines are DNA. The black lines are genes. The code determines the **characteristics** of every living thing.

What Are Genes?

Each human cell contains 50,000 to 100,000 small parts called genes. Each gene controls a different trait, such as eye color or height. Genes get passed on from **generation** to generation. A baby **inherits** half its genes from its mother and half from its father. So, a baby inherits a quarter of its genes from each grandmother and a quarter from each grandfather.

Genes and People

Unless you are an identical twin, you are unique. This means that nobody else has exactly the same genes as you, not even your brothers and sisters.

Genes control all your traits. One gene controls skin color. Three genes control eye color.

---

bar code, a group of thin and thick lines on a product, which a computer in a store reads to find the price
characteristics, traits; qualities
generation, all the people who are about the same age in a family
inherits, gets; receives

252

▲ A model of DNA that is found in cells

▲ Identical twins share the same genes.

How Traits Are Inherited

Children often look like their parents in some ways. They can also look like their aunts or uncles, their grandparents, and their great-grandparents. The following traits are often inherited:

- eye color
- hair color
- dimples ②
- widow's peak
- cleft chin

Dimples are small hollows in the skin. Some people get them around their mouth when they smile. A cleft chin is a dimple in the chin. A hairline that comes to a point in the middle of your forehead is called a widow's peak.

BEFORE YOU GO ON . . .

① Where is DNA found?

② What are some traits that people inherit?

HOW ABOUT YOU?
- Name two traits you or someone you know inherited from a parent or grandparent.

GRACIELA SEGOVIA'S FAMILY

▲ This family tree shows how family members share traits.

253

CRITICAL THINKING 🔑

Have students respond orally or in writing to these questions:
- Genetically speaking, would you like to be an identical twin? Why or why not? *(Answers will vary.)*
- Which physical traits of yours or of someone you know can be traced back to parents or grandparents? *(Answers will vary.)*
- Do you think doctors should be allowed to change people's genes? Why or why not? *(Possible answer: No. Genetic changes might cause new health problems.)*

MODELING THE READING STRATEGY

Previewing: Remind students that before they read an informational article, it is helpful to preview the text. Have students preview the subtitle, photos, and captions on page 254. Then ask them to tell what this section of the article is about.

Viewpoint

Have students look at the family tree on page 253 and discuss how it helps them understand the information about genetics.

EXTEND THE LESSON

Invite students to interview a family member about physical traits that run in their family. Encourage students to take notes and gather photographs if possible. Have students create a class book in which they write about their families and provide pictures. The book can have an illustrated cover that is designed by the class.

REACHING ALL STUDENTS

LANGUAGE LEVELS

Beginning: Have student groups study and discuss the family tree on page 253. Ask them to identify the members of the family and the inherited traits that are depicted. Bring the class back together and discuss which traits appear to be most common from generation to generation. Then have students identify some other traits that are inherited.

Advanced: Review the format for taking notes on page 239. Provide students with index cards to take notes. Ask students to use the format on page 239 to take notes about DNA, genes, and inherited traits. Encourage students to share their research with the class when they have completed their note cards.

DNA and Solving Crimes

Forensic scientists are people who study crimes by looking at **evidence**. Many forensic scientists use scientific or medical tests to solve crimes. One test is for DNA. A sample of blood, hair, or other body **tissue** found at the scene of a crime is tested. The DNA from the sample can be matched to a suspect's DNA to find out if he or she **committed the crime**.

▲ A scientist studies a DNA sequence.

In recent years, many people have been released from prison after DNA tests proved that they were **innocent**. Law students at the Wisconsin Innocence Project **investigate** about twenty to thirty criminal cases at any given time. In 2001, the project was responsible for the release of a Texas prisoner, Chris Ochoa. He was serving a life sentence for a 1988 murder. DNA tests on samples found on the victim proved that Ochoa did not commit the crime. He was innocent. Chris Ochoa spent twelve years in prison for a crime he didn't commit.

▲ Chris Ochoa and the students who helped to free him

DNA testing is now a very important tool in criminal investigation, and it is going to be more important in the future. More forensic scientists are going to use DNA tests to help make sure the right people are punished for their crimes.

---

evidence, proof
tissue, material from the body, such as skin and muscle
committed the crime, did something wrong or illegal
innocent, not guilty
investigate, look into; research

BEFORE YOU GO ON . . .

1 What can scientists test to find DNA?

2 How did DNA testing help Chris Ochoa?

HOW ABOUT YOU?

• Would you like to be a forensic scientist? Why or why not?

254

SPELLING MINILESSON

Schwa

Explain that the schwa sound /ə/ can be represented by any vowel and is most commonly found in an unstressed syllable, as in the word a̱dopt. Tell students that there are no patterns that can help them determine which vowel represents the schwa sound—they must use their memory to spell these words. Explain that knowing about the schwa sound can help them avoid the trap of using *i* to spell every schwa sound.

Write these words on the board and have students identify the vowel that represents the schwa sound: *a̱round, sent̲ence, recipe, fo̲rensic, suppo̲se.*

Then write the following words from page 254 on the board: *given, commit, about, victim.* Give students five minutes to study the spelling of the words. Then erase the words from the board. Dictate the words, and have students write them in their notebooks. Correct the spellings as a class and invite students to tell which vowel represents the schwa in each word. *(giv̲en, com̲mit, inno̲cent, crimi̲nal)*

Link the Readings

Reread "DNA, Genes, and Traits" and think about the excerpt from *The Time Warp Trio: 2095*. Then copy the chart into your notebook and complete it.

Title of Selection	Type of Text (Genre)	Fiction or Nonfiction	Purpose of Selection	Invention That Helps People
From *The Time Warp Trio: 2095*			*to entertain*	
"DNA, Genes, and Traits"	*science article*			

DISCUSSION

Discuss in pairs or small groups.

1. One of the girls in 2095 looks very much like Joe's sister. Why is this fact important?
2. Everyone has his or her own special code called DNA. How is this fact important in *The Time Warp Trio: 2095* excerpt? How is it important in real life?

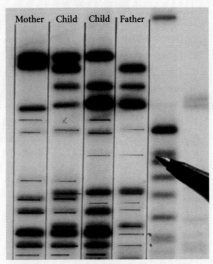

▲ The bands in these DNA sequences show that both children share some bands with each parent, proving that they are related.

255

REFLECTION

Read the headings of the Reflection chart aloud with students and discuss the chart headings. Have students copy the chart into their notebooks and complete it independently or with a partner. Encourage students to reread the selections as needed. Have students discuss their answers when the charts are complete. Then ask:

1. Which reading selection is nonfiction? ("DNA, Genes, and Traits")
2. What is the purpose of the excerpt from *The Time Warp Trio: 2095*? (to entertain)

DISCUSSION

Have volunteers take turns reading the Discussion questions. Encourage other students to paraphrase the questions. Have students answer the questions in pairs or small groups. If students have trouble with the second question, ask them to reread page 247 of the novel excerpt, in which the girls reveal their identity and the author says, "Everything suddenly made sense. That's why they looked so much like us."

CRITICAL THINKING

Have students think about the science article "DNA, Genes and Traits" and the information that the boys learn about their descendants in *The Time Warp Trio: 2095*. Then have students think about life in the future. Ask, *How do you picture life in the future for your own descendants? What might they look like? What kinds of things will they be able to do that you have not yet seen in your lifetime?*

REACHING ALL STUDENTS

LANGUAGE LEVELS

Beginning: Have students define each Reflection chart heading. Remind students that nonfiction readings are based on facts that can be proved and that fiction stories are made up by the author. Then complete the Reflection chart together, writing and revising student ideas on an overhead projector.

Advanced: As students work to complete the Reflection chart, have them focus on the last column. Tell students that before they can list an invention on the chart, they must tell a partner at least one way that the invention helps people. If they cannot think of a way the invention is useful, they should not list it on the chart.

GRAMMAR

Read aloud the explanations of ways to express future plans and predictions. Then have student volunteers read the examples in each box. Make sure students understand that the verb *be* can appear in different forms, such as *is, are*, or *am*. Point out that depending on the subject of the sentence, the phrase used to express future plans can be *is going to, are going to,* or *am going to.*

Form student pairs, and have partners complete the Practice exercises in their notebooks. After correcting the sentences as a class, have each pair write and read aloud three new sentences, using *be going to.*

SCAFFOLDING

Write the following phrases on the board and have students read them aloud:

> *I am*
>
> *She is*
>
> *They are*

To each phrase, add *reading.* Together, read the sentences aloud. Then change the sentences to *going to read.* Explain that the sentence *I am reading* is in the simple present. Tell students that the sentence *I am going to read* is in the simple future.

Connect to Writing

GRAMMAR

Using *be going to* for the Future
Use ***be going to* + base form of the verb** to talk about future plans.

> **I'm going to visit** my grandparents this weekend.
> My parents **are going to talk** to my teacher tonight.

Will and *be going to* have the same meaning when making predictions about the future.

> Forensic scientists **will help** solve more crimes using DNA tests.
> Forensic scientists **are going to help** solve more crimes using DNA tests.

Practice
Write sentences in your notebook using the words below and a form of *be going to.*

Example: Helen (visit me) on Friday.
  Helen is going to visit me on Friday.

1. My sister (call) home this evening.
2. Joanie, Freddi, and Samantha (buy) new antigravity disks next week.
3. I (see) the doctor tomorrow morning.
4. We (watch) my sister play tennis after school.
5. He (stay) home tonight.
6. My grandfather (fix) his car this weekend.
7. Forensic scientists (do) more DNA tests in the future.
8. Ricardo and Luz (travel) in Mexico this summer.
9. Joe (buy) a computer next month.
10. "We're (blow up)," said Sam.

256

SKILLS FOR WRITING

Making Sentence Outlines
The first and second steps in writing a research report are choosing a topic and researching it. The third step is organizing the facts you found in your research in an outline. One type of outline is called a sentence outline. In a sentence outline, you group facts together under main ideas and supporting ideas.

Look at this sentence outline about the Skycar M400. Then answer the questions.

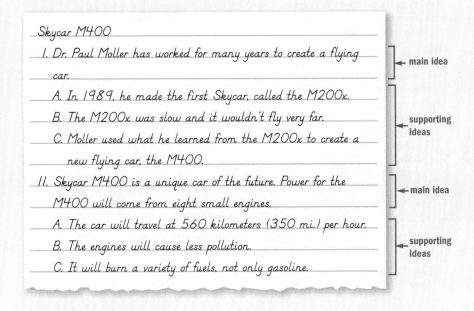

Skycar M400

I. Dr. Paul Moller has worked for many years to create a flying car. ← main idea

A. In 1989, he made the first Skycar, called the M200x.
B. The M200x was slow and it wouldn't fly very far. supporting ideas
C. Moller used what he learned from the M200x to create a new flying car, the M400.

II. Skycar M400 is a unique car of the future. Power for the M400 will come from eight small engines. ← main idea

A. The car will travel at 560 kilometers (350 mi.) per hour.
B. The engines will cause less pollution. supporting ideas
C. It will burn a variety of fuels, not only gasoline.

1. What is the first main idea?
2. Do the sentences under it support it?
3. What is the second main idea?
4. Do the sentences under it support it?

257

WRITING ASSIGNMENT

Sentence Outlines

Have a volunteer read aloud the assignment and step 1. Ask students to tell a partner what they will be writing. Then have students reread "DNA, Genes, and Traits" silently to find the main ideas.

WRITING STRATEGY

Read the Writing Strategy section aloud. Discuss the outline's form, explaining how to use Roman numerals for main ideas and capital letters for supporting details. Have students answer the questions below the outline. Then read step 2 aloud. Tell students they will write a sentence outline about the selection "DNA, Genes, and Traits."

Model how to complete an outline by working on an overhead projector. Ask students how many Roman numerals they will need to show the main ideas of this article. *(five)* Then have students write the headings in the article as the main ideas in their outlines. Next, have students read and do step 3 with partners. Work with them to complete the first supporting detail. Record it in outline form below Roman numeral I. *(Possible detail: DNA is found in cells.)* Have partners complete the outline together.

USING THE EDITING CHECKLIST

Have students read the Editing Checklist and use it to revise their outline. Remind them to place each main idea before its supporting details.

WRITING ASSIGNMENT

Sentence Outlines
You will make a sentence outline of the text "DNA, Genes, and Traits" on pages 252–254.

1. **Read** Reread the sentence outline on page 257. Note how the writer used main ideas and supporting ideas.

Writing Strategy: Outline
Follow this outline to organize the information in the article. Try to have at least two supporting details under each main idea. This will help you know whether you need to find more information about your topic.

Outline
 I. Main Idea
  A. Supporting Detail
  B. Supporting Detail
  C. Supporting Detail
 II. Main Idea
  A. Supporting Detail
  B. Supporting Detail
 III. Main Idea
  A. Supporting Detail
  B. Supporting Detail

1. How many main ideas are there in this research report?
2. How many supporting details are there about the first main idea?

---

2. **Make an outline** Use the sentence outline on page 257 and the outline above as models. Start your outline by filling in the main ideas from the article "DNA, Genes, and Traits." The headings can be the main ideas for your outline.

3. **Write** Write supporting ideas under each main idea in your outline. How many main ideas do you have?

EDITING CHECKLIST

Did you . . .
▶ list the main ideas first?
▶ find at least two supporting details for each main idea?
▶ remember to indent the details?
▶ use any sentences in the future?

258

PART REVIEW 2

Check Your Knowledge

Language Development

1. How did your purpose differ in reading the excerpt from *The Time Warp Trio: 2095* and "DNA, Genes, and Traits"?

2. What is dialogue? What are quotation marks? Give examples.

3. What is science fiction? Why is *The Time Warp Trio: 2095* science fiction?

4. What is the reason to make a sentence outline when you write a report?

5. What information is included in an outline?

6. Give an example of *be going to* to talk about future plans.

Academic Content

1. What new science vocabulary did you learn in Part 2? What do the words mean?

2. What do you call the chemical code found in every cell?

3. Where are genes located and what do they do?

4. How do forensic scientists use DNA to help solve crimes?

259

ASSESS

You can assess students' knowledge of the unit in several different ways.

Portfolio: Students can answer the Check Your Knowledge questions as a class assignment. Students can include their answers in their portfolios.

Traditional: Students can complete the Check Your Knowledge questions as a quiz. After students complete Check Your Knowledge, use the Assessment Package. Students can complete the Part Test on pages 73–76. For further practice, have students complete the Test Preparation worksheets.

Performance: Ask students to answer the Check Your Knowledge questions with a partner. Have partners meet with you to discuss their responses. Guide students to take turns speaking and interjecting additional reasons for their answers.

TEST-TAKING TIP

Remind students to read test questions carefully, looking for signal words, such as *give an example,* that tell the reader that specific details are needed in the answer. See the Test Preparation pages in the Assessment Guide for additional test-taking strategies.

METACOGNITION

Tell students to read their answers to the Check Your Knowledge questions softly to themselves to be sure that they are complete and make sense. Encourage students to revise their answers, if necessary.

REACHING ALL STUDENTS

LANGUAGE LEVELS

Beginning: Have students write the information for their outline on separate sentence strips, one strip for each main idea or supporting detail. Encourage them to organize the sentence strips in order of appearance in the article. After students have organized their strips, have them transfer the information to their notebooks.

Advanced: Have students work with a partner to revise their outlines. Ask students to read aloud the first draft of their outline to a partner. Then have them describe how each detail relates to each main idea. Encourage students to make changes if they discover unclear sentences, incomplete sentences, or detail sentences that do not relate to the main idea.

T259

Put It All Together

EXTEND THE LESSON

Read the Put It All Together section on pages 260–263, which reviews and consolidates concepts, skills, and strategies from both parts of the unit, with an emphasis on listening, speaking, and writing skills.

LISTENING AND SPEAKING WORKSHOP

Have volunteers read aloud the workshop directions, paraphrasing each step. Have students work in small groups to brainstorm inventions that could help future students. Have the presenting student practice with the group before the final presentation. Ask the class for feedback.

COOPERATIVE GROUPING

Once groups reach step 4, invite them to practice in front of another group before presenting to the class. Ask the group that is viewing the practice session to offer constructive advice about organization, clarity, visuals, and so on.

TEACHING THE TIPS

Speaking Tips: Ask three students to each read a different tip. Model the tips, and have students practice them in their groups.

Listening Tip: After having a volunteer read the tip aloud, remind students that it is best to review what they hear when the speaker pauses, not when the speaker is making other important points.

OBJECTIVES

Integrate Skills
- Listening/ Speaking: *Presentation*
- Writing: *Research report*

Investigate Themes
- Projects
- Further reading

LISTENING and SPEAKING WORKSHOP

PRESENTATION

You will give a presentation on an invention that will help students in the future.

1 **Think about it** Think about inventions that help you now, such as computers and calculators. What inventions would help students in the future? Write some ideas for future machines that would help you in school.

Work in small groups. Compare and discuss your ideas for future inventions. Choose one invention that you all think would help many students.

2 **Organize** Choose one group member to present the report to the class. Work together to write a description of your invention. Make a large drawing of the invention that the speaker can point to as he or she is talking. Make note cards that the speaker can look at while describing the invention.

3 **Practice** Listen carefully to your group speaker as he or she practices presenting the report. Make suggestions on how to make the presentation better.

4 **Present and evaluate** Present your group's report to the class. Then invite students to ask questions about the invention. After each speaker finishes, evaluate the presentation. Was each speaker's explanation and drawing clear? Do you have any suggestions for improvement?

SPEAKING TIPS

- Stand up straight, and speak loudly and clearly. Try to speak slowly.
- Point to your drawing to emphasize important information.
- Make eye contact with your classmates. Talk to your audience, not to your drawing.

LISTENING TIP

As you listen to a report, review in your mind the speaker's main ideas. This helps you pay attention to the speaker and to remember the important points.

260

RESEARCH SKILLS

Print: Before assigning the research report, ask the school or local librarian to set aside plenty of reference books that are appropriate for intermediate ESL/ELL students and to generate a list of web addresses and expert contacts so that students can complete their research. Give students ample class time or freedom from other homework so they can conduct their research.

WRITING WORKSHOP

RESEARCH REPORT

In a research report, the writer gathers and presents information about a topic from different sources, such as reference books, the Internet, and interviews. The writer's purpose is to explain a topic or to answer a question about it.

A good research report includes the following characteristics:

- a topic or question that the writer investigates and explains
- a main idea that gives the writer's purpose for the research report
- information about the topic from different sources, stated in the writer's own words
- clearly organized facts that explain the topic and support the writer's main ideas
- a list of the writer's sources

You will write a three-paragraph research report on a topic about the future. Research one of the topics from the list below, or choose another topic that interests you.

DNA Testing	Future Travel
Cars of the Future	Robots
Space Stations	Future Entertainment
A Space Colony	Cities of the Future
Computers	Future Schools

1 **Prewrite** Look up the topic in reference books and on the Internet to find information. Next, take notes about the topic and subtopics. Write them on note cards. If necessary, reread how to take notes in Skills for Writing on page 239. Then organize your note cards by main ideas. Write a sentence outline for your research report. Review how to write a sentence outline in Skills for Writing on page 257.

WRITING TIP

As you do research, narrow your topic. For example, the topic "Cars of the Future" is too broad because there are too many different kinds of cars. To narrow your topic, ask yourself questions such as "What are the characteristics of one future car?" or "What makes this future car unique?" The answers to these questions will help you choose the main idea of your report.

261

WRITING WORKSHOP

Research Report

Read aloud the opening paragraph and list of research report characteristics. Have students explain the writing task in their own words. Briefly discuss each topic on the list to clarify its meaning. Then display the student model on an overhead projector and read it aloud. Ask volunteers to point out the following elements: title, paragraph indents, topic sentences, details, and conclusion. Additional practice activities can be found in the **Workbook** and **CD-ROM.**

PROCESS WRITING

Read step 1 aloud. Guide each student to choose a topic narrow enough to fit the parameters of the assignment. Have student pairs review how to take notes and create note cards as described on page 239. Have students work independently to do research and make note cards, and create a sentence outline. Meet with students individually to help them complete each task. Then guide students to use the model report, their note cards, and their outline to complete the writing assignment.

TEACHING THE TIP

Writing Tip: Read aloud the Writing Tip with students. After students finish their draft, have them read their report. Ask, *Does any part of your report lack details? Where can you get more information?* Provide additional time for students to gather information as needed.

REACHING ALL STUDENTS

LANGUAGE LEVELS

Beginning: Help students practice the Listening Tip by reading aloud a recipe. Read slowly and clearly, pausing to give students time to think about what you said. Then have students describe in their notebooks how to make the food item. Invite students to discuss how using the Listening Tip helped them remember what they heard.

Advanced: Have students practice the Speaking Tip by describing a recent personal experience. Have them first tell the experience keeping their voice as soft and flat as possible. Then have them retell the experience loudly and clearly and with expression. Finally, invite class members to give the speaker feedback.

LEARNING MODALITIES

Kinesthetic: As students plan their presentation, have them take turns acting out how to use their group's invention. Other group members should watch and listen for ideas that describe the invention and its use. These ideas can be added to their final report.

Put It All Together

CREATING BETTER WRITERS

Conventions: Call on a volunteer to read aloud the call-outs in the margin of the writing sample. Have students identify the narrowed topic, discuss the main idea of the opening paragraph, and list facts that support the writer's main idea.

Before students revise their reports, explain that good writers are always aware of writing *conventions* when they revise their work. One good way to remember five important writing conventions is to use CUPPS: *C*apitalization, *U*sage, *P*unctuation, *P*aragraphing and *S*pelling. Following these conventions will help to ensure that students' writing is clear and easy to follow.

Write the following organizing tips on the board. Tell students to use the tips as they revise their writing.

- State the topic of your report clearly in the opening paragraph.
- Check that the transitions between paragraphs create a bridge, or link, from one idea to the next.
- Make sure every detail adds a little more information about the main idea.
- Write a strong concluding paragraph that brings together all the important ideas.

Before you write a first draft of your report, read the following model. Notice the characteristics of a research report.

> Thomas José Harding
>
> Skycar M400: Car of the Future
>
> Dr. Paul Moller has a dream: to design, manufacture, and sell a flying car. In 1989, his company made a flying car called Skycar M200x. The M200x was slow and didn't fly very far. Dr. Moller then developed the Skycar M400. He believes that it will be the car of the future.
>
> Skycar M400 is going to have some amazing features. It will take off and land like a helicopter. Skycar M400 will travel at a top speed of 560 kilometers (350 mi.) per hour and will get about 32 kilometers (20 mi.) to a gallon of gasoline.
>
> The first M400 cars will have human pilots, but later models will be computer-driven. The first Skycar M400 will cost about $1 million, but Dr. Moller believes it will cost only about $60,000 to mass produce the car.
>
> Sources:
>
> www.moller.com/skycar/
>
> Future, by Michael Tambini, Dorling Kindersley, New York, 1998
>
> www.howstuffworks.com/flying-car2.htm

The writer has narrowed his topic to a specific car.

He clearly states the main idea of his report.

He includes facts to explain and support his main idea.

He includes information from several sources and lists the sources.

262

2 **Draft** Use your sentence outline and
the model to write your research report.

3 **Edit** Work in pairs. Trade reports. Use
the editing checklist to evaluate each
other's writing.

EDITING CHECKLIST

Did you . . .

▶ narrow your research to a specific
topic or question?

▶ state the main idea of your research?

▶ include information from several
sources?

▶ state information in your own words?

▶ organize your report clearly, using two
or three main ideas?

▶ include a list of your sources?

▶ use correct grammar and
punctuation?

4 **Revise** Revise your report. Add or
rearrange information to make your
report easier to read and
understand.

5 **Publish** Share your research report
with your teacher and your
classmates. If possible, show
pictures that illustrate your topic and
any important person or people
connected to the topic.

▲ A solar-powered car of the future

263

USING THE EDITING CHECKLIST

Have students read aloud the Editing
Checklist. Have them work in pairs to read
it again and use it to revise their writing.
Remind students that the details in their
report must support the main idea.

ASSESS

Portfolio: Include the research report in
students' assessment portfolios for
comparison with later assignments.

REACHING ALL STUDENTS

LANGUAGE LEVELS

Beginning: Hold periodic conferences with
individual students so you can check their
progress as they choose and narrow a topic,
do the research, and complete the note-taking
and outlining portion of the writing
assignment.

Advanced: Remind students that details are
what hold a reader's interest. Encourage
students to find and include at least three
interesting details that are relevant but still
make the report fun to read.

Unit Projects

PROJECTS

Work in pairs or small groups. Choose one of these projects.

1. With your group, talk about ideas for a science fiction story. What would be a good time period for the story? What scientific facts do you want to include? What are some things that will happen? Then draft your story. Include some dialogue.

2. Find out more information about the inventions listed on the timeline on page 226. Look for facts in magazines, reference books, and on the Internet. Make a visual aid about the invention you research and share your information with the class.

3. Paint or draw a picture of what you think certain people, places, or objects might look like 100 years from now. Create an art gallery of the future in the classroom to display the pictures.

4. With a family member, look through old and current photo albums. Discuss traits that have been passed on to several members of your family like hair or eye color. Look for features that are unique to your family.

5. Invite a forensic scientist to speak to the class about tools that are used to gather and test evidence. Before the person comes, brainstorm questions to ask him or her after the talk.

6. Create a comic strip about characters who live in the future. Show what they look like, where they live, and how they travel. You can make your comic strip funny or serious. Place the comic strips together in a class comic book.

▲ The Hamm family of Dallas, Texas, includes five sets of twins and one "single" child.

264

Further Reading

To find out more about the theme of this unit, choose from these reading suggestions.

Robotz, **Stephen Munzer** This encyclopedia of robots in fact and fiction covers robots past, present, and future. You'll get tips on building your own robots, learn about artificial intelligence, and be treated to a glimpse of future robots.

The New Way Things Work, **David Macaulay** This beautifully illustrated book contains a wealth of information about how things work, from everyday items, such as keys and can openers, to the most complex, including compact disks, computer hard drives, and the Internet. The explanations are easy to understand and fun to read.

Outernet: Friend or Foe?, **Steve Barlow and Steve Skidmore** It all started with a birthday present—what appeared to be a laptop computer. But Jack, Loaf, and Merle are about to discover that this laptop is much more than they imagined. They accidentally connect to an intergalactic Internet, called the Outernet, via a lost Server. There they encounter the evil Tyrant and his henchmen (the FOES) who are trying to take over the Outernet to use its powers to control the galaxy.

A Wrinkle in Time, **Madeleine L'Engle** In this story, Charles Wallace, Meg Murry, and their mother go off to rescue Meg and Charles Wallace's father, who mysteriously disappeared while he was experimenting with time travel. Their voyage takes them on an exciting trip through space, battling the forces of evil.

A Wind in the Door, **Madeleine L'Engle** Charles Wallace, Meg Murry's six-year-old brother, is very ill. To save him, Meg, Charles Wallace, and their friend Calvin O'Keefe go off on an extraordinary journey into galactic space—both fantastic and frightening—where they battle evil. This book is a companion to *A Wrinkle in Time.*

265

REACHING ALL STUDENTS

LANGUAGE LEVELS

Beginning: Invite beginning students to draw a labeled diagram of the invention they choose to research for Project 2. Have students display and describe their diagram as a way of sharing their information.

Advanced: For Project 1, encourage students to find science fiction books and skim through them, noting the kind of mood that is conveyed and the settings that are common to the stories. *(The mood is often tense or suspenseful; common settings are fictitious planets, space stations, cities of the future.)* Invite students to use some of these elements in their story.

Glossary

ACTIVE VOICE /ak′tiv vois/
A verb is in the active voice when its subject is the performer of the action: *The firefighters rescue people from the building.*

ADJECTIVE /aj′ik tiv/
An adjective describes nouns (people, places, animals, and things) or pronouns. In the sentence *I have a blue car*, the word *blue* is an adjective.

ADVERB /ad′vèrb/
An adverb usually describes the action of a verb, such as how an action happens: *The boy runs quickly.* The adverb *quickly* describes the verb *runs.* Several adverbs, such as *always, usually, often, sometimes,* and *never,* are called frequency adverbs: *She never found her necklace.*

ALLITERATION /ə lit′ə rā′shən/
Alliteration is the poetic use of two or more words that begin with the same sound. Writers use alliteration to draw attention to certain words or ideas, to imitate sounds, and to create musical effects.

ANALYZING HISTORICAL CONTEXT
/an′ə līz ing hi stôr ə kəl kon′tekst/
Sometimes the historical context, or the political and social events and trends of the time, plays a key role in a story setting. For example, in *The Diary of Anne Frank: The Play*, the historical context is the experience of the Jews in Holland during World War II. As you read, ask yourself what effect the historical setting has on the characters and the action. This will help you understand both the characters and the action better.

ARTICLE /är′tə kəl/
An article is a piece of nonfictional writing that is usually part of a newspaper or magazine.

AUTOBIOGRAPHY /ò′tə bī og′rə fē/
An autobiography is the story of the writer's own life, told by the writer, usually in the first person. It may tell about the person's whole life or only a part of it. Because autobiographies are about real people and events, they are nonfictional. Most autobiographies are written in the first person.

BASE FORM /bās fôrm/
The base form, or simple form, of a verb has no added ending (*-s, -ing, -ed*). *Talk* is the base form of the verb talk. (Other forms of *talk* are *talks, talking,* and *talked.*)

BIOGRAPHY /bī og′rə fē/
A biography is a nonfictional story of a person's life told by another person. Most biographies are written about famous or admirable people.

CHARACTER /kar′ik tər/
A character is a person or an animal that takes part in the action of a literary work.

CHARACTERIZATION
/kar′ik tər ə zā′shən/
Characterization is the creation and development of a character in a story. Writers sometimes show what a character is like by describing what the character says and does.

COMPARATIVE /kəm par′ə tiv/
A comparative is an adjective or adverb used to compare two things. Most one-syllable adjectives and some two-syllable adjectives add *-er* for comparatives: *Bigger* is the comparative form of *big.* Most adjectives of two or more syllables use *more* for comparatives: *This rose is more fragrant than that one.* (*See also* Superlative.)

266

COMPARE AND CONTRAST
/kəm pâr′ and kən trast′/
When you compare and contrast texts, you consider what is similar about the texts (compare) and what is different (contrast).

COMPOUND SENTENCE
/kom′pound sen′təns/
A compound sentence is made up of two simple sentences that are joined by a conjunction, such as *and, but,* and *or.*

CONJUNCTION /kən jungk′shən/
A conjunction connects words, groups of words, and sentences. The words *and, but, so,* and *or* are conjunctions.

CONTRACTION /kən trak′shən/
A contraction is a short form used to join two words together. For example, the contraction of *I am* (the verb *be* and the subject pronoun *I*) is *I'm.* The contraction of *you are* is *you're.* In a contraction, an apostrophe replaces one or more letters. Contractions are used in speaking and informal writing.

DIALOGUE /dī′ə lȯg/
A dialogue is a conversation between characters. In novels, short stories, and poems, dialogue is usually shown by quotation marks to indicate a speaker's exact words. In a play, dialogue follows the names of characters, and no quotation marks are used.

DIARY /dī′ə rē/
A diary is a book in which you write each day about your personal thoughts, things that happened to you, or about things that you did.

DISTINGUISHING FACT AND OPINION
/dis ting′gwish ing fakt and ə pin′yən/
A fact is a statement someone can prove. An opinion is a belief that cannot be proved. Distinguishing fact and opinion means seeing the difference between what is a fact and what is an opinion in a text.

EXCERPT /ek′sėrpt/
An excerpt is a short passage or section taken from a longer text, such as a letter, a book, an article, a poem, a play, a speech, etc.

FABLE /fā′bəl/
A fable is a brief story or poem, usually with animal characters, that teaches a lesson, or moral. The moral is usually stated at the end of the fable.

FICTION /fik′shən/
Fiction is prose writing that tells about imaginary characters and events. Short stories and novels are works of fiction.

FLASHBACK /flash′bak/
A flashback is a scene within a story that interrupts the sequence of events to tell about something that happened in the past.

GENRE /jän′rə/
A genre is a division or type of literature. Literature is commonly divided into three major genres: poetry, prose (fiction and nonfiction), and drama (plays).

HISTORICAL FICTION
/hi stȯr′ə kəl fik′shən/
Historical fiction, such as a historical novel, combines imaginary elements (fiction) with real people, events, or settings (history).

267

INFORMATIONAL TEXT
/in′fər mā′shən əl tekst/
An informational text is a nonfiction text. It is about real facts or events. The purpose of an informational text is to inform the reader about real facts, people, or events.

IMPERATIVE /im per′ə tiv/
An imperative is the form of a verb used for giving an instruction, a direction, or an order: *Give me the ball. Turn to the right. Come here!*

INTERVIEW /in′tər vyü/
An interview is an occasion when a famous person is asked questions about his or her life, opinions, etc.

LETTER /let′ər/
A letter is a written communication from one person to another. In personal letters, the writer shares information and his or her thoughts and feelings with one other person or group.

MAKING INFERENCES
/ma′king in′fər ans es/
Figuring out a writer's meaning when the writer suggests something rather than presenting information directly is called making an inference.

MOOD /müd/
Mood, or atmosphere, is the feeling created in the reader by a literary work or passage. The mood can be sad, funny, scary, tense, happy, hopeless, etc.

MYSTERY /mis′tər ē/
A mystery is something that is difficult to understand or explain. In a mystery story, the characters as well as the readers are given clues, or hints, to solve, or figure out, the mystery.

MYTH /mith/
A myth, like a fable, is a short fictional tale. Myths explain the actions of gods and heroes or the origins of elements of nature. Their purpose is to entertain and instruct. Every ancient culture has its collection of myths, or mythology, that is passed from parents to children as part of the "oral tradition."

NARRATIVE /nar′ə tiv/
A narrative is a story that can be either fiction or nonfiction. Novels and short stories are fictional narratives. Biographies and autobiographies are nonfiction narratives. In a personal narrative, the writer tells about something he or she experienced.

NARRATOR /nar′ā tər/
A narrator is a speaker or character who tells a story. The narrator sometimes takes part in the action while telling the story. Other times, the narrator is outside the action and just speaks about it.

NONFICTION /non fik′shən/
Nonfiction is prose writing that tells about real people, places, objects, or events. Biographies, reports, and newspaper articles are examples of nonfiction.

NOTING CAUSES AND EFFECTS
/nōt′ing kȯz′ əz and ə fekts′/
Noting causes and effects as you read can help you better understand a text. Most fiction and nonfiction texts tell about events. Why an event happens is a cause. What happens as a result of a cause is an effect. The words *so* and *because* often signal causes and effects.

268

NOUN /noun/

A noun is the name of a person, thing, place, or animal. *Plane, building,* and *child* are common nouns. *Robert, Chicago,* and *Puerto Rico* are proper nouns.

NOVEL /nov′əl/

A novel is a long work of fiction. Novels contain such elements as characters, plot, conflict, and setting. The writer of novels develops these elements.

PASSIVE VOICE /pas′iv vois/

In the passive voice, the subject of the sentence receives the action: *The ball was caught by the outfielder.*

PERSONIFICATION
/pər son′ə fə kā′shən/

Personification is giving human traits to animals or inanimate objects.

PLAY /plā/

A play is a story performed by people in a theater.

PLAYWRIGHT /plā′rīt/

A playwright is a person who writes plays.

PLOT /plot/

A plot is a sequence of connected events in a fictional story. In most stories, the plot has characters and a main problem or conflict. After the problem is introduced, it grows until a turning point, or climax, when a character tries to solve the problem. The end of the story usually follows the climax.

POEM /pō′əm/

A poem is a piece of writing that uses a pattern of lines and sounds to express ideas, emotions, etc.

POINT OF VIEW /point ov vyü/

A narrator tells a story from his or her point of view. In the first-person point of view, the narrator tells the story using *I* and *my.* In the third-person point of view, the narrator tells someone else's story using *he* or *she,* and *his* or *her.*

PREDICTING /pri dikt′ ing/

Predicting means guessing what will happen next in a text. Predicting includes looking for clues, thinking about what you already know, and asking yourself, "What will happen next?"

PREPOSITION /prep′ə zish′ən/

A preposition is a short connecting word, such as *to, with, from, in,* and *for* that is always followed by a noun or pronoun: *Amy's mother drives her to school. Amy walks back from school with friends.* Prepositions of location tell where something is: *The apple is on the table. The sun is between the mountains. The shoes are under the bed. The bag is next to it.*

PRESENT PROGRESSIVE
/prez′nt prə gres′iv/

A verb in the present progressive describes an action that is happening now: *I am eating my lunch. It is raining today.*

PREVIEWING /prē′vyü′ ing/

Previewing a text is looking at the text to get a general idea about what it contains before reading it more closely. Previewing includes thinking about what you already know about the subject; looking at the title, headings, photographs, and illustrations.

PRONOUN /prō′noun/

A pronoun is a word used instead of a noun, to avoid repeating the noun: *Carlos goes to school. He likes it. He* replaces the proper noun *Carlos*; *it* replaces the noun *school.*

269

PROSE /prōz/
Prose is the ordinary form of written language. Most writing that is not poetry, drama (plays), or song is considered prose. Prose is one of the major genres of literature and occurs in fiction and nonfiction.

PUNCTUATION /pungk′chü ā′shən/
Punctuation is the set of signs or marks, such as periods (.) and commas (,), used to divide writing into phrases and sentences, to make their meaning clear. Other punctuation marks indicate questions (?), exclamations (!), pauses (. . .), etc.

RHYME /rīm/
Rhyme is the repetition of sounds at the ends of words. Many poems contain end rhymes, or rhyming words at the ends of lines.

SENTENCE /sen′təns/
A sentence is a group of words with a subject and a verb. A sentence can stand alone.

SETTING /set′ing/
The setting of a literary work is the time and place of the action. The setting includes all the details of a place and time—the year, the time of day, even the weather. The place may be a specific country, state, region, community, neighborhood, building, institution, or home. In most stories, the setting serves as a context in which characters interact. Setting can also help create a feeling, or atmosphere.

SHORT STORY /shôrt stôr′ē/
A short story is a brief work of fiction. Like a novel, a short story presents a sequence of events, or plot. A short story usually communicates a message about life or human nature.

SIMPLE PAST /sim′pəl past/
Verbs in the simple past are used to tell about an action that happened in the past and is completed: *The boy ate the apple. The girl walked up the hill.*

SKIMMING /skim′ing/
Skimming a text is reading it very quickly to gain a general understanding of it. Skimming involves reading the first and second paragraphs quickly, reading only the first sentences of the following paragraphs, and reading the last paragraph quickly.

SONG /sȯng/
A song is a piece of music made especially for singing.

STAGE DIRECTIONS /stāj də rek′shənz/
Stage directions are notes included in a play to describe how the work is to be performed or staged. Stage directions are usually printed in italics and enclosed within parentheses or brackets. Some stage directions describe the movements and costumes, as well as the emotional states and ways of speaking of the characters.

SUMMARIZING /sum′ə rīz′ ing/
Summarizing is restating the main ideas of a text in a shorter form. A way of summarizing is to read a text, reread each paragraph or section, put the text aside, and write the main ideas in one's own words in a sentence or two. Summarizing can help you understand a text better.

270

SUMMARY /sum′ə rē/
A summary is a brief statement that gives
the main points of an event or literary work.

SUPERLATIVE /sə pėr′lə tiv/
A superlative is the form of an adjective or
adverb used to compare three or more
things. Most one-syllable adjectives and
some two-syllable adjectives add -est for
superlatives: *Biggest* is the superlative form
of *big*. Most adjectives of two or more
syllables use *the most* for superlatives. (*See
also* Comparative.)

SUSPENSE /sə spens′/
Suspense is a feeling of uncertainty about
the outcome of events in a literary work.
Stories with suspense make the readers ask,
"What will happen next?"

TIME PHRASE /tīm frāz/
Time phrases tell the reader when an event
happened: *Yesterday, we went to see a
movie. Last night, we watched television.
Next week, we will go to see my
grandmother.*

VERB /vėrb/
A verb is the word or words in a sentence
that describe an action, a fact, or a state:
Tom is eating his lunch (action). *New York
has many tall buildings* (fact). *Mary feels
sleepy* (state).

VISUALIZING /vizh′ ü ə līz′ ing/
Visualizing means imagining or picturing in
your mind the characters, events, and places
in a text.

271

Index

272

274

275

276

277

Acknowledgments

Carol Mann Agency. "He Was the Same Age as My Sister" by Mieke C. Malandra, from *I Thought My Father Was God, and Other True Tales,* from NPR's National Story Project, edited and introduced by Paul Auster, 2001. Reprinted by permission of the Carol Mann Agency.

Cinco Puntos Press. "Why Rattlesnake Has Fangs" by Cheryl Giff from *And It Is Still That Way*, collected by Byrd Baylor. Copyright © 1998. Reprinted by permission of Cinco Puntos Press.

Discovery Communications, Inc. "Interview with an Astronaut: Dan Bursch." Copyright © 2000 Discovery Communications, Inc. All rights reserved. www.discovery.com. Reprinted by permission of Discovery Communications, Inc.

Flora Robert, Inc. Excerpt from *The Diary of Anne Frank: The Play* by Frances Goodrich and Albert Hackett, newly adapted by Wendy Kesselman. Copyright © 2001 (revised) the Anne Frank-Fonds, Actors Fund of America, the Dramatists Guild Fund, Inc., New Dramatists. Copyright © 2002, the Anne Frank-Fonds, Actors Fund of America, the Dramatists Guild Fund, Inc., New Dramatists. Used by permission of Flora Robert, Inc.

Harcourt, Inc. "Grass," from *The Complete Poems of Carl Sandburg*. Copyright © 1970, 1969 by Lilian Steichen Sandburg, Trustee. Reprinted by permission of Harcourt, Inc.

HarperCollins Publishers. "Stolen Rope," "The Cookie Jar," and "School Days," from *More True Lies* by George Shannon. Copyright © 1991 by George W. B. Shannon. Used by permission of HarperCollins Publishers.

Hyperion Books. Excerpt from *Lator, Gator* by Laurence Yep. Copyright © 1995 Laurence Yep. Reprinted by permission of Hyperion Books for Children.

Newfront Productions, Inc. "The Case of the Surprise Visitor" and "The Case of the Defaced Sidewalk" by Carol Farley, and "The Case of the Disappearing Signs" by Elizabeth Dearl. Originally appeared on MysteryNet.com Kids Mysteries Site. Copyright © 1996, 2002 Newfront Productions, Inc. Reprinted by permission of Newfront Productions, Inc.

United Feature Syndicate, Inc. Peanuts reprinted by permission of United Feature Syndicate, Inc.

Viking Penguin. Excerpts from *Time Warp Trio: 2095* by Jon Scieszka. Copyright © 1995 by Jon Scieszka. Used by permission of Viking Penguin, an imprint of Penguin Putnam Books for Young Readers, a division of Penguin Putnam, Inc. All rights reserved.

Viking Penguin. Excerpts from *Zlata's Diary* by Zlata Filipović. Copyright © 1994 Editions Robert Laffont/Fixot. Used by permission of Viking Penguin, a division of Penguin Putnam, Inc.

Warner Bros. Publications U.S., Inc. "The Wind Beneath My Wings" by Larry Henley and Jeff Silbar. Copyright © 1982 Warner House of Music and WB Gold Music Corp. All rights reserved. Used by permission of Warner Bros. Publications U.S., Inc., Miami, FL 33014.

Westminster John Knox Press. Excerpt from *A Boat to Nowhere* by Maureen Crane Wartski. Copyright © 1980 Maureen Crane Wartski. Used by permission of Westminster John Knox Press and the author.

278

Credits

Illustrators: Mike DiGiorgio 130, 131; **L. R. Galante** 4, 20, 22, 58, 66, 76, 92, 120, 121 left, 122, 142, 154; **Tim Haggerty** 106, 108; **John Hovell** 140, 156-161 bkgrd., 162; **Inklink Firenze** 94, 110; **Dom Lee** 68-69, 71, 72; **Tom Leonard** 121 right; **Jeffrey Lindberg** 112, 114, 115, 116, 117; **Lee MacLeod** 244, 246, 247, 249; **Mapping Specialists** 136, 144, 164, 165; **Ron Mazellan** 59, 60; **Gail Piazza** 253; **Barry Rockwell** 14-15, 16, 19; **Phil Scheuer** 102, 103, 104; **Andrea Wesson** 24, 26, 28, 30.

Photography

COVER: Panel top, Geoff Brightling; middle, Stone/Getty Images; middle, Hulton-Deutsch Collection/CORBIS; bottom, PhotoDisc/Getty Images; background, Fergus O'Brien/Taxi/Getty Images; inset left, North Carolina Museum of Art/CORBIS; inset right, NASA.

UNIT 1: 2 top, British Museum; 2 middle, Dorling Kindersley; 2 bottom, British Museum; 2 inset, Ariel Skelley/CORBIS; 2-3 David Turnley/CORBIS; 3 top, Dorling Kindersley; 3 bottom, Chuck Savage/CORBIS; 6 Dorling Kindersley; 7 top, Johannes Laurentius/Bildarchiv Preussischer Kulturbesitz; 7 bottom, Dorling Kindersley; 8 top, Dorling Kindersley; 8 left, Dorling Kindersley; 8 right, Dorling Kindersley; 9 right, Dorling Kindersley; 9 left, Dorling Kindersley; 10 top, Michael T. Sedan/CORBIS; 10 bottom, Dorling Kindersley; 11 right, Dorling Kindersley; 11 left, Dorling Kindersley; 12 Dorling Kindersley; 15 Mary Evans Picture Library; 18 Dorling Kindersley; 21 Dorling Kindersley; 29 Joanne Ryder; 32 all, Dorling Kindersley; 33 all, Dorling Kindersley; 34 all, Dorling Kindersley; 35 Dorling Kindersley; 39 Dorling Kindersley; 41 Allsport Concepts/Getty Images; 43 top, PhotoDisc/Getty Images; 43 bottom, Dorling Kindersley; 44 Dorling Kindersley.

UNIT 2: 46 top, NASA; 46 middle, NASA; 46 middle, Abbas/Magnum Photos; 46 bottom, Wolfgang Kaehler/CORBIS; 46 inset, Duomo/CORBIS; 46-47 Galen Rowell/CORBIS; 47 bottom foreground, Jonathan Blair/CORBIS; 48 left, Reuters Newmedia/CORBIS; 48 right, Reuters Newmedia/CORBIS; 48 bottom, Wally McNamee/CORBIS; 50 Reuters Newmedia/CORBIS; 51 Bettmann/CORBIS; 52 top, Stephen Hird/Reuters/Timepix; 52 middle, Bettmann/CORBIS; 52 bottom, Bettmann/CORBIS; 53 top, Bettmann/CORBIS; 53

bottom, Scala/Art Resource; 54 top, NASA; 54 bottom AFP/CORBIS; 55 inset, Didrik Johnk/CORBIS Sygma; 55 bottom, John Noble/CORBIS; 57 Peter Turnley/CORBIS; 60 Photo courtesy of the author; 61 Jess Stock/Getty Images; 65 Julie Habel/CORBIS; 67 Peter Turnley/CORBIS; 73 Courtesy Maureen Crane Wartski; 74 Jose L. Pelaez/CORBIS; 77 Republished with permission of Globe Newspapers, Inc.; 78 top, Jon Chase/Harvard News Office; 78 bottom, Republished with permission of Globe Newspapers, Inc.; 79 Jon Chase/Harvard News Office; 83 Bettmann/CORBIS; 85 Skjold Photographs; 87 Dorling Kindersley; 88 all, Dorling Kindersley.

UNIT 3: 90 top, Geoff Brightling; 90 middle, Stone/Getty Images; 90 middle, Hulton Deutsch Collection/CORBIS; 90 bottom, PhotoDisc/Getty Images; 90 foreground, Stone/Getty Images 90 inset, HO/Reuters/Timepix; 90-91 National Geographic/Getty Images; 91 bottom, Roman Soumar/CORBIS; 91 center inset, Stone/Getty Images; 91 inset, Dorling Kindersley; 93 Dorling Kindersley; 94 bottom, Space Imaging; 95 top, Roger Wood/CORBIS; 95 bottom, Taxi/Getty Images; 96 top, Adam Woolfitt/CORBIS; 96 bottom, Stone/Getty Images; 97 top, The Griffith Institute, Oxford; 97 bottom, Erich Lessing/Art Resource; 98 top, New Zealand Herald/CORBIS Sygma; 98 bottom, AP/Wide World Photos; 99 left, Bettmann/CORBIS; 99 right, Dorling Kindersley; 100 Dorling Kindersley; 104 © 1997 Rick Olson; 109 PhotoDisc/Getty Images; 117 Photos courtesy of the authors; 118 Dorling Kindersley; 124 Reprinted by permission of United Features Syndicate, Inc.; 125 Dorling Kindersley; 127 PhotoDisc/Getty Images; 129 Dorling Kindersley; 132 all, Dorling Kindersley.

UNIT 4: 134 middle, David Turnley/CORBIS; 134 middle, Private collection Edward Lamprich; 134 bottom, CORBIS; 134 foreground, Dorling Kindersley; 134 inset, Hulton-Deutsch Collection/CORBIS; 134-135 Reuters New Media/CORBIS; 135 foreground, Jon Jones/CORBIS Sygma; 138 Hulton/Archive/Getty Images; 139 left, Timepix; 139 right, Hulton/Archive/Getty Images; 141 top left, Hulton/Archive/Getty Images; 141 top right, Dorling Kindersley; 141 bottom, Dorling Kindersley; 141 middle, Bettmann/CORBIS; 142-143 AP/Wide World Photos; 142 bottom, Bettmann/CORBIS; 145 The Art Archive/Imperial War Museum; 147 Private collection Edward Lamprich; 148 top, AP/Wide World Photos; 148 bottom, Stuart

Credits

Photography

COVER: Panel top, Geoff Brightling; middle, Stone/Getty Images; middle, Hulton-Deutsch Collection/CORBIS; bottom, PhotoDisc/Getty Images; background, Fergus O'Brien/Taxi/Getty Images; inset left, North Carolina Museum of Art/CORBIS; inset right, NASA.

FRONT MATTER: 7 top, Taxi/Getty Images; 7 bottom, Steve Chenn/CORBIS; 9 top, Dorling Kindersley; 12 bottom left, Dorling Kindersley; 12 bottom right, PhotoDisc/Getty Images; 14 bottom, Dorling Kindersley.

INTERLEAF SPREADS: T2A top, Michael T. Sedan/CORBIS; T2A bottom, Dorling Kindersley; T2B Allsport Concepts/Getty Images; T46A top, Wally McNamee/CORBIS; T46 bottom, Dom Lee (artist); T46B Scala/Art Resource; T90A top, North Carolina Museum of Art/CORBIS; T90A bottom, Dorling Kindersley; T90B PhotoDisc/Getty Images; T134A top, Dorling Kindersley; T134A bottom, Private collection Edward Lamprich; T134B Bettmann/CORBIS; T178A top, Hulton /Archive/Getty Images; T178A bottom, Reuters Newmedia/CORBIS; T178B © 2002 www.kids-guernica.org/Kaoru Mizuguchi; T222A top, Geoff Tompkinson/Photo Researchers; T222A bottom, AP/Wide World Photos; T222B Courtesy of Moller International.

Franklin/Magnum Photos; 153 Imperial War Museum/ Dorling Kindersley; 156 Alexandra Boulat/SIPA Press; 157 Alexandra Boulat/SIPA Press; 158 Françoise de Mulder/CORBIS; 159 Alexandra Boulat/SIPA Press; 160 Paul Lowe/ Magnum Photos; 161 top, Les Stone/CORBIS Sygma; 161 bottom, Otto Lang/CORBIS; 163 Alexandra Boulat/ SIPA Press; 166 top, Adam Woolfitt/CORBIS; 166 middle, Thouvenin/Photo Researchers; 166 bottom, Tim Page/ CORBIS; 167 Reuters New Media/CORBIS; 171 Alamany & Vicens/CORBIS; 173 Merrilee Thomas/Tom Stack & Associates, Inc.; 175 Dorling Kindersley; 176 Swim Ink/CORBIS.

UNIT 5: 178 top, Flip Schulke/CORBIS; 178 middle, Mansell/Timepix; 178 bottom, Bettmann/CORBIS; 178 inset, Lowell Georgia/CORBIS; 178-179 CORBIS; 179 foreground, Reuters Newmedia/CORBIS; 180 top left, George Hall/CORBIS; 180 top right, Tony Freeman/ PhotoEdit; 180 bottom left, Yoav Levy/Phototake; 180 bottom right, Pearson Education; 182 top, Erich Lessing/ Art Resource; 182 bottom, Mansell/Timepix; 183 top, CORBIS; 183 bottom, AP/Wide World Photos; 184 top, Hulton/Archive/Getty Images; 184 bottom, PhotoEdit; 185 AP/Wide World Photos; 186 top, Francesco Zizola/ Magnum Photos; 186 bottom, David & Peter Turnley/ CORBIS; 187 David Turnley/CORBIS Sygma; 189 Jim Zuckerman/CORBIS; 190 background, Mark A. Johnson/ CORBIS; 190 inset, Greg Gorman/Warner Brothers Records; 191 top, Sebastião Salgado/Contact Press Images; 191 bottom, AFP/CORBIS; 192 top, CORBIS; 197 SPL/Photo Researchers; 198 Hulton/Archive/Getty Images; 199 Wolfgang Kaehler/CORBIS; 200 top, AP/Wide World Photos; 200 bottom, Hulton/Archive/Getty Images; 203 all, Hulton/Archive/Getty Images; 205 Hulton/Archive/Getty Images; 206 Hulton/Archive/Getty Images; 208-209 John Bigelow Taylor/Art Resource/ARS; 208 left, Hulton/Archive/Getty Images; 210 © 2002

www.kids-guernica.org/Kaoru Mizuguchi; 211 Dorling Kindersley; 215 Eyewire/Getty Images ; 216 Nicola Sutton/Life File/Getty Images/Photodisc; 219 David H. Wells/CORBIS; 220 top, Dorling Kindersley; 220 bottom, © Joan Marcus.

UNIT 6: 222 top, Joseph Sohm/Chromosohm/CORBIS; 222 middle, NASA; 222 bottom, Courtesy of Moller International; 222-223 top, NASA; 222-223 bottom, NASA; 222 inset, NASA; 222 foreground, David Lawrence/CORBIS; 223 top, Toshiyuki Aizaw/Reuters/ Timepix; 223 bottom, Steve Chenn/CORBIS; 224 top left, PhotoDisc/Getty Images; 224 top right, National Motor Museum at Beaulieu; 224 bottom left, Museum of Flight/CORBIS; 224 bottom right, Hulton/Archive/Getty Images; 226 top, Digital Art/CORBIS; 226 middle, AP/Wide World Photos; 226 bottom, Roger Ressmeyer/ CORBIS; 227 top, Jacques M. Chenet/CORBIS; 227 bottom Richard Davies/Foster & Partners; 228 top, Forrest J. Ackerman Collection/CORBIS; 228 bottom, Courtesy of Moller International; 229 AFP/CORBIS; 230 top, Gianni Dagli Orti/CORBIS; 230 left, AP/Wide World Photos; 230 right, Photograph of Solotrek™ is courtesy of Trek Aerospace © 2002 Trek Aerospace, Inc.; 231 Detlev van Ravenswaay/Photo Researchers; 232 Department of Electrical & Electronic Engineering, University of Portsmouth, England; 233 NASA; 234 NASA; 235 NASA; 237 NASA; 241 NASA; 242 Roger Harris/Photo Researchers; 249 James E. Schuck; 250 The Image Bank/Getty Images; 251 Forrest J. Ackerman Collection/CORBIS; 252 top, Digital Art/CORBIS; 252 bottom, Mary Kate Denny/PhotoEdit; 254 top, Geoff Tompkinson/Photo Researchers; 254 bottom, Wisconsin Innocence Project/University of Wisconsin Law School; 255 David Parker/Photo Researchers; 259 Tek Image/Photo Researchers; 263 Corbis/Sygma; 264 Bettmann/CORBIS.

280